Going Public

How to Order:

Single copies may be ordered from Prima Publishing, P.O. Box 1260BK, Rocklin, CA 95677; telephone (916) 786-0426. Quantity discounts are also available. On your letterhead, include information concerning the intended use of the books and the number of books you wish to purchase.

Going Public

Everything You Need to Know to Successfully Turn a Private Enterprise into a Publicly Traded Company

Frederick D. Lipman

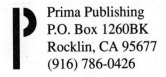

Prima Publishing
P.O. Box 1260BK
Rocklin, CA 95677
(916) 786-0426

Production by Robin Lockwood, Bookman Productions
Copyediting by Toby Wraye
Typography by Arrow Connection
Jacket design by Paul Page Design

Library of Congress Cataloging-in-Publication Data

Lipman, Frederick D.
    Going public : everything you need to know to successfully turn a private enterprise into a publicly traded company / Frederick D. Lipman.
      p. cm.
    Includes index.
    ISBN 1-55958-425-4
    1. Going public (Securities)—United States. 2. Going public (Securities)—Law and legislation—United States. 3.Corporations—United States—Finance. I. Title.
HG4963.L56 1994
658.15'224—dc20   93-23557
                                          CIP

94 95 96 97 98 RRD 10 9 8 7 6 5 4 3 2 1

Printed in the United States of America

To my wife, Gail

Acknowledgments

I want to acknowledge the helpful comments and editorial efforts of the following of my partners at the Philadelphia office of the law firm of Blank, Rome, Comisky & McCauley:

Chapters 1 and 2: Fred Blume;
Chapters 3 and 4: Barry H. Genkin;
Chapters 5 and 6: Richard J. McMahon;
Chapter 7: James J. Bowes;
Chapter 8: Alan L. Zeiger;
Chapter 9: G. Michael Stakias;
Chapters 10 and 11: Arthur H. Miller;
Chapter 12: Lawrence R. Wiseman;
Chapter 13: Sol B. Genauer.

I absolve the editors from any responsibility for any errors in this book.

I appreciate the comments given to me with respect to Chapter 11 by Paige Thompson of the New York Stock Exchange, Michael S. Emen of the American Stock Exchange, and Katharine Cox of NASDAQ. Charles Bennett of the National Association of Securities Dealers, Inc. was kind enough to review the abbreviated description of the Corporate Financing Rule of the NASD.

Helpful suggestions for this book were made by Ted Kaminer of Gruntal & Co., Inc. and my son, L. Keith Lipman. I also want to thank Bruce Goldberg of Coopers & Lybrand for his examples of companies that had initial public offerings without significant revenues or earnings.

I also want to thank Martin Chazin, a paralegal, who prepared Appendices 2 through 4. I also acknowledge the ever cheerful and invaluable assistance of Kit Boyle, our librarian. Last but not least, I owe a special debt to my secretary, Terie Cotten, for unusual dedication and patience.

Contents

Going Public

Introduction

Going public is a milestone for a growing company. Public companies can typically raise capital more cheaply and easily than private companies, with far fewer operational restrictions. Founders of public companies can retain their control positions and still sell their own stock to diversify their investments. Upon death, the founder's estate has a liquid asset to pay death taxes, without being forced to sell the company.

Even if you cannot sell your personal stock in your company's initial public offering (IPO), you can usually start selling your own stock under Rule 144 of the Securities Act of 1933 as early as six months after the IPO without incurring any new registration costs. Rule 144 permits you to personally sell at least 1 percent of the outstanding stock every three months. In addition, your personal stock may be sold in registrations subsequent to your IPO.

Greater growth is possible for public companies than private companies because of their access to larger pools of capital. It is no coincidence that most of the *Fortune* 500 companies are publicly-traded. Nor is it an accident that many of the *Fortune* 300 families' fortunes resulted from their association with founders of public companies. A recent example is William Gates, III, the founder of Microsoft, who at age 36 was (according to *Forbes*)[1] the richest man in America with a net worth in excess of $6 billion.

Private companies, like public companies, can also raise growth capital through their internally generated funds, bank loans, and private placements of their securities. However, unlike public companies, private companies cannot offer private placement investors the liquidity of the public market place. This lack of liquidity generally results in a lower valuation for the company than a comparable public company and limits the overall amount of available growth capital.

There are, however, a number of significant disadvantages to going public. Chief among these disadvantages are the pressure to show earnings growth and the additional management, accounting, legal, and printing costs of both the IPO and subsequent compliance with federal and state securities laws. A complete description of the advantages and disadvantages is contained in Chapter One of this book.

A successful IPO requires careful advance planning beginning as early as five years before the IPO target date. Most businessmen begin planning for the IPO shortly before the target date. This is too late. A wise entrepreneur will obtain advice from experienced SEC (Securities and Exchange Commission) professionals well in advance of the target date to maximize the benefits of the IPO. Suggestions for advanced planning, such as adopting stock option plans, are contained in Chapter Two of this book.

A successful IPO also requires the careful selection of an underwriter and clever marketing of the IPO (described in Chapters Three and Four of this book) as well as lucky timing to fit within an IPO "window" in the stock market. The stock market's appetite for an IPO is extremely variable. IPO windows tend to open and close quickly.

Chapter Five of this book discusses the preparation of a prospectus.

The traditional IPO is a strange process. A company may spend several hundred thousand dollars before an underwriter will legally commit itself to buy even one share of stock. Although underwriters will estimate the price at which the securities can be sold early in the registration process, they will not legally commit themselves until the SEC declares the registration statement effective. This is after most of your out-of-pocket costs have been incurred. The public offering price will be determined based upon market conditions existing at the time the SEC declares the registration statement effective. These market conditions may be drastically different than those existing at the time the IPO process began.

Thus, even the best advanced planning and the most prudent selection of an underwriter may not be sufficient to insure a successful IPO. In IPOs, it is better to be lucky than smart.

Chapters Six through Ten of this book describe some nontraditional methods of going public, including self-underwritten and best efforts offerings, mergers with public shells, and spin-offs.

Chapters Eight and Nine of this book describe the new Regulation A offering and SCOR (Small Corporate Offering Registration) offerings, respectively. SCOR is the new $1 million "do-it-yourself" offering.

Chapter Eleven describes the requirements for trading on Small Cap NASDAQ and the NASDAQ National Market as well as national securities exchanges.

Chapters Twelve and Thirteen of this book describe some of the consequences of being public and Rule 144, respectively.

Chapter Fourteen is the exciting story of the 1986 Microsoft IPO.

Chapter One

The Advantages
and Disadvantages

The Advantages

The major advantages of being public are as follows:

1. Lower Cost of Capital

A public company has more alternatives for raising capital than a private company. A private company, once it has exhausted its bank lines, generally raises additional equity and subordinated debt capital from institutional investors. These institutional investors, such as venture capital funds, insurance companies, and others, usually require very stiff terms including significant operational restrictions.

In contrast, a public company has the additional alternative of going to the public market place. The public market place typically does not demand the same stiff terms. This results in less dilution to the existing shareholders and fewer operational restrictions.

Investors will value two identical companies, one private and the other public, quite differently. Investors in the private company will discount the value of its equity securities by reason of their "illiquidity," that is, the inability to readily sell them for cash.

The availability of the public capital alternative also permits the

5

public company greater leverage in its negotiations with institutional investors. Many institutional investors prefer investing in public companies since they have a built-in "exit," that is, they can sell their stock in the public market.

2. Personal Wealth

A public offering can enhance your personal net worth. Stories abound of the many millionaires and multi-millionaires created through public offerings. Even if you don't realize immediate profits by selling a portion of your existing stock during the initial offering, you can use publicly-traded stock as collateral to secure loans.

For approximately six months after the IPO, the underwriter will restrict you from selling your personal stock. Thereafter, you can sell stock under Rule 144. Rule 144 permits you to personally sell up to 1 percent of the total outstanding stock of the company every three months, or if higher, one week's trading volume. The sales have to be in unsolicited brokerage transactions or transactions with brokerage firms that make a market in your stock. You also will have to publicly report these sales. Thus, it may not be desirable for you to utilize Rule 144 too frequently for fear of giving the investment community the impression that you are "bailing out."

Approximately one or two years after your IPO, you may have another registered public offering in which you sell a greater amount of your holdings than in the IPO. You generally can only do so if your company's earnings have grown since your IPO.

3. Competitive Position

Many businesses use the capital from the IPO to enhance their competitive position. The additional capital resources permit greater market penetration.

Some businesses have only a short window of opportunity. For example, a technology-based company can use the IPO proceeds to achieve a dominant position in the marketplace well before its underfinanced competitors.

Customers like to deal with well-financed businesses. A strong balance sheet is a good marketing tool.

6

4. Prestige

You and your co-founders gain an enormous amount of personal prestige from being associated with a company that goes public. Such prestige can be very helpful in recruiting key employees and in marketing your products and services.

5. Ability to Take Advantage of Market Price Fluctuations

The market price of public company stock can fluctuate greatly. These fluctuations may relate to overall stock market trends and have nothing to do with your company's performance. The stock market from time to time tends to unreasonably overprice your stock or severely underprice it.

During the period that the market severely underprices your stock, your company has the ability to repurchase the stock in the stock market at these depressed prices. Likewise, during the period that the market unreasonably overprices your stock, your company can sell stock on very favorable terms. None of these opportunities are available to a private company.

6. Enhanced Ability to Grow Through Acquisitions

Underwriters prefer companies that can use the IPO proceeds to grow the business. You can use the cash proceeds from the IPO to effectuate acquisitions, which can help your company grow faster. A publicly-traded company may also grow by using its own stock to make acquisitions. This option is generally not available to a private company, which is forced to use cash or notes for acquisitions. Private company stock is not attractive to a seller because it lacks liquidity.

The ability to grow through stock acquisitions may permit your company to use pooling-of-interest accounting for acquisitions. An acquiring company using pooling-of-interest accounting can reflect, as part of its own reported income, the income the acquired company earned even before the date of the acquisition. Pooling accounting also avoids the reduction of your company's future income caused by goodwill amortization resulting from the acquisition and the extra depreciation resulting from writing fixed assets of the acquired company up to their current values. If pooling accounting is available, no goodwill is created and no write-up of fixed assets is required.

7

Spectacular increases can occur in your company's reported earnings per share as a result of pooling accounting for acquisitions. This could occur, for example, where your company's stock is valued at 20 times earnings and you can use your stock to effectuate mergers based on paying 10 times the acquired company's earnings. After the merger, your stock price will presumably reflect the acquired company's earnings multiplied by 20.

Since your company's stock will trade for a multiple of your reported earnings per share, significant increases in your reported earnings per share can, in turn, result in dramatic increases in your company's stock price.

7. Enhanced Ability to Borrow; No Personal Guarantees

When your company sells stock, it increases its net worth and improves its debt-to-equity ratio. This should allow your company to borrow money on more favorable terms in the future.

Banks often require the principals of private companies to personally guarantee bank loans made to their companies. Once your company is public, banks and other financial institutions are less likely to require any personal guarantees.

8. Enhanced Ability to Raise Equity

If your company continues to grow, you will eventually need additional permanent financing. If your stock performs well in the stock market, you will be able to sell additional stock on favorable terms.

9. Attracting and Retaining Key Employees

Stock options offered by emerging public companies have much appeal and can help you to recruit or retain well-qualified executives and to motivate your employee-shareholders.

10. Liquidity and Valuation

Once your company goes public, your stock will have a market and you will have an effective way of valuing that stock. Subject to Rule 144 (see Chapter Thirteen), you can sell whenever the need arises.

You can easily follow your stock prices. The market will quote prices daily, and the newspaper may even print them.

11. Estate Planning

Many private companies have to be sold upon the death of their founder in order to pay death taxes. This may prevent you from passing the ownership of your private company to your family or to key employees.

Founders of private companies sometimes fund death taxes by maintaining large life insurance policies on their lives. However, the premiums paid on these life insurance policies can be a significant drain on the business. These premiums are not deductible for federal income tax purposes.

If you publicly trade your company's stock, your estate will have a liquid asset with which to pay death taxes.

The Disadvantages

The major disadvantages are as follows:

1. Expense

The cost of going public is substantial, both initially and on an ongoing basis. As for the initial costs, the underwriters' discount or commission can run as high as 10 percent or more of the total offering. Additionally, you can incur out-of-pocket expenses, which typically range from $150,000 to $500,000 for even a small offering of $10 million of your securities. (See Chapter Four for more information on these initial expenses.) If your IPO is cancelled at the last minute because of adverse market conditions or other reasons, you will be liable for substantial costs.

On an ongoing basis, regulatory reporting requirements, stockholders meetings, investor relations, and other expenses of being public can run from $25,000 to $100,000 or more annually. This is in addition to your management time, which can be considerable. For example, the cost of printing and distributing your annual and quarterly reports, proxy statements, and stock certificates can be extremely expensive.

9

In addition, you may need to hire additional financial and accounting personnel to help prepare your company's financial disclosures. Likewise, you may need to hire a shareholder relations employee and to upgrade the quality of existing financial and accounting employees. These are all additional hidden costs of going public.

A number of smaller public companies have developed methods of minimizing their ongoing costs of being public. These methods include the judicious use of outside professionals, sending bare-bone annual and quarterly reports to shareholders, using inexpensive techniques to reproduce and mail these shareholder reports (e.g., third class mail), avoiding expensive shareholders' meetings, and so on. Minimization of such expenses can reduce your ongoing costs to just $20,000 per year.

2. Pressure to Maintain Growth Pattern

After going public there will be considerable pressure to maintain the growth rate you have established. If your sales or earnings deviate from an upward trend, investors may become apprehensive and sell their stock, driving down its price. You may not have the capital with which to buy back the stock at these depressed prices. As a result, you will have unhappy stockholders.

Additionally, you will have to begin reporting operating results quarterly. People will evaluate the company on a quarterly, rather than annual, basis. This will intensify the pressure and shorten your planning and operating horizons significantly. The pressure may tempt you to make short-term decisions that could have a harmful, long-term impact on the company.

3. Disclosure of Information

Your company's operations and financial situation are open to public scrutiny. Information concerning the company, officers, directors, and certain shareholders—information not ordinarily disclosed by privately-held companies—will now be available to competitors, customers, employees, and others. You legally must disclose such information as your company's sales, profits, your competitive edge, material contracts with major customers, and the salaries and perquisites of the chief executive officer and certain highly-paid executive officers. You must disclose it not only when you initially go public but also on a continuing basis thereafter.

10

The SEC (Securities and Exchange Commission) staff has a procedure to authorize confidential treatment for documents you file. However, you must apply to the SEC early in the IPO registration process to avoid holding up the IPO. Very sensitive information can typically be excluded from public scrutiny.

The SEC mandated disclosures should not be a major concern to most businesses. Your competitors may already possess a lot more information about you than you realize. Customers, suppliers, and ex-employees may have already revealed this information to them. Many companies already provide some financial information to business credit agencies, such as Dun & Bradstreet. Although public companies disclose much more financial information than private companies, the additional information is not necessarily a competitive disadvantage.

In general, the SEC requires public companies to disclose information that is material to investors. You do not have to disclose information about specific customers for your products unless the customer's purchases are such a high percentage of your total sales as to be material to investors. Likewise, you do not normally have to disclose the exact profitability of specific products, provided that the product lines do not constitute a separate industry segment for financial reporting purposes.[2] The SEC gives management reasonable discretion in determining whether its business includes separately reportable industry segments. Accordingly, it is usually possible to avoid disclosure of the exact profitability of separate product lines.

4. Loss of Control

If a sufficiently large proportion of your shares is sold to the public, you may lose control of the company. Once your company is publicly-held, the potential exists for further dilution of your control through subsequent public offerings and acquisitions. Likewise, you may be subject to a hostile tender offer.

You can alleviate this disadvantage by the careful insertion of anti-takeover provisions in your charter or by creating two classes of stock with disproportionate voting rights. Although there are few, if any, anti-takeover defenses that are completely, legally foolproof, some defenses can in practice be very effective against raiders. Defenses that deprive the raiders of voting power or that otherwise penalize the raiders are particularly effective.

Many underwriters will object to unusual anti-takeover defenses in

11

the charter of IPO companies. Such defenses may make it more difficult to attract certain institutional investors. Underwriters who do not seek institutional investors will usually be more relaxed about these clauses.

What is a "normal" anti-takeover defense and what is "unusual" is typically a matter of negotiation with the underwriter. For example, some underwriters will object to the staggering of the terms of the members of the board of directors so that all directors are not elected each year. Others will not. In general, anti-takeover provisions, which are part of state law and which require special shareholder action to opt-out of, will usually be accepted by underwriters.

Even if anti-takeover defenses cannot be inserted into your charter prior to your IPO, you can usually amend your charter after your IPO to insert these defenses. You should accomplish this before your personal stock ownership falls below 50 percent of the outstanding stock.

5.   *Shareholder Lawsuits*

Public companies and their directors, officers, and control persons can be sued by their shareholders.

Shareholder class action lawsuits typically follow a significant drop in the market price of your company's stock caused by adverse news about your company. The theory of these suits is that your company knew or should have known of the adverse news and had a duty to publicize it at an earlier date than the date the news actually became public. The lawsuit will allege that failure to publicize the information earlier constitutes "fraud-on-the-market."

Overly optimistic or exaggerated statements contained in your company's reports to shareholders, or in press releases, are usually cited in these lawsuits to support their allegations. These statements are typically the result of a misguided attempt to generate interest in your company.

Public companies can prevent such law suits, or at least win them if brought, only by a careful program of promptly disclosing adverse news to the trading markets and by avoiding overly optimistic or exaggerated comments in shareholder and press releases. This requires that you be sensitive to the need for such disclosures.

Since everyone makes a mistake occasionally, it is a good idea to obtain liability insurance for directors and officers. Such insurance can cost anywhere from $15,000 to $100,000 per year or more in addition to the out-of-pocket expenses described earlier. However, some private companies maintain this insurance, but usually at lower cost. Thus, only consider the extra insurance premium costs of being public a disadvantage of an IPO.

6. Estate Tax Disadvantage

One of the advantages of an IPO is to create sufficient liquidity to pay death taxes. However, there is a concomitant disadvantage. It is more difficult to obtain a low estate tax valuation for a publicly-traded stock than for the stock of a private company. This is true because the public market tends to value stocks on a multiple of earnings basis, rather than a book value basis.

Chapter Two

Advanced Planning

Long term advanced planning is absolutely essential for a successful IPO. The following are ten suggestions for companies considering a future IPO, although not all of them are appropriate for all companies:

1. Develop an Impressive Management and Professional Team

Underwriters look for companies with impressive management teams. Reputable underwriters will shy away from one-man companies.

Your chief financial officer must be an impressive as well as competent person. This is particularly true if your CFO will be the main contact person for investment analysts after your IPO.

The assembly of your management team should not occur on the eve of your IPO. If you have a weakness in management, the time to upgrade your key employees is several years before your IPO target date.

It may be prudent to obtain an objective evaluation of you and your management team by a reputable management consultant.

Your auditor and your attorneys must also be impressive to the investment community. Hire accounting firms and law firms that have the SEC background and expertise to guide you up to and through the IPO.

2. Adopt a Stock Option Plan

You should adopt a stock option plan as early as five years before the target date for your IPO.

There are three primary advantages to granting options this early:

- You can grant options to yourself and your key employees at low exercise prices. Options should be issued with exercise prices equal to the appraised market value of your shares on the grant date to avoid accounting charges to your earnings. The earlier the options are granted in your company's growth cycle, the lower will be the appraised market value of your shares and, consequently, the lower the option exercise price.

- The prospect (even long-term) of an IPO will be an incentive for your existing key employees and permit you to attract new key employees with stock options. Many stories circulate about key employees who became instant millionaires with their stock options after an IPO.

- The options will reduce the dilution of your equity when the IPO occurs, since underwriters usually do not consider a reasonable number of outstanding options in valuing your company.

Most companies adopt a stock option plan on the eve of their IPO. This is the wrong time to adopt a stock option plan, since the options then have to be granted at the higher "market value" caused by your earnings growth and the imminent IPO. Moreover, you have lost the golden opportunity to incentivize your key employees and attract new key employees during the years preceding the IPO.

Suppose you never have an IPO? The company may make the stock options granted not exercisable unless and until there is a public offering. If your company never has a public offering, the options would expire unexercised.

A stock option is a great incentive device for key employees, whether your company is private or public. It gives key employees a proprietary interest in helping your company grow. It may lower the amount of cash compensation you pay to retain and attract key employees. If you desire to compensate your employee option holders even if your company never has an IPO, you can provide for cash payments to cancel these options.

How is your market value determined? An independent appraiser

16

should be used to determine the market value of a company whose stock is not publicly traded. The cost of such an appraisal can, with some shopping, be obtained for as little as $10,000 or possibly lower.

What should be the duration of the stock options? The stock options granted to your key employees can have a term of up to ten years and still have the benefit of incentive stock option treatment under the Internal Revenue Code. If you want incentive stock option treatment for your own options, you, generally, will not be able to give yourself an option having a term in excess of five years and your option price will have to be 110 percent of market.

Since the duration of the option may be more important to you than the tax benefits, consider giving yourself a non-incentive stock option having a ten year term issued at market value (not 110% of market). The loss of the tax benefits can be more than made up for by the additional five year term and the lower option price.

What happens if your key employees terminate their employment before the IPO? Any good stock option plan should contain a provision which terminates the option to the extent then unexercised upon an employee leaving, with or without cause, or after being fired. If employment terminates before the IPO and the option is not exercisable until the company goes public, the employee would have no further rights upon his termination.

If your stock option plan permits the employee to exercise an option before the IPO, and the employee has exercised a stock option before the termination, the option should contain a "call" provision permitting the company to buy back the stock. The "call" price should equal the option exercise price paid per share plus an amount necessary to compensate the employee for his loss of interest on the cash he paid to the company to exercise the option. If you are more generous, you might pay the employee an amount to reflect the per share increase in the book value of the option stock since the date of option grant, or some other appropriate measurement of his contribution to the company.

Why not grant stock options on the eve of the public offering with exercise prices that are below your proposed public IPO offering price? The problem with this strategy is that it raises the eyebrows of the underwriters and the investment community. Options issued on the eve of the IPO at below the IPO price rewards management even if the investment community suffers because the market price never happens to rise above the IPO price.

17

Moreover, the issuance of a stock option on the eve of an IPO with an exercise price below your *proposed* public offering price may result in accounting charges against the income of the company which could reduce the *actual* public offering price of your stock.

The SEC accounting staff may require accounting charges for options issued within one year of the IPO at prices below the IPO price. The SEC will typically require the company to justify these price differentials by variations in the valuation of the company between the date of the option grants and the IPO date.

For example, assume that your *proposed* IPO public offering price is expected to be based on a valuation of your company equal to 25 times your company's projected income after taxes. If your company grants stock options on the eve of the IPO at an exercise price below your stock's current market value (which is presumably your *proposed* IPO public offering price), your projected income would be reduced as a result of the accounting charge arising from issuance of the below market stock options. For each dollar of reduction in your projected income, your company's valuation could be reduced by 25 times the reduction. As a result, your company must either issue more shares to raise the same amount of money or issue the same number of shares at a lower *actual* IPO public offering price per share.

3. Grow Your Business with an Eye to the Public Market Place

Growing your business with an eye on the public market place requires you to become familiar with publicly-held companies similar to your own business. If you are engaged in two or more businesses, become familiar with publicly-held companies in each of your businesses.

You should pay particular attention to the price-earnings multiple of these similar public companies. The price-earnings multiple is obtained by dividing the market price of the stock by the earnings per share for the prior four quarters. This figure is regularly published by most financial newspapers.

If the price-earnings multiple of one of your two businesses is very low and is much higher for the other business, focus your attention on growing the business with the higher price-earnings multiple. Your growth efforts will receive greater reward by concentrating them on the business with the most potential.

Underwriters are particularly interested in businesses which are dominant in their field. Again, focus your efforts in becoming dominant in a niche business.

How Large Must My Company Be? Do you think that the company whose summarized financial information is presented below, is a good or bad candidate for a traditional firm commitment IPO?

| | *Fiscal Year Ending in* | | | |
	1989	*1990*	*1991*	*1992*
Product Revenues	$297,601	$437,578	$234,621	$523,197
Net Loss	(250,084)	(482,160)	(475,226)	(608,994)

	March 31, 1991	*March 31, 1992*
Total Assets	$133,331	$ 578,734
Total Liabilities	646,640	1,699,022
Working Capital (Deficit)	(394,830)	(1,442,259)
Stockholders' Equity (Deficit)	(513,309)	(1,120,288)

If you guessed that this company could not possibly qualify for a traditional IPO, you are wrong. This company, called "Palomar Medical Technologies, Inc.," completed a $6.6 million public offering in December 1992. Palomar Medical Technologies, Inc. was organized to design, manufacture and market lasers, delivery systems, and related disposable products for use in medical and surgical procedures.

In December 1992, a $17 million IPO was completed for Ultralife Batteries, Inc. The company, which develops, manufactures and markets lithium batteries, reflected revenues of approximately $1.5 million and a loss of approximately $1,660,000 for its last complete fiscal year prior to the IPO.

Do you think that the following company can qualify for a $24 million IPO?

| | *Fiscal Year Ending in* | | | |
	1989	*1990*	*1991*	*1992*
Net Sales	—	—	—	$53,890
Net Loss	(837,064)	(1,489,026)	(3,363,188)	(3,492,703)

In February 1993, the company described above closed a $24

million IPO. The lead underwriters were Morgan Stanley & Co. and Kidder, Peabody & Co., both prestigious underwriters. The company is named "Cyberonics." Its business is to design, develop, and bring to market medical devices which provide a novel therapy, vagus nerve stimulation, for the treatment of epilepsy and other debilitating neurological disorders.

Some underwriters *say* that they will not consider any company for an IPO unless the company has an income after taxes of at least $1 million during the last fiscal year. *The $1 million earnings level is really a rule of thumb which is often violated by those who advocate it.* In computing the $1 million earnings level, underwriters will normally permit you to add to your income the interest you will save in paying off debt from the IPO proceeds.

The larger underwriters generally require a minimum IPO of $10 million to $15 million in order to permit them to earn a reasonable profit. To achieve that level IPO, the valuation of your company after the IPO must be in the $20 million to $30 million range (including the IPO proceeds in the valuation), since underwriters generally do not wish to sell more than 50 percent of your company stock in the IPO. The so-called $1 million rule of thumb really is a shorthand method of telling prospective IPO candidates that their valuations must be high enough to permit at least a $10 to $15 million initial public offering.

Whether or not your company ever reaches the $1 million earnings level, it may still be a good IPO candidate. Many companies which have no earnings whatsoever, but great growth potential, go public with national underwriters. Your future growth potential is much more important to an underwriter than your current earnings. Many national, regional and local underwriters will underwrite your offering without regard to your earnings level.

Even very large and prestigious national underwriters will occasionally underwrite a company with minimal or no earnings or large losses, and great growth potential. This is particularly true in "hot" industries, such as environmental companies. But it is not limited to these industries.

Start-up companies with proven management teams are also taken public by prestigious underwriters. A "proven management team" means that they have successfully grown another company. For example, do you think that Bill Gates would really have difficulty finding an underwriter if he started another company?

In 1992, there were approximately 140 Firm Commitment IPOs involving less than $10 million.[3] These IPOs were underwritten by smaller and less well-known underwriters. In addition, there was a large but unknown number of nontraditional public offerings (described more fully in Chapters Six through Ten). Therefore, the mere fact that your company's valuation (including the IPO proceeds) does not permit a $10 million offering should not discourage you from seeking this alternative for raising growth capital.

According to a 1992 SEC release, a significant percentage of public companies have a market capitalization, assets and revenues of less than $5 million. The following are the SEC charts:

Public Companies—Classified by Market Capitalization

Market Capitalization	Cumulative Number and Percentage of Public Companies
Less than $5 million	3,003 (38%)
Less than $10 million	3,909 (49%)
Less than $15 million	4,393 (55%)
Less than $20 million	4,756 (60%)
Less than $25 million	5,017 (63%)

Public Companies—Classified by Assets

Assets	Cumulative Number and Percentage of Public Companies
Less than $5 million	2,325 (25%)
Less than $10 million	2,961 (32%)
Less than $15 million	3,326 (36%)
Less than $20 million	3,612 (39%)
Less than $25 million	3,769 (41%)

Public Companies—Classified by Revenues

Revenues	Cumulative Number and Percentage of Public Companies
Less than $5 million	1,845 (22%)
Less than $10 million	2,494 (29%)
Less than $15 million	2,937 (35%)
Less than $20 million	3,287 (39%)
Less than $25 million	3,562 (42%)

It is clear from these charts that many public companies are relatively small.

Growth Strategies

Reaching a high earnings level does give your company access to many more underwriters and lowers the percentage of the company you must sell in the IPO. Therefore, you should develop a strategy to maximize your earnings.

Your growth strategy might include the expansion of your product lines or entering into related businesses. This takes time. Your strategy might also include a merger with another company in your industry. Some IPO candidates merge on the effective date of the IPO. They fund the merger with the proceeds from the IPO or possibly use stock which is registered in the IPO.

Underwriters like companies that are showing growth through acquisitions. Identifying potential merger targets and negotiating transactions with them is not something easily done on the eve of the IPO.

Obviously, it is better to grow through bank loans and internally generated capital. However, that is not always possible. Identifying and negotiating with private capital investment sources takes careful advanced planning. Your growth strategy might require you to obtain additional private capital several years before the IPO target date.

4. Show Earnings Growth Before You Go Public

Private companies are typically operated in a manner to minimize income taxes. As a result, they tend to adopt policies which reflect the lowest possible taxable income.

Investors are interested in the growth of accounting earnings. You may have the greatest business in the world, but if you do not show your accounting earnings because of your minimization of taxes, you will not get the best price for your stock when you do go public. You may not even be able to have an IPO at all if you do not show sufficient earnings.

Underwriters also look at earnings trends to make certain that a consistent history of earnings growth over several years is reflected prior to the IPO. The investment community is justifiably suspicious of companies which show earnings for only one fiscal year just prior to the IPO target date.

Therefore, for at least two to three fiscal years prior to your IPO target date, you should begin showing earnings growth for financial accounting purposes. This is not always inconsistent with minimizing taxes, since different policies can be adopted for both tax and accounting purposes (e.g., taking accelerated depreciation for tax purposes but not for accounting purposes). Your accountant can retroactively adopt new accounting policies which will assist you in reflecting earnings.

One method of reflecting accounting earnings is to reduce share-holder-officer salaries. If you do not want to reduce your lifestyle, you should consider paying a dividend to make up for the short-fall. A dividend can have adverse tax effects if your company has not made a Subchapter S election. Therefore, you should consider becoming a Subchapter S corporation as part of your IPO planning. (There are other advantages to a Subchapter S election mentioned in Recommendation 9 below.)

5. Obtain Audited or Auditable Financial Statements

The SEC normally requires audited income statements for three years[4] in order to go public, if you or a predecessor have been in business that long. It may not be possible, on the eve of the IPO, to retroactively obtain audited financial statements. This is particularly true if sales of inventory account for a significant portion of your revenues and no auditor has ever observed your inventory.

Therefore, it is preferable to obtain either currently audited financial statements or to obtain "auditable" financial statements, that is, financial statements which are capable of being audited retroactively at the time of your IPO.

6. Clean Up Your Act

Public companies operate in a fishbowl. If you engage in illegal or other questionable practices as a private company, you may have created contingent liabilities for your company which may have to be publicly disclosed in the IPO registration statement. No one will buy the securities of a company which may have significant contingent liabilities resulting from questionable practices.

It is wise to stop any questionable practices many years before your IPO target date. Indeed, the statute of limitations on causes of action for commercial bribery, for understatement of federal income taxes (e.g., as a result of inventory cushions, paying relatives who do not work, etc.), may be as long as six years and could be even longer in certain cases.

It is strongly recommended that you stop any such questionable practices well before the date you plan to go public. Besides, you'll sleep better at night.

7. Establish Two Classes of Stock or Other Anti-Takeover Defenses

It is never too early to establish two classes of stock or other anti-takeover defenses. The longer the company has operated with these anti-takeover defenses, the more likely the company will be able to retain them in the IPO. However, there is no guarantee that any anti-takeover defenses can survive the negotiations with the underwriter.

The best takeover defense is two classes of common stock. The first class of common stock, call it Class A common stock, would be intended to be sold in the IPO and have the right to elect only a small percentage of the members of the board or perhaps none at all.[5] The second class of stock, call it Class B common stock, would elect a majority of the board of directors and, at the option of the holder, be convertible into Class A common stock, usually on a one for one basis. Both Class A and Class B stock would be issued to the founder, with the majority of the shares being Class A stock. If stock options are granted, the options should be granted in the Class A stock so as to avoid dilution of control.

Other anti-takeover clauses can also be established as well. These could include staggering election of directors by classifying the terms of the members of the board of directors, prohibiting removal of the board of directors except for cause, multiple director votes to the founders, etc.

Particularly valuable are clauses which prohibit purchase of more than a specified percentage (e.g., 10 percent) of the company's stock without board permission and permitting the company to repurchase at a loss to the investor any excess shares acquired without board permission. Although these clauses have not been legally tested, their very appearance in your charter has a deterrent effect.

Even if the potential underwriter objects to anti-takeover clauses, almost none will object to changing your company's state of incorporation. Changing your state of incorporation to such states as Nevada and Pennsylvania can dramatically increase the protection given to management from unwanted offers. Contrary to popular opinion, states such as Delaware may not be as protective against unfriendly suitors as some of these other states.

No underwriter likes to have anti-takeover clauses in the IPO. If your IPO is marginal, it is likely that few (if any) anti-takeover clauses will survive underwriter scrutiny since they add unneeded marketing problems to the IPO.

If the IPO cannot be sold with major anti-takeover clauses, then consideration should be given to installing such anti-takeover clauses at the first annual shareholders' meeting after the company has gone public. In many states, the shareholder votes of the founders can be counted to approve anti-takeover amendments to the charter. However, establishing two classes of stock is much more difficult, if not impossible, once the company has gone public.

When interviewing potential underwriters, questions should be asked as to whether or not the existence of two classes of stock or other anti-takeover clauses would prevent their underwriting the IPO. Most underwriters, in their eagerness to obtain the business, are willing to accept any reasonable anti-takeover clauses if such provisions are contemplated at the time they are hired.

8. Select Your Own Independent Board Members

Consideration should be given to appointing independent directors to your board prior to the IPO. Such independent directors can, if they have outstanding credentials, help establish the credibility of your management team to potential underwriters. They can also be helpful in introducing you to potential underwriters and guiding you through the IPO process.

Public companies are expected (and are required by stock exchange and NASDAQ/National Market rules) to have an independent audit committee of their board of directors. The underwriters will insist upon the appointment of independent directors in order to "dress-up" the prospectus for the investment community.

You will need independent directors for the IPO anyway. Therefore, why not obtain the benefit of their knowledge even before the IPO? Appointing them to your board before the IPO also gives you a chance to evaluate them as directors. It may also forestall a request by the underwriters to have their own designees appointed to the board. However there is no assurance of this. Even if you never have an IPO, many private companies find that having independent directors on their board is helpful since they can give dispassionate advice in the operation of your business.

Some potential directors would prefer to be appointed to an "Advisory Committee," rather than to your board of directors, because of liability concerns. If the person has outstanding credentials and the company does not maintain liability insurance for directors and officers, you may wish to accommodate their request. However, it should be understood that the person will join your board of directors when the IPO occurs since, presumably, the company will then purchase directors and officers liability insurance.

Most outside directors will accept a small stock option if you do not wish to pay them in cash for their services.

9. Create Insider Bail-Out Opportunities

Underwriters of IPOs are very wary of permitting founders of the company to sell any significant amount of their present stock in the IPO. It looks like a bail-out.

Subchapter S

A Subchapter S corporation creates unique bail-out opportunities. A "Subchapter S corporation" is a corporation which has elected to be taxed similar to a partnership or sole proprietorship Subchapter S of the Internal Revenue Code of 1986 (as amended). The shareholders of a Subchapter S corporation are personally taxed on the corporation's income for federal income tax purposes.

Underwriters will typically not object to the withdrawal from the corporation of this previously taxed income upon the closing of the IPO. Of course, the company must still be reasonably funded after the withdrawal.

The withdrawal is in reality a dividend to the insider. It is typically justified by the fact that the income was previously taxed to the shareholders.

Shareholders of non-Subchapter S corporations (so-called C or regular business corporations) have much greater difficulty convincing underwriters to permit a dividend on the eve of a IPO. Yet, economically, such dividends are very similar to a Subchapter S withdrawal.

Appendix 1 contains excerpts from the 1992 prospectus for the IPO of *Today's Man,* a retailer of men's clothing. The "Use of Proceeds" section on page 7 of Appendix 1 reflects the effect of the Subchapter S election.

Insider Debt

Underwriters are less concerned with the company using part of the proceeds of the IPO to pay debts or other obligations to an insider, provided the debt or other obligation is incurred in a legitimate transaction.

For example, the insider may enter into a long-term patent license or real estate lease with the company and use a portion of the IPO proceeds to fund the license or lease payments. Likewise, the insider may sell property to the company provided it is normally used in company operations.

Alternatively, if payments to the insider, license, lease or sale were originally funded with bank debt, underwriters generally do not object to the repayment of the bank debt with the IPO proceeds. This may be true even if the insider is a personal guarantor of the bank debt.

However, the sale of insider stock to the company would raise eyebrows unless the sale resulted from the retirement of one of several founders of the company.

Obviously, if the debts or other obligations to the insider are incurred shortly before or upon the closing of the IPO, it looks more like a disguised bail-out. Therefore, any insider transaction should generally be effected well before the IPO. Equally importantly, only a small portion of the IPO proceeds should typically be used for this purpose.

10. Take Advantage of IPO Windows, Fads, and IPOs of Similar Companies

IPO windows quickly open and close. Your short term planning should take advantage of these windows. You may prefer to have your IPO in 6 months or a year. However, in 6 months or a year there may be no market for IPOs.

Your plans must be flexible enough to take advantage of these windows.

The table on the next page shows the great variations in the number of firm commitment IPO underwritings from year to year which are declared effective by the SEC.

Fads often develop in IPOs when investor interest is high. For example, biotechnology and environmental issues are currently popular. If your company has a product line which can be fitted within a fad, you may want to change your IPO target date to take advantage of this fad.

27

Particular attention should be paid to IPOs of other companies in your industry. If another company in your business recently had a successful IPO, underwriters will be eager to market your company's public issue. This is particularly true if the current market price of the stock of the similar company is above its initial public offering price. Your stock will be attractive to underwriters since they can market your IPOs to potential investors with the analogy of the prior successful IPO.

To keep track of IPOs, particularly in your industry you might consider subscribing to a publication called *Going Public: The IPO Reporter.* (For information concerning subscriptions call (212) 227-1200.)

YEAR	NUMBER OF IPOs	DOLLAR VALUE OF IPOs (In Millions)
1970	238	583.7
1971	253	1,071.7
1972	496	2,202.7
1973	96	1,433.9
1974	9	98.8
1975	6	189.4
1976	40	337.2
1977	32	221.6
1978	38	225.4
1979	62	398.4
1980	149	1,387.1
1981	348	3,114.7
1982	122	1,339.1
1983	686	12,466.4
1984	357	3,868.9
1985	355	8,497.6
1986	726	22,211.3
1987	556	26,847.3
1988	291	23,807.5
1989	254	13,706.1
1990	213	10,117.4
1991	402	25,144.2
1992	605	39,947.1
1993*	363*	27,532.5*

*Through July 13, 1993.
Source: Securities Data Co.

Chapter Three

The World of Underwriters

The major marketing steps of your company's IPO involve the following:

- Attracting an Underwriter
- Selecting an Underwriter
- Creating the Prospectus
- Road Shows

Marketing your IPO also requires understanding of the following topics, which are interwoven with the marketing process:

- The Valuation of Your Company
- The Underwriter's Letter of Intent
- Types of Underwritings
- The Cost of the IPO
- Due Diligence
- Press Releases and Publicity
- The Major Participants and Timetable
- The Registration Process
- The Pricing Meeting
- Execution of Underwriting Agreement and Effective Date
- Closing

This chapter covers the attraction and selection of the underwriter. Chapter Four discusses the rest of the marketing steps.

What You Should Know About Underwriters

National Underwriters

Firms that underwrite IPOs range enormously in size and prestige and other characteristics. The so-called national underwriters fall into two categories.

The first category includes underwriters that have retail distribution capabilities around the country by reason of their widespread retail brokerage operations as well as an institutional sales capacity. These firms are colloquially called "wire-houses." Examples of such national firms include: Merrill Lynch & Co.; Dean Witter Reynolds, Inc.; PaineWebber Incorporated; Prudential Securities Incorporated; Smith Barney, Harris Upham & Co., and others.

The second category includes national underwriters that are primarily focused on institutional sales and have few (if any) retail brokerage operations. This category includes: Goldman, Sachs and Co.; Salomon Brothers, Inc.; The First Boston Corporation; and many other excellent firms.

There are two major divisions composing national underwriting firms: (1) the investment banking division; and (2) the institutional sales and retail brokerage division. The investment banking division raises capital, both privately and publicly, arranges mergers and acquisitions, and provides financial consulting and valuation services, such as fairness opinions, offensive and defensive strategies in connection with tender offers, proxy contests, and the like. The investment banking division generates its revenues by charging a fee based on a percentage of the new capital raised or on a percentage of the value of a merger or acquisition, or by charging a fee for its consulting or valuation services.

The institutional sales and brokerage division of these national underwriters generates its revenues primarily through commissions earned on institutional sales and trades of already outstanding equity and debt securities as well as new offerings. In recent years, the investment banking divisions have generated substantially more revenue per employee than the brokerage divisions.

The Chinese Wall

A so-called "Chinese Wall" must legally exist between the investment banking and institutional sales and brokerage division. The law limits the amount and kind of information that the two divisions may share. Investment bankers receive confidential information about issuers of publicly-traded securities and their acquisition and other targets. This confidential information, if publicly revealed, may significantly affect the market prices of the securities of these companies. The Chinese Wall is designed to prevent the disclosure of this market sensitive information by the investment banking division to the other parts of the firm.

The Institutional Bias

As an incentive to the institutional sales and retail brokerage division to sell an IPO underwritten by the investment banking division, larger brokerage fees are typically paid to the individual brokers who generate institutional and retail sales of the IPO securities. This is necessary because it takes more selling effort and time to sell an untested IPO security than to sell normally traded securities.

A far larger percentage commission is paid to brokers who make retail sales (e.g., sales to individuals) of IPO securities than to brokers who make institutional sales. The commission percentage paid to brokers who make institutional sales is typically lower on sales of both IPO and non-IPO securities because of the greater bargaining power of these institutions.

Underwriters typically charge a discount equal to 6 percent to 10 percent of the IPO public offering proceeds. For example, for a $10 million public offering of common stock, $600,000 might be the underwriters' discount. This means that the underwriter purchases the company's common stock issue for $9,400,000 and resells the issue to the public for $10 million. You must also provide underwriters an expense allowance to cover their out-of-pocket expenses.

The gross profit of $600,000, less out-of-pocket expenses not covered by the expense allowance, typically divides three ways:

1. Amounts paid to both retail and institutional brokers that sell the IPO securities (including brokers for underwriting syndicate members)
2. Amounts credited to the investment banking division of the underwriters and paid to its key employees, usually as year-end bonuses

3. Amounts paid to the underwriting firms themselves

The bias of underwriters toward institutional sales of IPO securities is evident from this profit division. Since institutional sales generate lower brokerage commissions, the more IPO securities placed with institutions, the greater is the underwriting profit available to the investment banking division and to the underwriting firms themselves.

In addition, institutional sales tend to be in much larger dollar amounts than retail sales to individuals. Thus, it is far easier to quickly sell an entire IPO to institutions than to individuals.

This built-in bias toward institutional sales means that, left unchecked, a high percentage of IPO securities will wind up in institutional hands. This may or may not be a desirable result for the company. For example, if five institutional investors collectively own 35 percent of your company's outstanding stock, this could threaten control of your company if the founders own significantly less than 50 percent of the outstanding stock.

Niche Underwriters

There are many excellent small underwriters who specialize in specific industries and have a national reputation in that industry. For example, Wessels, Arnold & Henderson specializes in the food industry and Equitable Securities Corporation concentrates in the hospital and medical field. The niche underwriters typically co-underwrite issues with other firms to lend strength and credibility to the underwriting syndicate.

All underwriters have certain industries in which they tend to specialize. A niche underwriter, however, usually specializes in a single industry.

Regional Underwriters

There are many excellent regional underwriters, that is, firms who have distribution capabilities in only one region of the country and do not have as strong a reputation outside their regions as do the national underwriters. These firms will typically co-underwrite the IPO issue with some of the other regional firms with complementary distributional capabilities in other regions.

There is only a blurry line between regional and national underwriters. Many hot "regional" underwriters soon achieve a national reputation and national underwriters lose their "national" reputation after a few flops.

Local Underwriters

There are many tiny local underwriting firms located throughout this country. They are characterized by distinct limits on the dollar size of the issue that they can handle and their local distributional capabilities. Many of these firms underwrite securities only on a "best effort" basis, that is, they never make a firm commitment to buy securities from the issuer, and they receive a commission only on the securities they actually sell.

These local underwriters are particularly useful if you are considering a nontraditional IPO (see Chapters Six through Ten). Brokers in smaller cities and towns have proven extremely adept at raising amounts in the range of $500,000 to $5,000,000. They are usually well-known in their local areas, and hop-nob with groups of wealthy investors from their city or town. These wealthy investors tend to follow the local underwriter into investments that the local underwriter sponsors.

Underwriting Syndicates

IPO underwriting is typically performed by a managing underwriter who forms a syndicate. Even national underwriters with strong national distributional capabilities form syndicates when they wish to hedge their financial risk or obtain a more diversified distribution capability. The syndication also helps attract other syndicate underwriters to make strong after-markets in the IPO securities.

It is not unusual to have two managing underwriters in an IPO and even more than two in a very large IPO. The advantage of two managing underwriters is the creation of greater distributional capability and after market interest. (Having analysts from two firms following your stock is better than only one.) The disadvantage is that the underwriting profits have to split between the firms, thereby decreasing the profit incentive to each managing underwriter. This can be a problem where the total dollar amount of the public issue is small. Since many IPOs have co-managing underwriters, it would seem that the advantage usually outweighs the disadvantage.

Every underwriting syndicate has one lead managing underwriter.

33

The lead managing underwriter is responsible for maintaining the books for the syndicate and is sometimes called the "book manager."

In the arcane world of investment banking, it is customary to have the lead managing underwriter's name on the left side of the face page of the prospectus and the other managing underwriter's name on the right side.

An underwriting syndicate should be distinguished from a selling group. Everyone in the underwriting group is a party to the underwriting agreement signed by your company. Members of the selling group are not. Although members of the underwriting syndicate may sell a portion of the shares they underwrite, they are not necessarily expected to sell such shares. The agreement among underwriters compensates each underwriter for assuming the underwriting risk rather than for actually selling shares.

The underwriting syndicate may be organized before or after you file the registration statement, whereas the selling group can only be formed after the filing.

"Prestigious" vs. "Nonprestigious" Underwriters

A number of academic studies[6] suggest that the investment banking industry is subject to a rigid hierarchy. These studies divide underwriters into two categories: prestigious and nonprestigious. The prestigious underwriters consist of "bulge bracket," "major bracket" and "sub-major bracket" underwriters. They base these upon a ranking scale established by comparing "tombstone announcements" of public offerings listed in *Investment Dealer's Digest* and *The Wall Street Journal* from January 1979 to December 1983.

According to these academics, the rank of the underwriter depends upon its position in these tombstone advertisements. Those underwriters closest to the top of the advertisement (excluding managing underwriters) are more prestigious than those at the bottom of the advertisement. They list underwriters of equal rank alphabetically.

Those in the upper brackets of the hierarchy enjoy a more prestigious and more lucrative position than their lower bracket counterparts. The hierarchy is reflected in the "tombstone announcements" of public offerings. Occasionally an underwriter will withdraw from a public offering in order to avoid being placed in too low a category in the tombstone.[7]

The illustration is an example of a tombstone that reflects this

2,000,000 Shares

TODAY'S MAN

Common Stock

Price $7.50 Per Share

Copies of the Prospectus may be obtained from such of the Underwriters as may legally offer these securities in compliance with the securities laws of the respective states.

ALEX BROWN & SONS INCORPORATED PAINEWEBBER INCORPORATED

DILLON, READ & CO. INC. KIDDER, PEABODY & CO. INCORPORATED LEHMAN BROTHERS

MONTGOMERY SECURITIES OPPENHEIMER & CO., INC.

PRUDENTIAL SECURITIES INCORPORATED ROBERTSON, STEPHENS & COMPANY SALOMON BROTHERS INC.

SMITH BARNEY, HARRIS UPHAM & CO. INCORPORATED WERTHEIM SCHRODER & CO. INCORPORTED DEAN WITTER REYNOLDS INC.

ADVEST, INC. ARNHOLD AND S. BLEICHROEDER, INC. WILLIAM BLAIR & COMPANY

FURMAN SELZ INCORPORATED GRUNTAL & CO., INCORPORATED JANNEY MONTGOMERY SCOTT INC.

LEGG MASON WOOD WALKER INCORPORATED McDONALD & COMPANY SECURITIES, INC. NEEDHAM & COMPANY, INC.

THE ROBINSON-HUMPHREY COMPANY, INC. SCOTT & STRINGFELLOW INVESTMENT CORP.

WESSELS, ARNOLD & HENDERSON WHEAT FIRST BUTCHER & SINGER CAPITAL MARKETS

BREAN MURRAY, FOSTER SECURITIES INC. DOMINICK & DOMINICK INCORPORATED FAHNESTOCK & CO., INC.

FIRST MANHATTAN CO. C.J. LAWRENCE INC. RAGEN MACKENZIE INCORPORATED STURDIVANT & CO., INC.

35

hierarchy. Ignore the two managing underwriters, Alex. Brown & Sons and PaineWebber Incorporated, when determining the tiers. The first tier starts with Dillon, Read & Co., Inc. and ends with Dean Witter Reynolds, Inc. ("Witter" being the last of this tier in alphabetical order). The second tier starts with Advest, Inc. and ends with Wheat First Butcher & Singer. The third tier starts with Brean Murray, Foster Securities Inc. and ends with Sturdivant & Co., Inc.

Academics have used these tiers to determine who is and who is not "prestigious." These scholars examined numerous tombstones over a period of time and use a prestige scale of 0 to 9 points, giving underwriters in the top tier of any tombstone 9 points and those in the bottom tier 0 points. The underwriters with the highest number of points are the most prestigious.

Unfortunately, all of the academic studies are out of date. However, a quick glance at a number of tombstone advertisements in *The Wall Street Journal* will quickly give you a good idea as to how underwriters rank themselves.

Academic scholars view underwriters as the certifiers of the quality of the information released by issuers. The investment banker is a "reputational intermediary."[8] The difference in prestige can affect the investor's confidence in a security according to these scholars. A 1992 study[9] concluded that it is in the issuing company's best interest to engage an underwriter with the most prestigious reputation so that prospective investors will give more credence to the company's prospects.

Underwriter Track Records

Appendix 2 contains a list of the names and addresses of the lead managing underwriters on all firm commitment IPO underwritings filed with the SEC that had a public offer date between January 1, 1990 and March 31, 1992. You can use this list to determine the frequency of IPOs by any given underwriter, the dollar amount of each IPO (excluding overallotment options), and the business of the company that had the IPO.

Appendix 3 contains a list of all firm commitment underwritings filed with the SEC during the same period that involved less than $10 million but did involve $5 million or more. Appendix 4 contains a similar list for IPOs that involve less than $5 million.

The number of IPOs in Appendices 3 and 4 will help debunk the myth that you cannot have an IPO that raises less than $10 million.

36

You can use Appendices 2, 3, and 4 for:

- Determining which underwriters are willing to serve as lead managing underwriters of an IPO.
- Determining the frequency with which these underwriters are willing to serve as lead managing underwriters.
- Determining the industries with which each lead managing underwriter has IPO experience.
- Determining which investment bankers are willing to underwrite IPOs involving less than $10 million (Appendix 3) and $5 million (Appendix 4).

If an investment banker proposes to underwrite your company and has not in the recent past served as lead managing IPO underwriter, you should carefully inquire as to their prior experience. It is possible that the investment banker has frequently been a managing IPO underwriter but is not frequently in the lead. However, the fact that they have not frequently been in the lead may mean that you should continue your search for a good lead underwriter.

The fact that an underwriter has not had prior experience in your industry should not automatically disqualify them. However, all other things being equal, if the proposed investment banker has had a successful IPO in your industry, it is more likely that your company's offering will be successful as well.

The following chart reflects the top seven lead managing underwriters of firm commitment IPOs filed with the SEC that had an offering date from January 1, 1990 to March 31, 1993:

Number of IPOs By Lead Managing Underwriters
January 1, 1990 through March 31, 1993

Lead Managing Underwriters (Top 7 Only)	*Number of IPOs*
1. Alex. Brown & Sons	89
2. Merrill Lynch	76
3. Goldman Sachs & Co.	58
PaineWebber	58
4. Morgan Stanley & Co.	57
5. Lehman Brothers	55
6. First Boston	48
7. Montgomery Securities	43

The only two firms listed that are willing to underwrite IPOs in the range of $15 million are Alex. Brown & Sons and Montgomery Securities. The remaining named underwriters typically are the leads on larger IPOs (as can be seen from Appendix 2).

For IPOs that exceed $5 million but are less than $10 million, the clear winner is D. H. Blair Investment Banking Corp. (see Appendix 3). For IPOs under $5 million, the clear winners are D. H. Blair Investment Banking Corp. and Thomas James Assoc., Inc. (see Appendix 4).

Since the appendices do not reflect managing underwriter experience other than the lead underwriter, avoid mechanical reliance upon them.

How to Attract Underwriters

If you have taken the right steps in planning your IPO, you will have no difficulty in attracting an underwriter.

Investment bankers create and maintain their reputations by underwriting companies whose securities do very well in the market place. Therefore, underwriters are interested in growth companies with competent management teams and that have special market niches. They generally seek companies that can use the proceeds of the offering to grow the business.

To be attractive to an investment banker, your company must have a growth plan that is thorough and impressive. Most underwriters expect a growth of 20 percent or more a year.

The business plan should contain detailed projections of your growth and descriptions of your business (including its birth and development) and the background of its management. You should articulate the major assumptions behind your projections. The business plan should also identify risk areas and describe ways your company can hedge these risks.

The company must have a "story" that is credible to the investment community. Reputable underwriters will thoroughly investigate every aspect of the story. They may contact major customers and suppliers and even competitors. They may contact your banker. They may interview key employees. You must be prepared to convincingly answer questions arising from this investigation.

Companies considering an IPO should seek the advice of their accountants, attorneys, and investment advisors in order to create a business plan that will appeal to an investment banker. They can help you anticipate what questions an underwriter will ask and assist you in preparing the responses.

When underwriters ask you questions they are also appraising your qualities as an executive. You must demonstrate a thorough grasp of your business and its problems. This cannot be over-emphasized. If you appear not to have the answer to an obvious question, but must research the question, the underwriter will wonder about your competency as an executive.

From the underwriter's viewpoint, management quality is the most important attribute of a potential IPO candidate. The underwriter's judgment of your executive talents and those of your management team will be crucial in the underwriting decision.

Underwriters are turned off by companies whose managements are looking to bail-out of their investment in the IPO. They want management to assume the same investment risks as the new investors in the IPO. It is possible for management to sell a small portion of its holdings in the IPO; however, they must justify even such small sales with a reason other than the risks of the business. For example, underwriters would usually not object management selling a small portion of shares to pay personal tax costs resulting from the IPO or other personal needs.

Occasionally, underwriters request principals of companies to sell personal shares to make the offering large enough to be effective. This is possible when the company does not need for its growth plan the extra funds derivable from selling more company stock.

Selecting an Underwriter

The right investment banker is a major factor in the success of your IPO. Some of the attributes you should look for are:

- *Reputation.* The better the reputation of your underwriter, the greater confidence investors will have in purchasing your securities.
- *Distribution Capability.* It is important to have a large and varied base of investors in your company. This helps generate interest in your securities.

- *Experience.*   It is helpful if the managing underwriter has had successful experience with companies in similar industries. This is particularly true if the stock of these other similar companies rose significantly above the IPO offering price after their IPOs.

- *Market-making Capability.*   After the completion of your IPO, it is important that there be a strong after-market in your securities. This increases liquidity to investors. Generally, the managing underwriter will make such a market and you should inquire as to the amount of resources the underwriter will devote to this task. You should inquire whether the managing underwriter has an analyst for your industry, the analyst's reputation (is the analyst listed in the *Institutional Investor* or the *Greenwich Survey*), and if they will periodically distribute research reports on your company's stock.

- *Flexibility in Accommodating Your Needs.*   If you desire to sell a small percentage of your own stock in the IPO, you should inquire whether that would be acceptable to the underwriters. Likewise, if you desire to retain two classes of stock and sell only the lesser voting class in the IPO, you should inquire if the underwriter will object.

The underwriter will, on the effective date of your registration statement, execute an underwriting agreement, with the closing typically within five to ten business days after the effective date. Underwriters will not commit to buying your securities until they are reasonably convinced they can resell them. Unfortunately, you incur almost all of the out-of-pocket costs of the IPO *before* the underwriter ever signs the underwriting agreement. Therefore it is important to chose an underwriter in whom you have great confidence. An ideal underwriter should value its reputation so much that it would absorb some losses on the IPO rather than completely abandon the IPO under adverse market conditions.

There are underwriters for every type of company. Some underwriters will not ordinarily handle IPOs, while other underwriters prefer IPOs. Some underwriters specialize in specific industries. Some underwriters will only handle companies that have revenues or earnings over certain minimum figures. One way to chose an underwriter is to find other companies in your industry that have gone public and identify their underwriters. An experienced securities lawyer and accounting firm may also be helpful in recommending an underwriter.

Ideally, the underwriter should be large enough to easily handle your IPO (either by itself or with a co-managing underwriter), but small enough that your business and goodwill is important to them. You should inquire whether the underwriter has a long-term commitment to research in your industry.

There are a variety of opinions as to whether "shopping" your IPO among underwriters is desirable. If you have only a marginally desirable IPO, you may have no choice but to shop your IPO. If you have a very desirable IPO, you may want to approach a few larger underwriters and create a competition among them. In general, it is best to select the most prestigious underwriter interested in your IPO who has sufficient interest to treat you as an important client.

You should carefully review the information on IPO underwriters contained in Appendices 2 through 4 of this book before making your selection.

Prior to finalizing your selection, check with at least five companies for which this same underwriter acted as lead IPO managing underwriter. Make certain at least two of the IPOs were very recent. Two of the IPOs should be one year and two years old, respectively, to determine the after-market support given by the underwriter under consideration.

Limits on Underwriter Compensation and Offering Expenses

Practically all underwriters are members of the NASD. The NASD prohibits its members from commencing a public offering until the NASD issues an opinion that it has no objections to the proposed underwriting. The NASD will object to any underwriters terms or arrangements that it considers to be "unfair or unreasonable."

The NASD lists the following factors (among others), which they consider when determining the maximum amount of underwriter compensation considered fair and reasonable:

- the offering proceeds
- the amount of risk assumed by the underwriters, which they

determine by (a) whether the offering is "firm commitment" or "best efforts" and (b) whether the offering is an IPO or not

- the type of securities being offered

The NASD determines the maximum amount of underwriters compensation on a case by case basis, and the NASD rules do not specify a specific maximum percentage.

Under the NASD Corporate Financing Rule (adopted in May 1992), it is "unreasonable" for an underwriter and related persons in a public offering (among other things):

- to receive securities as underwriting compensation in an aggregate amount greater than 10 percent of the dollar amount of securities offered to the public (excluding the overallotment option, securities constituting underwriter compensation, and the like);
- to receive any non-accountable expense allowance in excess of 3 percent;
- to receive any accountable expense allowance that includes payment for general overhead, salaries, supplies, or similar expenses of the underwriters incurred in the normal conduct of business.

Underwriters and related persons include underwriters, underwriter's counsel, financial consultants and advisers, finders, members of the selling and distribution group, any member participating in the public offering, and any and all other persons associated with or related to, as well as members of the immediate family, of any of the aforementioned persons.

The NASD rule also contains complicated formulas for valuing warrants given to underwriters by the company and regulates the terms of these warrants. The rules also deem unreasonable any overallotment option of more than 15 percent of the amount of securities offered in a firm commitment underwriting.

The NASD's Corporate Financing Department (the Department) has direct responsibility for the review of underwriting compensation. To ensure compliance with the compensation guidelines, the Department reviews public offerings before their effective dates and aggregates all items of value proposed to be received by underwriters and related persons. The Department then compares the total compensation, expressed as a percentage of offering proceeds, to the appropriate guideline applicable to the offering. For the Department to issue an opinion expressing "no objections" to the underwriting compensation, such compensation must be equal to or less than the maximum applicable guideline.

To predict levels of underwriting compensation accurately, the Department analyzed the amount of compensation received, as disclosed in the final offering document or prospectus, for 874 corporate equity offerings filed with the Department during calendar year 1991. All items of underwriting compensation received by underwriters and related persons were considered, including: cash discounts or commissions; accountable and non-accountable expense reimbursements; warrants, options, cheap stock, and other securities and rights to acquire securities received by underwriters and related persons; finders fees paid for introducing the underwriter and the issuer; rights of first refusal; financial consulting and advisory fees; and all other items of value received in connection with the offering.

The offerings were organized into three categories: 402 firm commitment IPOs, 380 firm commitment secondary offerings, and 92 best efforts offerings. For each of the three categories, the staff performed a regression analysis to predict expected amounts of compensation for certain size offerings in each category.

The illustration on page 44 reflects the results of the Department's study and indicates the gross proceeds of the offering (in millions of dollars) and the typical predicted percentage of gross proceeds, exclusive of any over-allotment option, that might be allocated to underwriting compensation for firm commitment IPOs, firm commitment secondary offerings, and best efforts corporate equity offerings. The amounts shown do not represent the compensation actually received in any one offering or the mathematical average for all offerings of a particular size reviewed during 1991. Such amounts also do not reflect the compensation originally proposed to be received when the offerings were filed with the NASD. However, the illustration does indicate the generally accepted level of compensation as determined by the Department.

Many underwriters will, prior to the IPO, raise private investment capital for your company. Under the NASD Corporate Financing Rule, all compensation and other items of value received within the six-month period prior to the filing of the IPO registration statement are presumed (subject to rebuttal) to be underwriting compensation. The NASD also examines all items of value received more than six months, but within

TOTAL UNDERWRITING COMPENSATION

Gross Dollar Amount of Offering (millions)	Firm Commitment Initial Offerings (%)	Firm Commitment Secondary Offerings (%)	Best Efforts Offerings (%)
$ 1	15.80%	14.57%	11.83%
2	14.31	12.91	10.72
3	13.44	11.94	10.07
4	12.82	11.26	9.61
5	12.34	10.72	9.26
6	11.95	9.56	8.96
7	11.62	9.12	8.72
8	11.33	8.76	8.50
9	11.08	8.45	8.32
10	10.65	8.18	8.15
11	9.90	7.95	8.04
12	9.18	7.74	7.86
13	8.49	7.56	7.73
14	7.82	7.39	7.61
15	7.59	7.24	7.50
16	7.55	7.10	7.40
17	7.52	6.97	7.30
18	7.48	6.85	7.21
19	7.45	6.74	7.12
20	7.42	6.63	7.04
25	7.29	6.20	6.68
30	7.19	5.86	6.39
35	7.10	5.60	6.14
40	7.02	5.37	5.93
45	6.95	5.19	5.74
50 or more	6.89	5.00	5.57

one year, of the filing of the IPO registration statement. Underwriters who raise private capital for your company will typically wait at least six months, and preferably one year, before commencing the IPO to avoid these rules.

State securities laws also impose varying limits on underwriting compensation and offering expenses. For the most part the NASD limits are more restrictive. However, unlike the NASD limitations, some states (including Alabama, Arkansas, Kansas, Nebraska, Oklahoma, South Dakota and Texas) restrictions on "offering expenses" can include legal and accounting fees and expenses paid by the company. However, the total offering expense limits in these states (ranging from 15 percent to 20 percent of the aggregate offering price) are usually high enough to avoid bumping into them.

The NASD also has adopted rules (the so-called "free riding rules") designed to restrict the purchase of so-called "hot issues" by NASD members and their directors, officers, employees, and other related persons. The purpose of these rules is to require a bona fide public distribution of "hot issues." A "hot issue" is an IPO in which trading opens at a premium above the public offering price.

The selection of an underwriter is a critical step in the process of raising public capital. Your selection will undoubtedly be affected by the valuation the underwriter initially gives to your company. The valuation of your company and the registration and marketing of your IPO are discussed next.

Chapter Four

Registering and Marketing the Traditional IPO

$\mathbf{O}$nce you have selected an underwriter, there are preliminary discussions concerning the valuation of your company, an underwriter's letter of intent is signed, and the registration process commences. The process ends with a closing at which you issue the shares and the company receives the net offering proceeds.

The Valuation of Your Company

Underwriters do not usually value your company until the "pricing meeting," which is held on the effective date of your registration statement or a few days thereafter. However, the underwriters should be able to determine the procedure for the valuation at the beginning of the IPO.

Generally, underwriters will look at comparable companies that are public and determine their price earnings multiple or their multiple of EBITDA (earnings before interest, taxes, depreciation and amortization). If a comparable company has been public for a while and its market price is 14 times its trailing earnings, for example, on the effective date of the IPO registration statement, it may be expected that your company will probably be valued at a 10% to 15% discount below the 14 multiple.

This discount provides an incentive for the institutional investors to buy your stock (as opposed to the stock of more seasoned public companies in your industry) on the grounds that your stock is a bargain.

If you are using IPO proceeds to discharge the company's bank or other indebtedness, the underwriter will typically permit you to increase your earnings or EBITDA by the pro-forma interest savings resulting from such discharge of debt.

Your adjusted earnings or EBITDA are then multiplied by the appropriate multiplier to value your company. For example, if the company's adjusted earnings or EBITDA is $2 million and the discounted multiplier is 12, the company will have a $24 million valuation prior to adjustment for the IPO proceeds. If the company wishes to raise $12 million from the sale of stock in the IPO, the company's overall valuation will be $36 million ($24 million plus $12 million) and 33⅓ percent of the outstanding stock of the company will be sold in the IPO.

There is a tendency of underwriters to underprice the stock in the initial public offering. Therefore, it may be wise to consider minimizing the total number of shares that you sell in the IPO. Obviously, you must balance this consideration against your capital needs at the time the offering goes into effect.

A slightly underpriced IPO has the advantage of permitting IPO investors to enjoy a price rise in the after market trading. This may stimulate investor interest in future public offerings by your company.

Underwriters generally tend to price the stock of initial public offerings at between $10 and $20 per share. Occasionally, they use an IPO price of $20 or more to create prestige for the issue. If the stock is priced below $5 per share, it would be considered "penny stock" and, therefore, subject to onerous SEC rules applicable to brokers. The institutional investment community also tends to shun "penny stock" issues.

To get to a price range of $10 to $20, you may need to change your stock capitalization (by stock splits or reverse stock splits) to achieve the desired IPO price, based upon the valuation for your company and the proportion of your company to be sold in the IPO.

In general, a minimum of 350,000 shares is sold in an IPO and preferably a number above 350,000 shares. The purpose of this minimum number is to make certain there is a sufficient "float" to permit an active trading market after the IPO.

Underwriter's Letter of Intent

Once you have selected an investment banker interested in an IPO, your company will sign a letter of intent. The letter of intent usually is not legally binding (except as noted below), but does express the basic business understanding of the parties.

The letter of intent will typically cover the following topics, among others:

- the expected offering price per share
- the amount of the underwriter's discount (or commissions in the case of a best efforts offering)
- overallotment option
- who is responsible for the payments of expenses, such as lawyers, accountants, printers, filing fees, and other expenses (is there an underwriter's expense allowance and is it accountable or nonaccountable)?
- any board members to be designated by the underwriter
- preferential rights on future financings by the company

Unless your company has very strong bargaining power, it is probably wise to agree to give the underwriter, if requested, a preferential right on future financings. However, it is also wise to limit that right to a period not exceeding three to five years and possibly condition that right on the sale of the company's stock in the IPO at or close to the price projected by the underwriter.

It is important for the company to designate counsel for the underwriter from a list of counsel approved by the underwriter. Since the company may ultimately pay the fees and costs of underwriter's counsel, the company should have input into this decision. The company should also attempt to designate the financial printer from an approved list submitted by the underwriters.

There may also be a clause inserted into the letter of intent that requires the company to pay the underwriters' counsel fees and other out-of-pocket expenses in the event the company decides to withdraw from the offering. At a minimum, this clause should be amended to insert a "not to exceed" figure. In addition, you may vary the maximum figure by whether the withdrawal occurs early or late in the registration process.

Occasionally, underwriters attempt to insert a clause in the letter of

49

intent providing that if the company is sold before the IPO effective date, and the company withdraws from the IPO, a commission on the sale price should be paid to the underwriter. Such clauses should be carefully reviewed with your counsel and, in appropriate cases, rejected.

Generally the letter of intent legally restricts any press releases or other publicity by the company concerning the offering without approval of the underwriter.

The letter of intent does not prevent the underwriter from withdrawing from the IPO. It should be made clear that the company will not reimburse the underwriter for its own counsel fees or other expenses if the underwriter withdraws without any breach by the company. The best safeguard to the company against the arbitrary withdrawal of the underwriter from the IPO is the underwriter's investment of time, counsel fees and costs in the IPO project as well as the damage to its reputation caused by an arbitrary withdrawal.

Types of Underwritings

There are generally two types of underwritings:

1. Firm Commitment.
2. Best Efforts.

Under a firm commitment underwriting, the underwriters agree to buy, at a fixed price, all the securities being sold at a discount from the public offering price. The underwriters then resell the securities to the public at the public offering price. If the underwriters do not resell all the securities, the underwriters assume the investment risk with regard to the unsold securities.

Under a best efforts commitment, the underwriters agree to use their "best efforts" to sell the securities. However, if they do not sell the entire amount to the public, they have no obligation to purchase the balance from the company. The underwriters merely act as agent for the issuer of the securities. They are never at risk if the securities are not sold.

There are several variations of the "best efforts" commitment. For example, the agreement may provide that a minimum number of securities must be sold or the purchase price is returned to the investors.

Most initial public offerings with national or regional underwriters are on a firm commitment basis. This is the traditional IPO underwriting. Indeed, "best efforts" initial public offerings are relatively rare and the financial markets would view them as a sign of weakness.

As previously noted, even a firm commitment underwriting is not "firm" prior to executing the underwriting agreement on the IPO registration statement's effective date.

The Cost of a Traditional IPO

The largest single cost of your IPO is the underwriters discount from the public offering price. In a firm commitment underwriting, this normally ranges from 7 percent to 10 percent of the public offering price. In a "best efforts" offering, the underwriter is paid a commission, which is based upon the public offering price and is the economic equivalent of the discount. All other factors being equal, the commissions in a best efforts underwriting should be slightly lower than the underwriter's discount since the underwriter assumes less risk.

Some underwriters, in addition, require the company to pay an expense allowance, which may or may not be on an accountable basis. This is a negotiated figure.

The company will also incur out-of-pocket costs for legal fees, accounting fees, and printing. Legal fees for your own counsel in an IPO are typically between $125,000 and $250,000. This figure usually includes a certain amount of corporate housekeeping that your company may have deferred for a number of years.

Accounting fees generally run between $75,000 and $125,000. However, they can be much higher if there are significant issues related to the audit.

Printing costs can run $50,000 to $150,000 or more, depending upon the length of the prospectus, whether or not you use pictures and color, and the extent of the revisions required. Since revisions can be very expensive, it is best not to commence printing until after you circulate a reasonably good draft to all parties.

Other out-of-pocket costs include SEC filing fees (1/29 of 1 percent of the maximum aggregate offering price), blue sky fees and costs ($15,000 or more depending on the number of states and the amount registered in each state), filing fees of the NASD ($500 plus .01 percent of the gross dollar amount of the offering with a maximum filing fee of $30,500), and registrar and transfer fees (generally $10,000 to $25,000).

If the underwriter withdrew very close to the effective date of the offering, it is possible your company could lose anywhere from $300,000 to $500,000.

The underwriter is liable for its counsel fees and costs and incurs significant executive time in any underwriting. Therefore, the underwriter has a significant investment it will lose if you or it abandons the offering at a late stage.

The following is the cost breakdown (excluding underwriters discount and expense allowance) contained in the $15 million 1992 IPO of "Today's Man," a clothing retailer, excerpts of whose prospectus you can read in Appendix 1:

Securities and Exchange Commission	
Registration Fee	$ 8,625
National Association of Securities Dealers, Inc. Fee.	3,360
Printing and Engraving Expenses	75,000
Accounting Fees and Expenses	100,000
Legal Fees and Expenses	150,000
Blue Sky Qualification Fees and Expenses	10,000
Transfer Agent and Registrar Fees and Expenses	10,000
Miscellaneous	43,015
TOTAL	$400,000

The underwriters' discount totalled $1,050,000. The overall aggregate offering costs of $1,450,000 ($400,000 plus $1,050,000) was approximately 10 percent of the $15 million offering (disregarding the over-allotment option).

Due Diligence

Under the Securities Act of 1933 ("1933 Act"), the company is absolutely liable if there are material misstatements or omissions contained in the registration statement at the time it becomes effective (unless the purchaser knew of the untruth).

In addition, the following persons are also liable to investors in such event, subject to the "due diligence" defense:

- Directors
- Officers who sign the registration statement (the principal executive, financial and accounting officers)

- The underwriters

- Experts (independent accountants and the like)

The due diligence defense permits the persons named above (excluding the company) to defend themselves from such liability if they have performed a reasonable investigation and have no reason to believe (and do not believe) that there were any material misstatements or omissions. With regard to the "expertized" portions of the registration statement (like audited financial statements), it is sufficient to establish a due diligence defense if these persons have no reason to believe (and do not believe) that there are any material misstatements or omissions.

The underwriters and their counsel spend much time and effort, both prior to filing the registration statement and after filing and prior to its effective date, in attempting to establish this due diligence defense.

The most famous case on the due diligence defense is *Escott v. Barchris Construction Corporation.*[10] This case arose out of a public offering by a company engaged in the construction of "bowling centers," the growth industry of the late 1950s and early 1960s. The investors sued the company and its directors, its officers who signed the registration statement, its auditors, and its underwriters. The court found material misstatements and omissions in both the financial and nonfinancial portions of the prospectuses (e.g., the backlog).

The court held that none of the defendants had established a due diligence defense. The court created different standards of due diligence based upon (a) whether a director was or was not an officer and (b) upon each defendant's background and expertise.

The decision in *Barchris* is also noteworthy in rejecting due diligence defense claims by the following directors with respect to the portions of the registration statements other than the audited financial statements:

- Two founding directors and officers, "each men of limited education" for whom the "prospectus was difficult reading, if indeed they read at all" had no diligence defense. The court stated that, "the liability of a director who signs a registration statement does not depend upon whether or not he read it or, if he did, whether or not he understood what he was reading."

- An outside director was liable even though he just became a director on the eve of the IPO and had little opportunity to familiarize himself with the company. The court found that the 1933 Act imposed liability on a director "no matter how new he is." The outside director was not permitted to rely on the statements of other directors and officers of the company who were "comparative strangers" without making further inquiry.

- An outside lawyer director who failed to check on his client's statements to him, which could "readily have been checked," including his client's overstatement of the company's backlog, was held personally liable.

Press Releases and Publicity

The following is a discussion of the restrictions on publicity during each of the following three time periods:

- Prior to Filing Registration Statement (the "Gun Jumping" Prohibition)
- After Filing Registration Statement and Prior to Its Effective Date
- After Effective Date of Registration Statement and During Continuation of Public Distribution

Prior to Filing Registration Statement ("Gun Jumping" Prohibition)

Section 5(c) of the 1933 Act generally makes it *unlawful* to offer to sell any security *prior to the filing* of a registration statement. This is the "gun jumping" prohibition. The purpose of this prohibition is to prevent issuers and other persons from arousing public interest in a securities offering prior to the filing of a registration statement.

The term "offer to sell" is broadly defined in Section 2(3) of the 1933 Act to include *"every attempt . . . to dispose of a security, for value."* Publicity that a company does not express as an offer may, nevertheless, be construed by the SEC as an offer if it is deemed to involve such an "attempt."

The SEC has taken the position that the release of publicity in

54

advance of a filing that has the *effect* of conditioning the public mind or arousing public interest in an issuer or in its securities constitutes an offer in violation of Section 5 of the 1933 Act. Upon discovery of such a violation, the SEC will usually delay the effective date of a registration statement in order to allow the effect of such publicity to dissipate.

The SEC has also taken the position that the prohibition against "offers" of securities prior to filing is not intended to restrict normal communications between issuers and their stockholders or the public with respect to important business or financial developments, provided such communications are consistent with the issuer's prior practice, are in the customary form, and do not include forecasts, projections, predictions or opinions as to value. Nor does the prohibition affect discussions with underwriters.

In order to determine whether a particular activity or statement by an issuer would constitute an unlawful offer, the facts and circumstances surrounding each activity or statement, including its content, timing, and distribution, must be analyzed. Since this determination often involves difficult legal issues, it is imperative that the company clear any proposed public disclosure with its counsel before its release. Such disclosures would include, but not be limited to, letters to shareholders, press releases, interviews, speeches, and advertisements. The SEC is particularly concerned with publicity that artificially stimulates the markets by whetting the public appetite for the security.

If your offering is a Regulation A offering (discussed in Chapter Eight), you can test-the-waters before filing provided that you comply with certain disclosure requirements, submit the offering material to the SEC, and do not accept any money. However, you may not raise more than $5 million.

After Filing Registration Statement and Prior to Its Effective Date

After the filing of a registration statement and before its effective date, you may make verbal offers to sell securities. Thus, the underwriters may conduct "road shows" during this period. However, during this period, *no written offers* may be made except by means of a statutory prospectus (the "red-herring" prospectus). The underwriters may also place Tombstone advertisements during this period.

You may not consummate any sales of securities during this period.

The prohibition of sales includes a prohibition on contracts of sale as well as the receipt of any portion of the securities' purchase price.

The release of publicity (particularly in written form) during this period also raises a question about whether the publicity is a selling effort by an illegal means, that is, other than by means of a statutory prospectus. Therefore, the company should continue to clear any proposed publicity with its counsel prior to its release.

After Effective Date of Registration Statement and During Continuation of Public Distribution

After the effective date of the registration statement, you may make both written as well as verbal offers. However, during the period of the public distribution of security, a copy of the final statutory prospectus must be delivered in connection with any *written* offer or confirmation or upon delivery of the security, whichever occurs first. You may use supplemental sales literature if you accompany it or precede it by a final statutory prospectus. You may consummate sales during the post-effective date period.

The release of publicity after the effective date and prior to completion of the public distribution likewise raises issues as to whether the publicity is a written offer or supplemental sales literature which must be accompanied by a final statutory prospectus. Therefore, your company should continue to clear any proposed public disclosure with its counsel until it completes the public distribution.

Major Participants and Timetable

The major participants in the IPO are as follows:

- Company: Typically, the CEO and CFO
- Company Counsel
- Underwriter
- Underwriter's Counsel
- Independent Auditors

A typical timetable for an IPO is contained in Appendix 5.

The Prospectus

Usually, the company's securities counsel drafts the IPO registration statement and then distributes it to the underwriter, the underwriter's counsel, the independent auditors, and the executives of the company. The prospectus is Part I of the registration statement. Part II contains other information, which although filed with the SEC, is not distributed to investors, such as a breakdown of the costs of the offering, indemnification rights of directors and officers, lists of exhibits, and certain financial statement schedules.

Generally the underwriters and others "wordsmith" the initial draft of the prospectus until it tells a convincing story to potential investors. This "word-smithing" process is sometimes a laborious and time consuming process and typically occurs at various meetings of all the parties. These "all hands" meetings may last through the night, especially those meetings held at the printers immediately prior to filing.

Of most concern to the underwriters are the business description section, the management discussion and analysis section, and the use of proceeds section of the prospectus. These sections must present a cohesive and convincing story to investors. Chapter Five of this book describes these sections in greater detail.

The Registration Process

Once you file the original IPO registration statement with the SEC, there is generally a quiet period until the SEC issues its letter of comment. Typically this occurs within 30 days after the filing. Although the SEC may determine not to review the IPO registration statement, this is relatively rare.

Once you receive the comment letter, you prepare revisions to the registration statement, along with supplemental explanations where required, and file an amendment to the registration statement. The SEC may require several amendments before it is willing to declare the registration statement effective.

State Securities Laws

The registration statement also has to be filed and ultimately cleared in the states in which offers and sales will be made. Almost all of the states have securities (blue-sky) laws. Some states will not clear IPOs that they consider too speculative or risky. This can occasionally cause serious problems for the marketing of the IPO.

The most common blue-sky problem is the prior sale by the company to insiders and promoters of stock at prices substantially below the IPO price ("cheap stock"). The states generally deem prior sales at 85 percent or less of the IPO price to be "substantially" below the IPO price. The cheap stock issue is typically raised with respect to companies that have no significant earnings or are in the development stage.

The usual justifications for cheap stock include:

- an increase in value of the company since the date of issuing cheap stock
- a low price for stock results from resale restrictions
- shares were sold to officers and employees at low prices in lieu of normal compensation
- the number of shares involved is de minimis

If the state securities administrator does not agree with the justification, some states require that the shares be escrowed until the achievement of certain earnings objectives by the company and cancelled if those earnings objectives are not satisfied in five or six years.

The IPOs, particularly of promotional or developmental stage companies, can also suffer from some of the following blue-sky problems:

- Some states may not register the stock if the company's existing capital is less than 10 percent of the aggregate offering price of the stock sold in the IPO, or if the total cash invested by promoters is less than 10 percent of the aggregate offering price.
- Some states look with disfavor on excessive numbers of warrants or stock options given to promoters and insiders.
- Some states object to excessive dilution (the difference between the IPO price and the pro forma net tangible book value per share after giving effect to the IPO) if the dilution to new investors exceeds 50 percent.

- Some states will object to insider loans.
- Some states will not register IPOs if the class of stock offered to the public either has no voting rights or less than proportional voting rights. Justifications for the unequal treatment include giving the IPO stock a dividend or liquidation preference.
- Some states object to "blank check" preferred stock, i.e., where the board of directors sets the terms of the preferred stock without shareholder approval.
- Some states object to a company having a negative net worth unless the company projects to show profits in a reasonable period of time.
- Some states limit the amount of expenses that you may incur in a public offering.

Most of these blue-sky problems surface in states that have merit review laws. These laws permit a state administrator to determine the substantive merits and fairness to investors of the IPO. This contrasts with the SEC review of IPOs under the 1933 Act, which (theoretically at least) considers only the adequacy of the disclosures. The states that currently apply these merit review standards the most strictly are Arizona, Arkansas, California, Iowa, Massachusetts, Missouri, Nebraska, North Carolina, Ohio, Oklahoma, Tennessee, Texas, and Wisconsin.

Road Shows

Sometime after the initial filing date and before the effective date, the underwriter will organize and schedule "road shows," which "showcase" the company's executives. These involve marketing meetings at various cities in the United States and possibly abroad with potential underwriting syndicate members, portfolio managers, securities analysts, brokers, and institutional investors.

A presentation is usually made by the company (with the underwriter providing assistance) and the audience is given the opportunity to ask questions. The underwriters will rehearse you on expected questions and the disclosure guidelines to which you must adhere.

The road shows (including one-on-one meetings with institutional investors) are usually hectic times for both the underwriter and the company's executives. They involve substantial traveling over a compressed time period, generally ranging from a week or two weeks. The road shows will educate the financial community about your company and generate interest in your IPO.

The Pricing Meeting

The "pricing meeting" firmly establishes the public offering price for your securities. This meeting typically occurs after the close of the market on the day prior to the effective date of the registration statement or within a few days thereafter.

The investment banker will recommend a public offering price based upon a number of factors. The most important factor is the price earnings multiples or EBITDA multiples of companies in the same industry that are of comparable size and capitalization and market conditions in general at the time of the pricing meeting.

It is important that you do your own homework in preparing for the meeting. You should be aware of the price/earnings ratios and EBITDA ratios of comparable companies and you should be prepared to negotiate with the underwriters. However, your bargaining power will usually be very limited. It is generally better to sell your company's stock slightly too cheaply than to have unhappy IPO investors because the aftermarket price falls below the IPO price.

Execution of Underwriting Agreement and Effective Date

The underwriters and your company execute the underwriting agreement on the date (or the evening before the date or a few days after) you expect the SEC to declare the IPO registration statement effective.

This is the first time the underwriters legally bind themselves to purchase your securities. They must purchase securities at a closing generally held five business days after the date of execution. The underwriting agreement is a complicated agreement and contains a number of "outs" for the underwriter. The most important "outs" are:

- A breach by the company of the warranties, representations, or covenants set forth in the underwriting agreement.
- The failure to deliver legal opinions, accountant's "cold comfort" letter, or other similar documents at the closing.
- An order issued by the SEC suspending the effectiveness of your registration statement.

The underwriting agreement may also contain an "over-allotment" option, also sometimes called a "green shoe." This option typically permits the underwriter to purchase up to a maximum of an additional 15% of the number of shares included in the basic offering. The underwriter can only exercise the option within 30 days of the public offering date. This option permits the underwriter to sell to the public more shares than the they must purchase under the underwriting agreement, and to cover their "short position" by exercising the over-allotment option.

On the date the SEC declares your IPO registration statement effective, you may list the stock or the stock may qualify for trading on an exchange or on NASDAQ. Chapter Eleven contains the requirements your stock must meet for listing on NASDAQ and the major stock exchanges.

You may also register your stock under Section 12 of the Securities Exchange Act of 1934. This registration makes your company subject to various periodic reporting requirements, proxy rules, tender offer rules, short-swing profit rules, and the like. For more information see Chapter Twelve.

Closing

The closing is generally held five business days after the execution of the underwriting agreement. At the closing, the company and other selling shareholders receive the check (typically in next-day funds) and the underwriters receives the company's securities.

Chapter Five

Preparing the Prospectus
for the Traditional IPO

The company, its counsel, and its accountants prepare the initial draft of the prospectus for the traditional IPO (as noted in Chapter Four). They submit this draft to the underwriters and their counsel for comment. Subsequently, they resubmit redrafts incorporating the comments to all parties. At "all-hands" meetings everyone reviews the redrafts to hone them into shape.

The preparation of a prospectus for the traditional IPO reflects the tension between two objectives: creating a good marketing document and avoiding legal liability.

Typically you can reconcile these conflicting objectives by tilting the disclosure in the "Prospectus Summary" and "Business" sections more toward the marketing objective. Although from a legal viewpoint it may be better to scatter risk factors throughout the document, marketing considerations typically prevail when drafting those two sections.

You can compromise the marketing/legal liability objectives by creating a separate section of the prospectus entitled "Investment Considerations," which contains risk factors related to the business. Frequent cross references are then made throughout the prospectus to the "Investment Considerations" section. Thus, you will notice prospectuses that contain an "Investment Considerations" section having the cross-reference words "See Investment Considerations" liberally sprinkled throughout the prospectus and particularly in their marketing oriented "Business" section.

SEC forms and rules dictate the contents of the prospectus for the traditional IPO. These forms and rules are elaborate and complicated. Here are the highlights.

SEC Registration Forms

You register the traditional IPO on a Form S-1 Registration Statement. It applies if no other registration statement form is applicable.

In 1992, the SEC adopted a special registration statement form for a "small business issuer." A small business issuer refers to a company and other issuer that:

- Has revenues of less than $25 million
- Has a public float of less than $25 million (if the issuer is publicly held, the aggregate market value of the securities held by non-controlling persons is less than $25 million)
- Is a U.S. or Canadian issuer
- Is not an investment company
- If a majority owned subsidiary, the parent corporation is also a small business issuer

Any "small-business issuer" can use Form SB-2 to register its securities. If, as a small business issuer, you have not previously registered more than $10 million in securities offerings in any continuous twelve month period (including the present transaction), you can use a Form SB-1 to register up to $10 million of securities to be sold for cash.

Advantages of Forms SB-1 and SB-2

The big advantages of Forms SB-1 and SB-2 over Form S-1 is that they require less specified disclosure and only two years of audited financial statements. Form S-1 requires three years of audited financial statements.

The purported advantage of Form SB-1 over Form SB-2 is that it permits a question and answer format (Form SB-2 requires a narrative format). For an example of the question and answer format, see the offering circular in Appendix 6.

The lesser disclosure requirements of Forms SB-1 and SB-2 may decrease overall preparation costs. However, it is not yet clear how material this cost reduction will be in view of the newness of these forms.

There are two major problems with Forms SB-1 and SB-2:

- It is unclear whether the professional investment community will accept the question and answer format of Form SB-1 and the fewer disclosures of both Form SB-1 and Form SB-2.
- Legal liability considerations may cause Forms SB-1 and SB-2 to look more like Form S-1, thereby destroying any cost savings.

Institutional investors and other members of the professional investment community are accustomed to a narrative format, not a question and answer format. Likewise, these investors may not be satisfied with the lesser disclosures of Forms SB-1 and SB-2. This is especially true for Form SB-2, which a small business issuer could use for a large dollar offering normally presented on a Form S-1. For example, a non-small business issuer must register a $15 million offering on the more elaborate Form S-1, whereas a small-business issuer can register the same $15 million offering on Form SB-2 with its fewer specified disclosures.

Just as a company tries to please customers with its marketing material, so must an underwriter accommodate the desire of the professional investment community. This community is used to the Form S-1 format. Old customs die hard!

Legal Concerns

Although the SEC made a good faith attempt to simplify disclosure for small business issuers, it did not modify its "anti-fraud" and other legal liability rules. Thus, Rule 408 under the 1933 Act still requires the disclosure of all other material information necessary to make the disclosures in Forms SB-1 and SB-2 not misleading. Merely complying with the explicit disclosure requirement of these forms does not insulate the company from liability.

Likewise, Sections 11 and 15 of the 1933 Act still make the company and its directors, officers, and other control persons liable for material misstatements or omissions in Forms SB-1 and SB-2. The liability of the company is absolute (unless the investors knew of the falsity). The personal liability of directors, officers, and other control persons applies even to material misstatements or omissions made in good faith, unless such persons can prove that in the exercise of reasonable care they could not have known of the material misstatements or omissions.

For example, Form S-1 requires the disclosure of products contributing more than 15 percent of the company's annual consolidated revenues (10 percent if the total consolidated revenues exceed $50 million per year). Forms SB-1 and SB-2 do not specifically require that disclosure.

If sales of a particular product constitute a disproportionately high amount of the company's revenues (say 25% of annual revenues) and such contribution is not disclosed, reasonable arguments can be made that the omission is material and creates legal liability. This is true even though neither Form SB-1 nor SB-2 specifically requests that information.

Sections of Form S-1 Prospectus

The following are the headings found in a typical IPO Prospectus that are part of the Form S-1 Registration Statement[11] and distributed to investors:

Prospectus Summary
The Company
Investment Considerations
Dividend Policy and Prior S Corporation Status [if applicable]
Use of Proceeds
Dilution
Capitalization
Selected Financial Data
Management's Discussion and Analysis of Financial Condition
    and Results of Operations
Business
Management
Certain Transactions
Principal Shareholders
Description of Capital Stock

Shares Eligible for Future Sale
Underwriting
Legal Matters
Experts
Additional Information
Financial Statements

From the viewpoint of the professional investment community, the sections entitled "Business," "Management Discussion and Analysis" ("MD&A") and "Use of Proceeds" are among the more important sections of the nonfinancial disclosures in the prospectus.

Business

The following are some of what you must have in the Business section of the Prospectus. (The "registrant" in SEC rules refers to the company or other entity registering the securities).

General Development of Business

This is a description of the general development of the business, its subsidiaries, and any predecessor(s) during the past five years, or such shorter period as the registrant may have been engaged in business. You must disclose information for earlier periods if material to understanding the general development of the business.[12]

No Prior Revenues

If the company has not received any prior revenues from operations during each of the past three fiscal years, you must provide a detailed description of your plan of operation.

Industry Segments

For each of the registrant's last three fiscal years or for each fiscal year the registrant has been engaged in business, whichever period is shorter, the company must state the amounts of revenue (with sales to unaffiliated customers and sales or transfers to other industry segments shown separately), operating profit or loss, and identifiable assets attributable to each of the registrant's industry segments.

Principal Products

The principal products produced and services rendered by the registrant in the industry segment and the principal markets for, and methods

67

of distribution of, the segment's principal products and services must be described. In addition, for each of the last three fiscal years, the company must state the amount or percentage of total revenue contributed by any class of similar products or services which accounted for 10 percent or more of consolidated revenue in any of the last three fiscal years or 15 percent or more of consolidated revenue, if total revenue did not exceed $50 million during any of such fiscal years.

The description should include the following:

- A description of the status of a product or segment (e.g., whether in the planning stage, whether prototypes exist), the degree to which product design has progressed or whether further engineering is necessary, if there has been a public announcement of, or if the registrant otherwise has made public information about, a new product or industry segment that would require the investment of a material amount of your company's assets or that otherwise is material. You are not required to disclose otherwise nonpublic corporate information, which would, if known, adversely affect your competitive position.

- Raw Materials. The sources and availability of raw materials.

- Patents, etc. The importance to the industry segment and the duration and effect of all patents, trademarks, licenses, franchises and concessions held.

- Seasonality. The extent to which the business of the industry segment is or may be seasonal.

- Working Capital Items. Tell how your company's industry's practices relate to working capital items (e.g., where the registrant is required to carry significant amounts of inventory to meet rapid delivery requirements of customers or to assure itself of a continuous allotment of goods from suppliers; where the registrant provides rights to return merchandise; or where the registrant has provided extended payment terms to customers).

- Dependence on Customers. Disclose how dependent the segment is upon a single customer or a few customers, the loss of any one or more of which would have a material adverse effect on the segment. "The name of any customer and its relationship, if any, with the registrant or its subsidiaries must be disclosed if sales to the customer by one or more segments are made in an aggregate amount equal to 10 percent or more of the registrant's consolidated revenues and the loss of such customer would have a material adverse effect on the registrant and its subsidiaries taken as a whole. You may include the names of other customers unless it would be misleading.

- Backlog. Give the dollar amount of backlog orders believed to be firm as of a recent date and as of a comparable date in the preceding fiscal year. Indicate what portion of this you reasonably expect you will not fill within the current fiscal year and give seasonal or other material aspects of the backlog.

- Competition. Describe the competitive conditions in the business including, where material, the identity of the particular markets in which your company competes, an estimate of the number of competitors, and your company's competitive position (if known or reasonably available). Identify the principal methods of competition (price, service, warranty or product performance, or the like) and explain the positive and negative factors pertaining to your competitive position.

- R&D. If it is material, give the estimated amount your company spent during each of the last three fiscal years on research and development activities. Use generally accepted accounting principles.

- Effects of Environmental Laws. You must disclose the material effects that compliance with federal, state, and local provisions regulating the discharge of materials into the environment, or otherwise relating to the protection of the environment, may have upon the company and its subsidiaries' capital expenditures earnings, and competitive position.

You should carefully review the "Business" section of the *"Today's Man"* prospectus (Appendix 1).

Management Discussion and Analysis

The SEC views the MD&A section as one of the most important sections of disclosure documents, because it helps to explain the financial results to the reader. As a result, several enforcement actions have been brought by the SEC based upon defective MD&As.

Underwriters also are concerned with the MD&A for different reasons. The MD&A and Business sections must dovetail. A reader of

69

the MD&A must be able to understand the financial results of the company's business as discussed under the "Business" section. In addition, the MD&A should explain the selected financial information that precedes it.

The MD&A must provide the reader with information with respect to the liquidity, capital resources, and results of company operations. It includes other information necessary to understanding the company's financial condition and the results of its operations.

The following are some of the highlights from the SEC rules as to what must be contained in the MD&A section of the Prospectus:

Liquidity[13]

The SEC requires the identification of any known trends or any known demands, commitments, events, or uncertainties that will result in or that are reasonably likely to result in the registrant's liquidity increasing or decreasing in any material way. If a material deficiency is identified, the course of action that the registrant has taken or proposes to take to remedy the deficiency should be indicated. Also, the company is required to identify and separately describe internal and external sources of liquidity, and briefly discuss any sources of liquid assets used.

Capital Resources

- The registrant's material commitments for capital expenditures as of the end of the latest fiscal period, and the general purpose of such commitments, and the anticipated source of funds needed to fulfill such commitments should be described.
- The registrant must describe any known material trends, favorable or unfavorable, in the registrant's capital resources. Any expected material changes in the mix and relative cost of such resources should be indicated. The discussion must consider changes between equity, debt, and any off-balance sheet financing arrangements.

Results of Operations

The information required by the SEC about the results of operations include the following: The registrant should describe any unusual or infrequent events or transactions or any significant economic changes that materially affected the amount of reported income from continuing operations and, in each case, indicate the extent to which income was so affected. In addition, any other significant components of revenues or

70

expenses that, in the registrant's judgment, should be described in order to understand the registrant's results of operations.

- Any known trends or uncertainties that have had or that the registrant reasonably expects will have material favorable or unfavorable impact on net sales or revenues or income from continuing operations should be described. If the registrant knows of events that will cause a material change in the relationship between costs and revenues (such as known future increases in costs of labor or materials or price increases or inventory adjustments), the change in the relationship must be disclosed.

- The discussion and analysis must focus specifically on material events and uncertainties known to management that would cause reported financial information not to be necessarily indicative of future operating results or of future financial condition. This would include descriptions and amounts of (A) matters that would have an impact on future operations and have not had an impact in the past, and (B) matters that have had an impact on reported operations and are not expected to have an impact upon future operations.

SEC Examples of MD&A Disclosure

The SEC has given companies examples of what it expects the MD&A to contain.

Liquidity Example

The following is an example given by the SEC of liquidity disclosure by a financially troubled company:

"The Company has violated certain requirements of its debt agreements relating to failure to maintain certain minimum ratios and levels of working capital and stockholders' equity. The Company's lenders have not declared the Company in default and have allowed the Company to remain in violation of these agreements. Were a default to be declared, the Company would not be able to continue to operate. A capital infusion of $4,000,000 is necessary to cure these defaults. The Company has engaged an investment banker and is considering various alternatives, including the sale of certain assets or the sale of common shares, to raise these funds.

"The Company frequently has not been able to make timely payments to its trade and other creditors. As of year-end and as of

71

February 29, 1988, the Company had past due payables in the amount of $525,000 and $705,000, respectively. Deferred payment terms have been negotiated with most of these vendors. However, certain vendors have suspended parts deliveries to the Company. As a result, the Company was not always able to make all shipments on time, although no orders have been cancelled to date. Were significant volumes of orders to be cancelled, the Company's ability to continue to operate would be jeopardized. The Company is currently seeking sources of working capital financing sufficient to fund delinquent balances and meet ongoing trade obligations."

Capital Resources Example

The following is an example given by the SEC of proper disclosure of planned capital expenditures necessary to maintain sales growth:

"The Company plans to open 20 to 25 new stores in fiscal 1988. As a result, the Company expects the trend of higher sales in fiscal 1988 to continue at approximately the same rate as in recent years. Management estimates that approximately $50 to $60 million will be required to finance the Company's cost of opening such stores. In addition, the Company's expansion program will require an increase in inventory of about $1 million per store, which are anticipated to be financed principally by trade credit. Funds required to finance the Company's store expansion program are expected to come primarily from new credit facilities with the remainder provided by funds generated from operations and increased lease financings. The Company recently entered into a new borrowing agreement with its primary bank, which provides for additional borrowings of up to $50 million for future expansion. The Company intends to seek additional credit facilities during fiscal 1988."

Results of Operation Example

In the following SEC example, the company analyzes the reasons for a material change in revenues and in so doing describes the effects of offsetting developments:

"Revenue from sales of single-family homes for 1987 increased 6% from 1986. The increase resulted from a 14% increase in the average sales price per home, partially offset by a 6% decrease in the number of homes delivered. Revenues from sales of single-family homes for 1986 increased 2% from 1985. The average sales price per home in 1986 increased 6%, which was offset by a 4% decrease in the number of homes delivered.

"The increase in the average sales prices in 1987 and 1986 is primarily the result of the Company's increased emphasis on higher priced single-family homes. The decrease in homes delivered in 1987 and 1986 was attributable to a decline in sales in Texas. The significant decline in oil prices and its resulting effect on energy-related business has further impacted the already depressed Texas area housing market and is expected to do so for the foreseeable future. The Company curtailed housing operations during 1987 in certain areas in Texas in response to this change in the housing market. Although the number of homes sold is expected to continue to decline during the current year as a result of this action, this decline is expected to be offset by increases in average sales prices."

Known Uncertainty Example

The following is an example given by the SEC of a "known uncertainty" which you must disclose in the MD&A:

"Facts: A registrant has been correctly designated a PRP by the EPA with respect to cleanup of hazardous waste at three sites. [A "PRP" is a potentially responsible party as designated by the Environmental Protection Agency under the Superfund Law]. No statutory defenses are available. The registrant is in the process of preliminary investigations of the sites to determine the nature of its potential liability and the amount of remedial costs necessary to clean up the sites. Other PRPs also have been designated, but the ability to obtain contribution is unclear, as is the extent of insurance coverage, if any. Management is unable to determine that a material effect on future financial condition or results of operations is not reasonably likely to occur.

"Based upon the facts of this hypothetical base, MD&A disclosure of the effects of the PRP status, quantified to the extent reasonably practicable, would be required. For MD&A purposes, aggregate potential cleanup costs must be considered in light of the joint and several liability to which a PRP is subject. Facts regarding whether insurance coverage may be contested, and whether and to what extent potential sources of contribution or indemnification constitute reliable sources of recovery may be factored into the determination of whether a material future effect is not reasonably likely to occur."

The foregoing example illustrates just how difficult MD&A disclosure can be.

General

An example of a typical MD&A section can be found in the *Today's Man* Prospectus dated June 4, 1992 (starting on page 11) which appears in Appendix 1.

As described above under "Business," if a company has separate business segments, revenues and profits of that segment must be separately disclosed. This disclosure can be harmful competitively. The accounting criteria for what is a separate segment are fairly vague and most companies successfully take the position that they do not have any significant separate segments apart from their main businesses.

Use of Proceeds

SEC rules require the disclosure of the proposed use of proceeds from the offering and, after the IPO, the actual use. The following are some of these SEC rules:

- The registrant must state the principal purposes for which the net proceeds to the registrant from the securities to be offered are intended to be used and the approximate amount intended to be used for each such purpose. Where the registrant has no current specific plan for the proceeds, or a significant portion thereof, the registrant must so state and discuss the principal reasons for the offering.

- Where less than all of the securities to be offered may be sold and more than one use is listed for the proceeds, the registrant must indicate the order of priority of such purposes and discuss the registrant's plans if substantially less than the maximum proceeds are obtained.

- If any material amounts of other funds are necessary to accomplish the specified purposes for which the proceeds are to be obtained, the registrant must state the amounts and sources of such other funds needed for each such specified purposes and the sources thereof.

- If any material part of the proceeds is to be used to discharge indebtedness, the registrant must set forth the interest rate and maturity of such indebtedness. If the indebtedness to be discharged was incurred within one year, the registrant must describe the use of the proceeds of such indebtedness other than short-term borrowings used for working capital.

- If any material amount of the proceeds is to be used to acquire assets (other than in the ordinary course of business), the registrant must describe briefly and state the cost of the assets, where such assets are to be acquired from affiliates of the registrant or their associates, the names of the persons from whom they are to be acquired and the principal followed in determining the cost to the registrant.

- Where the registrant indicates that the proceeds may, or will, be used to finance acquisitions of other businesses, the identity of such businesses, if known, or, if not known, the nature of the businesses to be sought, the status of any negotiations with respect to the acquisition, and a brief description of such business must be included.

An example of the use of proceeds section can be found on page 7 of the *"Today's Man"* prospectus.

Other Important Sections of the Prospectus

The following are other important SEC Regulation S-K disclosure items (excluding financial statements and information) to include in an IPO prospectus on Form S-1:

Item 103 Legal proceedings
Item 202 Description of registrant's securities
Item 304 Changes in and disagreements with accountants on accounting and financial disclosure
Item 401 Directors, executive officers, promoters, and control persons
Item 402 Executive compensation
Item 403 Security ownership of certain beneficial owners and management
Item 404 Certain relationships and related transactions
Item 503 Summary information, risk factors, and ratio of earnings to fixed charges
Item 505 Determination of offering price
Item 506 Dilution
Item 509 Interest of named experts and counsel

The executive compensation disclosures required by Item 402 apply to the chief executive officer at the end of the last completed fiscal

75

year, regardless of compensation level. It also applies to the company's four most highly compensated executive officers (other than the CEO) at the end of the last completed fiscal year whose total annual salary and bonus exceeds $100,000. The executive compensation rules are complex and a delight to insomniacs and anyone who enjoys completing *The New York Times* crossword puzzle.

The only major exclusion from these compensation disclosures is perquisites (fringe benefits) provided they do not exceed the *lesser* of $50,000 or 10 percent of the total annual salary and bonus. In addition, nondiscriminatory group medical, life, and similar group plans generally made available to all salaried employees escape disclosure.

Particular attention should also be paid to Item 404, which requires extensive disclosure of transactions (or series of similar transactions) with or involving the company or any of its subsidiaries in which a director, executive officer, 5% stockholders and members of their immediate family had a *direct or indirect* material interest. "Immediate family" includes a person's spouse, parents, children, siblings, mothers and fathers-in-law, sons and daughters-in-law, and brothers and sisters-in-law.

Complying with Item 404 requires a very careful review of all transactions that involve insiders or their immediate families during the prior three years. There are limited exclusions from the required disclosures (e.g. transactions involving $60,000 or less) that are narrowly interpreted by the SEC and conservative securities lawyers.

A prospectus is a complicated and exhausting document to prepare. It requires a relentless attention to detail. Hundreds of hours of time will be required to be spent by your chief financial officer and your attorneys and accountants.

Your involvement will also require a significant time commitment. You must be prepared to continue to manage and operate your business while spending inordinate amounts of time on the prospectus preparation process.

Chapter Six

Nontraditional Methods of Going Public

A traditional IPO is underwritten on a firm commitment basis and filed with the SEC. Many companies, which cannot qualify for a traditional IPO, can still raise growth capital through a nontraditional IPO.

What Are Nontraditional IPOs?

Nontraditional IPOs include:

- Self underwritten offerings and offerings on a best-efforts basis through broker-dealers.
- Mergers with a publicly-held shell corporation.
- Spin-offs.

Chapters Seven through Ten discuss these nontraditional offerings.
Chapter Seven covers self underwritten and best efforts offerings. Two special types of self underwritten and best efforts offerings, namely Regulation A and SCOR offerings, are covered in Chapter Eight and Nine, respectively.

Turn to Chapter Ten to read about mergers with a publicly held shell corporation and spin-offs.

Why Can't a Company Qualify
for a Traditional IPO?

Companies do not qualify for traditional IPOs because they are too small, are not in a "hot" industry, and have unproven management or growth potential. Although many small or start-up companies that are in hot industries can qualify for a traditional IPO even if they have no revenue, a small company that is in an unexciting business will have difficulty finding a willing underwriter.

In the last few years, at various times, the market has considered environmental, biotechnology, technology and health care companies hot. However, a small company with management that has proven successful in prior businesses may still be a candidate for an IPO, even though its industry is not "hot."

Other major reasons for a company being disqualified from a traditional IPO include the following:

- Your industry's growth prospects are questionable.
- The company cannot use the minimum amount of proceeds raised from the traditional IPO (typically $10 million less IPO costs). Institutions are typically not interested in investing in IPOs in which the gross proceeds are less than $10 million.
- The management of the company is not impressive to the investment community.
- There are problems with the background of the promoters of the company (SEC or other governmental investigations are pending, civil fraud suits are unresolved, criminal convictions, and the like).
- Other traditional IPOs in the same industry performed poorly.
- The public markets are saturated with public offerings of similar businesses.
- There is no market for IPOs.

The market for traditional IPOs is very cyclical. At the height of the cycle, many more companies can qualify for a traditional IPO than at its low point.

If your company is a questionable candidate for a traditional IPO, it may be best to time your IPO to correspond with the high point in the cycle. This is easier said than done.

Some companies have made so-called "quiet filings" (unadvertised) with the SEC. At the mid-point of the cycle, these companies then requested an accelerated SEC effective date of the IPO registration when (they think) the IPO cycle is on the upswing. The cycles in traditional IPOs also affect the marketability of nontraditional self-underwritten or best efforts offerings. However, the cycle effect is not as direct. The IPO cycles have a lesser effect on shell mergers and spin-offs.

Why Consider a Nontraditional IPO?

Some financial consultants advise companies, if they cannot qualify for a traditional IPO, to not go public. Some consultants go so far as to say that, if you cannot attract a prestigious underwriter, you should not go public.

The primary objections to a nontraditional IPO are:

1. If the company waits until it is large enough to qualify for a traditional IPO, it will receive a better price for its stock.
2. There is not an active and liquid market for the stock after a nontraditional IPO.

The soundness of this advice depends upon the company's other alternatives. If the company has no other method of raising needed growth capital than a nontraditional IPO, it is certainly bad advice not to explore that alternative.

However, even companies that can raise growth capital privately should explore nontraditional IPOs. The low valuation placed on the company by private investors may result in too great an equity dilution of the founders. In some cases, the "illiquidity discount" is so large that the founders lose control of the company. This loss of control may occur on the first round of private financing, but it is more likely lost as subsequent rounds of needed financing are sought from venture capitalists or other private investors.

Even companies that can generate growth capital through internal earnings should consider a nontraditional IPO.

If your business is technology based, that technology may only have a limited lifespan until someone improves on the technology. The capital generated from a nontraditional IPO can assist such a company in imme-

79

diately exploiting the technology and becoming a significant market force. Staying private may merely result in your losing an opportunity that has a short window.

Many companies fade because their competition is much better capitalized. Staying private when your competitors are raising public capital may result in a weakening of your market position. This has proven especially true in retail businesses. Consider companies, such as Blockbuster Video, that have dominated their market with gigantic, retail stores. Levitz Furniture is a good 1970s example of this same phenomenon. Capital is a key weapon in competition.

It is true that nontraditional IPOs sometimes result in weak or nonexistent public markets. Even traditional IPOs sometimes suffer from similar problems. However, the presence of a reputable underwriter in a traditional IPO helps provide market support.

It is therefore extremely important to be certain that there will be an active and liquid marketplace after the nontraditional IPO.

Are There Any Advantages of Nontraditional IPOs over Traditional IPOs?

Even companies that qualify for a traditional IPO may decide that they do not want to risk the large expenditures required prior to obtaining a firm commitment from an underwriter. Until the underwriter makes a firm commitment, there is no assurance as to what the valuation of the company will be. Thus, the company does not have any guarantee as to the minimum proceeds of the IPO.

Many underwriters tend to give a company too high a valuation estimate when the company is selecting an underwriter. The underwriters know they are competing with other underwriters for the IPO, and that the valuation estimate given by an underwriter is a major factor in determining whether that underwriter is ultimately selected by the company. Hence, there is an inherent tendency to inflate the valuation estimate.

A nontraditional IPO, such as a shell merger, permits the company to precisely know its valuation prior to incurring substantial expenditures. Hence, the company knows how much equity it must give up to the promoter of the shell prior to incurring major expenditures. There are, however, other disadvantages to a shell merger you must weigh against this particular advantage.

80

A self-underwritten or best efforts offering permits the company to establish its own valuation within reasonable limits. The market will determine whether that valuation is correct. If it is too high, the securities will not sell.

In a traditional IPO, sophisticated institutional investors, to whom the underwriter markets the securities, play a crucial role in determining valuation. This is because a significant portion of the underwritten offering is typically sold to such institutional investors.

A self-underwritten or best efforts offering is typically marketed to retail buyers. Retail buyers tend to be less sophisticated than institutional investors. As a result, self-underwritten or best efforts offerings can generally be marketed at higher valuations, resulting in less equity dilution.

Notwithstanding this advantage of self-underwritten and best efforts offerings, very few companies that qualify for a traditional IPO will seek this alternative. Marketing your company's securities is difficult and time consuming. Most executives are better off using their time to run their own business instead of marketing their company's securities.

Chapter Seven

Self Underwritings and Best Efforts Public Offerings

Some companies go public by registering and selling their own stock. Such companies may also pay commissions to broker-dealers who sell their stock. In some cases, broker-dealers will enter into formal best efforts underwriting arrangements with the company in which they agree to use their best efforts to sell the company's stock.

Marketing

Self-underwriting requires a very significant marketing effort by management, which can interfere with normal business operations of the company. The success of these offerings is far from assured. However, where alternative capital sources are not available, or are available at too steep a price, this route should be seriously considered.

Any company that attempts a non-traditional IPO must have a thoughtful marketing plan to sell its securities. The absence of a firm commitment underwriting makes such a marketing plan imperative.

Marketing may be performed through licensed broker-dealers or through officers and full-time employees of the company, or both.

Brokers-Dealers

Many local and regional brokers are willing to assist companies in marketing their IPOs. No prestigious underwriting firm, whether national or regional, will typically be interested in such marketing.

It is in your best interest to make certain that the broker pays the most attention to your offering. The sales commissions negotiated with local and regional brokers must be sufficiently high to incentivize their marketing efforts. Your IPO will typically be competing with other IPOs and securities offerings for the attention of the broker. So it is usually not wise to unduly reduce sales commissions. Brokers tend to concentrate their efforts where their reward is the highest.

It is a truism that securities are sold, not bought. Someone has to induce the customer to buy your securities. The customer will not call you, except in unusual circumstances. The broker's endorsement of your offering is an effective selling technique. It is much more effective than touting your own company's investment merits. The third party endorsement, which the broker provides to your securities offering, is an essential part of the marketing plan.

As noted, the NASD and state securities laws place limits on the amount brokers can charge for securities offerings. The brokers must clear the amount of sales commissions and other compensation (warrants and others) with the NASD prior to commencing their selling efforts. The harder the marketing effort will be for the broker, the closer the overall compensation will approach the maximum permitted by the NASD.

Officers and Employees

Officers and employees can be effective spokespersons for the company in its self-marketing efforts. If the company suffers from a severe capital shortage, officers and employees are motivated by the desire to sell securities in order to retain their jobs. Thus, they tend to be much more energetic in their selling efforts. However, officers and employees must be carefully trained to avoid statements not contained in the prospectus.

Care must be taken to comply with applicable federal and state registration and licensing requirements for brokers, dealers, and securities salespersons. To avoid federal registration, the officers and employees doing the selling should be full-time employees primarily performing duties other than selling securities and no portion of their compensation should be based upon such sales.

The states vary as to their licensing requirements. Merely being exempt from federal licensing does not exempt the officer and employee from state licensing.

Since the federal exemption (contained in Rule 3a4-1 under the Securities Exchange Act of 1934) and any applicable state exemptions are complicated, the company should seek advice from a securities lawyer.

After-Market Trading

You must structure a nontraditional IPO so that your company's stock will qualify for trading on NASDAQ or, better yet, the NASDAQ National Market or a national securities exchange (see Chapter Eleven). Brokers willing to make a market in your stock must be lined up in advance of your nontraditional IPO. Such brokers must have an incentive to continue as active market-makers.

Special SEC rules apply to brokers in connection with the sale of penny stock. A penny stock is a stock selling for less than $5 per share. Many brokers prefer not having to comply with the recordkeeping provisions of these SEC rules. Accordingly, it is preferable to structure your company's capitalization to avoid having to sell the stock for less than $5 per share.

To avoid unreasonable spreads between the "Bid" and "Asked" prices (the brokers' profit) for your stock, at least three brokers should be making an active market in your stock.

Legal Considerations

The sale of securities is a highly regulated transaction. You must comply with both federal and state securities laws. These laws regulate the necessity of registering the securities, the registration and licensing of brokers, and dealers and salesman. They also create remedies for material misstatements and omissions in connection with the offer and sale of securities. Criminal penalties apply to flagrant violations.

The company is absolutely liable for material misstatements or omissions in offerings registered under the 1933 Act (unless the investor knew of the material misstatement or omission). The 1933 Act typically also makes directors, officers and other controlling persons of the company personally liable if the company violates the law. For example, under Section 15 of the 1933 Act, controlling persons can be personally liable for material misstatements and omissions made by the company in connection with the offer or sale of securities. The liability can extend even to honest mistakes unless the company and the controlling persons can prove that they exercised reasonable care.

Nontraditional IPOs tend to be more dangerous than traditional IPOs. In a traditional IPO, the underwriter is very sophisticated and represented by knowledgeable counsel. This is not always true in non-traditional IPOs. Many local underwriters and brokers are not terribly sophisticated and do not seek advice from securities lawyers.

As a result, these local underwriters and brokers have a higher risk of inadvertently violating the myriad rules applicable to them than are sophisticated national and regional underwriters.

To protect itself, the company should enter into a selling agreement with a local underwriter or broker-dealer that contains (among others) the following clauses:

- Warranties and representations by the broker-dealer of its compliance with federal and state securities laws and NASD rules.
- Covenants that the broker-dealer will continue to comply with during the period of the securities offering.
- Indemnification rights for the company if the broker-dealer fails to do so.

All parties typically prepare the disclosure documents (the prospectus, offering, circular, etc.) in a traditional IPO with greater care than in a nontraditional IPO. This is due partly to the discipline imposed by counsel for underwriters of the IPO who are highly adverse to risk.

You should employ sophisticated securities lawyers to prepare the disclosure documents and monitor the offering. You should use the same care as is typical in the traditional IPO.

Protecting Your Personal Assets

In view of the potential personal liabilities of control persons under federal and state securities laws, consider doing the following:

- If state law exempts jointly owned property from creditors of either spouse, transfer the assets of the control person into the names of the control person and the control person's spouse.
- Transfer assets of the control person to his or her spouse (provided the marriage is strong).
- Take great care in preparing disclosure documents and in selling securities.
- Use sophisticated professionals to assist the company. The company's auditor must be trained in securities law and be a member of the SEC Practice Section of the American Institute of Certified Public Accountants. The Company's lawyer should be an experienced securities lawyer.

How Does the Company Choose Which Offering It Wants?

The type of offering you choose depends on the following factors:

- How much money do you wish to raise?
- Does your marketing plan require you to generally solicit potential customers?
- Where do you wish to sell the securities?

More important than the dollar amount is the method of marketing the offering to customers. If you want to be able to approach strangers or to advertise in newspapers, you cannot use offerings that prohibit general solicitation. Thus, you cannot use private offerings if your marketing plan assumes that you need to employ these marketing methods.

In private offerings, the SEC prohibits any solicitation of any investor with whom the company or its broker does not have a pre-existing relationship.

If you need the ability to solicit investors in more than one state, then an intrastate offering is inappropriate for your company. Consequently, you must register your offering with the SEC or use a Regulation A offering.

Most self underwritten and best efforts offerings are for less than $5 million. Accordingly, your practical choices are to use a Regulation A or an intrastate offering registered with one state. If the offering is for $1 million or less, the SCOR offering may permit you to avoid federal registration and to file a question and answer SCOR form with the state.

Unlimited Dollar Amount Offerings

You can register self underwritings and best efforts offerings in an unlimited dollar amount on Form S-1. If the company is a small business issuer, it can register these offerings in an unlimited dollar amount on Form SB-2 in the same manner as traditional IPOs. As you may recall, the primary requirements for a small business issuer are that the company have revenues of less than $25 million and a public float of less than $25 million.

A company can alternatively register an unlimited dollar amount of their stock with a state securities commission in an intrastate offering (offers and sales limited to one state) if the company otherwise legally qualifies. No federal registration is required for intrastate offerings.

A company can also sell an unlimited dollar amount of their stock to accredited investors[14] and up to 35 sophisticated and experienced investors pursuant to Rule 506 of Regulation D of the Securities and Exchange Commission. Rule 506 is a so-called "safe-harbor" which if complied with, will automatically satisfy the private placement exemption (Section 4(2)) from the registration provisions of the 1933 Act. However, state securities laws must still be satisfied.

Even if you don't comply with Rule 506, your private placement may still be exempt from registration under the private placement exemption contained in Section 4(2) of the 1933 Act. However, unlike intrastate offerings and Forms S-1 and SB-2, you cannot use general advertising and general solicitation in both a Rule 506 offering and in a private placement under Section 4(2).

Limited Dollar Amount Offerings

Companies can also raise limited dollar amounts of funds using the following form and federal registration exemptions:

88

- Form SB-1 (up to $10 million) for small business issuers.
- Regulation A (up to $5 million, including not more than $1.5 million to be received by selling securityholders). (Regulation A is not limited to small business issuers.)
- Rule 505 of Regulation D (up to $5 million), but limited to certain accredited investors plus up to 35 nonaccredited investors.
- Rule 504 of Regulation D (up to $1,000,000).

Regulation A offerings and Rule 504 offerings permit general advertising and general solicitation, unlike Rule 505 offerings.

All of the foregoing federal offering exemptions require either registration or an exemption from applicable state securities laws. Thus, if your company wishes to take advantage of these dollar limited federal exemptions, your company must choose states to market company securities that have hospitable securities laws.

Rule 504 offerings are typically registered under state securities laws by filing a Form U-7 also known as SCOR (Small Corporate Offering Registration).

Offerings Permitting General Advertising and Solicitation

General advertising and solicitation is only permitted by the following IPO registration forms:

- Form S-1
- Form SB-1 and SB-2 (limited to small business issuers)
- Intrastate offering (solicitation limited to one state)
- Regulation A offering
- Rule 504/SCOR offering

Summary of Public and Private Offering Choices

The following is a summary of the public offering choices and the private offering choices for raising capital in self-underwritten and best efforts offerings.

The Public Offering Choices

General solicitation is permitted and there is no investor qualification for these offerings:

1. Public Offerings Registered with SEC
   Primary Advantages: Better terms for founder than private placements. Unlimited marketing where blue-skied; no investor qualification.
   Primary Disadvantage: Cost (typical range: firm commitment underwriting: $350,000 to $500,000; self-underwritten $100,000 to $250,000, but less for a Form SB-1 or SB-2; plus underwriting discount and commissions and expense allowance). Audited financials required.
2. Public Intrastate Offerings Registered in One State
   (exempt from federal registration)
   Primary Advantages: Same as above. No federal review required.
   Primary Disadvantages: Can only be marketed in one state.
3. Public Regulation A Offerings
   (exempt from federal registration, but federal review required)
   Primary Advantages: Can "test-the-waters" before filing. Audited financial statements not required for federal review, unless otherwise available (however, states may still require audited financials); less disclosure required than in SEC registered offerings; can use question and answer format; unlimited marketing where blue-skied.
   Primary Disadvantages: Limited to $5 million in 12 months, including no more than $1.5 million in non-issuer resales; still must be reviewed by both federal and state regulators; professional help required; cost in excess of $50,000 (typical range: $75,000 to $150,000).
4. Public Rule 504/SCOR Offerings
   Primary Advantages: Same as Regulation A, except no federal review required, and unaudited financial statements permitted in most states; can be completed without professional help and is therefore least expensive of all offering forms.
   Primary Disadvantages: Limited to $1 million in 12 months; still must be reviewed by state regulators; higher risk of defective disclosure and personal liability if prepared without professional help.

The Private Placement Choices

In the following offerings, no general solicitation is permitted and marketing is limited to qualified investors with whom there is a preexisting relationship with the company or broker soliciting the sale:

1. Rule 505

   Primary Advantages: Can sell to 35 unsophisticated persons and unlimited number of accredited investors[15]; no federal review required and may be exempt from many state reviews.
   Primary Disadvantages: Limited to $5 million in 12 months; no general solicitation permitted; professional investors may extract onerous terms because of illiquidity.

2. Rule 506/Section 4(2)

   Primary Advantages: Unlimited dollar amount can be sold to 35 sophisticated and experienced investors and an *unlimited* number of accredited investors; no federal review required and may be exempt from many state reviews.
   Primary Disadvantages: No general solicitation permitted; professional investors may extract onerous terms because of illiquidity.

Chapter Eight describes the Regulation A offering. Chapter Nine describes the SCOR offering.

Chapter Eight

Regulation A:
The $5 Million Offering

Regulation A is an exemption from the registration requirements of the federal Securities Act of 1933. Complying with Regulation A does not exempt the company from having to meet state securities law requirements.

Do not assume that because you have qualified your company's offering under Regulation A, that you can sell it in any state you want. There is little comfort in being arrested by the state police instead of the FBI.

Regulation A offerings are exempt from federal registration, but not from federal review. You must submit an offering statement to the SEC (either the national office in Washington, D.C. or a regional SEC office). You must wait for comments and comply with such comments prior to the SEC declaring the offering statement effective. In this respect, there is very little difference between a traditional IPO registered with the SEC and a Regulation A offering.

The primary advantages of a Regulation A over a registered offering are:

- You can "test-the-waters" prior to going to the expense of preparing the offering statement.
- Audited financial statements are not required for federal review, unless otherwise available (however, states may still require audited financials to satisfy state securities laws).

- Less disclosure is required.
- You can use a question and answer format in offering circular.

Testing-the-Waters

The major advantage of the Regulation A offering is that you can determine if there is any investor interest *prior* to incurring significant legal, accounting, and printing costs. Unlike a registered offering, you may solicit indications of interest prior to preparing or filing a Regulation A offering statement with the SEC.

This testing-the-waters rule permits the company to publish or deliver a simple written document or make a scripted radio or television broadcast to determine if there is investor interest. The company can say anything it wishes in the test-the-waters document or script, with two exceptions:

- The document or script cannot violate the anti-fraud laws
- The document or script must contain certain required disclosures

The written document or script of the broadcast must identify the chief executive officer of the company and identify briefly and in general its business and products. The document or script must also state that no money is being solicited and, if sent, will not be accepted. Moreover, the document or script must indicate that an indication of interest involves no obligation or commitment of any kind by the investor and that no sales will be made until a completed offering circular is delivered.

The inability to legally bind investors, or to even escrow their money, are serious drawbacks to the utility of the test-the-waters rule. A period of three or more months may pass between the date the investors express their interest until the date the complete offering circular has cleared the SEC and become available for distribution. Investors who initially express their interest in the investment may change their minds in the interim.

The utility of using radio, television, or newspaper marketing is also questionable. Traditionally, securities are sold by personal recommendation of brokers, friends, barbers, and the like. Investors typically follow these recommendations because they are theoretically given privately to the proposed customer. The customer has a sense of being favored with exclusive information not available to the public. The public nature of radio, television, or newspaper marketing may detract from the investor appeal of the company's securities.

Despite these handicaps, the ability to solicit indications of interest without incurring major expense can be very useful. The rule permits any written document provided to the potential investor to contain a coupon, returnable to the company. The coupon would reveal the name, address and telephone number of the prospective investor. This permits the accumulation of a potential investor list, which can be useful after the offering circular has cleared the SEC.

Once the company submits the written document or script to the SEC, the company can orally communicate with the potential investor. This permits a sales pitch by telephone. Obviously, all communications are subject to the anti-fraud provisions of federal and state securities laws.

Any solicitation to purchase a security must satisfy state as well as federal securities laws. It is not clear at this time whether the states will adopt similar test-the-waters rules. Until they do so, the federal rule is useless.

Apart from testing-the-water rules, the rules relating to when offers and sales of securities under a Regulation A offering may be made are similar to those applicable to a traditional IPO.

Who Can File Under Regulation A?

The following are the major requirements for any company that wishes to file a Regulation A offering statement:

- The company must be organized in the United States or Canada.
- The company must not be a public company (it must not file reports under Section 13 or 15(d) of the Securities Exchange Act of 1934).
- The company must not be a development stage company that either has no specific business plan or purpose or has indicated that its business plan is to merge with an unidentified company.

It should be noted that development stage companies which do have a specific business plan (other than merging with some unidentified company) do qualify for Regulation A.

Bad Boy Disqualification

Rule 262 of Regulation A contains a "bad boy" provision disqualifying certain companies from filing under Regulation A. The provision is waivable by the SEC upon a showing of good cause.

The bad boy provision is very broad and denies use of Regulation A in the following situations, among others:

- Any director, officer, 10% shareholder, promoter, underwriter, or any partner, director, or officer of an underwriter:
    1. was convicted within 10 years prior to filing of certain felonies or misdemeanors relating generally to securities;
    2. is subject to a court, SEC or U.S. postal service order enjoining certain activities relating to securities or use of the mails to make false representations;
    3. is suspended or expelled from membership in certain securities associations.
- The company, or any of its predecessors, or any affiliated issuer, or any underwriter have had certain problems with the SEC or others within the past five years.

How Much Money Can Be Raised?

Your company may raise a maximum of $5,000,000 in cash and other consideration under Regulation A. In computing the $5,000,000 figure, you must subtract the aggregate offering price for all securities sold within twelve months before the start of the Regulation A offering. Thus, you may raise a maximum of $5,000,000 every twelve months (plus the time necessary to offer and sell the securities).

Regulation A also permits receiving up to $1,500,000 cash or other consideration by all selling security holders. However, your company may not make affiliate resales if it has not had net income from continuing operations in at least one of its last two fiscal years.

You must subtract the amount sold by selling securityholders in computing the $5,000,000 limit. Thus, if selling securityholders sell $1,500,000 of their securities, the company can only sell $3,500,000 during the relevant twelve-month period.

There are complicated rules in computing the $5,000,000 limit, particularly the "integration" rules. For example, securities sold in a private placement within six-months after the completion of the Regulation A offering may have to be integrated with the Regulation A, thereby destroying the exemption. An experienced securities lawyer can assist you in navagating these complicated rules.

Offering Statement and Offering Circular

You file a Regulation A offering statement with the SEC's regional office in the region in which the company's principal business operations are or are proposed to be conducted. Alternatively, you may file the offering statement with the SEC's national office in Washington, D.C.

The Regulation A offering statement is analogous to a registration statement for a fully registered offering. The Regulation A offering circular is analogous to the prospectus, which you would include in a registration statement for a fully registered offering.

The offering circular must include a balance sheet as of the end of the most recent fiscal year and statements of income, cash flows, and other stockholders equity for each of the two fiscal years preceding the date of the balance sheet. You must prepare financial statements in accordance with generally accepted accounting principals in the U.S., but these do not need to be audited; however, if audited financial statements are available, you must provide them.

The company has the option of preparing the offering circular in a question and answer format. If the company has audited financial statements and does not need to "test-the-waters," the company should consider the alternative of filing a Form SB-1. The use of a Form SB-1, which registers securities under the 1933 Act (versus the Regulation A exemption), may actually make it easier to qualify the offering under state securities laws.

Appendix 6 contains excerpts from a Regulation A offering circular prepared in the question and answer format and filed by Real Goods Trading Corporation with the Securities and Exchange Commission. You may obtain a copy of the full offering circular from the Washington Service Bureau (202-508-0600).

Outline of Regulation A

A. Overview

1. This regulation grants an exemption from the registration provisions of the 1933 Act for public offerings of securities of no more than $5 million in a 12 month period, including no more than $1.5 million in non-issuer resales.
2. The non-financial portions of the Regulation A offering circular, which is included in the Regulation A offering statement, can be prepared in question and answer format.
3. Except as provided by the "test-the-waters" provisions, no offers may be made until a Regulation A offering statement is filed with the SEC and no sales may be made until the offering statement has been qualified and an offering circular is delivered.
4. Pursuant to the "test-the-waters" provisions, an issuer may obtain indications of interest in a proposed offering prior to filing an offering statement; however, no solicitation or acceptance of money nor any commitment to purchase is permitted until the offering statement is qualified. Copies of any written document must be submitted to the SEC.
5. The company and its controlling persons remain liable for material misstatements and omissions in the offering statement or the offering circular.

B. Issuer and Offering Requirements

1. The issuer:
   a. must be organized in the U.S. or in Canada;
   b. must not be a reporting company nor an investment company;
   c. must not be a development stage company that either has no specific business plan or purpose, or has indicated that its business plan is to merge with an unidentified company or companies;
   d. may not be issuing fractional undivided interests in oil or gas rights or similar interests in other mineral rights; and
   e. must not be disqualified because of administrative or court orders as set forth in Rule 262.
   Note: Rule 262 provides that if the issuer, any of its predecessors or any affiliated issuer, any of its directors, officers, general

partners or 10% equity owners, any promoter, any underwriter or partner, director or officer of such underwriter are subject to certain specified civil, criminal, or administrative actions the exemption provided by Regulation A will not be available. The Rule provides that the SEC, upon a showing of good cause, may waive the disqualification provisions.

2. The aggregate amount offered and sold in reliance on the Regulation A exemption may not exceed $5 million in any 12 month period. Not more than $1.5 million of such amount may be offered and sold by selling securityholders and no affiliate resales are permitted if the issuer has not had net income in at least one of its last two fiscal years.

    Note: (1) In computing the aggregate amount offered, sales made in the preceding 12 months in reliance on Rule 504, Rule 505 or any other Section 3(b) exemptions (excluding Regulation A), or sales made in violation of the 1933 Act, need not be included.

    (2) If securities are offered for both cash and non-cash consideration, the offering price should be based on the cash price. If the securities are not offered for cash, the offering price should be based on the value of consideration as established by bona fide sales of that consideration or, in the absence of sales, on the fair value as determined by an accepted standard.

3. Integration

    a. There is a specific safe harbor provision relating to integration that states that offers and sales made in reliance on Regulation A will not be integrated with any *prior* offers or sales. It further provides that there will be no integration with *subsequent* offers or sales that are (1) registered under the 1933 Act, (2) made in reliance on Rule 701 (stock option plans and certain other compensatory benefit plans) or Regulation S (foreign sales), (3) made pursuant to an employee benefit plan, or (4) made more than six months after the Regulation A offering is completed.

    b. If the safe harbor rule does not apply to particular offers or sales, such offers and sales still may not be integrated depending upon the particular facts and circumstances. *See* Securities Act Release No. 4552 (November 6, 1962).

C. *Offers Prior to and After Filing and Qualification of Offering Statement*

1. Prior to Filing: Test-the-Waters Rule
    a. Prior to the filing of the offering statement, an issuer may publish or deliver a written document or make scripted radio or television broadcasts to determine whether there is any interest in the securities intended to be offered. A copy of this document should be submitted to the SEC's regional office for the region in which the issuer's operations are or are proposed to be conducted or with the SEC's main office in Washington, D.C.
    b. The written document or script of the broadcast must:
        (1) state that no money or other consideration is being solicited and, if sent in response, will not be accepted;
        (2) state that no sales of the securities will be made or commitment to purchase accepted until delivery of an offering circular that includes complete information about the issuer and the offering;
        (3) state that an indication of interest made by a prospective investor involves no obligation or commitment of any kind; and
        (4) identify the chief executive officer of the issuer and identify briefly and in general its business and products.
    c. No sales may be made until 20 days after the last publication or delivery of the document or radio or television broadcast.
    d. Any written document may include a coupon, returnable to the issuer, indicating interest in a potential offering.
    e. If an issuer has a bona fide change of intention and decides to register an offering after using the test-the-waters process, it must wait at least 30 days before filing a registration statement with the SEC.
2. After Filing and Before Qualification: After seven copies of the offering statement have been filed with the SEC's regional office in the region in which the issuers principal business operations are or are proposed to be conducted or with the SEC's office in Washington, D.C., the following activities are permissible:
    a. Oral offers may be made and copies of the preliminary offering circular may be delivered to prospective investors. The preliminary offering circular must be clearly marked as

such, must contain substantially the same information as the final offering circular, and must indicate that no securities may be sold until a final offering circular is delivered.

    b. Advertisements indicating only (1) the name of the issuer, (2) the amount being offered and the offering price, (3) the general type of the issuer's business and (4) the general character and location of its property may be used, if they state from whom an offering circular may be obtained.

3. After Qualification: After the offering statement has been qualified, oral offers and written offers, if accompanied or preceded by an offering circular, may be made if a preliminary or final offering circular is furnished to the purchaser at least 48 hours prior to the mailing of the confirmation and a final offering circular is delivered with the confirmation, unless it has previously been delivered.

D. *Information Required to Be Disclosed in Offering Circular*

1. The offering circular must include a balance sheet as of the end of the most recent fiscal year and statements of income, cash flows, and other stockholders equity for each of the two fiscal years preceding the date of the balance sheet.

2. For non-financial disclosure, the issuer may choose from three options:

    a. A question and answer format substantially similar to the SCOR document used by many states to register securities for small offerings may be used by a corporate issuer.

    b. The traditional Regulation A format, which is similar to a prospectus used in a registered offering, may be used by any issuer.

    c. Any issuer may choose to furnish the information required by Part I of Form SB-2.

3. The offering circular, which is a part of the offering statement, must include the narrative and financial information required by Form 1-A in a clear, concise, and understandable manner, and the cover page of every offering circular must include a legend indicating the SEC has not passed upon the merits or given its approval to any securities offered.

101

4. The offering statement must be signed by the issuer, its chief executive officer, chief financial officer, a majority of the members of its board of directors and any selling securityholder. A $500 fee must be paid with the initial filing of the offering statement.

E.   *Filing and Qualification of Offering Statement*

An offering statement is qualified without SEC action twenty days after filing, unless a delaying notification is included providing that it must only be qualified by order of the SEC.

F.   *Sales*

No sale of securities can be made until:

1. The Form 1-A offering statement has been qualified;
2. A preliminary offering circular or final offering is furnished to the prospective purchaser at least 48 hours prior to the mailing of the confirmation of sale to that person; and
3. A final offering circular is delivered to the purchaser with the confirmation of sale, unless it has been delivered to that person at an earlier time.

G.   *Sales Material and Subsequent Reports Regarding Sales and Use of Proceeds*

1. Advertisements and other sales material may be used as indicated in Section C of this outline. Copies of such material should be filed with the office of the SEC where the offering statement was filed when the material is first published or delivered.
2. The issuer should report information concerning the amount of securities sold and the use of proceeds every six months after the offering statement has been qualified until substantially all of the proceeds have been applied or within 30 days after the completion of the offering, whichever is the latest event.

H. *Substantial Good Faith Compliance Defense*

1. Rule 260 provides that a failure to comply with a term, condition or requirement of Regulation A will not result in the loss of the exemption for any offer or sale to a particular individual, if the person relying on the exemption establishes:
   a. the condition violated was not intended to protect the complaining individual;
   b. the failure to comply was insignificant to the offering as a whole (issuer requirements, aggregate offering limitations, and the requirements to file an offering statement and deliver an offering circular are always significant to the offering as a whole); and
   c. a good faith and reasonable attempt was made to comply with all of the requirements of Regulation A.
2. Rule 260 preserves the SEC's right to pursue any failure in compliance regardless of significance.

103

Chapter Nine

SCOR: The $1 Million Do-It-Yourself Offering

Approximately 38 states, officially or unofficially, permit the use of a simplified question and answer format when raising funds pursuant to federal Rule 504.

This simplified form is the "SCOR" form (small corporate offering registration) or Form U-7 (also known as "ULOR" or uniform limited offering registration). It is also called "Registration Form U-7."

The purpose of the "SCOR" form is to *reduce* the legal and accounting costs of preparing extensively documented reports. In general, the "SCOR" form has been praised as being "user-friendly." Many corporate executives have filed this form without incurring significant outside professional costs.

The states in conjunction with the American Bar Association's State Regulation of Securities Committee developed the SCOR offering to facilitate raising capital by small businesses. The SCOR offering permits a company to raise $1,000,000 within approximately twelve months without federal review of the offering documents. It only requires a state review. However, the company must file a Form D with the SEC, with a copy to the state, in order to use the SCOR form.

Theoretically, the small businessman can respond to the SCOR question and answer format himself, or with the advice of a general legal practitioner, and does not need the assistance of a securities law specialist. The SCOR form is then filed with the state or states in which the securities are to be sold. Accordingly (so goes the theory), the company can minimize the cost of preparing the SCOR form to less than $5,000 and possibility even less than $1,000.

This theory is somewhat questionable since the SCOR form is not exempt from the anti-fraud provisions of federal and state securities laws. As noted, these anti-fraud provisions can impose personal liability on the control persons of the company, including its directors and officers.

In addition, the SCOR form contains a number of sophisticated questions that may be beyond the knowledge of the company's officers or their general counsel. For example, question 45 of the form is as follows:

"Describe any other material factors, either adverse or favorable, that will or could affect the Company or its business (for example, discuss any defaults under major contracts, any breach of bylaw provisions, etc.) or which are necessary to make any other information in this Disclosure Document not misleading or incomplete."

The answer to this question requires a knowledge of what facts or circumstances the courts view as "material." Small business owners proceed at their peril if they try to answer these questions without assistance of a securities law specialist.

It should also be noted that both federal and state securities laws provide for criminal sanctions for flagrant violations.

In light of these considerations, some companies are using sophisticated law firms to help prepare the SCOR form, at costs ranging from $15,000 to $30,000.

It is true, however, that the exemption of the SCOR offering from federal registration by Rule 504 (discussed below) helps to minimize the costs of the offering. Also, the practice in this area has evolved into a system where state examiners play a large role in assisting companies with their SCOR document.

Federal Registration Exemption

Rule 504 under the 1933 Act provides an exemption from the registration provisions of federal law for certain offerings up to $1,000,000. The registration exemption, however, does not also exempt the offering from the anti-fraud and personal liability provisions of the law (as noted above).

Rule 504 permits a qualified non-public company to raise up to $1 million, less the aggregate offering price of all securities sold by the company within 12 months before the start of and during the Rule 504 offering (subject to certain exceptions). Rule 504 does not require any specific disclosure to be made, and the offering circulars (prospectuses) are not subject to federal regulatory review.

More importantly, Rule 504 does not prohibit a general solicitation of investors to market the offering. Thus, marketing may be accomplished by cold telephone calls and radio, television, and newspaper advertising without violating the registration provisions of the 1933 Act. This contrasts with the marketing of private placements, which prohibit general solicitations.

Of course, the company must satisfy the requirements of state securities laws before the use of a general solicitation. The states generally prohibit any general solicitation *prior* to the clearance of the SCOR form. However, the states are rethinking this issue in light of the "test-the-waters" rules for Regulation A offerings.

The business must file a Form D with the SEC not later than 15 days after the first sale of securities. The date of filing is the date on which the business mails the form by registered or certified mail to the SEC's principal office in Washington, D.C. or the date the SEC otherwise receives it.

State Securities Laws

Although Rule 504 does not require any specific disclosure to investors, most state securities laws do.

Eligibility to Use SCOR

To use the SCOR form:

- The company must be incorporated in the United States or its possessions.
- The company cannot be engaged in petroleum exploration or production or mining or other extractive industries.
- "Blind pool" offerings and other offerings for which the specific business or properties cannot now be described are ineligible.

107

- The securities can only be sold by the company, and not by selling securityholders.
- The offering price for common stock must be equal to or greater than $5 per share.[16]
- The company must believe or have reason to believe that all selling agents are appropriately registered.
- A bad boy provision (similar to the Regulation A bad boy provision) disqualifies certain companies from eligibility to file SCOR.
- The aggregate offering price cannot exceed $1 million less the aggregate offering price for all securities sold within twelve months before the start of and during the offering.
- The company cannot be an investment company or be subject to the reporting requirements of the Securities Exchange Act of 1934.
- The company must have filed a Form D.

Financial Statements

Rule 504/SCOR offerings in most states do not require audited financial statements, but only "review" financial statements, if all of the following requirements are satisfied:

- The company has not previously sold securities by means of advertising, mass mailings, public meetings, cold call telephone solicitation, or any other method directed toward the public.
- The company has not been previously required under federal or state securities laws to provide audited financial statements in connection with any sale of its securities.
- The aggregate amount of all previous sales of securities by the company (exclusive of debt financings with banks and similar commercial lenders) must not exceed $1,000,000.
- The amount of the present offering does not exceed $500,000.

However, the SCOR form requires the company to agree to provide annual financial statements to investors for five years after the date of the SCOR offering. If at the end of any fiscal year, the company has more than 100 securityholders, it *must* have the financial statements audited. In this respect, the SCOR form is less desirable than a Regulation A offering, which does not require the company to provide audited financial statements to investors after completing the offering.

Offers and Sales

The business cannot offer or sell securities pursuant to the SCOR offering until the state declares the registration effective. The business cannot make pre-effective offers under the SCOR offering form. Thus, there is no testing-the-waters, as with Regulation A.

Escrow

If the proposed business of the company requires a minimum amount of proceeds to commence business, the SCOR form requires an escrow of all proceeds received from investors until the company raises the minimum amount. The escrow must be with a bank or a savings and loan association or other similar depository institution.

The Regulation A offering does not require an escrow. However, state securities officials could still require such an escrow under the Regulation A offering in order to permit offers and sales in a particular state.

States Adopting SCOR

There are approximately 38 states in which the SCOR form was officially or unofficially recognized as of April 1993. They include: Alaska, Arizona, Arkansas, California, Colorado, Connecticut, Georgia, Idaho, Indiana, Iowa, Kansas, Kentucky, Louisiana, Maine, Massachusetts, Michigan, Mississippi, Missouri, Montana, Nevada, New Hampshire, New Jersey, North Carolina, North Dakota, Ohio, Oklahoma, Oregon, Pennsylvania, South Carolina, South Dakota, Tennessee, Texas, Vermont, Virginia, Washington, West Virginia, Wisconsin, Wyoming.

Instructions and Form

Appendix 7 is Form U-7, which contains the SCOR form. Note that the SCOR form and the Regulation A question and answer form are very similar. In fact, the Regulation A question-and-answer form was based in part on the SCOR form. Therefore, a business can use the Regulation A offering circular contained in Appendix 6 that illustrates the method of answering similar SCOR questions.

Chapter Ten

Mergers with Publicly Held Shell Corporations and Spin-Offs

Shell mergers and spin-offs provide a company the opportunity to create a public market place for its stock. A public market place facilitates raising additional capital and helps to avoid the "illiquidity discount" applicable to the valuation of private companies.

A company does not automatically raise capital because its stock has become publicly traded by reason of a shell merger or spin-off. Therefore, companies that consider this nontraditional route should try to have investors lined up to invest in the company the moment its stock becomes publicly traded.

Recently, Dollar Time Group, Inc. (discount stores) and Prins Recycling Corp. (recycling) had private offerings under Rule 506/Section 4(2), which closed simultaneously with their shell mergers. This permitted these companies to negotiate better terms for the private offering than would otherwise have been possible.

Many major underwriters will decline to handle a traditional IPO that raises less than $10 million. This is partly due to the lack of institutional interest in these smaller IPOs. Another reason is that many major underwriters cannot make enough underwriting profit from these smaller IPOs to justify their effort and risk. At least one major underwriter has sought to solve this problem by doing private placement/shell mergers where less than $10 million in capital is required. The underwriter effort and risk in these private placement/shell mergers is significantly less than in a traditional IPO.

Typically, simultaneously with the shell merger or spin-off, a company registers the stock of the merged or spun-off company under Section 12 of the 1934 Act and the merged or spun-off company becomes a reporting company (see Chapter Twelve).

Shell Mergers

There are a number of promoters who acquire or form publicly-held shell corporations. These entities are called "shells" because they conduct no business whatsoever, but do have a large number of shareholders. Some of these shells have significant capital. Many shells have no capital whatsoever. Some shells have tax loss carryovers from a prior business.

To become part of a shell, your corporation typically merges into a publicly-held shell corporation. Prior to the merger you and the shell's promoter negotiate a percentage of the shell's stock that you would receive in the merger in exchange for the stock of your company, which you personally own. The percentage you receive depends upon whether the shell has capital or not and the relative valuation of your company. If the shell has no capital, the shell stock you receive in the merger would typically equal 80 percent to 95 percent of the total outstanding stock.

The chart on the following page illustrates the process.

The promoters of the shell typically have a relationship with broker-dealers who will make a market in the shell stock after the merger and will assist in raising additional capital. The promoters of the shell typically receive warrants and stock in the merged company. The promoter's stock ownership is included in the public stock ownership after the merger in the above table. If the shell has cash or other assets, the ownership by the public and promoters after the merger increases proportionately.

After the merger, your company does not suffer the illiquidity discount.

SHELL MERGERS

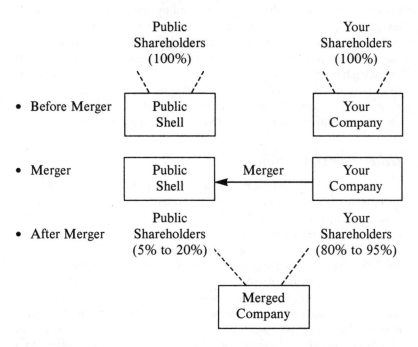

Advantages

There are four major advantages of the shell merger. It is a less expensive method of going public, and if the shell has capital, you will know before the shell merger precisely how much equity you must give up for that capital. (As you may recall, in the traditional IPO, you do not have assurance as to how much capital you will actually receive until the effective date of the IPO, after you have already spent substantial sums.) After the merger, the existence of a public trading market in your company's stock is very useful in attracting additional capital, since the market provides immediate liquidity for the investor. And finally, if the shell has a tax loss carryover, that carryover, subject to significant limitations, may be available to shelter the taxable income of your business.

Disadvantages

There are also major disadvantages of the shell merger. If the shell has no capital, you still have no assurance until after the merger as to how much capital you can raise and what valuation the market will give to your company. Some shells are promoted by less than the best quality broker-dealers, who typically maintain large spreads between the "Bid" and "Asked" prices for your stock (enlarging their profits or commissions). There is a certain stigma to shell mergers, which may prevent financing by some of the traditional capital sources; however, your company may not have qualified for financing by such traditional sources even if no shell merger ever occurred. As a final consideration, the shell may have undisclosed liabilities that your business will inherit.[17]

Other Considerations

The depth of the public market after the shell merger is crucial to the success of any further capital raising efforts. If only one broker/dealer is making a market in the stock after the shell merger, investors will be rightfully leery of the market's liquidity.

You should carefully investigate the background of the promoters of public shells prior to engaging in any shell merger. An ounce of prevention is worth a pound of cure.

As noted, a recent phenomenon is the coupling of a private placement of securities with a shell merger. The private placement permits the company to raise capital simultaneously with the shell merger. The shell merger creates a liquid market for the private placement securities. As a result, the investors typically can justify a higher valuation for the company since there is no need for an illiquidity discount.

Spin-Offs

There are two types of spin-offs:

- Subsidiary spin-offs
- Spin-offs of unaffiliated company stock

Subsidiary Spin-offs

In 1992, according to *Financial World,* there were seventeen spin-offs of subsidiaries or divisions of existing publicly held companies. For example, the stock of GFC Financial Corp., a subsidiary of The Dial Corp., was recently spun-off to the Dial stockholders. GFC Financial

114

stock thereby became publicly held by the Dial stockholders and publicly traded. Also, the same market makers and broker-dealer network for Dial stock became available to GFC Financial and its new public stockholders.

In 1991, Quaker Oats spun-off the stock of Fisher Price, the fourth largest toy company in the United States, to the shareholders of Quaker Oats.

These spin-offs are motivated by various considerations such as:

- The desire to remove loss operations from the parent's financial statements
- The desire to permit investors in the parent to invest solely in one industry (a so-called "pure stock play")
- To create value for the parent's shareholders.

The "spin-off" can be free of federal income taxes to the shareholders if certain requirements are satisfied.

Another form of spin-off involves the issuance of "tracking stock." Tracking subsidiary stock is typically a special class of common stock issued by a parent corporation. It should provide a return on investment linked to the performance of a subsidiary. General Motors Class E and H shares are an example.

Spin-offs of Unaffiliated Companies

An unaffiliated company can create a spin-off in two steps:

1. The company gives a small percentage of the stock to a publicly held sponsoring company without charge.
2. The sponsoring company then declares a dividend in that stock payable to the shareholders of the sponsoring company.

The dividend makes the spun-off company a publicly traded company. Its public shareholders are the shareholders of the sponsoring company. Hopefully, the stock of the spun-off company will qualify for NASDAQ. Ideally, market makers and other broker-dealers interested in the stock of the sponsoring company will also become interested in the stock of the spun-off company.

Spinning off of the stock of an unaffiliated company is relatively rare. The primary reason is the sponsoring company's concern for its image and legal liability.

115

Should the spun-off company fail, the sponsoring company may have unhappy shareholders. This may be true even though the shareholders of the sponsoring company did not pay a cent for the spun-off stock!

There are several SEC interpretations that indicate the sponsoring company may be a "statutory underwriter" of the spun-off company's stock. As a result, the sponsoring company may have legal liability for material misstatements or omissions made by the spun-off company.

To avoid the legal liability as a statutory underwriter, the sponsoring company should acquire the stock to be spun-off without a view of its distribution. Typically, a two year period between the date of acquisition of the stock by the sponsoring company and the date of the spin-off will avoid statutory underwriter liability.

The SEC's position on underwriter liability seriously undermines the willingness of civic minded sponsoring companies to assist smaller, local start-up companies to become publicly held. It is hoped that, in the proper factual circumstances, the SEC will reconsider its position and permit these socially desirable spin-offs.

Chapter Eleven

Trading on NASDAQ and National Securities Exchanges

It is an important marketing tool for your IPO if you can state in your prospectus or offering circular that you intend to have the company's common stock listed for trading on a national securities exchange or on NASDAQ.

The major places your company can trade its stock are:

- New York Stock Exchange
- American Stock Exchange—the listing may be for either the regular American Stock Exchange or for the Emerging Company Market Place (ECM) of that exchange
- The NASDAQ Stock Market (NASDAQ)—the listing may be for either Small Cap NASDAQ or NASDAQ National Market (NM)
- Other national and foreign stock exchanges

If your company's stock does not qualify for any of the foregoing, it will be quoted in the so-called "Pink Sheets."[18] The Pink Sheets are inter-dealer quotations distributed by the National Quotation Bureau, Inc. or similar quotation services operating on a regional basis. The quotations will only appear when a broker or dealer inserts a "bid" price or "asked" price in the Pink Sheets. The Pink Sheets stock are the least actively traded securities.

The NASDAQ system refers to the electronic inter-dealer quotation system operated by NASDAQ, Inc., a subsidiary of the NASD. To qualify for the NASDAQ NM a security must first qualify for inclusion in the NASDAQ system and then meet special requirements for designation as a NM security.

NASDAQ publishes last sale prices for stock traded on the national stock exchanges and on Small Cap NASDAQ and NM. However, only "Bid" and "Asked" prices are available for "Pink Sheet" stocks.

Both NASDAQ and the national securities exchanges charge listing fees and annual fees with the New York Stock Exchange having the highest original listing fees. Although the New York Stock Exchange is still the most prestigious market, you must weigh the expense of original listing on that market against that prestige.

Initial Listing Requirements

The following table compares the listing criteria for NASDAQ NM (Alternative 1 or 2), The New York Stock Exchange, The American Stock Exchange (Alternative 1 or 2), ECM, and Small Cap NASDAQ.

The table is current as of July 1993. All the exchanges and NASDAQ continue to compete for listings from which they derive revenue. Accordingly, the listing standards are constantly being revised to reflect competitive conditions as well as changes in the market place.

Over-the-Counter Market vs. Exchanges

The over-the-counter (OTC) market encompasses all non-exchange traded securities. It is the second largest market in the world. The only larger market is the New York Stock Exchange.

The OTC market has two distinct sub-groups of securities:

- Those quoted on NASDAQ (either Small Cap NASDAQ or NM)
- Those quoted in the Pink Sheets

COMPARISON OF LISTING CRITERIA

NASDAQ NATIONAL MARKET, NYSE, AMEX, AMEX ECM, AND REGULAR NASDAQ

	Nasdaq National Market Alt. 1	Nasdaq National Market Alt. 2	NYSE	AMEX Alt. 1	AMEX Alt. 2	ECM (Non-Nasdaq Companies)	ECM (Companies Presently Traded in Nasdaq)	Regular Nasdaq
Total Assets	N/A	$12,000,000	N/A	N/A	N/A	$4,000,000 [4]	$2,000,000	$4,000,000
Net Tangible Assets [1]	$4,000,000	See Footnote 1	$18,000,000	$4,000,000	$4,00,000	$2,000,000	None	None
Stockholders Equity			None	None	None		$1,000,000 [5]	$2,000,000
Public Float	500,000	1,000,000	1,100,000	500,000	500,000	250,000 [4]	250,000	100,000
Pre-Tax Income	$750,000	None	$2,500,000 [2]	$750,000	None	None	None	None
Net Income	$400,000	None	None	None	None	None	None	None
Shareholders [3]	800/400 [4]	400	2,000	800/400	800/400	300	300	300
Market Value of Float	$3,000,000	$15,000,000	$18,000,000	$3,000,000	$15,000,000	None	None	$1,000,000
Total Market Value	N/A	N/A	N/A	N/A	N/A	$2,500,000 [5]	$2,500,000	N/A
Bid Price	$5	$3	$3 "	$3	None	$3 [5]	$1 [6]	$3
Market Makers	2	2	N/A	N/A	N/A	N/A	N/A	2
Operating History	N/A	3 years	3 years	N/A	3 years	None	None	None

1   Net Tangible Assets shall mean total assets (excluding goodwill) minus total liabilities.

2   Pre-tax income of $2 million in each of the preceding 2 years is also required or, alternatively, aggregate pre-tax income of $6.5 million for the preceding 3 years together with (a) $4.5 of pre-tax income for first preceding year and (b) some after tax income for second and third preceding years.

3   The rules vary as to whether old lot holders (less than 100 shares) count as shareholders.

4   The issuer has a minimum of 800 shareholders if the issuer has between 500,000 and 1 million shares publicly held, or a minimum of 400 shareholders if the issuer has either (i) over 1 million shares publicly held or (ii) over 500,000 shares publicly held and average daily trading volume in excess of 2,000 shares per day for the six months preceding the date of application.

5   The ECM permits companies to list with $3 million in total assets and only a $2 price per share if the public float is 400,000 shares and the total market capitalization is $10 million.

6   The ECM permits companies to list with a price of less than $1 per share if they have equity of $2 million.

The OTC market is a dealer market. One or more dealers making markets in any particular OTC stock enter quotations either in NASDAQ or in the Pink Sheets. There is no single "specialist" in the stock of OTC companies maintaining a book on such stocks. Likewise, there is no auction of any OTC stock conducted by any specialist.

The market-makers compete with each other as to the price at which they are prepared to buy (the Bid) and the price at which they are prepared to sell (the Ask) the securities for which they act as market-maker. The market makers revenues are the differences between the Bid and Ask price. NASDAQ claims that, on average, each security listed on NASDAQ has approximately 11 market makers.

The stock exchanges trade securities in "a continuous two-sided auction market." In this market, each security trade on an exchange occurs at one designated place on the floor of that exchange called a "post." At each post there are one or more exchange members who are registered with that exchange as specialists in one or more securities. The larger exchanges allocate each equity security to a single specialist. They award these specialists, in effect, a monopoly right to make a market in that security on the exchange floor. The specialist, in return, undertakes certain responsibilities. If other markets simultaneously trade the security (NASDAQ or other exchanges), the specialist must compete with these other markets.

With respect to the securities for which they specialize, specialists perform the dual functions of brokers and dealers. In the capacity as a broker, the specialist holds and executes buy and sell orders for others. Generally these orders are forwarded to the specialist by exchange members. The orders may be "market" orders (buy or sell a security at the best current market price), but they are usually "limit" orders (orders to buy or sell a security at a specific price) or "stop" orders.

The primary mechanism used by the specialist to handle limit and stop orders is the specialist's "book." The specialist is the only broker who has the "book." Limit and stop orders are entered into the book in the sequence in which the specialist receives them with the appropriate price, number of shares, and the name of the firm that forwarded the order. The specialist usually charges a commission for this activity.

The specialist's second function is to act as a dealer to the extent necessary to maintain fair and orderly markets. As a dealer, the specialist is responsible for purchasing and selling securities in a manner that contributes to the maintenance of a fair and orderly auction market in the specialist's assigned security or group of securities.

Which Is Best?

There is significant controversy over the relative merits of a dealer market (NASDAQ) vs. an auction market (the stock exchanges). The "best" market provides reasonable price stability for your company's stock and avoids excessive dealer mark ups.

Theoretically, a specialist market should provide better protection against wild price fluctuations and unreasonable mark-ups. However, the specialist system (as did the NASDAQ) operated inconsistently during the 1987 stock market crash. Many of the specialists were inadequately capitalized and could not provide price stability in the face of the wave of sell orders that occurred in October 1987. Since 1987, there has been some improvement in the specialist system.

If your company is stuck with a poor specialist on an exchange, you may try to change the specialist or, alternatively, qualify your company's securities on Small Cap NASDAQ or NM. However, if only a small number of dealers make a market in your company's stock on Small Cap NASDAQ or NM, it is more likely that you will get better results from an exchange listing.

If a large number of well capitalized dealers make a market in your company's stock on NASDAQ or NM, these markets can, as a result of dealer competition, provide reasonable protection against wild price gyrations or unreasonable dealer mark-ups.

In general, exchange specialists have affirmative obligations to maintain a fair and orderly market in their stocks. OTC market makers have no affirmative obligations to continue to make markets and can withdraw at any time. However, a NASDAQ market maker who withdraws its quotations may not again register as a market marker in that security for 20 business days.

Stocks listed on the New York and American Stock Exchanges receive greater coverage in the media than Small Cap NASDAQ securities. Typically, there is greater brokerage firm research in newly listed securities on the New York or American Stock Exchanges compared to Small Cap NASDAQ securities.

Tick Rule and Short-Selling

Exchange listed securities are subject to the "tick rule." This rule prohibits short-selling except on "plus-ticks" or on "zero-plus ticks."

A plus tick is a trade at a price greater than the immediately preceding transaction and a zero-plus tick is a trade at a price greater than the last transaction at a different price.

For example, the exchange permits a short-sale at 20 as a plus-tick if the prior trade was 19⅞ and as a zero-plus tick if the two prior trades were 19⅞ and 20, respectively. However, it would prohibit a short-sale at 20 if the prior tick was 20⅛ or if the two prior ticks were 20⅛ and 20, respectively.

There is currently no tick rule on NASDAQ or NM. As a result, the stock exchanges argue that they have better protection against short-selling than NASDAQ or NM. NASDAQ has proposed its own "short-sale" rule for NM securities but had not adopted the proposal as of July 1993.

Extensive short-selling ("bear raids") can have a disastrous effect on the price of your company's stock. The tick rule does not prevent short-selling per se. A persistent short-seller can easily accumulate a large short position despite the tick rule. Likewise, the tick rule does not prevent short sellers from impeding a justified rise in the price of your company's stock. However, the tick rule will assist in preventing dramatic market price declines resulting from bear raids.

Small Cap NASDAQ vs. American Stock Exchange (ECM)

If your choice is between Small Cap NASDAQ and the American Stock Exchange (ECM), you should seriously consider the ECM. The American Stock Exchange (ECM) is more prestigious than Small Cap NASDAQ and the specialist system may provide a better market for your company's stock. In addition, your company's stock will receive better media coverage.

Listing and maintenance fees on ECM should be carefully compared to Small Cap NASDAQ fees prior to making your final decision.

Cost

The following table shows the original listing fees and continuing annual fees for each of the major markets, assuming the company has 1 million outstanding shares.

	NASDAQ NATIONAL MARKET	NYSE	AMEX	ECM	REGULAR NASDAQ
Original Listing Fees	$10,000	$53,000[1]	$10,000	$5,000	$6,000
Annual Fees	$ 5,250	$15,700[1]	$ 6,500	$6,500	$4,000

[1]Based on a minimum public float of 1.1 million shares

Maintenance Criteria

Both NASDAQ and the stock exchanges have "maintenance criteria" your company must satisfy to continue trading your stock. Once listed, your company's common stock is easier to retain than it was to initially qualify. For example, to have your stock continue to be designated as an NM security your common stock, preferred stock, shares or certificates of beneficial interest of trusts, and limited partnership interests in foreign or domestic issues must have:

- 200,000 shares publicly held.
- A market value of publicly held shares of $1 million.
- The issuer's net tangible assets be at least:
  $2 million if the issuer has sustained losses from continuing operations and/or net losses in two of its three most recent fiscal years; or
  $4 million if the issuer has sustained losses from continuing operations and/or net losses in three of its four most recent fiscal years.
- 400 shareholders or 300 shareholders of round lots.
- $1 Bid Price
- Rights and Warrants—Common stock of issuer must continue to be designated.
- Market Makers—At least two authorized NASDAQ market makers.

In addition, should an issuer file under any of the sections of the Bankruptcy Act or announce that its board of directors has authorized liquidation and is committed to proceed, the issuer's securities must not remain designated as an NM security unless the public interest and the protection of investors would be served by continued designation.

The maintenance requirements for Small Cap NASDAQ and ECM are as follows.

SMALL CAP NASDAQ MAINTENANCE REQUIREMENT

Number of Market Makers	2[1]
Bid Price	$1.00[2]
Public Float (shares)	100,000
Public Float (market value)	$250,000
Total Assets	$200,000
Capital and Surplus (equity)	$1,000,000
Total Shareholders	300

[1] If there is only one market maker for 10 consecutive days, the issuer has 30 days in which to find an additional market maker.
[2] If the Bid Price is below $1, the issuer will still qualify if the public float (market value) is $1 million and capital and surplus (equity) is $2 million.

ECM MAINTENANCE REQUIREMENT

	Regular	Alternate
Total Assets	$2 million	$2 million
Capital & Surplus	$1 million	$2 million
Market Value	$500,000	$1 million
Public Float	250,000 shares	250,000 shares
Public Shareholders	300	300
Minimum Price	$1	Under $1

Corporate Governance Requirements

There are a number of corporate governance requirements applicable to companies listed on NASDAQ or national securities exchanges. However, there are no corporate governance requirements for Small Cap NASDAQ.

The most important governance requirements applicable to NM securities are:

124

- Two independent directors must be on the board of directors.
- The board of directors must have an independent audit committee.
- There must be annual shareholder meetings, with minimum governance requirements and solicitation of prices.
- The company must prohibit conflicts of interest.

In addition, the market may require shareholder approval for the issuance of securities when:

a. the company establishes a stock option or purchase plan pursuant to which officers or directors may acquire stock,

b. the issuance will result in a change in control,

c. the issuance is in connection with certain acquisitions or public offerings involving 20 percent or more of the common stock or total voting power, or

d. the issuance is in connection with an acquisition in which a director, officer, or substantial shareholder of the company has a 5% or greater interest.

Also, NM severely restrict creating two classes of stock after the IPO or other disenfranchising proposals.

These corporate governance requirements of each market may significantly influence your choice of markets. For example, the New York Stock Exchange and NM restrict the creation of two classes of stock after the IPO. The American Stock Exchange does not. If you are considering adopting this control device, the American Stock Exchange or Small Cap NASDAQ may be a better choice.

Small Cap NASDAQ does not require shareholder approval to issue 20 percent or more of your authorized but unissued stock. Most state laws only require director approval. As noted, NM generally requires such shareholder approval. Such shareholder approval requires a proxy solicitation and can be expensive due to the extensive SEC disclosure requirements for your proxy statement.

Accordingly, if you plan an acquisition or financing that requires the issuance of 20 percent or more of your company's stock, you might decide to hold off qualifying the company for NM and remain on Small Cap NASDAQ until your company issues 20 percent or more of its shares.

Getting Your Stock in the Newspaper

If your stock is traded on NASDAQ (either NM or Small Cap NASADQ) or the New York or American Stock Exchange lists it, its price will regularly appear in *The Wall Street Journal*. This assumes, of course, that there is trading in your stock on any particular day.

Newspapers other than *The Wall Street Journal* vary with regard to their practices of publishing stock quotations. In general, almost all newspapers that publish stock quotations include the New York Stock Exchange, American Stock Exchange and NM. Some newspapers will also carry stocks of local interest as discussed below.

Local Quotations Program

Recently, NASDAQ developed a Local Quotation Program. To include your stock in the Local Quotations List there must be sufficient shareholder interest reflected by the number of shareholders residing in the area and other fair and reasonable standards.

All NASDAQ securities are eligible for inclusion in the Local Quotations List. However, even non-NASDAQ securities can be eligible for inclusion on a case-by-case basis in the Local Quotations Program if:

a. The bid price for a security is at least $2.00, or the issuer reports total assets of not less than $2,000,000 and capital and surplus of not less than $1,000,000 and may continue to be included so long as it continues to report total assets of not less than $750,000 and capital and surplus of not less than $375,000.

b. The issuer makes prompt and full disclosure of all material corporate developments.

c. The issuer annually submits to its shareholders a balance sheet and income statement.

d. The issuer imprints CUSIP[19] numbers on all stock certificates.

Other Methods to Obtain Newspaper Coverage

If your stock does not qualify for listing on NASDAQ or a national securities exchange, you may still be able to obtain newspaper coverage by listing your stock on a national stock exchange located in your local area such as the *Boston Stock Exchange, Chicago Board Options Exchange, Inc., Cincinnati Stock Exchange, Chicago Stock Exchange, Pacific Stock Exchange, Inc.,* and the *Philadelphia Stock Exchange, Inc.*

Chapter Twelve

Being Public

General

After the completion of your IPO, your company and its directors, officers, and principal stockholders will be subject to certain duties under various provisions of the Securities Exchange Act of 1934 ("1934 Act"), if *any* of the three following events occur:

1. If your company had, at any fiscal year end, assets exceeding $5 million and a class of equity securities held of record by 500 or more persons. (Section 12(g))
2. If a national securities exchange lists a class of your company's securities for trading. (Section 12(b))
3. If your company *voluntarily* registered a class of its equity securities under Section 12(g) of the 1934 Act. (This registration might have occurred in order to qualify your stock for trading on Small Cap NASDAQ or NM.)

Section 12 of the 1934 Act *requires* the registration of equity securities under that section (a) once an issuer has over 500 shareholders and over $5 million in assets or (b) upon the listing of the security for trading on a national securities exchange.

Registration under Section 12, whether required or voluntary, invokes other sections of the 1934 Act, including those dealing with filing reports with the SEC on Forms 10-K (yearly), 10-Q (quarterly) and

8-K (periodically) under Section 13 of the 1934 Act, the proxy and tender offer rules (Section 14 of the 1934 Act), and the short-swing profit rules (Section 16 of the 1934 Act).

Companies who register debt or equity securities under the 1933 Act and have more than 300 debt or equity securityholders are also required under Section 15(d) of the 1934 Act to file reports on Forms 10-K, 10-Q and 8-K.[20]

In 1991, there were over 12,000 issuers filing reports with the SEC because of Section 12 and Section 15(d) of the 1934 Act.

The forms for registering a class of equity securities under Section 12 depend upon whether your company is a small business issuer and whether your company registered its IPO under the 1933 Act.

The annual and quarterly report forms for small business issuers are called Form 10-KSB and Form 10-QSB, respectively. If your company is an SEC reporting company because it filed a 1933 Act Registration Statement for an IPO, a simple disclosure form is all it needs to submit.

In general, if your company acquired more than 500 shareholders through gradual accretion over a period of time without filing a 1933 Act Registration Statement, your company must file a rather extensive disclosure document (similar to a Form S-1 or a Form SB-1 for a small business issuer) once it acquires more than $5 million in assets at the end of any fiscal year.

Many companies with over $5 million in assets attempt to avoid costs of registration under Section 12(g) and subsequent reporting costs by attempting to limit their number of shareholders to a figure below 500. This is accomplished by buying back stock for the company's treasury, by placing charter or bylaw restrictions on transfers, and by taking other measures.

Occasionally, in the absence of restrictions, sophisticated shareholders will attempt to secure bargaining leverage on companies by threatening to make family gifts sufficient to raise the number of shareholders to 500 or above, unless the company buys back the shareholder's stock at a premium. Therefore, companies that do not wish to be subject to this type of intimidation may wish to insert charter or bylaw restrictions on these activities.

Some companies complete their IPOs and have less than 500 shareholders and never voluntarily register under Section 12(g) of the 1934 Act or have their securities registered in a national securities exchange. The above provisions and other provisions of the 1934 Act discussed in the remainder of this chapter (Forms 3, 4 and 5, the "short-swing" profit rules, and Schedules 13D and 13G) are, therefore, not applicable to such companies or their directors, officers, and principal shareholders. However, these companies and their directors, officers, and principal shareholders are still subject to the anti-fraud and anti-manipulative provisions of the 1934 Act, such as Rules 10b-5 and 10b-6 below.

Brief Summary

The following is a brief summary of the personal duties of directors, officers, and principal shareholders under the 1934 Act described in the remainder of this chapter, expressed in do's and don'ts:

Do

- File a Form 3 Report within 10 days after becoming a director, officer, or more than 10 percent stockholder of the company.
- File a Form 4 Report within 10 days after the end of any calendar month in which a change occurred in your beneficial ownership of any equity security of the company.
- File a Form 5 Report within 45 days after the end of the company's fiscal year disclosing all transactions and holdings, if any, not previously disclosed during such year.
- File a Schedule 13D if during any 12-month period you acquire more than 2 percent of any class of equity securities registered under the 1934 Act and if, after such acquisition, you beneficially own more than 5 percent of such class and promptly file any required material amendments to Schedule 13D.
- File a Schedule 13G within forty-five days after the end of any calendar year if you beneficially own more than 5 percent of any class of equity securities registered under the 1934 Act at year end and have been exempt from filing a Schedule 13D.
- Consult with the company's counsel or any personal attorney who specializes in securities law before engaging in any transaction in the securities of the company. Supply a copy of all reports filed with the SEC to the company's counsel.

Don't

- Within a 6-month period, make any purchase and sale, or sale and purchase, of any equity securities of the company if such transaction results in a "short-swing" profit.

- Make any short sales of the company's equity securities or sales against the box.
- Utilize material confidential information of the company for purposes of trading in the company's securities or engage in other manipulative or deceptive devices.
- Tip confidential information of the company to others.
- Bid for or purchase any security of the company, or any right thereto, while you or the company are participating in a public distribution of such securities.
- Violate the provisions of the Foreign Corrupt Practices Act of 1977.
- Participate or aid or abet others in a violation of the 1934 Act or conspire to commit such violation.
- Sell restricted or control securities (as defined in Chapter Thirteen) unless you comply with Rule 144 of the 1933 Act or other applicable exemption from the 1933 Act.

Form 3, Form 4 and Form 5 Reports— Section 16(a) of the 1934 Act[21]

Section 16(a) of the 1934 Act requires a more than 10 percent beneficial owner of any class of equity securities registered under the 1934 Act, and all directors and officers of the issuer of such security, to file a Form 3 Report disclosing the amount of equity securities of such issuer of which they are beneficial owners.[22] They must file the Form 3 Report on or before the effective date of the registration of the company's securities or, if later, within 10 days after they become a director, officer, or more than 10 percent beneficial owner. The term "equity securities" includes not only common stock but also (among other things) debt securities convertible into common stock, or having a right attached to subscribe for common stock, warrants, and certain stock options.[23]

If a change in beneficial ownership of any equity security of the company occurs during any calendar month, the person must file a Form 4 Report within 10 days after the end of that calendar month unless the change in beneficial ownership is exempt from reporting. A change of beneficial ownership could occur not only because of a sale or purchase of equity securities, but also as a result of a gift, a stock dividend, a stock split, the receipt of certain stock options, the purchase or sale of a put, call, or convertible securities, or as a result of a change in the nature of the ownership, such as a change from indirect ownership through a trust or corporation to direct ownership.[24] The beneficial owner must file a Form 4 Report even though the net result of all securities transactions during the calendar month results in no change at the end of the month.[25]

A person must file a Form 5 Report within 45 days after the end of the company's fiscal year. In this report the person must disclose (i) all exempt transactions not previously reported during the year and (ii) all holdings and transactions that should have been reported during the most recent fiscal year (during the two most recent fiscal years with respect to the first Form 5 Report) but which were not reported.[26] You do not need to complete a Form 5 Report if all transactions and holdings otherwise required to be reported on the Form 5 were previously reported.[27]

You must file reports on Form 3, Form 4 and Form 5 with the SEC and with each national securities exchange listing or having registered any class of equity securities of the company (if any).[28] The law does not consider reports filed until they are actually received by the SEC or the exchange; however, the law deems reports transmitted to a delivery service that guaranteed delivery by the due date to be timely filed.[29] Therefore, reports must be mailed for filing within sufficient time prior to their due dates so that the SEC and the exchange can receive them within the required time period. The company must also send an original or duplicate of each report simultaneously to the person designated by the company to receive such filings or to the company's corporate secretary if no person is designated.[30]

Reports filed on Form 3, Form 4 and Form 5 are public information and the SEC publishes a monthly summary of such reports, which is publicly distributed. The summary is scrutinized by individuals interested in instituting lawsuits against directors, officers, and more than 10 percent beneficial owners under Section 16(b) of the 1934 Act to recover "short-swing" profits. The company must disclose in its proxy statement and Form 10-K annual reports the names of any person who failed to file a Form 3, Form 4 and Form 5 Report on time, or who failed to disclose any holdings or transactions during the prior fiscal year.[31] Finally, SEC monetary fines for filing violations by a reporting person can be assessed under recently adopted legislation.[32]

133

Liability for Short-Swing Profits—
Section 16(b) of 1934 Act[33]

Section 16(b) permits the company (with certain exceptions) to recover any profit realized by a director, officer, or more than 10 percent beneficial owner from any sale and purchase, or purchase and sale, of any equity security (whether or not registered under the 1934 Act) of the company within a period of less than 6 months—these are "short-swing" profits. A short-swing profit occurs when within a period of less than 6 months, there is either a purchase and subsequent sale of the equity security at a higher price or there is a sale and subsequent purchase of the equity security at a lower price. Liability for short-swing profits may be imposed even though no equity security of the company was registered under the 1934 Act at the time of the initial purchase or sale,[34] but was at the time of the corresponding sale or purchase and even though the purchaser or seller was not a director or officer or more than 10 percent beneficial owner at both the time of the purchase and the sale.[35]

An action to recover short-swing profits may be instituted by the company or by the owner of any security of the company if the company refuses to bring suit within 60 days after request or fails to prosecute the action diligently. A security holder bringing the suit need not have been a security holder at the time of the transaction in question.[36] Thus, it is possible for an individual who discovers a short-swing profit from the published information, to buy one share of stock and bring a suit in the name of the company, even though the company refuses to bring such suit. One motivation for bringing this suit might be that the individual's attorney would be entitled, as an attorney's fee, to a portion of the profits that the director, officer, or more than 10% beneficial owner was required to pay back to the company.[37]

The terms "sale" and "purchase," as interpreted by the regulations of the SEC and the courts under Section 16, have been applied to transactions that are not customarily considered sales or purchases. For example, the receipt of a stock option is considered a "purchase" for purposes of Section 16(b),[38] unless the option is exempt by reason of being granted pursuant to a plan approved by shareholders and otherwise meeting the conditions set forth in Rule 16b-3. If employees sell stock within six months before or after the date of the receipt of the nonexempt option, they may incur liability under Section 16(b).

Other situations not customarily thought of as "sales" and "pur-

134

chases," but nevertheless may constitute "sales" or "purchases" under Section 16(b), include certain mergers,[39] the sale or purchase of preferred stock convertible into common stock, debentures or warrants convertible into common stock,[40] and the exercise for cash of certain stock appreciation rights.[41] For example, the court may deem a merger to involve the "sale" of the security being surrendered in the merger and the "purchase" of the security acquired in the merger. Thus, if the company is involved in a merger in which the company's shares are to be surrendered for shares of another issuer, the company's directors, officers, and more than 10 percent beneficial owners should avoid purchases of shares of the company within six months of the date of the merger. Since the merger may also involve the "purchase" of the securities acquired in the merger, sales of such securities within six months before or after the merger could also create Section 16(b) liability.

Section 16(b) covers purchases or sales of equity securities that you "beneficially own." A person is considered the beneficial owner of any security if he, directly or indirectly, through any contract, arrangement, understanding or otherwise, has or shares the opportunity, directly or indirectly, profits from any transaction in such securities.[42] As a result, you are deemed to "beneficially own" many securities that you do not legally own. For example, you generally are presumed to "beneficially own" securities legally owned by your spouse or minor children and certain relatives of yours or your spouse who share the same home.[43] Thus, if you live with your mother-in-law, her purchases or sales may be matched with your own to impose Section 16(b) liability upon you. If you have the right to vest title in yourself to securities legally owned by another person, either immediately or at some future time, you may "beneficially own" such securities.

You cannot avoid liability under Section 16(b) by establishing that the particular share certificates sold (or purchased) are not the same ones purchased (or sold) within the same six-month period.[44] The court may deem a purchase or sale to have occurred on the trade date or the date a legally binding contract to purchase or sell is entered into, and not necessarily on the date of closing or settlement.[45]

Under present law, with certain exceptions, if there is a series of purchases and sales within a six-month period, the recoverable profit is computed by matching the highest sale price with the lowest purchase price of the same quantity; then the next highest sale price is matched with the next lowest purchase price, etc.[46] As a result of this method of computing profits, a defendant suffered a judgement of approximately

135

$300,000 even though the defendant had an *actual loss* on his series of purchases and sales.[47]

A purely objective standard is generally used under Section 16(b) to determine whether or not liability exists, that is, whether there is a sale and purchase or purchase and sale within a six-month period. It is irrelevant that the director, officer, or more than 10% beneficial owner acted in good faith, or innocently, or lacked any improper intent, or used material non-public information.[48] This objective standard has been tempered only in unusual situations that could not possibly allow for insider speculation and profiteering on non-public information.[49]

Short Sales and Sales Against the Box— Section 16(c) of 1934 Act

Under Section 16(c) of the 1934 Act,[50] a director, officer, or more than 10% beneficial owner is prohibited (with certain exceptions) from selling any equity security of the company which the director, etc. does not own ("short-sales") or, if owned, from failing to make delivery against the sale within 20 days thereafter, or to place it in the mails or other usual channels of transportation within five days after the sale ("sales against the box"). Persons violating this provision may, in addition to any civil liabilities, be subject to criminal penalties under Section 32(a) of the 1934 Act.[51]

Personal Use of Inside Information— Rule 10b-5 Under 1934 Act

Transactions in securities of the company by insiders may involve not only the provisions of Section 16 of the 1934 Act but also the anti-fraud and anti-manipulative provisions of the 1933 and 1934 Acts as well. The most significant of these is Rule 10b-5 under the 1934 Act, which is the rule upon which the SEC based its complaint in the famous Texas Gulf Sulphur case.[52]

Rule 10b-5 generally makes it unlawful for any person, directly or indirectly, by the use of any means or instrumentality of interstate commerce or of the mails or of any facilities of any national securities exchange, to employ any manipulative or deceptive device in connection with the purchase or sale of securities. The most common example of the application of Rule 10b-5 is the use by an insider, for the purpose of trading in the company's securities, of information pertaining to the company that is not publicly available (confidential information) and which is material. The courts would deem the use of such material confidential information for trading purposes generally manipulative or deceptive in connection with the purchase or sale of securities.[53] Assuming the buyer with whom the insider dealt was not aware of this material confidential information, the buyer would have the right to rescind the purchase or sale or seek damages from the insider.[54]

Rule 10b-5 differs from Section 16(b) in numerous ways, among which are the following:

- Unlike Section 16(b), it is not necessary under Rule 10b-5 to have both a purchase and a sale in order to render the insider liable. Thus, even though you made a purchase only or a sale only, if you utilized material confidential information you would be liable under Rule 10b-5 even though you had no liability under Section 16(b). Also, if you purchased in January and sold in September of the same year, you would avoid Section 16(b) liability, but if either the January purchase or the September sale involved the utilization of material confidential information, you would nevertheless be liable under Rule 10b-5.[55]

- Rule 10b-5 generally extends to all persons having material confidential information, whereas Section 16(b) applies only to directors, officers and more than 10% beneficial owners. Your secretary would be deemed an insider subject to Rule 10b-5 liability if the secretary traded on or tipped material confidential information even though the secretary would have no liability under Section 16(b). The courts have interpreted the term "insider" when used in conjunction with Rule 10b-5 to include, with certain exceptions, all persons possessing material confidential information of the company, regardless of their position with or relation to the company.[56]

- Rule 10b-5 applies to all securities of the company (whether debt or equity), whereas Section 16(b) applies only to equity securities of the company.

- It is generally a defense against Rule 10b-5 liability to show that you did not know or have reason to know of material confidential information of the company at the time of your trading.[57] The fact that you did not possess or utilize material confidential information of the company in trading is generally no defense to Section 16(b) liability.

- It is generally a defense to Rule 10b-5 liability, but not to Section 16(b) liability, if you prove that the person with whom you dealt possessed the same material confidential information that you did.[58]

In order to be liable under Rule 10b-5, it is necessary that you know or have reason to know that the confidential information is "material" and that it was obtained or used in breach of a fiduciary duty. What is material information and whether or not such information was obtained or used in violation of a fiduciary duty are of course difficult questions to determine. Courts have considered as material any information that the average prudent investor would consider important.[59]

There are many occasions on which you have information that is not then available to the public. You may, for example, have access to the financial statements of the company that have not yet been publicly released. Making any purchase or sale of any company security during the period after such financial information is available to you, but before such statements are made generally available to the public, would create an inference that you had acted on the basis of this material confidential information.

There are periods of time in which prudence would dictate that you refrain from any trading in the company's securities, even though you do not possess any material confidential information or even though your possession of material confidential information does not influence your trading. False appearances of your use of material confidential information can be as harmful to you and the company as its actual utilization. One of the most crucial times during which to avoid trading is right before the publication of financial information that the court may be deem material. Likewise, you should avoid trading immediately prior to the public announcement of any material corporate development, such as the receipt or loss of a large contract, an acquisition or merger, a stock split or stock dividend, a public offering, exchange, or tender offer, a change in dividend rates or earnings, a call for redemption, a new product or discovery, and the like. Your trading should not commence simultaneously with the public announcement; rather, you should continue to refrain from trading until the trading market has had a chance to absorb the public announcement (usually 48 hours). As a general rule, you should avoid trading at any time there is a pending material corporate development of which the trading market has no knowleddge.

Recent judicial decisions and SEC enforcement actions have extended the reach of Rule 10b-5 to situations where a person, although not an insider in the traditional sense, acquires or uses material confidential information unlawfully, in breach of a fiduciary duty to someone other than the person with whom the person traded.[60] In addition, in 1984 President Reagan signed the Insider Trading Sanctions Act (ITSA). Under ITSA, the SEC may, among other things, bring an action seeking a penalty not to exceed three times the profit gained or the loss avoided by an unlawful purchase or sale against (1) any person who purchases or sells securities while in possession of material, non-public information in violation of the 1934 Act and the rules adopted thereunder, and (2) any person who, by communicating material, non-public information to such other person, aids and abets another in the purchase or sale of securities while in possession of material, non-public information.[61]

One purpose of Rule 10b-5 is to ensure that neither party to a trade has an unfair advantage insofar as his knowledge of all material facts relating to the company. It is possible that the company may have disclosed certain facts concerning a material corporate development but not have disclosed them completely—the "half-truth problem."[62] An insider knowing the full story and who engages in trading will likewise be liable in the same manner as though the public did not have any information at all.

Rule 10b-5 and other rules and sections of the 1934 Act and 1933 Act also prohibit various types of manipulative or deceptive devices that do not depend on the utilization of material confidential information by insiders. For example, creating a false appearance of active trading in the company's stock by entering matching buy and sell orders or engaging in a series of transactions to raise or depress the price of a security for the purpose of inducing the purchase or sale of security by others would violate Rule 10b-5 as well as rules and sections of the 1934 Act and 1933 Act.

The violation of Rule 10b-5 can result in both civil and criminal liability. The civil liability may include a suit to recover any profits earned by the insider or, where appropriate, any profits lost by the person with whom he traded. The suit may be in the form of a direct suit by the person with whom the trade occurred or may be a suit by any stockholder (even though not on the other end of the trade) to recover for the company any profits realized by the insider. In addition, the SEC has brought civil injunctive proceedings against insiders trading on material confidential information. Finally, there is a possibility of criminal liability under Section 32(a) of the 1934 Act, although the courts have reserved for very serious cases.

Tipping of Material Confidential Information— Rule 10b-5 Under 1934 Act

Rule 10b-5 not only prohibits the utilization by insiders of confidential information for their own trading purposes, but also prohibits tipping by the insider of such confidential information to others. The Texas Gulf Sulphur case[63] established the principle that the insider who does the tipping is liable not only for personal profits but also for any profits realized by the tippee. In addition, it may be possible that the tipper would be held liable for the profits or losses of the entire class of buyers or sellers during the period between the time of the initial tip and the time that the tipped information is finally made public. If the tipper is a director, officer, or other employee of the company, the company may also be liable.[64]

In any event, it is clear that you should avoid casual cocktail party conversations concerning the company except to the extent that your conversation relates only to publicly available information. As a director, officer, or principal stockholder, you will be constantly pressed for information concerning the company by friends, relatives, business associates, brokers, and analysts. It is important that you either refrain from giving any information or be very careful to stick to only publicly available information. In this connection, you should know that the SEC has brought actions against corporations and their officers for disclosing material confidential information to brokers or analysts prior to releasing such information to the public.[65]

Schedules 13D and 13G—
Sections 13(d) and 13(g) of 1934 Act

Section 13(d) of the 1934 Act[66] provides that any person who, after acquiring the beneficial ownership (directly or indirectly) of any equity security of a class registered under the 1934 Act, is a beneficial owner of more than 5 percent of such class must, within 10 days after such acquisition, file a Schedule 13D with the issuer of the security, with each exchange on which the security is traded, and with the SEC.

There are various exemptions to this requirement. The most important exemption is that Schedule 13D does not have to be filed if the acquisition of the security, when taken together with all other acquisitions of securities of the same class by the same person during the preceding 12 months, does not exceed 2 percent of such class of securities.[67] For example, if you own 3% of the common stock of the company registered under the 1934 Act and, within a 12-month period, increase your ownership of the common stock by more than 2%, you must file a Schedule 13D within 10 days after you have exceeded the 2% limit.

When two or more persons act as a group for the purpose of acquiring, holding, or disposing of securities of the company, such group is considered a single person for Section 13(d) purposes.[68] If you become part of such a group, the court will deem the group to have acquired beneficial ownership of the securities of its members and, if the 5% threshold is met, the group will have to file a Schedule 13D within 10 days after its formation.[69]

If any material change occurs in the facts set forth in the Schedule 13D you previously filed, you must file an amendment to the Schedule.[70] The SEC deems material acquisition or disposition of beneficial ownership of securities in the amount equal to 1 percent or more of the class of securities. Acquisitions or dispositions of less than 1 percent may be material, depending on the circumstances. Please note that you must file a Schedule 13D even though the transaction in the securities was reported on a Form 4 Report.

You can be the beneficial owner of securities that you do not legally own. For purposes of Sections 13(d) and 13(g) of the 1934 Act, you beneficially own securities which you (directly or indirectly) have, or which you share with others either by voting power (the power to direct the voting of the securities) or investment power (the power to direct the disposition of the securities). In addition, if you have the right to acquire beneficial ownership of the security within the next 60 days (e.g., by the exercise of a stock option or warrant, conversion of a security, or revocation or automatic termination of a trust or discretionary account), you beneficially own the security.[71] Thus, if you own 4% of the common stock of the company and have stock options exercisable within the next 60 days for more than 1% of such stock, you must file a Schedule 13D within 10 days.

If you are not required to file a Schedule 13D because of an exemption, and you are the beneficial owner of more than 5% of a class of securities registered under the 1934 Act at the end of the calendar year, then the law may require you to file a Schedule 13G with the issuer of the security and with the SEC within 45 days of the end of that calendar year.[72]

Trading During Distribution of Securities— Rule 10b-6 Under the 1934 Act

Rule 10b-6 prohibits various persons, including the company, from certain types of trading activities during the time a distribution of the company's securities is being made in which they participate. The term "distribution" is not defined in the 1934 Act, but includes any registered or unregistered public sale of the securities of the company.[73] The SEC may deem you carried on a distribution when the company is issuing its securities in an acquisition or merger or pursuant to an "earnout" granted in a previous acquisition, or otherwise.

Rule 10b-6 prohibits participants in the distribution from bidding for or purchasing any security that is the subject of a distribution, any security of the same class or series, or any right to purchase any such security (e.g., a warrant or call), or attempting to induce any person to purchase any such security or right until they complete the distribution (subject to certain exceptions). Under certain circumstances, the Rule 10b-6 prohibitions may apply to directors, officers, and principal stockholders of a corporation engaged in a distribution of securities, whether or not such directors, officers, or principal stockholders are themselves engaged in the distribution.[74] There is a great deal of uncertainty as to the date when a distribution begins and when the SEC would deem it to have ended. In case of question, it is best to consult with counsel.

The purpose of Rule 10b-6 is to forestall any attempt to manipulate securities prices by means of bids or purchases during the course of a public distribution of such securities. The effect of bids for, or purchases of, securities being distributed may be to artificially inflate the price of the distributed securities above the price that would have prevailed in a free and open market.

Foreign Corrupt Practices Act of 1977— Sections 13(b)(2) and 30A of 1934 Act

The Foreign Corrupt Practices Act of 1977[75] amended the 1934 Act to impose certain accounting standards on public companies and to prohibit "corrupt" foreign payments by or on behalf of United States corporations (whether or not public), business entities, citizens, nationals, and residents.

Accounting Standards

Under the accounting standards, the company must make and keep books, records, and accounts, which in reasonable detail accurately and fairly reflect the transactions and dispositions of the assets of the company.

The company must also devise and maintain a system of internal accounting controls sufficient to provide reasonable assurance that the company executes all transactions in accordance with management's general or specific authorization. It must record the transactions as necessary to permit preparation of financial statements in conformity with generally accepted accounting principles or any other criteria applicable to such statements and to maintain accountability for assets. The accounting controls must permit access to assets only in accordance with management's general or specific authorization. And, it must compare the recorded accountability for assets with the existing assets at reasonable intervals and the company must take appropriate action with respect to any differences.

The government enacted the 1934 Act's requirements with regard to the maintenance of books and records and a system of internal control largely in response to disclosures that many United States corporations had established "off-the-book" accounts and "slush funds." However, the requirements apply to all public companies, whether or not they engage in foreign business or employ slush funds.

Keep in mind that the writers of the 1934 Act directed the accounting standards at the accuracy of the company's books, records, and accounts, not its financial statements. Thus, even though the company has not paid foreign bribes and even though its published financial statements may be accurate in all respects, it could nonetheless be in violation of the 1934 Act if, for example, its books and records improperly characterized the nature of a perfectly legitimate item of expense.

The accounting standards of the 1934 Act do not impose personal duties upon you. However, prudence would dictate that you should periodically review the company's accounting systems, including its system of internal controls, with the company's auditors. You may, of course, delegate this function to the Audit Committee of the Board of Directors. However, neglect of this review function can have serious consequences to you as well as the company.

Foreign Bribes

The Foreign Corrupt Practices Act of 1977 also proscribes and criminalizes foreign corrupt payments. Generally speaking, the 1934 Act makes it illegal for any public company, as well as any officer, director, employee, or stockholder acting on behalf of the company, to pay, promise to pay, or authorize the payment of money or anything of value to:

- any official of a foreign government or instrumentality of a foreign government,
- any foreign political party,
- any candidate for foreign political office, or
- any person the company knows or has reason to know will make a proscribed payment or will promise to make or authorize payment of a proscribed payment,
- if the purpose is to induce the recipient to: (a) use personal influence with the foreign government or instrumentality; (b) influence the enactment of legislation or regulation by that foreign

government or instrumentality; or (c) refrain from performing any official responsibility, in each case, for the purpose of obtaining or retaining business for or with, or directing business to, any person.

In order to fall within the 1934 Act's proscriptions, the payment, or promise or authorization of payment, must be corrupt, that is, whether or not it is legal under the laws of the foreign jurisdiction, the payers must intend to induce the recipients to use their official position for the benefit of the persons offering the payment or their clients. The 1934 Act prohibits not only the payment of, but also the promise or authorization of, a corrupt foreign payment. Therefore, you can violate the law even if the payment is never in fact made. Since a corrupt payment requested by the foreign official (rather than offered to him) involves a decision to accede to the request, it is not a defense that the payment was requested. However, if the foreign official extorts payments and you pay them to protect physical assets from capricious destruction, you are not within the ambit of the 1934 Act. In addition, "grease payments" (payments to ministerial or clerical employees of foreign government or agencies to speed them in the performance of or encourage them to in fact perform their duties) are not prohibited by the 1934 Act.

It is clear that, if authorized, the making of a foreign corrupt payment by a foreign subsidiary of a United States company is prohibited by the 1934 Act. The law also prohibits payments to an agent (even one who is not himself subject to the 1934 Act) when it is known or should be known that they will be used to make corrupt payments.

If the company engages in foreign transactions, particularly those involving an agent, it should exercise great care to secure documentation proving that it did not violate the 1934 Act. It is prudent to secure an affidavit from any commissioned agents attesting to their compliance with the 1934 Act. Obviously, such an affidavit is useless if company officials have reason to know that it is false.

Violations of the corrupt payment provisions of the 1934 Act are punishable by fines against corporations or business entities of up to $1,000,000 and, for individuals who violate the 1934 Act, fines of up to $10,000 and imprisonment of up to five years or both. The 1934 Act further provides that fines imposed on an individual violator cannot be paid, directly or indirectly, by the company for whose benefit the bribe was paid or promised.

145

Participants, Aiders and Abettors, Conspirators and Controlling Persons

The company has numerous duties under the 1934 Act. Besides the duty under Rule 10b-5 to immediately and fully disclose material corporate developments, the company must file various reports with the SEC, including quarterly and annual reports and reports due within 15 days or more after certain events occur. If the company has a meeting of security holders, the company must file proxy material with the SEC. The company must comply with the accounting and payment provisions of the Foreign Corrupt Practices Act of 1977. These are only a few examples.

You may be personally liable if the company violates any of its duties under the 1934 Act and you either directly or indirectly (using agents or other means) participate or aid and abet in such violations or conspire to commit such violations or if you are a person who controls the company (unless you acted in good faith and did not directly or indirectly induce the act constituting the violation).[76] For example, if the company violates the 1934 Act by sending out a false or misleading press release or by filing with the SEC a false or misleading document, and you helped prepare that press release or other document, you could be liable as a participant, aider and abettor, and possibly as a conspirator. Likewise, if you participate or aid and abet in a violation of the 1934 Act by another person (such as a director, officer, or other employee of the company), or conspire with such person to commit the violation, you will be liable for that person's violation.

You may be liable as a participant in a violation of the 1934 Act even though you had no intent to deceive anyone but were merely negligent in not discovering and remedying the violation. For example, a director may be liable for unknowingly approving the use of a false and misleading, management proxy statement, if the director should, by the exercise of due care, have discovered the violation.[77] A director cannot immunize himself from liability by remaining ignorant of corporate affairs.

To be liable as an aider and abettor, you must generally have knowledge of an illegal course of conduct by another person and perform some affirmative act which assists the violator, either directly or indirectly. Mere inaction will generally not make you liable as an aider and abettor unless you have some legal duty in the situation to take action, such as if your inaction encourages the violator to continue the illegal course of conduct.[78]

The SEC has taken the position that directors and officers of a public company may have a legal responsibility for the company's noncompliance with the 1934 Act as well as other securities laws. On occasion, particularly where aider and abettor liability is not clear, the SEC publishes and publicly disseminates reports on the alleged derelictions of directors who were not sufficiently vigilant in their supervision of management.[79] Where the SEC can prove aider and abettor liability, possible criminal actions may be brought.

If you are personally liable as a participant, aider or abettor, or conspirator in the company's violation of the 1934 Act, you may be entitled to indemnification from the company, depending upon the nature of the violation and your participation in the violation.

The company should never send out a press or shareholders' release or file a document with the SEC unless the company's counsel has first reviewed it, since the company will be liable if a violation occurs and any participants, aiders and abettors, conspirators and, under certain circumstances, controlling persons.

Conclusion

As you can see, the applicable provisions of the 1934 Act (and, as you will find, Rule 144 of the 1933 Act discussed in Chapter Thirteen) are extremely complicated. The worst thing that you can do is to try to be your own lawyer. The old saying that a person who represents himself has a fool for a client is particularly applicable in dealing with the securities laws.

Your personal liability for violating the "do's and don'ts" of this chapter can range from an injunction entered against you by the SEC to criminal actions in appropriate cases. Under the Racketeer Influenced and Corrupt Organizations Act of 1970, as amended (RICO), shareholders of your company can sue you for triple damages for your violation of the securities laws. These private damage actions are becoming more frequent as the courts liberalize the requirements. For example, under the "fraud-on-the-market" theory, a shareholder may sue even if you can prove that the shareholder never read the company's disclosure document alleged to be false.

The utilization of one common sense rule should help to prevent you from violating the 1934 Act or Rule 144 of the 1933 Act: ALWAYS CONSULT WITH THE COMPANY'S COUNSEL OR ANY PERSONAL ATTORNEY WHO SPECIALIZES IN SECURITIES LAW PRIOR TO ENGAGING IN ANY TRANSACTION IN THE COMPANY'S SECURITIES. The consultation should be sufficiently in advance of the proposed transaction so that counsel has the time to properly advise you of the proposed transaction's consequences. The problems under the 1934 Act and 1933 Act are sufficiently complicated so that even the most expert counsel requires ample time to research and review the securities problems that you present.

You should supply a copy of all reports filed with the SEC by you or your counsel to the company's counsel.

Chapter Thirteen

Rule 144 of 1933 Act

The 1933 Act prohibits (among other things) the use of any means or instruments of transportation or communication in interstate commerce or of the mails to make any offer of securities of a company unless a registration statement is filed. It also prohibits any sale of securities unless a registration statement is effective. There are numerous securities and transaction exemptions from these prohibitions. The most common transactional exemptions are private placement transactions and transactions by or involving persons who are not issuers, underwriters, or dealers. A person who distributes control securities or restricted securities may be an underwriter under the law and subject to the registration provisions of the 1933 Act, unless that person complies with Rule 144 or some other applicable exemption from the registration provisions of the 1933 Act.

Control securities are securities of the company held by persons or groups controlling the company (e.g., a large stockholder or group of stockholders), controlled by the company (e.g., a subsidiary), or under common control with the company. For example, if a controlling stockholder of the company buys the company's securities on the open market or otherwise acquires securities of the company (by private purchase, gift or other ways), such securities are control securities.

The court may deem a person part of a "control group" of the company even though he does not personally own a significant amount of the company securities and even though the person does not in fact control the company. For example, the court might decide that a close relative of a controlling stockholder is part of a control group, especially if the relative is also a director of the company. Under such circumstances, the courts would consider all company securities held by the relative control securities. In some companies, the court may view all directors and officers as a group as constituting a control group.

Restricted securities are securities acquired in nonpublic offerings (generally private placements), directly or indirectly, from the company, from holders of control securities, or from other holders of restricted securities. For example, securities you acquire under a stock option plan, properly not registered under the 1933 Act because of the private placement exemption, are restricted securities.

Your security may be both a control security and a restricted security if, for example, you recently purchased the security from the company in a private placement performed by a person in a control relationship with the company. A control security ceases to be a control security when a person not in a control relationship with the company acquires it, but it may nevertheless continue to be a restricted security.

You cannot publicly sell control securities and restricted securities unless a current registration statement is in effect under the 1933 Act or Rule 144 or some other exemption from the registration provisions of the 1933 Act is available.

Two-Year Holding Period
for Restricted Securities

Rule 144 provides, among other things, if all conditions of the rule are met, that after two years has elapsed from the date you acquire restricted securities from the company or from a person or group in a control relationship with the company, you may sell limited amounts of restricted securities during successive three-month periods either in brokers' transactions or directly to market makers. Rule 144, likewise, lets you sell limited amounts of control securities that are not also restricted securities during successive three-month periods in brokers' transactions or directly to market makers without compliance with the two-year holding period. The permission to sell is conditional: there must be adequate current public information available concerning the company and the seller must file a notice on Form 144 (subject to exceptions) concurrently with the sale.

The purpose of the two-year holding period for restricted securities is to prevent the holder of restricted securities from acting as a conduit for the distribution of securities by the company[80] or by a person or group in a control relationship with the company. If you purchase the restricted securities from the company or such control person, the two-year period does not begin until you pay the full purchase price or other consideration to the company or control person. If a promissory note is given for all or a portion of the purchase price of the restricted securities, the issuance of that promissory note would not be deemed to be full payment of the purchase price, and accordingly, the 2-year holding period would not commence, unless the promissory note (a) provided for full recourse against the purchaser, (b) was secured by collateral (other than the restricted securities purchased) having a fair market value which, at all times until the note was paid, was at least equal to the unpaid balance of the note,[81] and (c) was paid in full before sale under Rule 144. If you acquire outstanding restricted securities from someone who is not in a control relationship with the company, you only need to hold the restricted securities for the balance of the two-year period, that is, the law does not require you to satisfy a new two-year period.

Certain restricted securities are given retroactive holding periods under the so-called "tacking" provisions of Rule 144. For example, securities you acquire from the company as a stock dividend, or pursuant to a stock split, reverse split, or recapitalization, the law deems acquired at the same time as the restricted securities on which the dividend was paid or the restricted securities involved in the split or recapitalization. Likewise, securities you acquire upon conversion of convertible debentures or convertible preferred stock generally have holding periods retroactive to the date the convertible debentures or preferred stock. Also, certain securities acquired by gifts and certain partnership distributions and pursuant to the earn-out and market-floor provisions of agreements of sale can obtain retroactive holding periods. These are only a few examples.

Amount Salable Under Rule 144

Rule 144 allows you to sell a limited amount of securities every three months under its "leakage" provisions.

The amount of restricted and control securities you sell in any three-month period must not exceed the greater of (a) 1% of the class outstanding (as shown by the most recent report or statement published by the company), (b) the average weekly volume of trading in that securities reported on all national securities exchanges and/or reported through the automated quotation system of a registered securities association during the 4 calendar weeks preceding the filing of Form 144,[82] or (c) the average weekly volume of trading reported through the consolidated reporting system during the four-week period. If, after filing a Form 144 covering a security traded on a national securities exchange, the average weekly trading volume of the security on all exchanges rises, you may file an amended Form 144 and sell the increased volume, provided you exclude your own trades from the new trading volume computations.

In computing the amount of restricted and control securities that you may sell under Rule 144 you must take into account the following:

1. If control securities (even though such securities are also restricted securities), all securities of the company, whether restricted, control or otherwise, sold for your account during the preceding three-month period count against your Rule 144 sales limit. If you sell restricted securities (but not control securities), only other restricted securities of the same class sold for your account during the preceding three months count against your Rule 144 sales limit.
2. Sales made by your spouse, or any relative of you or your spouse who shares the same home, count as sales by you.
3. Sales made by any trust or estate in which you or any person referred to in paragraph 2 above collectively own 10% or more of the total beneficial interest, or of which any such person serves as trustee, executor or in any similar capacity, count as sales by you.
4. Sales by any corporation or other organization (except the company) in which you or any of the persons specified in paragraph 2 are the beneficial owners collectively of 10% or more of any class of equity securities, or 10% or more of the equity interest, count as sales by you.
5. Sales by any person from whom you received the restricted or control securities as a gift or as a partnership distribution within the last two years count as sales by you.
6. Sales by any person to whom you gave a gift or made a partnership distribution of restricted or control securities within the last two years count as sales by you.

152

7. Sales by other persons with whom you are acting in concert for the purpose of selling restricted or control securities count as sales by you. In this connection, it would be wise to avoid any agreements with other holders of restricted or control securities as to the method of disposition of the securities unless you are prepared to have their sales count against your Rule 144 sales limit, and vice versa.

The foregoing list is not intended to be exhaustive and other sales may in a given situation count against your Rule 144 sales limit.

Adequate Public Information

The permission to sell restricted and control securities under Rule 144 is conditional upon there being adequate current information available to the public with regard to the company. Without discussing the various nuances of this requirement, it should be noted that you must represent to the SEC in your Form 144 that you do not know of any material adverse information with regard to the current or prospective operation of the company that has not been publicly disclosed. If you have any reason to believe that any report the law requires your company to file under Sections 13 or 15(d) of the 1934 Act has not been filed, the law prohibits you from engaging in Rule 144 sales.

Manner of Selling

There are strict limitations on the manner of selling under Rule 144 with which you should be familiar. You must not solicit or arrange for the solicitation of orders to buy the restricted or control securities in anticipation of or in connection with your Rule 144 sale. Nor may you make any payment in connection with the offering or sale of these securities to any person other than the broker who executes your sell order.

Furthermore, with one exception, your securities must be sold in broker's transactions, as defined in Rule 144. This requires, among other things, that the broker does no more than execute your order as agent, receives no more than the usual customary broker's commissions, and

153

neither solicits nor arranges for the solicitation of customers' orders to buy the securities in anticipation of or in connection with the transaction. The exception to this rule is that you may bypass the broker and deal directly with so-called "market makers." Market makers include any dealers who, with respect to a particular security, hold themselves out (by entering quotations in an inter-dealer communication system or otherwise) as being willing to buy and sell such security for their own accounts on a regular or continuous basis.

Form 144

Concurrently with any Rule 144 sale, you must file (subject to exceptions)[83] a Form 144 with the SEC and, if any national securities exchange admits the security to trading, with the principal national securities exchange listing the security. The person filing a Form 144 must have a bona fide intention to sell the securities covered in that form within a reasonable time after the filing of the form.

Exemption for Restricted Securities Held Three Years

There is an exception to compliance with certain of the provisions of Rule 144 for restricted securities that you beneficially own for three years. Restricted securities, which are beneficially owned for at least three years by persons who are not and have not been for the previous three months controlling persons of the company, you may sell without restriction as to volume or the manner of sale without filing a Form 144[84] and whether or not there is adequate information about the company. For purposes of computing the 3 year period, you may include the holding period of the donor of any restricted securities you receive as a gift and the holding period of any partnership from which you receive a partnership distribution.[85]

Control Securities

There is no three year rule for control securities. The leakage and other provisions of Rule 144 are applicable perpetually to control securities. To sell more control securities than the leakage provisions permit, the control securities must be either registered under the 1933 Act or sold in a private placement or another transaction exempt from the registration provisions of the 1933 Act.

Conclusion

Rule 144 is a complicated rule. You should not engage in a Rule 144 sale without consulting a securities lawyer. Many companies and stock transfer agents require a legal opinion before permitting a Rule 144 sale. Therefore, you should consult a securities lawyer in sufficient time before the proposed trade date for the Rule 144 sale so the lawyer can complete the necessary paperwork.

Chapter Fourteen

The Story of an IPO

The following story of the Microsoft 1986 IPO* provides you with a realistic picture of the traditional IPO process, laced with all of its tensions and suspense. The process starts with the business decision by Microsoft to go public and ends with a sharp rise in the after market trading price of its stock (which reflects the tendency to underprice IPOs). In between are the selection of underwriters, the all-hands meetings, the due diligence and registration process, the hectic road shows, the last minute haggling over underwriters' compensation, and the finalization of the IPO offering price.]

Going public is one of capitalism's major sacraments, conferring instant superwealth on a few talented and lucky entrepreneurs. Of the more than 1,500 companies that have undergone this rite of passage in the past five years [1981 through 1985], few have enjoyed a more frenzied welcome from investors than Microsoft, the Seattle-based maker of software for personal computers. Its shares, offered at $21 on March 13, zoomed to $35.50 on the over-the-counter market before settling back to a recent $31.25. Microsoft and its shareholders raised $61 million. The biggest winner was William H. Gates III, the company's co-founder and chairman. He got only $1.6 million for the shares he sold, but going public put a market value of $350 million on the 45%

*Fortune, July 21, 1986. Reprinted Fortune magazine; © 1986 Time Inc. All rights reserved.

stake he retains. A software prodigy who helped start Microsoft while still in his teens, Gates, at 30, is probably one of the 100 richest Americans.

Gates thinks other entrepreneurs might learn from Microsoft's experience in crafting what some analysts called "the deal of the year," so he invited *Fortune* along for a rare inside view of the arduous five-month process. Companies hardly ever allow such a close look at an offering because they fear that the Securities and Exchange Commission might charge them with touting their stock. Answers emerged to a host of fascinating questions, from how a company picks investment bankers to how the offering price is set. One surprising fact stands out from Microsoft's revelations: Instead of deferring to the priesthood of Wall Street underwriters, it took charge of the process from the start.

The wonder is that Microsoft waited so long. Founded in 1975, it is the oldest major producer of software for personal computers and, with $172.5 million in revenues over the last four quarters, the second largest after Lotus Development. Microsoft's biggest hits are the PC-DOS and MS-DOS operating systems, the basic software that runs millions of IBM personal computers and clones. The company has also struck it rich with myriad versions of computer languages and a slew of fast-selling applications programs such as spreadsheets and word-processing packages for IBM, Apple, and other personal computers.

Yet Microsoft stood pat when two of its arch competitors, Lotus and Ashton-Tate, floated stock worth a total of $74 million in 1983. Nor did it budge in 1984 and 1985, when three other microcomputer software companies managed to sell $54 million of stock. The reasons were simple. Unlike its competitors, Microsoft was not dominated by venture capital investors hungry to harvest some of their gains. The business gushed cash. With pretax profits running as high as 34% of revenues, Microsoft needed no outside money to expand. Most important, Gates values control of his time and his company more than personal wealth.

Money has never been paramount to this unmarried scion of a leading Seattle family, whose father is a partner in a top Seattle law firm and whose mother is a regent of the University of Washington and a director of Pacific Northwest Bell. Gates, a gawky, washed-out blond, confesses to being a "wonk," a bookish nerd, who focuses single-mindedly on the computer business though he masters all sorts of knowledge with astounding facility. Oddly, Gates is something of a ladies' man and a fiendishly fast driver who has racked up speeding tickets even in the sluggish Mercedes diesel he bought to restrain himself. Gates left Harvard after his sophomore year to sell personal computer makers on using a version of the Basic computer language that he had written with Paul Allen, the co-founder of Microsoft. Intensely competitive and often aloof and sarcastic, Gates threw himself into building a company dedicated to technical excellence. "All Bill's ego goes into Microsoft," says a friend. "It's his firstborn child."

Gates feared that a public offering would distract him and his employees. "The whole process looked like a pain," he recalls, "and an ongoing pain once you're public. People get confused because the stock price doesn't reflect your financial performance. And to have a stock trader call up the chief executive and ask him questions is uneconomic— the ball bearings shouldn't be asking the driver about the grease."

But a public offering was just a question of time. To attract managers and virtuoso programmers, Gates had been selling them shares and granting stock options. By 1987, Microsoft estimated, over 500 people would own shares, enough to force the company to register with the SEC. Once registered, the stock in effect would have a public market, but one so narrow that trading would be difficult. Since it would have to register anyway, Microsoft might as well sell enough shares to enough investors to create a liquid market, and Gates had said that 1986 might be the year. "A projection of stock ownership showed we'd have to make a public offering at some point," says Jon A. Shirley, 48, Microsoft's pipe-smoking president and chief operating officer. "We decided to do it when we wanted to, not when we had to."

In April 1985 Gates, Shirley, and David F. Marquardt, 37, the sole venture capitalist in Microsoft (he and his firm had 6.2% of the stock), resolved to look into an offering. But Gates fretted. To forestall sticky questions from potential investors, he first wanted to launch two important products, one of them delayed over a year, and to sign a pending agreement with IBM for developing programs. He also wanted time to sound out key employees who owned stock or options and might leave once their holdings became salable on the public market. "I'm reserving the right to say no until October," Gates warned. "Don't be surprised if I call it off."

By the board meeting of October 28, held the day after a roller-skating party for Gate's 30th birthday, the chairman had done his soundings and felt more at ease. The board decided it was time to select underwriters and gave the task to Frank Gaudette, 50, the chief financial officer, who had come aboard a year before. Gaudette was just the man to shepherd Microsoft through Wall Street. He speaks in the pungent

159

tones of New York City, where his late father was a mailman, and prides himself on street smarts. He had already helped manage offerings for three companies, all suppliers of computer software and services.

Aspiring underwriters, sniffing millions in fees, had been stroking Microsoft for years. They had enticed the company's officers to so-called technology conferences—bazaars where entrepreneurs, investors, and bankers look each other over. They had called regularly at Microsoft, trying to get close to Gates and Shirley. Gaudette had been sitting through an average of three sales pitches or get-acquainted dinners a month.

Gaudette proposed that since Microsoft was well established, it deserved to have a "class Wall Street name" as the lead underwriter. This investment firm would put together the syndicate of underwriters, which eventually was to number 114. It would also allocate the stock among underwriters and investors and pocket giant fees for its trouble. Gaudette suggested a "technology boutique" co-manager the offering to enhance Microsoft's appeal to investors who specialize in technology stocks.

Narrowing the field of boutiques was easy. Only four firms were widely known as specialists in financing technology companies: Alex. Brown & Sons of Baltimore, L.F. Rothschild Unterberg Towbin of New York, and two San Francisco outfits, Hambrecht & Quist and Robertson Colman & Stephens. Culling the list of Wall Street names took longer. Microsoft's managers concluded that some big firms, including Merrill Lynch and Shearson Lehman, had not done enough homework in high tech. The board pared the contenders to Goldman Sachs, Morgan Stanley, and Smith Barney. It also included Cable House & Ragen, a Seattle firm that could be a third co-manage if Gates and Shirley decided that pleasing local investors was worth the bother. "Get on the stick," Shirley told Gaudette. "Keep Bill and me out of it—we can't spend the time. Give us a recommendation in two or three weeks."

Early in November, Gaudette called the eight investment bankers who had survived the first cut. "I need half a day with you," he said. "Take your best shot, then wait for me to call back. I'll have a decision before Thanksgiving. But remember, it's my decision—don't try going around me to Bill or Jon." Gaudette made up a list of questions, ranging from the baldly general—"Why should your firm be on the front cover of a Microsoft prospectus?"—to the probingly particular, such as, "How would you distribute the stock, to whom, and why?"

After a whirlwind tour of New York, Baltimore and San Francisco,

160

Gaudette made his recommendations to Gates and Shirley on November 21. Then he took off for a ten-day vacation in Hawaii, a belated celebration of his 50th birthday in the 50th state. No decision would be announced until his return. The investment bankers turned frantic. Theirs is a who-do-you-know business, and they mobilized their clients, many of them Microsoft customers or suppliers, to besiege Gates and Shirley.

Gaudette had methodically ranked the investment houses on a scale of 1 to 5 in 19 different categories. But he also stressed that any candidate could do the deal and that the chemistry between Microsoft and the firms would finally determine the winners. Among the major houses, Gaudette had been most impressed by Goldman Sachs, which tightly links its underwriting group with its stock traders and keeps close tabs on the identity of big institutional buyers. For those reasons, Gaudette thought Goldman would be especially good at maintaining an orderly market as Microsoft employees gradually cashed in their share.

On December 4, after conferring with Gates and Shirley, Gaudette phoned Eff W. Martin, 37, a vice president in Goldman's San Francisco office who had been calling on Microsoft for two years. "I like you guys," Gaudette said, "and Microsoft wants to give you dinner on December 11 in Seattle. Do you think you can find time to come?"

Dinner at the stuffy Rainer Club was awkward. The private room was large for the party of eight, and one wall was a sliding partition ideal for eavesdropping. Most of the party were meeting each other for the first time; however well they got along could make or break the deal. Microsoft's top dogs didn't make things easy. Gates, who had heard scare stories about investment bankers from friends like Mitchell Kapor, chairman of Lotus Development, was tired and prepared to be bored. Shirley was caustic, waiting to know exactly what Goldman imagined it could do for Microsoft.

For nearly an hour everyone stood in a semicircle as Martin and three colleagues explained their efforts to be tops in financing technology companies. An Oklahoman by birth and polite to a fault, Martin labored to kindle some rapport. But it was not until talk turned to pricing the company's stock that Gates folded his arms across his chest and started rocking to and from, a sure sign of interest. At the end of dinner, Martin, striving to conclude on a high note, gushed that Microsoft could have the "most visible initial public offering of 1986—or ever."

"Well, they didn't spill their food and they seemed like nice guys," Gates drawled to his colleagues afterward in the parking lot. "I guess we should go with them." He and Shirley drove back to Microsoft head-quarters, discussing co-managing underwriters. Gaudette leaned toward Robertson Colman & Stephens. But Alex. Brown had been cultivating Microsoft longer than any other investment banking house. . . . Three days later the board quickly blessed the selection of Goldman Sachs and Alex. Brown.

The offering formally lumbered into gear on December 17 at an "all-hands meeting" at Microsoft. It was the first gathering of the principal players: the company with its auditors and attorneys as well as both managing underwriters and their attorney. Some confusion crept in at first. Heavy fog, a Seattle specialty, delayed the arrival of several key people until early afternoon. One of Microsoft's high priorities was making its prospectus "jury proof"—so carefully phrased that no stockholder could hope to win a lawsuit by claiming he had been misled. The company had insisted that the underwriters' counsel be Sullivan & Cromwell, a hidebound Wall Street firm. Gaudette was miffed to see that the law firm had sent only an associate, not a partner.

The 27-point agenda covered every phase of the offering. Gates said the company was contemplating a $40-million deal. Microsoft would raise $30 million by selling two million shares at an assumed price of around $15. Existing shareholders, bound by Gate's informal rule that nobody should unload more than 10% of his holdings, would collect the other $10 million for 600,000 or so shares. The underwriters, as is customary in initial public offerings, would be granted the option to sell more shares. If they exercised an option for 300,000 additional shares of stock held by the company, almost 12% of Microsoft's stock would end up in public hands, enough to create the liquid market the company wanted.

Gates had thought longest about the price. Guided by Goldman, he felt the market would accord a higher price-earnings multiple to Microsoft than to other personal computer software companies like Lotus and Ashton-Tate, which have narrower product lines. On the other hand, he figured the market would give Microsoft a lower multiple than companies that create software for mainframe computers because they generally have longer track records and more predictable revenues. A price of roughly $15, more than ten times estimated earnings for fiscal 1986, would put Microsoft's multiple right between those of personal software companies and mainframers.

A host of questions came up at the all-hands meeting. Both Shirley and Gates were concerned that going public would interfere with Microsoft's ability to conduct business. Shirley wondered whether all three of Microsoft's top officers would be needed for the "road show," meetings at which company representatives would explain the offering to stockbrokers and institutional investors. Gates tried to escape the tour by saying, facetiously, "Hey, make the stock cheap enough and you won't need us to sell it!"

Microsoft's attorney, William H. Neukom, 44, a partner at Shidler McBroom Gates & Lucas—the Gates in the title being Bill's father, William H. Gates—raised another matter. The company would have to tone down its public utterances, he said, lest it appear to be "gun jumping," or touting the stock. Press releases could no longer refer to certain Microsoft programs as "industry standards," no matter how true the phrase. Neukom would review all the company's official statements, which came to include even a preface Gates was writing for a book on new computer technologies.

The most tedious part of taking the company public was writing a prospectus. It was a task rife with contradictions. By law Microsoft's stock could be sold on the basis of information in this document. If the SEC raised big objections to the preliminary version, Microsoft would have to circulate a heavily amended one, inviting rumors that the deal was fishy. However cheerful or gloomy the prospectus, many investors would fail to read it before buying. Then if the market price promptly fell, they would comb the text for the least hint of misrepresentation in order to sue. Still, the prospectus could not be too conservative. Like all such documents, it had to be a discreet sales tool, soft-pedaling weaknesses and stressing strengths, all the while concealing as much as possible from competitors.

Even before Microsoft had picked its underwriters, Robert A. Eshelman, 32, an attorney at Shidler McBroom, had started drafting the prospectus. That task took all of January. "As usual," says one of the investment bankers, "it was like the Bataan death march." Neukom, who had just left Shidler McBroom to join Microsoft, spent the first week of 1986 with Eshelman, sketching in ideas about the company's products and business. Two days a week for the next three weeks, many of the people who had been at the all-hands meeting reconvened at Microsoft's sleek headquarters in a Seattle suburb to edit the prospectus.

At the first sessions, on January 8 and 9, the underwriters brought along their security analysts to help conduct a "due diligence" examination, grilling the company's managers to uncover skeletons. Gaudette was mollified that Sullivan & Cromwell had now furnished a partner from its Los Angels office, Charles F. Rechlin, 39. Gaudette had met

163

him years before in New York but was bowled over by how much he had changed. Rechlin was 40 pounds lighter and sported shoulder-length hair and a fierce sunburn.

For ten hours Gates, Shirley, and other managers exhaustively described their parts of the business and fielded questions. Surprisingly, the Microsoft crew tended to be more conservative and pessimistic than the interrogators. Steven A. Ballmer, 30, a vice president sometimes described as Gate's alter ego, came up with so many scenarios for Microsoft's demise that one banker cracked: "I'd hate to hear you on a bad day."

By late January only one major item remained undecided—a price range for the stock. The bull market that began in September had kept roaring ahead, pushing up P/E multiples for other software companies. The underwriters suggested a price range of $17 to $20 a share. Gates insisted on, and got, $16 to $19. His argument was ultraconservative: $16 would guarantee that the underwriters would not have to go even lower to sell the shares, while a price of $20 would push Microsoft's market value above half-a-billion dollars, which he thought uncomfortably high. "That was unusual," says Christopher P. Forester, head of Goldman Sach's high-technology finance group. "Few companies fight for a lower range than the underwriter recommends."

On February 1 a courier rushed the final proof of the prospectus to Los Angeles for Sullivan & Cromwell's approval and continued on to Washington, D.C., with 13 copies. Two days later Microsoft registered with the SEC, the underwriters sent out 38,000 copies of the prospectus, and the lawyers began waiting anxiously for comments from the regulators.

Gates coped with concerns of a different sort. Relatives, friends and acquaintances of Microsoft's managers—from Gate's doctor to a high school chum of Gaudette's—called begging to buy stock at the offering price. Except for about a dozen people, including Gates's grandmother and his former housekeeper, who wanted small lots for sentimental reasons, Gates turned most of them down. "I won't grant any of these goofy requests," he said. "I hate the whole thing. All I'm thinking and dreaming about is selling software, not stock."

Rehearsals for the road show dramatized how differently Gates and Gaudette approached the process of going public. Neukom, Microsoft's in-house attorney, had admonished Gates to say nothing to anybody that deviated from the prospectus or added new information. At Goldman Sachs's New York offices for a February 7 rehearsal, Gates wondered to himself, "With my mouth taped, what's the point of giving a speech?" Addressing about 30 investment bankers and salesmen, he assumed an uncharacteristic, robotic monotone while covering Microsoft's key strengths. He became annoyed when one critic commented, "It's a great first effort, but you can put more into it." Snapped Gates: "You mean I'm supposed to say boring things in an exciting way?"

Gaudette, however, was in his element. He praised and repraised the company's record, studding his talk with cliches and corny jokes. "When it comes to earnings," he exclaimed, showing a graph of quarterly change, "the pavement is bumpy, but the road goes only one way—up!" Describing Microsoft's $72 million in stockholders' equity and its lack of long-term debt, Gaudette teased Goldman Sachs with a competing investment house's slogan: "We made our money the old-fashioned way: We earned it!"

The road show previewed in Phoenix on February 18, and over the next ten days played eight cities, including engagements in London and Edinburgh. Halfway through, the pageant took on an almost festive air. Gates relaxed a bit, having been able to push his products as well as his stock at various ports of call. In London, Eff Martin of Goldman escorted the party to the Royal Observatory at Greenwich, found tickets for the smash musical Les Miserables, and arranged admittance to Annabel's, a popular club. Gates danced the night away with Ruthann Quindlen, a security analyst for Alex. Brown.

Festivity was appropriate. Every road show meeting attracted a full house, and many big institutional investors indicated they would take as much stock as they could get. By the end of February, the Dow Jones industrial average had passed 1700. In London, Martin told Gaudette that Goldman's marketing group considered the Microsoft issue very hot. The $16 to $19 price range would have to be raised, he said, and so would the number of shares to be sold.

The underwriters had wanted to come to market while euphoria from the road show ran high. But the SEC held the starting flag. On March 4 and 5 an SEC reviewer phoned in the commission's comments on the preliminary prospectus to Eshelman. The SEC had picked all sorts of nits, from how Microsoft accounted for returned merchandise to whether Gates had an employment contract (he does not). Its major concern appeared to be that the underwriters allocate shares widely enough to make the offering truly public and not just a bonanza for a handful of privileged investors. Eshelman was relieved. "It was a thorough review," he says, "but it was nothing to make my stomach drop."

165

On March 6 Microsoft's lawyers and auditors called the SEC to negotiate changes. Meanwhile, the company persuaded two stockholders to sell an additional 295,000 shares. The next day, as the lawyers pored over proofs of a revised prospectus at the San Francisco office of Bowne & Co., the financial printers, Gaudette zestfully battled to raise the price. Eff Martin of Goldman, who had flown up to Seattle that morning, had good news. The "book" on Microsoft—the list of buy orders from institutional investors—was among the best Goldman had ever seen. The underwriters expected the stock to trade at $25 a share, give or take a dollar, several weeks after opening. A sounding of big potential buyers showed that an offering price of $20 to $21 would get the deal done.

Gates asked Martin to leave while he conferred with Shirley and Gaudette. This was a different Gates from the one who two months before thought $20 too high. "These guys who happen to be in good with Goldman and get some stock will make an instant profit of $4," he said. "Why are we handing millions of the company's money to Goldman's favorite clients?" Gaudette stressed that unless Microsoft left some money on the table the institutional investors would stay away. The three decided on a range of $21 to $22 a share, and Gaudette put in a conference call to Goldman and Alex. Brown.

Eric Dobkin, 43, the partner in charge of common stock offerings at Goldman Sachs, felt queasy about Microsoft's counterproposal. For an hour he tussled with Gaudette, using every argument he could muster. Coming out $1 too high would drive off some high-quality investors. Just a few significant defections could lead other investors to think the offering was losing its luster. Dobkin raised the specter of Sun Microsystems, a maker of high-powered microcomputers for engineers that had gone public three days earlier in a deal co-managed by Alex. Brown. Because of overpricing and bad luck—competitors had recently announced new products—Sun's shares had dropped from $16 at the offering to $14.50 on the market. Dobkin warned that the market for software stocks was turning iffy.

Gaudette loved it. "They're in pain!" he crowed to Shirley. "They're used to dictating, but they're not running the show now and they can't stand it." Getting back on the phone, Gaudette crooned: "Eric, I don't mean to upset you, but I can't deny what's in my head. I keep thinking of all that pent-up demand from individual investors, which you haven't factored in. And I keep thinking we may never see you again, but you go back to the institutional investors all the time. They're your

166

customers. I don't know whose interests you're trying to serve, but if you're playing both sides of the street, then we've just become adversaries."

As negotiations dragged on, Shirley became impatient. Eshelman, the securities lawyer from Shidler McBroom, was waiting in San Francisco to get a price range so he could send an amended prospectus off to the SEC. Finally Gaudette told Dobkin, "I've listened to your prayers. Now you're repeating yourself, and it's bullshit." The two compromised on a range of $20 to $22, with two provisos: Goldman would tell investors that the target price was $21 and nothing less, and Dobkin would report Monday on which investors had dropped out.

Monday's news was mixed. Six big investors in Boston were threatening to "uncircle"—to remove their names from Goldman Sach's list. Chicago and Baltimore were fraying at the edges—T. Rowe Price, for instance, said it might drop out above $20—while the West Coast stood firm. The market had closed flat, worrying Goldman's salesmen. But their spirits revived the next day as the Dow surged 43 points. Gaudette, now confident that he and Dobkin could agree on a final offering price, flew with Neukom to San Francisco to pick up Martin, and the three boarded a red-eye flight for New York.

Sleepless but freshly showered and shaved, Gaudette reached Goldman Sachs's offices at 11 o'clock on Wednesday, March 12. Neukom walked over from Sullivan & Cromwell, where the other lawyers were preparing the last revision of the prospectus. After lunch the two Microsoft officers went to Dobkin's office and patched Shirley and Marquardt into a speakerphone.

The conferees had no trouble agreeing on a final price of $21. The market had risen another 14 points by noon. The reception for a $15 offering that morning by Oracle Systems, another software company, seemed a favorable omen: The stock had opened at $19.25. About half the potential dropouts, including T. Rowe Price, had decided to stay in.

The only remaining issue was the underwriting discount, or "spread"—the portion of the price that would go to the underwriters to cover salesmen's commissions, underwriting expenses, and management fees. Having agreed fairly easily over dollars, the two sides bogged down over pennies.

Microsoft had always had a low spread in mind, no more than 6.5% of the selling price. That was before negotiators at Sun Microsystems, where Marquardt is a director, wangled 6.13% on a $64 million offering. Gates wanted Microsoft to get at least as good a deal on its offering. But he had gone to Australia, where he was difficult to reach. In theory Gaudette lacked authority to go above 6.13%, or just under $1.29 a share.

Dobkin opened with an oration. He touched on what other Goldman clients had paid, noting that Sun's spread was off the bottom of the charts. He suggested that the managing underwriters deserved healthy compensation; after all, their marketing efforts had raised Microsoft's offering price 20%. Goldman's best offer, Dobkin said, was 6.5%, or $1.36 a share. But if pushed very hard and given no alternative, it might, just to keep things amicable, go as low as $1.34. Having given away $26,000—each penny of the spread was worth $31,000—Dobkin and his contingent left the room to let Microsoft's side confer.

When they returned, Gaudette declared that Bill Gates had given definite orders: no more than $1.28. Besides, he argued, Microsoft was a much easier deal to handle than Sun. As to the underwriters' marketing efforts, selling more shares at a higher price was its own reward since it automatically increased the money in their pockets.

At 3:30 the two sides were stalemated, Goldman Sachs now at $1.33 and Microsoft at $1.30. They were arguing over all of $93,000 in a total fee of more than $4 million, and pressure was building. The market was turning flat and would close in minutes. Members of the syndicate were clamoring to know whether the deal was done. Dobkin kept reiterating his arguments. "Eric, you're wasting my time," Gaudette sighed wearily, donning his coat. "I'm going to visit me sainted mother in Astoria. When you've got something to say, send a limo to pick me up." With that, the Goldman team left the room.

Dobkin returned alone and closed the door. "Sometimes these things go better with fewer people," he observed. Gaudette insisted he lacked authority to go higher. "All I can do is try to get another penny from Jon," he said. "But I'm calling him just one more time, so don't screw up." "Make the call," Dobkin said.

Gaudette caught Shirley as he was leaving a Bellevue, Washington restaurant to buy a car for his daughter as a 16th birthday gift. The lowest spread they could get, Gaudette said, was $1.31. Though it was above Sun's spread, it was way below what any other personal computer software company had achieved. Shirley approved. Neukom beckoned Dobkin back into the room, and Gaudette uttered one phrase that betokened his assent to $1.31: "It's a go!" Dobkin hugged Gaudette. David Miller, a beefy ex-football player who was Goldman's syndicate manager for the offering, thundered down the stairs to his office bellowing to his assistant, "Doreen, we have a deal!"

Gaudette saved his cheers for the next morning. At 8 a.m. a courier had delivered Microsoft's "filing package" to the SEC—three copies of the final prospectus and a bundle of exhibits, including the underwriters' agreement to buy the shares, which had been signed only hours earlier. The commission declared at 9:15 that Microsoft's registration was effective. On the trading floor at Goldman Sachs, Gaudette heard a trader say, "We're going to shoot the moon and open at 25!"

At 9:35 Microsoft's stock traded publicly on the over-the-counter market for the first time at $25.75. Within minutes Goldman Sachs and Alex. Brown exercised their option to take an extra 300,000 shares between them. Gaudette could hardly believe the tumult. Calling Shirley from the floor, he shouted into the phone, "It's wild! I've never seen anything like it—every last person here is trading Microsoft and nothing else."

The strength of retail demand caught everyone by surprise. By the end of the first day of trading, some 2.5 million shares had changed hands, and the price of Microsoft's stock stood at $27.75. The opportunity to take a quick profit was too great for many institutional investors to resist. Over the next few weeks they sold off roughly half their shares. An estimated one-third of the shares in Microsoft's offering has wound up in the hands of individuals.

In the wake of Microsoft's triumph, Gates still fears that being public will hurt the company. No longer able to offer stock at bargain prices, he finds it harder to lure talented programmers and managers aboard. On the other hand, his greatly enriched executives have kept cool heads. Shirley, who cleared over $1 million on the shares he sold, has been the most lavish. He bought a 45-foot cabin cruiser, traded in two cars for fancier models, and may give in to his daughter's pleas for an exotic horse. Gates used part of the $1.6 million he got to pay off a $150,000 mortgage and may buy a $5,000 ski boat—if he finds time. One vice president who raked in more than $500,000 can think of nothing to buy except a $1,000 custom-made bicycle frame; a programmer who received nearly $200,000 plans to use it to expand his working hours by hiring a housekeeper.

That's just the kind of attitude Gates prizes. Constantly urging people to ignore the price of Microsoft's stock, he warns that it may become highly volatile. A few weeks after the offering, strolling through the software development area, he noticed a chart of Microsoft's stock price posted on the door to a programmer's office. Gates was bothered. "Is this a distraction?" he asked.

[Note: The "distractions" that Bill Gates' feared apparently did not affect the future growth and prosperity of his company. Since the 1986 IPO, Microsoft has grown to the point where today it is a dominant force in the software and computer industry.]

Appendix 1

Excerpts from
Today's Man Prospectus
dated June 4, 1992

2,000,000 SHARES

TODAY'S MAN®

COMMON STOCK

All of the shares of Common Stock offered hereby are being sold by Today's Man, Inc. (the "Company" or "Today's Man"). Prior to this offering, there has been no public market for the Common Stock of the Company. See "Underwriting" for the factors considered in determining the initial public offering price.

See "Investment Considerations" for a discussion of certain factors that should be considered by prospective investors.

THESE SECURITIES HAVE NOT BEEN APPROVED OR DISAPPROVED BY THE SECURITIES AND EXCHANGE COMMISSION OR ANY STATE SECURITIES COMMISSION NOR HAS THE SECURITIES AND EXCHANGE COMMISSION OR ANY STATE SECURITIES COMMISSION PASSED UPON THE ACCURACY OR ADEQUACY OF THIS PROSPECTUS. ANY REPRESENTATION TO THE CONTRARY IS A CRIMINAL OFFENSE.

	Price to Public	Underwriting Discounts and Commissions	Proceeds to Company(1)
Per Share........................	$7.50	$.525	$6.975
Total(2)........................	$15,000,000	$1,050,000	$13,950,000

(1) Before deducting expenses of the offering estimated at $400,000.

(2) The Company has granted the Underwriters a 30-day option to purchase up to 300,000 additional shares solely to cover over-allotments, if any. To the extent that the option is exercised, the Underwriters will offer the additional shares at the Price to Public shown above. If the option is exercised in full, the total Price to Public, Underwriting Discounts and Commissions and Proceeds to Company will be $17,250,000, $1,207,500 and $16,042,500, respectively. See "Underwriting."

The shares of Common Stock are offered by the several Underwriters, subject to prior sale, when, as and if delivered to and accepted by them, and subject to the right of the Underwriters to reject any order in whole or in part. It is expected that delivery of the shares will be made at the offices of Alex. Brown & Sons Incorporated, Baltimore, Maryland, on or about June 11, 1992.

ALEX. BROWN & SONS
INCORPORATED

PAINEWEBBER INCORPORATED

The date of this Prospectus is June 4, 1992.

PROSPECTUS SUMMARY

The following summary is qualified in its entirety by the more detailed information and financial statements, including the notes thereto, appearing elsewhere in this Prospectus.

The Company

Today's Man is a leading operator of menswear superstores specializing in tailored clothing, furnishings and accessories and sportswear. The Company currently operates a chain of 14 superstores in the Greater Philadelphia, Washington, D.C. and New York markets. The Company seeks to be the leading menswear retailer in each of its markets by providing a broad and deep assortment of moderate to better, current-season, brand-name and private label merchandise at everyday low prices which the Company believes are typically 30% to 40% below regular prices charged by traditional department stores and menswear retailers. The Company provides these everyday low prices to its customers through economies provided by large volumes of preplanned inventory purchases and lower initial mark-ups. The Company generated net sales of $489 per square foot of selling space in its superstores in fiscal 1991.

The Company's superstores are usually located near major shopping malls. A 25,000 square foot superstore typically offers 80,000 items, including approximately 8,000 suits, 3,000 sportcoats, 15,000 dress shirts, 15,000 ties and 10,000 pairs of dress and casual pants. Today's Man creates an efficient and pleasant shopping experience to appeal to its core customers. The Company places great emphasis on providing an attractive, brightly lit and clean shopping environment, a courteous sales staff, professional on-premises tailoring and efficient cashiers.

The Company opened its first store in 1971 in Philadelphia and has focused since 1984 on developing and refining its superstore concept. Recognizing the success of other category-dominant retailers as well as the fragmented nature of the menswear retailing industry, the Company replaced the five smaller stores it operated in 1984 with its current 14 superstores, ranging in size from approximately 18,000 to 33,000 gross square feet. The Company has positioned itself for continued growth by developing an experienced management team with significant national retail experience, constructing a modern distribution center and implementing an integrated management information system.

The Company plans to open new superstores in the Greater New York and Washington, D.C. markets through fiscal 1994 to achieve operating and advertising efficiencies, and in new markets thereafter. The Company opened a new superstore in Wayne, New Jersey in March 1992 and has signed leases to open two additional superstores in the second half of fiscal 1992 in Fairfax, Virginia and Stony Brook, New York. In fiscal 1993, the Company expects to open four or five new superstores and has signed a lease to open a new superstore in Huntington, New York in the first half of fiscal 1993. The Company has identified a number of other large metropolitan markets which should support multiple Today's Man superstores. The Company believes its management team and information systems and central headquarters and distribution center are capable of supporting substantial growth in net sales without commensurate increases in selling, general and administrative expenses.

The Offering

Common Stock offered hereby	2,000,000 shares
Common Stock to be outstanding after offering (1)	9,300,000 shares
Use of proceeds	To finance new store openings, to reduce debt, to pay a distribution of S Corporation earnings and for working capital.
Proposed NASDAQ/NMS symbol....................	TMAN

(1) Excludes options to purchase 200,000 shares of Common Stock granted under the Company's Employee Stock Option Plan and Director Stock Option Plan at the initial public offering price. See "Management — Stock Option Plans."

3

Summary Financial and Operating Data
(In thousands, except per share and operating data)

	Fiscal Year				
	1987	1988	1989 (1)	1990	1991
Statement of Income Data:					
Net sales	$52,418	$78,020	$91,848	$93,361	$108,744
Executive equity plan expense (2)	—	—	229	188	2,959
Income from operations	2,273	3,256	2,620	3,375	2,851(3)
Income before income taxes	1,758	1,871	975	1,888	856
Net income	1,748	1,805	908	1,838	408
Pro forma (4):					
Income tax provision	759	782	396	755	338
Net income	999	1,089	579	1,133	518
Net income per share	0.14	0.16	0.08	0.16	0.07(3)
Weighted average shares outstanding (5)	7,021	7,021	7,021	7,021	7,249
Operating Data:					
Net sales per square foot of selling space (6)	$402	$452	$456	$438	$489
Increase (decrease) in comparable store sales (7)	13.9%	4.4%	4.0%	(2.1)%	7.3%
Number of stores (8):					
Open at beginning of period	7	8	11	12	11
Opened during period	1	3	1	—	2
Closed during period	—	—	—	1	—
Open at end of period	8	11	12	11	13(9)

	February 1, 1992	
	Actual	As Adjusted(10)
Balance Sheet Data:		
Working capital	$10,610	$12,910
Total assets	52,637	54,937
Long-term debt and capitalized leases, less current maturities	13,682	5,898
Shareholders' equity	11,940	20,010

(1) The fiscal year ended February 3, 1990 consisted of 53 weeks. The operating data presented herein for that year have been adjusted to a comparable 52-week basis by eliminating the 53rd week.

(2) Represents the net expense attributable to the Company's executive equity plan and related issuance of shares of Common Stock to participants in the plan as the result of its termination in fiscal 1991.

(3) Excluding the executive equity plan expense, a non-cash charge which will not be incurred in future years due to the termination of the plan, income from operations and pro forma net income per share for fiscal 1991 would have been $5.8 million and $0.32, respectively.

(4) For each of the fiscal years presented, the Company was an S Corporation and, accordingly, was not subject to federal and certain state corporate income taxes. The pro forma information has been computed as if the Company were subject to federal and all applicable state corporate income taxes for each of the fiscal years presented. See "Management's Discussion and Analysis of Financial Condition and Results of Operations—General."

(5) The Company would have had to issue 694,229 shares of Common Stock, at the initial public offering price of $7.50 per share, to pay the majority shareholder: (i) a $3.5 million distribution of previously taxed S Corporation earnings to be paid from the proceeds of this offering and (ii) a $1.2 million distribution to fund his remaining tax liability resulting from S Corporation earnings paid in fiscal 1991 and fiscal 1992 from internally generated funds. Had these shares been issued, pro forma net income for fiscal 1991 would have remained $0.07 per share. See "Dividend Policy and Prior S Corporation Status" and "Use of Proceeds."

(6) Calculated using net sales generated from superstores open for the entire fiscal year divided by the square feet of selling space of such stores. Selling space does not include tailoring, check-out and administrative areas or stock rooms.

(7) Superstores are included in the comparable store sales calculation beginning in their fourteenth full month of operation. Accordingly, the calculation does not include a store's first full month of operation, which typically has an abnormally high volume of sales resulting from the store's grand opening promotion. Stores relocated to a larger facility are not included in the comparable store sales calculation until the beginning of their fourteenth full month of operation at their new locations.

(8) Relocations of older, smaller stores to larger facilities do not constitute new store openings.

(9) In March 1992, the Company opened its fourteenth store in Wayne, New Jersey.

(10) Adjusted to give effect to the sale of the 2,000,000 shares of Common Stock offered hereby by the Company and application of the estimated net proceeds therefrom. See "Use of Proceeds."

As used in this Prospectus, "fiscal 1987," "fiscal 1988," "fiscal 1989," "fiscal 1990," "fiscal 1991," "fiscal 1992," "fiscal 1993" and "fiscal 1994" refer to the Company's fiscal years ended or ending January 30, 1988, January 28, 1989, February 3, 1990, February 2, 1991, February 1, 1992, January 30, 1993, January 29, 1994 and January 28, 1995, respectively.

All information in this Prospectus has been adjusted to give effect to stock splits effective prior to the date of this Prospectus and, unless otherwise indicated, assumes no exercise of the Underwriters' over-allotment option.

4

THE COMPANY

The Company was incorporated in Pennsylvania in 1971 as Feld & Sons, Inc. and changed its name to Today's Man, Inc. in March 1992. The Company's executive and administrative offices are located at 835 Lancer Drive, Moorestown West Corporate Center, Moorestown, New Jersey 08057 and its telephone number is (609) 235-5656.

INVESTMENT CONSIDERATIONS

In addition to the other information contained in this Prospectus, the following factors should be considered carefully in evaluating an investment in the Common Stock offered by this Prospectus.

Dilution. Purchasers of the Common Stock offered hereby will experience an immediate dilution in pro forma net tangible book value of $5.41 per share. See "Dilution." Of the net proceeds of this offering, $3.5 million will be used to pay a distribution of previously taxed S Corporation earnings to Mr. David Feld, the Company's principal shareholder, and $3.5 million will be used to reduce the outstanding balance of the subordinated loan payable to Barclays Bank, PLC ("Barclays") from $7.0 million to $5.0 million and to repurchase a portion of the warrants and rights to receive Common Stock issued to Barclays in connection with its subordinated loan so that Barclays will receive 279,000 shares upon exercise of the remaining warrants and stock rights contemporaneously with the consummation of this offering. See "Use of Proceeds."

Growth Strategy. The Company's growth over the next several years depends principally on its ability to open new stores in its existing markets and to operate those stores profitably. The Company's ability to open stores on a timely basis will depend upon the Company's ability to identify suitable store sites, obtain leases for those sites on acceptable terms, construct or refurbish the sites and hire and train skilled store managers and personnel. There can be no assurance that new stores will generate sales volumes comparable to those of the Company's existing stores. Moreover, the opening of additional stores in existing markets may have the effect of attracting customers from existing stores. See "Business – Strategy." Although the Company's existing stores generally have experienced increases in net sales in recent years, there can be no assurance that comparable store sales will increase in the future. Subject to compliance with certain financial covenants contained in its loan agreements, the Company is permitted to open up to three stores in fiscal 1992 and up to five stores per year in fiscal 1993 and thereafter. See "Management's Discussion and Analysis of Financial Condition and Results of Operations."

Recent Entry into Greater New York Market. The Company opened its first two stores in the Greater New York market in 1991. Although to date these stores have generated sales volumes comparable to the Company's Philadelphia and Washington, D.C. stores, there can be no assurance that these sales volumes will continue or that additional stores to be opened in this market will achieve comparable sales volumes. The Company opened its third store in this market in March 1992.

Small Store Base. The Company currently operates a chain of 14 superstores, a majority of which are located in the Greater Philadelphia market. Consequently, the results achieved to date by the Company's relatively small store base may not be indicative of the results of a larger number of stores in the Company's existing markets or in new markets in which the Company may open stores. Furthermore, due to the Company's relatively small store base, one or more unsuccessful new stores, or a decline in sales at an existing store, would have a more significant effect on the Company's results of operations than would be the case if the Company had a larger store base.

Declining Unit Sales of Men's Tailored Clothing. On a national basis, unit sales of men's tailored clothing have been declining over many years. The Company believes that this decline can be attributed primarily to men allocating a lower portion of their disposable income to tailored clothing as a result of less frequent changes in tailored clothing fashions, a relaxation of dress codes by many employers and a more casual lifestyle. The Company also believes that this decline has contributed to a consolidation among retailers of men's tailored clothing and that this consolidation has been a factor in the increases in sales volumes at Today's Man superstores. There can be no assurance that the Company will continue to be able to maintain or increase its sales volume or maintain its profitability as further consolidation of the industry occurs and as the unit sales of men's tailored clothing continue to decline. See "Business – Strategy."

5

Control by Majority Shareholder. Following completion of this offering, Mr. David Feld will own approximately 68.8% of the outstanding Common Stock. Accordingly, Mr. David Feld will continue to be able to elect all of the members of the Company's board of directors and determine the outcome of all shareholder votes. See "Principal Shareholders" and "Description of Capital Stock."

Relationship with Suppliers; Foreign Currency Fluctuations. The Company's business is dependent upon its ability to purchase both brand-name and private label merchandise in large quantities and at attractive prices. During fiscal 1991, approximately 43% of the dollar volume of all merchandise purchased by the Company was purchased from ten vendors, and approximately 25% of the dollar volume of all merchandise was purchased from overseas vendors. While the Company believes that alternative sources of supply are available, any disruption in the Company's sources of supply could have an adverse effect on its business. See "Business—Purchasing." Moreover, although the Company historically has been able to hedge its exposure to fluctuations in the relationship between the dollar and various foreign currencies through forward exchange contracts, the Company could incur additional expense if its hedging strategy were unsuccessful in the future. See "Management's Discussion and Analysis of Financial Condition and Results of Operations."

Dependence on Senior Management. The success of the Company's business will continue to be dependent upon Messrs. David Feld, Wasserman, Shenkman and the other members of senior management. The loss of the services of one or more of these individuals could have a materially adverse effect upon the Company's business. The Company's continued growth also will depend upon its ability to attract and retain additional skilled management personnel and store managers. See "Management."

Seasonality and General Economic Conditions. The Company's business is affected by the pattern of seasonality common to most apparel retailers. Historically, the Company has generated a significant portion of its net sales and the majority of its profits during its fourth fiscal quarter, which includes the Christmas selling season, and has incurred losses in its first and third fiscal quarters. See "Management's Discussion and Analysis of Financial Condition and Results of Operations—Seasonality and Quarterly Results." The Company's operating results may be adversely affected by unfavorable local, regional or national economic conditions, especially those affecting the Mid-Atlantic Region where all of the Company's stores are located. During recessionary periods, consumers can be expected to reduce their spending on discretionary items such as menswear.

Competition. The retail menswear business is highly competitive with respect to price, quality and style of merchandise and store location. The Company faces competition for customers and store locations from large national and regional department stores, various full-price menswear chains, a number of off-price specialty retailers as well as local department stores, catalog retailers and local menswear stores. Many of these competitors have significantly greater financial and other resources than the Company. The retailing business is affected by changes in consumer tastes, demographic trends and the type, number and location of competing stores. In the future, the Company may experience increased competition from menswear retailers attempting to imitate the Company's strategy. See "Business—Competition."

Absence of Public Market and Determination of Offering Price. Prior to this offering, there has been no public market for the Company's Common Stock. Consequently, the initial public offering price has been determined through negotiation between the Company and the Representatives of the Underwriters. See "Underwriting" for a description of the factors considered in determining the initial public offering price. There can be no assurance that an active trading market for the Common Stock will develop after this offering or, if developed, that such market will be sustained. Although the Representatives of the Underwriters intend to act as market makers in the Common Stock, they have no obligation to do so and may discontinue market making activities at any time.

Restrictions on Cash Dividends. The Company does not anticipate paying any cash dividends in the foreseeable future because it intends to retain its earnings to finance the expansion of its business. The Company's loan agreements impose certain restrictions on the Company's ability to pay cash dividends. See "Dividend Policy and Prior S Corporation Status."

Shares Eligible for Future Sale. Sales of substantial amounts of the Common Stock in the public market following this offering could adversely affect the market price of the Common Stock and make it more difficult for the Company to sell its equity securities in the future at a time and price which it deems appropriate.

6

Beginning 180 days after the date of this Prospectus, approximately 6,524,678 restricted shares of the Common Stock will be eligible for sale under Rule 144 and 496,322 shares will be eligible for sale under Rule 701, subject in certain cases to the volume and other limitations set forth in Rule 144. See "Shares Eligible for Future Sale."

DIVIDEND POLICY AND PRIOR
S CORPORATION STATUS

The Company does not anticipate paying any cash dividends in the foreseeable future because it intends to retain its earnings to finance the expansion of its business. The Company's loan agreements impose certain restrictions on the Company's ability to pay cash dividends.

From January 1, 1987 to January 30, 1992, the Company was subject to taxation under Subchapter S of the Internal Revenue Code of 1986, as amended (the "Code"). As a result, the net income of the Company, for federal and certain state income tax purposes, was reported by and taxed directly to Mr. David Feld, the Company's sole shareholder at such time, rather than to the Company. Primarily to provide funds to pay his tax obligations, the Company made cash distributions to Mr. David Feld aggregating $431,700 and $120,000 on account of the Company's S Corporation earnings in calendar years 1989 and 1990, respectively, and will have made cash distributions aggregating $1,203,400 by April 15, 1992 on account of the Company's S Corporation earnings in calendar year 1991 pursuant to a tax indemnification agreement. Upon consummation of this offering, the Company intends to use $3.5 million of net proceeds to pay a distribution to Mr. David Feld, representing a portion of undistributed S Corporation retained earnings previously taxed to him. In addition, a cash distribution will be made to Mr. David Feld in fiscal 1992 to pay his tax obligation resulting from the Company's S Corporation earnings for the period January 1, 1992 through January 30, 1992 pursuant to a tax indemnification agreement. Based on tax rates currently in effect, the Company expects that its aggregate tax expense plus the distribution to Mr. Feld for this period will not exceed 39.5% of the Company's income before income taxes in fiscal 1992. See "Management—Certain Transactions—Tax Indemnification Agreement."

USE OF PROCEEDS

The net proceeds to the Company from this offering are estimated to be $13.6 million ($15.6 million if the Underwriters' over-allotment option is exercised in full), after deducting estimated offering expenses and underwriting discounts and commissions. Of the net proceeds, (i) $4.25 million will be used to repay the outstanding balance of a bank term loan, (ii) $3.5 million will be used to pay a distribution of previously taxed S Corporation earnings to Mr. David Feld, and (iii) $3.5 million will be used to reduce the outstanding balance of the subordinated loan payable to Barclays Bank, PLC ("Barclays") from $7.0 million to $5.0 million and to repurchase a portion of the warrants and stock rights issued to Barclays in connection with its subordinated loan so that Barclays will receive 279,000 shares upon exercise of the remaining warrants and stock rights contemporaneously with the consummation of this offering. The $2.3 million of remaining net proceeds will be used to finance new store openings and for working capital, which may include the temporary reduction of borrowings under the Company's revolving credit facility (estimated to be $6.0 million as of the closing of this offering). Pending such uses, the net proceeds will be invested in short-term investment grade securities.

The bank term loan bears interest at the lead bank's prime rate plus 1.25% (7.75% as of February 1, 1992). The Barclays subordinated loan currently bears interest at 14% (to be reduced to 10.5% upon consummation of this offering). The revolving credit facility bears interest at the lead bank's prime rate plus 1% (7.5% as of February 1, 1992). The proceeds of the bank term loan and the Barclays subordinated loan were used to discharge existing debt and the proceeds of the revolving credit facility were used to discharge existing debt, for working capital and to open new stores. See "Management's Discussion and Analysis of Financial Condition and Results of Operations—Liquidity and Capital Resources" and "Management—Certain Transactions."

The Company anticipates that it will open a total of three superstores in fiscal 1992 (one of which has already been opened) and four or five superstores in fiscal 1993. The Company believes that its current sources of capital, together with the proceeds of this offering and internally generated funds, will be adequate to meet the Company's expansion plans through fiscal 1993. Total expenditures for a new store, including capital expenditures, pre-opening expenses and net working capital, are expected to range from $2,200,000 to $3,000,000 per store.

7

DILUTION

The net tangible book value of the Company at February 1, 1992 was $11,217,700, or $1.60 per share of Common Stock. Net tangible book value per share represents the amount of total tangible assets of the Company less total liabilities, divided by the number of shares of Common Stock outstanding. After giving effect to the sale by the Company of 2,000,000 shares of Common Stock offered hereby and the application of the estimated net proceeds therefrom, the pro forma net tangible book value of the Company at February 1, 1992 would have been $19,426,000, or $2.09 per share of Common Stock. This represents an immediate increase in the pro forma net tangible book value of $0.49 per share of Common Stock to existing shareholders and an immediate dilution in pro forma net tangible book value of $5.41 per share of Common Stock to new investors. The following table illustrates this dilution on a per share basis:

Assumed price to public		$7.50
Net tangible book value per share before offering	$ 1.60	
Increase per share attributable to new investors	0.49	
Pro forma net tangible book value per share after offering		2.09
Dilution to new investors		$5.41

The following table sets forth the number of shares of Common Stock issued by the Company and the total effective consideration and effective price per share (based upon independent appraisals) for the shares issued to participants upon termination of the Company's Executive Equity Plan prior to this offering and to Barclays upon the consummation of this offering and the price to be paid by the new investors in this offering:

	Shares		Total Effective	Effective Price
	Number	Percent	Consideration	Per Share
Executive equity plan participants	496,322	5.3%	$ 3,374,900	$6.80
Barclays	279,000	3.0%	1,235,000	4.43
New investors	2,000,000	21.5%	15,000,000	7.50

8

SELECTED FINANCIAL DATA
(In thousands, except per share data)

The following selected financial data, except pro forma amounts, for fiscal 1987, 1988, 1989, 1990 and 1991 have been derived from the Company's financial statements which have been audited by Ernst & Young, independent auditors. Pro forma adjustments have been shown to reflect the income tax provision which would have been made had the Company been subject to federal and all state income taxes for all periods presented. The information set forth below should be read in conjunction with "Management's Discussion and Analysis of Financial Condition and Results of Operations" and the financial statements of the Company and Notes thereto included elsewhere in this Prospectus.

	Fiscal Year				
	1987	1988	1989 (1)	1990	1991
Statement of Income Data:					
Net sales	$52,418	$78,020	$91,848	$93,361	$108,744
Cost of goods sold	33,803	49,883	60,296	61,035	70,526
Gross profit	18,615	28,137	31,551	32,326	38,219
Selling, general and administrative expenses (2)	16,342	24,881	28,703	28,764	32,408
Executive equity plan expense (3)	—	—	229	188	2,959
Income from operations	2,273	3,256	2,620	3,374	2,851(4)
Interest expense and other income, net	515	1,385	1,645	1,486	1,995
Income before income taxes	1,758	1,871	975	1,888	856
Income taxes	10	66	67	50	448
Net income	$ 1,748	$ 1,805	$ 908	$ 1,838	$ 408
Pro Forma Income Data (5):					
Income tax provision	759	782	396	755	338
Net income	$ 999	$ 1,089	$ 579	$ 1,133	$ 518
Net income per share	$ 0.14	$ 0.16	$ 0.08	$ 0.16	$ 0.07(4)
Weighted average shares outstanding (6)	7,021	7,021	7,021	7,021	7,249
Balance Sheet Data (at end of period):					
Working capital	$ 2,247	$ 6,746	$10,010	$11,600	$ 10,610
Total assets	20,909	33,812	38,346	43,887	52,637
Long-term debt and capitalized leases	5,696	14,216	17,526	17,775	13,682
Shareholders' equity	3,828	5,437	5,913	7,631	11,940

(1) The fiscal year ended February 3, 1990 consisted of 53 weeks.

(2) Includes buying and occupancy expenses.

(3) Represents the net expense attributable to the termination of the Company's executive equity plan and related issuance of shares of Common Stock to participants in the plan as the result of its termination in fiscal 1991.

(4) Excluding the executive equity plan expense, a non-cash charge which will not be incurred in future years due to the termination of the plan, income from operations and pro forma net income per share for fiscal 1991 would have been $5.8 million and $0.32, respectively.

(5) For each of the fiscal years presented, the Company was an S Corporation and, accordingly, was not subject to federal and certain state corporate income taxes. The pro forma information has been computed as if the Company were subject to federal and all applicable state corporate income taxes for each of the fiscal years presented.

(6) The Company would have had to issue 694,229 shares of Common Stock, at the initial public offering price of $7.50 per share, to pay the majority shareholder: (i) a $3.5 million distribution of previously taxed S Corporation earnings to be paid from the proceeds of this offering and (ii) a $1.2 million distribution to fund his remaining tax liability resulting from S Corporation earnings paid in fiscal 1991 and fiscal 1992 from internally generated funds. Had these shares been issued, pro forma net income for fiscal 1991 would have remained $0.07 per share.

10

179

MANAGEMENT'S DISCUSSION AND ANALYSIS OF
FINANCIAL CONDITION AND RESULTS OF OPERATIONS

General

The Company opened its first store in 1971 in Philadelphia and has focused since 1984 on developing and refining its superstore concept. In accordance with this strategy, the Company replaced its five smaller stores that existed in 1984 with its current 14 superstores, which range in size from approximately 18,000 to 33,000 gross square feet. The Company has positioned itself for continued growth by developing an experienced management team with national retail experience, constructing a modern distribution center and implementing an integrated management information system. From fiscal 1987 to fiscal 1991, net sales and income from operations (excluding executive equity plan expense) increased at compound annual rates of 20.0% and 26.4%, respectively.

The Company entered its first market outside Greater Philadelphia in fiscal 1987 with the successful opening of a new superstore in the Greater Washington D.C. market. This superstore generated higher net sales than any other Today's Man superstore in fiscal 1988, its first full year of operation. In fiscal 1988 and fiscal 1989, the Company opened four new superstores, increasing its store base by 50%. Net sales increased by 75.2% from fiscal 1987 to fiscal 1989.

In fiscal 1990, the Company focused on assimilating this large percentage increase in stores into its operations, on achieving continued improvement in the execution of its strategies and on securing additional financing to support its continued growth. The Company also made the strategic decision in fiscal 1990 to close a store it opened in the Philadelphia market in September 1989 due to the store's negative effect on the sales of nearby Today's Man superstores.

In fiscal 1991, the Company reinitiated its expansion efforts by entering the Greater New York market with the opening of two new superstores. The Company also generated comparable store sales increases of 7.3% despite a recessionary economic environment and increased its income from operations (excluding executive equity plan expense) by 63.1% from the fiscal 1990 level.

The Company opened a new superstore in Wayne, New Jersey in March 1992 and has signed leases to open two additional superstores in the second half of fiscal 1992. Beginning in fiscal 1993, the Company expects to open four or five new superstores per year. The Company anticipates that new stores will contribute to the Company's income from operations in their first full year of operation although such contributions are not expected to be material. The Company believes its management team and information systems as well as its central headquarters and distribution facilities are capable of supporting substantial growth in net sales without commensurate increases in selling, general and administrative expenses.

From fiscal 1987 to fiscal 1991, the Company was subject to taxation under Subchapter S of the Code. As a result, the net income of the Company, for federal and certain state income tax purposes, was reported by and taxed directly to Mr. David Feld, the Company's sole shareholder at such time, rather than to the Company. Accordingly, the Company has calculated the pro forma income tax provision, pro forma net income and pro forma income per share for each year presented herein as if the Company were a C Corporation subject to federal and all applicable state income taxes. The effective tax rates used in calculating the pro forma income tax provision were 40.6%, 40.0% and 39.5% for fiscal 1989, 1990 and 1991, respectively. The Company's status as an S Corporation was terminated January 30, 1992 and, as a result, the Company incurred a $372,000 additional income tax expense in fiscal 1991 due to the recording of a net deferred tax liability. See Note 7 of Notes to Financial Statements.

The Company does not provide post retirement healthcare benefits and, accordingly, is not subject to the provisions of Statement of Financial Accounting Standards 106.

11

Results of Operations

The following table sets forth for the periods indicated the percentages which the items in the Company's Statements of Income bear to net sales.

	Fiscal Year		
	1989	1990	1991
Net sales	100.0%	100.0%	100.0%
Cost of goods sold	65.6	65.4	64.9
Gross profit	34.4	34.6	35.1
Selling, general and administrative expenses	31.3	30.8	29.8
Executive equity plan expense	0.2	0.2	2.7
Income from operations	2.9	3.6	2.6
Interest expense and other income, net	1.8	1.6	1.8
Income before income taxes	1.1	2.0	0.8
Pro forma income tax provision	0.5	0.8	0.3
Pro forma net income	0.6%	1.2%	0.5%

Fiscal Years 1991 and 1990

Net sales. Net sales of $108,744,000 in fiscal 1991 represented an increase of $15,383,000 or 16.5% over net sales of $93,361,000 in fiscal 1990. This increase was attributable to the opening of two new stores in the New York market in fiscal 1991 which accounted for $14,104,000 in net sales in fiscal 1991 and an increase in comparable store sales of 7.3%. The comparable store sales increase was primarily due to higher unit sales volumes. The increase in net sales was partially offset by the closing of a store in the Philadelphia market at the end of fiscal 1990.

Gross profit. Gross profit as a percentage of net sales increased to 35.1% in fiscal 1991 from 34.6% in fiscal 1990. This improvement was primarily attributable to: (i) less shrinkage due to the implementation of an anti-theft electronic merchandise tagging system and an emphasis on increased associate awareness and (ii) reduced markdowns as a result of improved inventory management. In accordance with the Company's strategy of attempting to increase unit sales by providing improved values to its customers, management does not plan to increase its gross profit as a percentage of net sales in the future.

Selling, general and administrative expenses. Selling, general and administrative expenses, which included pre-opening expenses of new stores, increased in the aggregate by $3,645,000 or 12.7% in fiscal 1991 but decreased as a percentage of net sales to 29.8% in fiscal 1991 from 30.8% in fiscal 1990. The increase in aggregate expenses was primarily due to the cost of operating an increased number of stores and the additional advertising and other expenses associated with the Company's entry into the New York market in fiscal 1991. The decrease as a percentage of net sales was primarily due to an increase in comparable store sales without a commensurate increase in these expenses as a result of management's greater focus on cost control. Pre-opening expenses for the two superstores opened in fiscal 1991 aggregated $326,300.

Income from operations. In fiscal 1991, the Company incurred a $2,959,000 non-cash charge attributable to the termination of its executive equity plan and the related issuance of Common Stock to the plan's participants with the result that income from operations declined in fiscal 1991. See "Management — Executive Equity Plan." Excluding this charge, the increase in income from operations from fiscal 1990 to fiscal 1991 would have been $2,247,000 or 63.1% to $5,810,000 or 5.3% of net sales in fiscal 1991 from $3,563,000 or 3.8% of net sales in fiscal 1990.

Interest expense and other income, net. Interest expense and other income, net increased by $509,000 in fiscal 1991 from fiscal 1990. Interest expense remained relatively constant in the aggregate in fiscal 1991 as compared to fiscal 1990 as a result of higher average borrowings at reduced average interest rates. The Company expects interest expense to decline in fiscal 1992. Net other income included foreign exchange gains of $372,000, reduced in fiscal 1991 by other nonrecurring expenses including the settlement of sales and use tax audits.

Income before income taxes. Income before income taxes decreased by $1,032,000 in fiscal 1991 as a result of executive equity plan expense. Excluding this expense, income before income taxes would have increased by $1,739,000 or 83.8% to $3,815,000 or 3.5% of net sales in fiscal 1991 from $2,076,000 or 2.2% of net sales in fiscal 1990.

12

181

Fiscal Years 1990 and 1989

Net sales. Net sales of $93,361,000 in fiscal 1990 represented an increase of $1,513,000 or 1.6% over net sales of $91,848,000 in fiscal 1989, which consisted of 53 weeks. Excluding the 53rd week in fiscal 1989, the increase in net sales would have been $2,568,000 or 2.8% over fiscal 1989. This sales growth was primarily attributable to increased sales from the Company's Cherry Hill store which was relocated and expanded in fiscal 1990 and a 7.5% comparable store sales increase at the Company's two Washington D.C. stores in fiscal 1990. This increase was partially offset by a comparable store sales decrease in the Philadelphia stores caused by the opening of a new store in the Philadelphia market in September 1989 which reduced net sales for a number of existing Today's Man superstores in that market. As a result of this negative effect, the Company closed this new store at the end of fiscal 1990.

Gross profit. Gross profit as a percentage of net sales increased to 34.6% from 34.4% in fiscal 1989. This percentage increase was attributable to: (i) reduced markdowns as a result of improved inventory management, (ii) less shrinkage and (iii) improved productivity in the stores' tailoring operations.

Selling, general and administrative expenses. Selling, general and administrative expenses remained relatively constant from fiscal 1989 to fiscal 1990. As a percentage of net sales, these expenses decreased to 30.8% in fiscal 1990 from 31.3% in fiscal 1989, primarily as a result of management's improved control of store and headquarters payroll expenses. The decrease was partially offset by increased occupancy expenses as a percentage of net sales due to the additional expenses associated with the store opened in the Philadelphia market in September 1989 that did not materially increase the Company's total net sales in that market in fiscal 1990. Pre-opening expenses for the one superstore opened in fiscal 1990 aggregated $24,600.

Income from operations. Income from operations increased by $755,000 or 28.8% to $3,375,000 or 3.6% of net sales in fiscal 1990 from $2,620,000 or 2.9% of net sales in fiscal 1989.

Interest expense and other income, net. Interest expense and other income, net decreased $159,000 in fiscal 1990 from fiscal 1989. Interest expense remained relatively constant in fiscal 1990 and fiscal 1989. Net other income increased in fiscal 1990 over fiscal 1989 levels primarily due to a gain on the sale of the lease of the former, smaller Cherry Hill store.

Income before income taxes. Income before income taxes increased by 93.6% to $1,888,000 or 2.0% of net sales in fiscal 1990 from $975,000 or 1.1% of net sales in fiscal 1989.

Liquidity and Capital Resources

The Company's primary sources of working capital are cash flow from operations and borrowings under its revolving credit facility. The Company had working capital of $10,010,000, $11,600,000 and $10,610,000 at the end of fiscal 1989, 1990 and 1991, respectively. Historically, the Company's working capital is at its lowest levels in the first and third quarters and increases sharply in the second and fourth quarters in anticipation of the peak selling seasons. The Company measures its inventory turnover by dividing sales by the retail value of the inventory averaged over 12 months. Inventory turnover was 2.43 times and 2.54 times in fiscal 1990 and fiscal 1991, respectively. Increases in inventory from year to year were due to new store openings and were accompanied by a corresponding increase in accounts payable.

In August 1991, the Company established a two year revolving credit facility with several banks that provides for maximum borrowings of $9,000,000. The amount outstanding under this facility was $2,500,000 at the end of fiscal 1991 and is expected to be $6,000,000 as of the consummation of this offering. This agreement and certain of the Company's other loan agreements contain restrictive covenants, including those related to the maintenance of net worth, tangible capital funds and financial ratios, the maintenance of voting control by Mr. David Feld, limitations on new store openings, the payment of cash dividends, incurrence of debt and capital expenditures. Also in August 1991, the Company entered into a $5,000,000, five year term loan with the same banks, repayable in twenty equal quarterly installments. The revolving credit facility bears interest at the lead bank's prime rate plus 1.0% and the term loan at the lead bank's prime rate plus 1.25%. At February 1, 1992, the balance on the term loan was $4,750,000. Prior to the consummation of this offering, the Company will make $500,000 in scheduled payments on this loan and will repay it in its entirety from the net proceeds of this offering. On the same date as the other loans, the Company entered into a $7,000,000, ten year, 14% subordinated loan with warrants and stock rights with Barclays. Giving effect to the amortization of the

13

warrants and stock rights over the term of this loan, the effective interest rate would be approximately 20.29%. The Company intends to use $3,500,000 of the net proceeds of this offering to reduce the outstanding balance of the Barclays loan from $7,000,000 to $5,000,000 and to repurchase a portion of the warrants and stock rights issued to Barclays in connection with the loan so that Barclays will receive 279,000 shares of Common Stock upon exercise of the remaining warrants contemporaneously with the consummation of this offering. At the same time, the interest rate on the Barclays loan will be reduced to 10.5% and the principal will be due in various annual installments through 1998.

Net cash provided by operating activities amounted to $127,000, $3,000,000 and $5,712,000 in fiscal 1989, 1990 and 1991, respectively. These amounts primarily represent net income plus depreciation, amortization and other non-cash charges.

Net cash used in investing activities amounted to $1,497,000, $1,296,000 and $2,884,000 in fiscal 1989, 1990 and 1991, respectively, to fund investments for: (i) new stores in fiscal 1989, 1990 and 1991, (ii) an anti-theft electronic merchandise tagging system in fiscal 1991 and (iii) a new central computer in fiscal 1991.

Net cash provided by or (used in) financing activities amounted to $1,261,000, ($1,362,000) and ($1,875,000) in fiscal 1989, 1990 and 1991, respectively, and consisted primarily of borrowings and repayments under the Company's various loan agreements as well as shareholder distributions primarily relating to S Corporation income tax obligations.

At February 1, 1992, the Company had a distribution payable to the principal shareholder of $926,000 to pay his tax obligations resulting from the Company's S Corporation earnings in calendar year 1991.

During fiscal 1991, Common Stock increased by $9,036,000 due to (i) reclassification of S Corporation retained earnings to Common Stock upon the termination of the Company's S Corporation status, (ii) the termination of the Executive Equity Plan and the concurrent issuance of 496,322 shares of Common Stock and (iii) warrants and stock rights issued to Barclays in connection with the subordinated loan agreement.

Management intends to negotiate a new bank facility during fiscal 1992. The Company believes that the sources of capital described above, together with the proceeds of this offering (after reduction of existing debt as set forth in "Use of Proceeds") and internally generated funds, will be adequate to meet the Company's anticipated needs through at least fiscal 1993, including commitments to open two additional superstores in fiscal 1992 and one in fiscal 1993. Total expenditures for a new store, including capital expenditures, pre-opening expenses and net working capital, are expected to range from $2,200,000 to $3,000,000 per store. See "Business — Expansion." The Company expects to spend approximately $850,000 in fiscal 1992 for expansion of the distribution center and improvements to existing stores. The Company also expects to repay the $1,000,000 subordinated debt to Mr. David Feld at such time as it is able to obtain the necessary consent from its bank lenders. This debt bears interest at 1.5% above the prime rate.

Seasonality and Quarterly Results

The Company's business, like that of most retailers, is subject to seasonal influences. A significant portion of the Company's net sales and profits are realized during the fourth fiscal quarter (which includes the Christmas selling season) and, to a lesser extent, during the second fiscal quarter. In addition, because the Company's cost of goods sold includes net alteration expense, the Company's gross profit as a percentage of net sales has historically been lower in the first and third fiscal quarters primarily as the result of a lower level of net sales being spread over fixed (primarily payroll) expenses related to tailoring operations. In addition, quarterly results are affected by the timing of the opening of new stores. Because of the seasonality of the Company's business, results for any quarter are not necessarily indicative of the results that may be achieved for a full fiscal year.

14

183

The following table sets forth certain unaudited quarterly results of operations for fiscal 1990 and 1991. The unaudited quarterly information includes all normal recurring adjustments which management considers necessary for a fair presentation of the information shown.

Fiscal 1991:	Fiscal Quarter Ended			
	May 4, 1991	August 3, 1991	November 2, 1991	February 1, 1992
	(In thousands, except per share amounts)			
Net sales	$20,247	$25,885	$22,370	$40,243
Cost of goods sold	13,205	16,739	14,670	25,912
Gross profit	7,042	9,146	7,700	14,331
Selling, general and administrative expenses	7,552	7,760	8,243	8,854
Executive equity plan expense	73	73	73	2,740
Income (loss) from operations	(583)	1,313	(616)	2,737(1)
Interest expense and other income, net	222	484	463	826
Income (loss) before income taxes	(805)	829	(1,079)	1,911
Pro forma income tax provision (benefit)	(318)	328	(426)	755
Pro forma net income (loss)	($ 487)	$ 501	($ 653)	$ 1,156
Pro forma net income (loss) per share	($ 0.07)	$ 0.07	($ 0.09)	$ 0.15(1)
Weighted average shares outstanding	7,021	7,021	7,477(2)	7,477(2)

(1) Excluding the executive equity plan expense, a non-cash charge which will not be incurred in future years due to the termination of the plan, income from operations and pro forma net income per share for the fourth quarter of fiscal 1991 would have been $5,404,000 and $0.37, respectively.

(2) Includes 456,000 shares which would be issued in connection with the warrants and stock rights issued to Barclays without giving effect to the amendment to the Barclays subordinated loan agreement.

Fiscal 1990:	Fiscal Quarter Ended			
	May 5, 1990	August 4, 1990	November 3, 1990	February 2, 1991
	(In thousands, except per share amounts)			
Net sales	$17,512	$24,571	$17,809	$33,469
Cost of goods sold	11,571	15,917	11,769	21,778
Gross profit	5,941	8,654	6,040	11,691
Selling, general and administrative expenses	6,712	7,685	6,979	7,388
Executive equity plan expense	47	47	47	47
Income (loss) from operations	(818)	922	(986)	4,256
Interest expense and other income, net	516	424	334	212
Income (loss) before income taxes	(1,334)	498	(1,320)	4,044
Pro forma income tax provision (benefit)	(534)	199	(528)	1,618
Pro forma net income (loss)	($ 800)	$ 299	($ 792)	$ 2,426
Pro forma net income (loss) per share	($ 0.12)	$ 0.04	($ 0.11)	$ 0.35
Weighted average shares outstanding	7,021	7,021	7,021	7,021

Inflation

The Company does not believe that inflation has had a material effect on the results of operations during the past three years. However, there can be no assurance that the Company's business will not be affected by inflation in the future.

15

Overview

Today's Man is a leading operator of menswear superstores specializing in tailored clothing, furnishings and accessories and sportswear. The Company currently operates a chain of 14 superstores in the Greater Philadelphia, Washington, D.C. and New York markets. The Company seeks to be the leading menswear retailer in each of its markets by providing a broad and deep assortment of moderate to better, current-season, brand-name and private label merchandise at everyday low prices which the Company believes are typically 30% to 40% below regular prices charged by traditional department stores and menswear retailers. The Company provides these everyday low prices to its customers through economies provided by its large volumes of preplanned inventory purchases and lower initial mark-ups. The Company generated net sales of $489 per square foot of selling space in its superstores in fiscal 1991.

Strategy

The menswear retailing industry is highly fragmented. Most traditional menswear retailers, such as department and menswear specialty stores, offer less selection of tailored menswear, initially at full retail prices. In response to the opportunities existing in the industry, Today's Man has adopted a strategy of consistently offering a large breadth and depth of merchandise at everyday prices below those charged by traditional menswear retailers. The greater consistency of in-stock merchandise offered by the Company also allows the Company to compete effectively with off-price menswear retailers. As Today's Man has gained market share and increased its purchasing volume, it has been able to attract higher quality brand-name and private label merchandise and provide greater savings to its customers. By passing along these improved values to its customers, the Company seeks to increase further its market share which, in turn, should create additional operating, advertising and purchasing efficiencies.

The key elements of the Company's strategy to expand its market share are:

Dominant Selection of Quality Menswear. Management believes its superstores have a larger selection of suits and furnishings and accessories, in terms of styles, sizes and price points, than any other menswear retailer in its markets. A 25,000 square foot Today's Man superstore typically offers 80,000 items, including approximately 8,000 suits, 3,000 sportcoats, 15,000 dress shirts, 15,000 ties and 10,000 pairs of dress and casual pants. The Company uses preplanned buying programs in order to maintain a consistent and large selection of moderate to better brand-name and private label menswear. The Company believes that this category dominance differentiates Today's Man from its competitors and permits it t chieve significant operating, advertising and purchasing efficiencies.

Price and Value Leadership. Management believes that the Company's prices are typically 30% to 40% below the regular prices charged by traditional department stores and menswear retailers. The Company's high unit sales volume contributes to operating efficiencies which permit it to pass along cost savings to its customers. Management believes that as the Company's unit sales volume continues to increase, it will be able to provide improved values to its customers by offering higher quality merchandise at sharper prices.

Aggressive Marketing Strategy. The Company's objective is to be the first choice among its target customers when they decide to shop for menswear by investing substantially in local print and, when cost efficient, television advertising. For example, in the Philadelphia market, where the Company has nine superstores, it is the leading television advertiser among menswear retailers. As the Company increases the number of superstores operating in its other markets, it intends to become a leading advertiser among menswear retailers in each of those markets.

Efficient Shopping Experience. The Company attempts to create a shopping experience tailored to the desires of its core customers who typically are unwilling to spend substantial time shopping for menswear. The Company's superstores are usually located near major shopping malls and offer ease of access and ample parking. In addition to its large, well-organized selection of merchandise designed to satisfy most of its core customers' clothing needs, the Company places great emphasis on providing an attractive, brightly lit and clean shopping environment, a courteous sales staff, professional on-premises tailoring and efficient cashiers.

16

Focus on Productivity. The Company has made significant efforts to upgrade its management personnel, management information systems and distribution center which have resulted in high sales per square foot and higher operating margins. The Company also emphasizes superior execution of its merchandising strategies and management controls in an effort to achieve continued productivity improvements.

Expansion. The Company plans to open new superstores in the New York and Washington, D.C. markets through fiscal 1994 to achieve operating and advertising efficiencies, and in new markets thereafter. The Company opened a new superstore in Wayne, New Jersey in March 1992 and has signed leases to open two additional superstores in the second half of fiscal 1992 in Fairfax, Virginia and Stony Brook, New York. In fiscal 1993, the Company expects to open four or five new superstores and has signed a lease to open a new superstore in Huntington, New York in the first half of fiscal 1993. The Company believes that its management team and information systems and its central headquarters and distribution center are capable of supporting substantial growth in net sales without commensurate increases in selling, general and administrative expenses.

Merchandising

Today's Man seeks to offer a larger selection and variety of menswear, in terms of styles, sizes and price points, than its competitors. The Company's merchandise assortment consists principally of tailored clothing (suits, sportcoats, slacks, formal wear and outerwear), furnishings and accessories (dress shirts, ties, belts, suspenders, underwear, socks, scarves and gloves) and sportswear (casual pants, sportshirts, sweaters and jackets). A 25,000 square foot superstore typically offers 80,000 items, including approximately 8,000 suits in American and European styles, 3,000 sportcoats, 15,000 dress shirts, 15,000 ties and 10,000 pairs of dress and casual pants. The core of the Company's merchandise offering is nationally recognized brand-name and designer label suits at prices typically ranging from $200 to $350. In fiscal 1991, approximately two-thirds of the Company's net sales were tailored clothing, with the balance approximately evenly divided between furnishings and accessories and sportswear.

The Company has product offerings in most of its merchandise categories under the Company's private labels, such as "Today's Man," "Brookcraft," "Amherst and Brock," "Torriani" and "Lamberti." Today's Man's private label programs are focused on high volume merchandise classifications and include products which can differentiate the Company from other retailers on the basis of price and quality. For example, the Company has introduced a line of dress shirts under its own "Today's Man" label which sell for $20. These button down or spread collar shirts, made from 100% pinpoint cotton oxford cloth, regularly sell for between $35 and $40 in department stores.

The Company's pricing strategy is to provide its customers superior value through everyday low prices on all of its products. Management believes that the Company's prices are generally 30% to 40% below the regular prices charged by traditional department stores and menswear retailers. Except for clearance sales in January and July, the Company does not use special sales to attract customers but instead promotes its everyday low prices. Consistent with its pricing strategy of offering everyday low prices, the Company has eliminated many of the "free" services offered by major department stores and traditional menswear retailers, such as gift wrapping and alterations, although the Company does offer full-service alterations generally priced at cost and provides gift boxes for a nominal charge.

Marketing and Promotion

The Company has identified as its core customers men between the ages of 25 and 54 with average household incomes of approximately $40,000 per year who routinely wear a suit to work. Based on consumer research conducted by the Company and an independent market research firm, management believes that most men shop no more than two to three times a year for tailored clothing. Important reasons men cite for selecting one menswear retailer over another include the ability to find their size, low prices, good selection of quality merchandise, helpful salespeople, ease of selection, efficient tailoring and quick check-out. Today's Man attempts to address these factors by offering a wide selection of merchandise at low prices in a comfortable and time-efficient shopping environment.

17

186

The Company seeks to be the first choice among its target customers when they decide to shop for clothes by investing substantially in local print and, when cost efficient, television advertising. For example, in the Philadelphia market, where the Company has nine superstores, it is the leading television advertiser among menswear retailers. Because of the high cost of television advertising in the New York market and the limited number of superstores the Company currently has there, to date the Company has relied primarily on newspaper advertisements. As the Company increases the number of its superstores in the Washington D.C. and New York markets and in new markets, it intends to become the leading advertiser among menswear retailers in each market.

The Company uses outside agencies as well as its own marketing department to prepare its advertising materials. In addition, the Company uses direct mail advertising to customers on its mailing list, including holders of its Today's Man credit cards.

Today's Man Superstores

The Company's superstores average approximately 25,000 gross square feet. Approximately three quarters of the area of each store is devoted to selling space, with the remaining portion used for tailoring, check-out, storage and administrative and employee areas. Today's Man superstores are usually located in a shopping center or freestanding building near a major shopping mall.

The Company places great emphasis on providing an attractive, brightly lit and well-organized shopping environment. The Company's stores have similar layouts, emphasizing efficient traffic flow, separation of distinct departments, merchandise presentation and ease of merchandise selection. Use of a similar store design facilitates the operational integration of new stores into the Company's centralized merchandising, distribution, management and accounting systems. The Company attempts to arrange its merchandise to provide a logical flow from department to department and regularly monitors its product layouts in an attempt to make shopping easier and to maximize sales per square foot.

The Company believes that a courteous and knowledgeable staff and efficient cashiers are important factors in attracting and retaining customers. The Company staffs each store with trained personnel, supported by an efficient check-out system and a full-function tailoring facility. The Company emphasizes to its employees the importance of customer service, courtesy and product knowledge through its training programs. The Company also believes that its typical customer prefers to shop without aggressive sales help and seeks assistance primarily to locate sizes or to coordinate styles and colors. Accordingly, Today's Man's sales associates are paid on a salaried rather than a commission basis. Sales associates in the tailored clothing departments are also eligible to earn incentive payments based on the total performance of that department.

Each store is managed by a store manager who is compensated by a base salary and a bonus based on the store's actual versus planned sales, shrinkage and other factors. Store managers have an average of 15 years of retail experience. Store managers report to one of two regional managers who in turn report to the Company's Vice President, Store Operations. All stores have one or more assistant managers, three to five clothing department heads (including the head of the tailoring department) and an average of 30 full-time and 14 part-time associates (including sales associates, tailors and cashiers). Most of the Company's tailored clothing associates have prior retail experience. Additional training is provided on the job by the store's assistant managers and department heads.

Full-function tailoring facilities are located at each store and are typically staffed by one fitter, six full-time and one part-time tailors and two pressers under the supervision of the head of the tailoring department and an assistant. As part of the Today's Man's efficient shopping experience, the Company seeks to provide professional alterations within one week. Because the Company views efficient and competitively priced tailoring as a means of attracting and retaining its core customers, the Company's tailoring services generally are priced at cost.

The Company maintains an appropriate level of security in each store based on local conditions. The Company believes that its shrinkage rate is well below the industry average.

18

187

Expansion

The Company plans to open new superstores in the Greater New York and Washington, D.C. markets through fiscal 1994 to achieve operating and advertising efficiencies, and in new markets thereafter. The Company has identified a number of other large metropolitan markets which should support multiple Today's Man superstores. The Company also seeks to increase sales in existing superstores through new product offerings, sharper pricing and better execution of its merchandising strategies.

The Company opened a 33,000 gross square foot superstore in a shopping center in Wayne, New Jersey in March 1992 and has signed leases to open two additional superstores in the second half of fiscal 1992, a 25,000 gross square foot store currently under construction in Fairfax, Virginia and an existing 26,200 gross square foot superstore in Stony Brook, New York. In fiscal 1993, the Company expects to open four or five new superstores and has signed a lease to open an existing 25,500 gross square foot superstore in Huntington, New York in the first half of fiscal 1993.

The Company selects new store sites after conducting market research and demographic analysis and bases its selection on many factors, including population density, age, household income, education, historical menswear sales in the market area and accessibility to the location from major traffic arteries. The Company has a store construction and facilities planning staff that supervises the construction or refurbishing of new store locations and the remodeling of existing stores.

The cost of leasehold improvements, furniture and fixtures for a typical Today's Man superstore has ranged from approximately $750,000 to $1.5 million per store, depending on the location and size of the store and the terms of the lease. Pre-opening expenses, which are expensed in the fiscal year of opening, have ranged from $125,000 to $175,000. Superstores have required between $1.7 and $2.4 million of opening inventory at cost, a large portion of which is financed through vendor trade credit. Nearly all of the Company's superstores have generated store-level operating profits and have contributed to the Company's income from operations in their first full year of operation although such contributions have not been material.

There can be no assurance that the Company will be able to open superstores in a timely manner as described above or that the Company will be able to operate profitably any new superstores.

Purchasing

The Company purchases most of its merchandise in large volumes through preplanned buying programs, which allow it to consistently offer a broad and deep selection of current-season, moderate to better brand-name and private label menswear at substantial savings to its customers. The Company typically does not purchase manufacturers' production overruns and does not seek return privileges or advertising and markdown allowances from its vendors.

The Company purchased merchandise from approximately 200 domestic and overseas manufacturers and suppliers during fiscal 1991. During that year, the top ten vendors by dollar volume accounted for approximately 43% of total purchases, but no vendor accounted for more than 9% of the Company's purchases. Of the Company's purchases by dollar volume in fiscal 1991, approximately 25% were from overseas vendors, primarily in U.S. dollars. In instances in which the Company makes purchases in foreign currencies, the Company enters into forward exchange contracts for all of its purchases in those currencies to hedge against currency fluctuations. Some of the Company's overseas purchases are financed by letters of credit. The Company expects that purchases from overseas vendors as a percentage of the total dollar volume purchased will continue to increase. The Company believes that its relationships with its vendors are excellent and that alternative domestic and overseas sources of supply are available for each category of merchandise it purchases.

The Company employs a Vice President of Merchandising and two specialty merchandise directors who supervise six buyers. The Company purchased approximately 3.2 million units of merchandise in fiscal 1991, of which approximately two-thirds were purchases of brand-name merchandise and the remainder were purchases of the Company's private label merchandise.

In recent years, the Company has placed great emphasis on product development, including the design of its own merchandise for sale under its private labels. A significant portion of the Company's private label merchandise is designed by the Company's in-house product development group. Company-designed products are made by manufacturers based upon the Company's quality and size specifications, often using

19

188

materials that the Company has purchased from other suppliers. The Company regularly inspects the manufacturing of its product development merchandise to maintain its quality standards. The Company believes that by designing its own private label merchandise and by dealing directly with manufacturers, it is able to offer fashionable merchandise at substantial savings to its customers. The Company does not own or operate any manufacturing facilities.

Distribution

The Company's distribution center is adjacent to the Company's executive and administrative offices in an office park in Moorestown, New Jersey. The distribution center is a modern 68,000 square foot facility constructed in 1987 that currently is being expanded by the landlord by an additional 48,000 square feet. This construction is expected to be completed in August 1992. The expanded facility will double the Company's merchandise processing potential to ten million units per year, increasing the number of superstores it is capable of serving using a single shift to approximately 30. The distribution facility could support more superstores by using more than one shift. The landlord, Mr. David Feld, also owns land adjacent to the distribution center which can be used for additional expansion. See " — Facilities" and "Certain Transactions — Leases."

Merchandise is generally shipped directly by common carriers to the distribution center or to ports or airports for pick up by the Company's trucks. Merchandise from local manufacturers is often picked up by the Company's trucks directly from the manufacturer. At the distribution center, merchandise is received, counted, ticketed with the Company's bar coded labels and sorted for distribution to the Company's stores. Whenever possible, merchandise is preticketed with the Company's bar coded labels by the Company's vendors prior to delivery to reduce processing time and expense. Deliveries are made from the distribution center to each store typically twice a week by the Company's trucks. Merchandise is usually shipped to the stores ready for immediate placement on the selling floor.

Management Information and Control Systems

The Company has placed substantial emphasis on upgrading and integrating its management information and control systems. The Company believes its management information and control systems are an important factor in enabling it to achieve its goal of superior execution of all aspects of the Company's operations.

The Company employs a nine person MIS group, including two programmers. Control of the Company's merchandising activities is maintained by a fully integrated point-of-sale (POS) inventory and management information system which permits management to monitor inventory and store operations on a daily basis and to determine weekly operating results by store. Each store is on-line with the Company's IBM RS/6000 computer system via IBM 4680 POS registers. By bar coding all merchandise and using POS scanners, inventories are automatically adjusted and sales recognized as customers check out. Today's Man has also installed a computerized purchasing system, allowing buyers to order merchandise in appropriate quantities and sizes based on each store's historical sales pattern and other variables. These closely linked systems track merchandise from order through sale, comparing actual to planned results and highlighting areas requiring management attention. The Company has recently implemented ARTHUR®, a merchandise planning system which facilitates seasonal planning by department and by store and provides data for financial planning. This system interacts with the Company's POS inventory management system.

The Company continues to enhance its management information and control systems. For example, the Company is implementing an electronic data interface (EDI) system with certain of its vendors which will allow it to place purchase orders electronically. It is expected that the Company will be on-line with a limited number of vendors during the second half of fiscal 1992.

Customer Credit

Today's Man customers may pay for their purchases with the Today's Man proprietary credit card, Visa, MasterCard, cash or check. Approximately two-thirds of all purchases are paid for by credit card, a growing portion of which is with the Today's Man credit card.

Today's Man credit cards are issued by a national bank, using the bank's credit standards, on a non-recourse basis to the Company. The Company has no liability to the card issuer for any bad debt expense, provided that credit card purchases are made in accordance with the issuer's procedures.

20

189

The Company, as part of its growth strategy, intends to seek to increase aggressively the number of Today's Man credit card holders while maintaining credit standards. As of February 1, 1992, the Company had issued approximately 72,000 Today's Man credit cards. The Company believes that its credit card is a particularly productive tool for targeted marketing and presents an excellent opportunity to analyze and better understand its customers' shopping patterns and needs.

Competition

The retail menswear business is highly competitive with respect to price, quality and style of merchandise and store location. The Company faces competition for customers and store locations from large national and regional department stores, various full-price menswear chains, a number of off-price specialty retailers as well as local department stores, catalog retailers and local menswear stores. Many of these competitors have significantly greater financial and other resources than the Company. The retailing business is affected by changes in consumer tastes, demographic trends and the type, number and location of competing stores. In the future, the Company may experience increased competition from menswear retailers attempting to imitate the Company's strategy. The Company believes that it generally compares favorably with its competitors with respect to the quality, depth and range of sizes and styles of merchandise, prices for comparable quality merchandise, customer service and store environment.

Associates

Today's Man places great importance on recruiting, training and motivating quality store level associates by such methods as promoting associates from within, offering bonuses for associates who recommend successful job applicants and holding monthly awards luncheons at corporate headquarters for top sales associates. Additionally, the Company has recently hired a director of training who will be responsible for further developing and implementing the Company's in-store and central training programs.

As of February 1, 1992, the Company had 517 full-time and 266 part-time associates. The Company also employs additional part-time clerks and cashiers during peak periods. None of the Company's associates is represented by a labor union. The Company believes that its relationship with its associates is good.

Legal Proceedings

The Company is involved in routine legal proceedings incidental to the conduct of its business. Management believes that none of these legal proceedings will have a materially adverse effect on the financial condition or results of operations of the Company. The Company maintains general liability insurance coverage in amounts deemed adequate by management.

In 1979, Mr. David Feld pleaded no contest to a misdemeanor charge related to his activities in response to an attempt by a labor union to organize the Company's warehouse employees, for which he received a full and unconditional pardon in 1991 from the President of the United States.

Trademarks

The Company owns all rights to the trademarks it believes are necessary to conduct its business as currently operated. The Company believes that no individual trademark or trade name, other than the Today's Man® trademark, is material to the Company's competitive position in the industry.

21

190

Facilities

The Company's executive offices and distribution center are housed in a 92,000 square foot building located in an office park in Moorestown, New Jersey. The Company leases the building from Mr. David Feld, pursuant to a lease expiring in 1998. Mr. David Feld has undertaken to construct a 48,000 square foot addition to the distribution center. The Company has committed to lease this addition upon completion, which is scheduled to occur in August 1992. See "Management — Certain Transactions — Leases."

The following table provides information regarding the Company's existing stores and planned stores under lease:

Store Location	Approximate Gross Square Feet	Year Of Opening
Greater Philadelphia Market:		
Center City Philadelphia, PA (1)	25,600	1980
Broomall, PA	17,800	1984
Deptford, NJ (1)	19,600	1985
Allentown, PA	22,700	1986
Montgomeryville, PA	22,100	1986
Northeast Philadelphia, PA	22,500	1987
King of Prussia, PA (1)	25,000	1988
Langhorne, PA (1)	25,000	1988
Cherry Hill, NJ	25,000	1990
Greater Washington, D.C. Market:		
Bailey's Crossroads, VA	26,000	1987
Rockville, MD	26,100	1988
Fairfax, VA (2)	25,000	1992
Greater New York Market:		
Paramus, NJ	30,000	1991
Carle Place, NY	33,000	1991
Wayne, NJ	33,000	1992
Stony Brook, NY (2)	26,200	1992
Huntington, NY (3)	25,500	1993

(1) Leased from David Feld. See "Management — Certain Transactions — Leases."

(2) Scheduled to open in the second half of fiscal 1992.

(3) Scheduled to open in the first half of fiscal 1993.

The Company leases all of its existing stores and anticipates that it will continue to do so. Unexpired lease terms range from three to twenty-nine years and no lease is scheduled to expire prior to 1995, assuming the exercise of options to renew in certain cases. Approximately one-half of the leases have percentage rent clauses, although none of the leases with Mr. David Feld have percentage rent clauses. The Company has collectively assigned most of its leases to secure its obligations under its revolving credit facility and term loan.

22

191

UNDERWRITING

Subject to the terms and conditions of the Underwriting Agreement, the Underwriters named below, through their Representatives, Alex. Brown & Sons Incorporated and PaineWebber Incorporated, have severally agreed to purchase from the Company the following respective number of shares of Common Stock at the initial public offering price less the underwriting discounts and commissions set forth on the cover page of this Prospectus:

Underwriter	Number of Shares
Alex. Brown & Sons Incorporated	550,000
PaineWebber Incorporated	550,000
Dillon Read & Co. Inc.	40,000
Kidder, Peabody & Co. Incorporated	40,000
Montgomery Securities	40,000
Oppenheimer & Co., Inc.	40,000
Prudential Securities Incorporated	40,000
Robertson, Stephens & Company	40,000
Salomon Brothers Inc.	40,000
Shearson Lehman Brothers Inc.	40,000
Smith Barney, Harris Upham & Co. Incorporated	40,000
Wertheim Schroder & Co. Incorporated	40,000
Dean Witter Reynolds Inc.	40,000
Advest, Inc.	30,000
Arnhold and S. Bleichroeder, Inc.	30,000
William Blair & Company	30,000
Furman Selz Incorporated	30,000
Gruntal & Co. Incorporated.	30,000
Janney Montgomery Scott Inc.	30,000
Legg Mason Wood Walker, Incorporated	30,000
McDonald & Company Securities, Inc.	30,000
Needham & Company, Inc.	30,000
The Robinson-Humphrey Company, Inc.	30,000
Scott & Stringfellow Investment Corporation	30,000
Wessels, Arnold & Henderson, L.P.	30,000
Wheat, First Securities, Inc.	30,000
Brean Murray, Foster Securities Inc.	10,000
Dominick & Dominick, Incorporated.	10,000
Fahnestock & Co., Inc.	10,000
First Manhattan Co.	10,000
C.J. Lawrence Inc.	10,000
Ragen MacKenzie Incorporated	10,000
Sturdivant & Co. Inc.	10,000
Total	2,000,000

33

192

The Underwriting Agreement provides that the obligations of the Underwriters are subject to certain conditions precedent and that the Underwriters will purchase all of the shares of Common Stock shown above if any of such shares are purchased.

The Company has been advised by the Representatives of the Underwriters that the Underwriters propose to offer the shares of Common Stock directly to the public at the initial public offering price set forth on the cover page of this Prospectus and to certain dealers at such price less a concession not in excess of $.30 per share. The Underwriters may allow, and such dealers may reallow, a concession not in excess of $.10 per share to certain other dealers. After the initial public offering, the offering price and other selling terms may be changed by the Representatives of the Underwriters.

The Company has granted to the Underwriters an option, exercisable no later than 30 days after the date of this Prospectus, to purchase up to 300,000 additional shares of Common Stock at the same price per share as the Company will receive for the 2,000,000 shares of Common Stock that the several Underwriters have agreed to purchase. To the extent that the Underwriters exercise such option, each of the Underwriters will have a firm commitment to purchase approximately the same percentage thereof that the number of shares of Common Stock to be purchased by it shown in the above table bears to 2,000,000, and the Company will be obligated, pursuant to the option, to sell such shares to the Underwriters. The Underwriters may exercise such option only to cover over-allotments made in connection with the sale of Common Stock offered hereby. If purchased, the Underwriters will offer such additional shares on the same terms as those on which the 2,000,000 shares are being offered.

The Underwriting Agreement contains covenants of indemnity and contribution among the Underwriters and the Company against certain civil liabilities, including liabilities under the Securities Act.

The Representatives of the Underwriters have advised the Company that the Underwriters do not intend to confirm sales to any accounts over which they exercise discretionary authority.

The Company, Mr. David Feld and officers, directors and certain employees of the Company have agreed that they will not, without the prior written consent of the Representatives of the Underwriters, offer, sell or otherwise dispose of any shares of Common Stock for a period of 180 days from the date of this Prospectus. The foregoing does not apply to issuances of Common Stock to employees pursuant to the Company's benefit plans, upon exercise of options granted under the Company's Stock Option Plans or as consideration for future acquisitions provided that any shares so issued may not be sold prior to the expiration of the 180 day period.

Prior to this offering, there has been no public market for the Common Stock of the Company. Consequently, the initial public offering price for the Common Stock has been determined by negotiations between the Company and the Representatives of the Underwriters. Among the factors considered in such negotiations were prevailing market conditions, the price-earnings ratios of publicly traded companies that the Company and the Representatives of the Underwriters believe to be comparable to the Company, the results of operations of the Company in recent periods, the market capitalizations and stages of development of other companies which the Company and the Representatives of the Underwriters believed to be comparable to the Company, estimates of the business potential of the Company, the present state of the Company's development and other factors deemed relevant.

Application has been made to have the Common Stock approved for quotation on the NASDAQ National Market System under the symbol TMAN.

34

193

LEGAL MATTERS

An opinion has been rendered by the law firm of Blank, Rome, Comisky & McCauley, Philadelphia, Pennsylvania, to the effect that the shares of Common Stock offered by the Company hereby, when issued and paid for as contemplated in this Prospectus, will be legally issued, fully paid and non-assessable. Certain legal matters will be passed upon for the Underwriters by Piper & Marbury, Baltimore, Maryland.

EXPERTS

The financial statements and schedules of Today's Man, Inc. at February 1, 1992 and February 2, 1991, and for each of the three fiscal years in the period ended February 1, 1992, appearing in this Prospectus and Registration Statement have been audited by Ernst & Young, independent auditors, as set forth in their reports thereon appearing elsewhere herein and in the Registration Statement, and are included in reliance upon such reports given upon the authority of such firm as experts in accounting and auditing.

ADDITIONAL INFORMATION

The Company has filed with the Securities and Exchange Commission (the "Commission"), Washington, D.C. 20549, a Registration Statement on Form S-1 under the Securities Act with respect to the Common Stock offered hereby. This Prospectus does not contain all of the information set forth in the Registration Statement and the exhibits and schedules thereto. For further information with respect to the Company and the Common Stock, reference is made to the Registration Statement, and the exhibits and schedules thereto, which may be inspected and copied at the public reference facilities maintained by the Commission at Room 1024, 450 Fifth Street, N.W., Washington, D.C. 20549. Copies of such materials can also be obtained at prescribed rates from the Public Reference Section of the Commission, Washington, D.C. 20549. Statements contained in this Prospectus as to the contents of any contract or other document are not necessarily complete and, in each instance, reference is made to the copy of such contract or document filed as an exhibit to the Registration Statement, each such statement being qualified in all respects by such reference.

35

194

No dealer, salesman or other person has been authorized in connection with any offering made hereby to give any information or to make any representation not contained in this Prospectus, and, if given or made, such information or representation must not be relied upon as having been authorized by the Company, the Selling Shareholder or any Underwriter. This Prospectus does not constitute an offer to sell or a solicitation of an offer to buy any security other than the shares of Common Stock offered hereby, nor does it constitute an offer to sell or a solicitation of an offer to buy any of the securities offered hereby to any person in any jurisdiction in which it is unlawful to make such an offer or solicitation. Neither the delivery of this Prospectus nor any sale made hereunder shall, under any circumstances, create any implication that the information contained herein is correct as of any date subsequent to the date hereof.

TABLE OF CONTENTS

Until June 30, 1992, all dealers effecting transactions in the Common Stock, whether or not participating in this distribution, may be required to deliver a Prospectus. This is in addition to the obligation of dealers to deliver a Prospectus when acting as Underwriters and with respect to their unsold allotments or subscriptions.

2,000,000 SHARES

TODAY'S MAN®

COMMON STOCK

PROSPECTUS

ALEX. BROWN & SONS
INCORPORATED

PAINEWEBBER INCORPORATED

June 4, 1992

Firm Commitment IPO Underwritings

filed with the SEC which were publicly
offered between January 1, 1990 and
March 31, 1993, listed by name
of lead managing underwriter

FIRM COMMITMENT IPO'S JANUARY, 1990 THROUGH MARCH, 1993[1]

LEAD UNDERWRITER & ADDRESS	ISSUER	PUBLIC OFFER DATE	OFFERING AMOUNT	BUSINESS
A.G. EDWARDS & SONS, INC. One North Jefferson St. Louis, MO 63103	Microtek Medical, Inc. Data Research Associates, Inc. Gencare Health Systems, Inc. Home Federal Savings Bank - MO	10/06/92 07/01/92 11/20/91 04/25/90	$ 14.2 million $ 10.5 million $ 30.0 million $ 2.1 million	Biomedical products Computer networks Managed health care Savings & loan
A.R. BARON & CO., INC. 1 Penn Plaza - Suite 4525 New York, NY 10119	Cypros Pharmaceutical Corp.	11/03/92	$ 6.3 million	Therapeutic drugs
A.S. GOLDMEN & CO., INC. 67 Wall Street New York, NY 10005-3192	Perma-Fix Environmental Services Managed-Health Benefits Corp. Princeton Dental Management Corp. Pet Products, Inc. Sports Heroes, Inc. Sports Media, Inc. Pamel Systems, Inc.	12/08/92 08/11/92 04/15/92 03/12/92 11/20/91 07/23/91 11/01/90	$ 8.0 million $ 6.2 million $ 4.2 million $ 4.3 million $ 4.5 million $ 3.8 million $ 4.0 million	Pollution control services Health care cost services Dental practices Beef dog treats Sports memorabilia Sports yearbooks Computer software
ADAMS, HARKNESS & HILL, INC. One Liberty Square Boston, MA 02109	Aseco Corp.	03/16/93	$ 14.3 million	Automated circuit tests
ADVEST, INC. 280 Trumbull Street Hartford, CT 06103	NPM Healthcare Products, Inc.	11/17/92	$ 14.0 million	Health products

IPO's of investment funds are not complete.

LEAD UNDERWRITER & ADDRESS	ISSUER	PUBLIC OFFER DATE	OFFERING AMOUNT	BUSINESS
ALEX. BROWN & SONS INCORPORATED 135 East Baltimore Street Baltimore, MD 21202	Brock Control Systems, Inc.	03/31/93	$ 23.7 million	Automated sales & marketing software
	McGraw, Inc.	03/19/93	$ 48.0 million	Intravenous solutions & hospital eqip.
	Microchip Technology, Inc.	03/19/93	$ 19.5 million	Microchips
	Energy Bio Systems Corp.	03/12/93	$ 14.4 million	Bio-technology processes
	Landstar Holding Corp.	03/05/93	$ 61.8 million	Truckload carrier
	MathSoft, Inc.	02/03/93	$ 32.5 million	Software products
	Capitol American Financial Corp.	12/18/92	$ 105.6 million	Insurance underwriter
	Trident Microsystems, Inc.	12/16/92	$ 51.0 million	Graphics products
	Fresh Choice, Inc.	12/08/92	$ 19.5 million	Restaurants
	Dial Page, Inc.	11/05/92	$ 16.5 million	Paging & messaging services
	Olicom A/S	10/22/92	$ 75.6 million	Network communications
	Alpha-Beta Technology, Inc.	10/16/92	$ 16.0 million	Carbohydrate ploymers
	Netrix Corp.	09/22/92	$ 33.0 million	Computer network products
	Layne, Inc.	08/20/92	$ 16.1 million	Water well drilling services
	Medic Computer Systems, Inc.	08/05/92	$ 20.0 million	Management systems
	Starbucks Corp.	06/26/92	$ 35.7 million	Specialty coffee importer
	Express Scripts, Inc.	06/09/92	$ 26.0 million	Health care management services
	Today's Man, Inc.	06/04/92	$ 15.0 million	Men's clothing stores
	Perspective Biosystems, Inc.	05/29/92	$ 17.5 million	Biomolecules analysis systems
	Stac Electronics, Inc.	05/07/92	$ 36.0 million	Data compression software
	Orthofix International, N.V.	04/24/92	$ 28.2 million	Fracture treatment devices
	Option Care, Inc.	04/15/92	$ 16.0 million	Home infusion therapy services
	America Online, Inc.	03/19/92	$ 23.0 million	Consumer on-line information
	Access Health Marketing, Inc.	02/21/92	$ 14.0 million	Information for the health care industry
	Advantage Health Corp.	02/14/92	$ 45.5 million	Medical rehabilitation services
	Target Therapeutics, Inc.	01/24/92	$ 40.5 million	Disposable medical devices
	Phycor, Inc.	01/22/92	$ 37.6 million	Medical clinics
	Granite Broadcasting Corp.	01/14/92	$ 21.0 million	Communications & broadcasting

199

LEAD UNDERWRITER & ADDRESS	ISSUER	PUBLIC OFFER DATE	OFFERING AMOUNT	BUSINESS
ALEX. BROWN & SONS INCORPORATED (continued)	Nuveen Premier Insured Muni Income Fund	12/19/91	$ 262.5 million	Closed-ended fund
	Nuveen Premeir Muni Income Fund	12/19/91	$ 262.5 million	Closed-ended fund
	Aramed, Inc.	11/27/91	$ 50.0 million	Pharmaceuticals
	Broderbund Software, Inc.	11/25/91	$ 35.8 million	Computer software
	Nuveen NY Quality Income Muni Fund	11/25/91	$ 322.5 million	Closed-ended fund
	Information America, Inc.	11/21/91	$ 14.5 million	On-line information services
	Nuveen Calif. Quality Income Muni Fund	11/20/91	$ 300.0 million	Closed-ended fund
	Wabash National Corp.	11/08/91	$ 37.8 million	Semi trailors
	Alteon, Inc.	11/01/91	$ 45.0 million	Pharmaceuticals
	IMRS	10/25/91	$ 40.0 million	Business information software
	Old Dominion Freight Line, Inc.	10/24/91	$ 25.0 million	General commodities trucking
	Nuveen Florida Qual Income Muni Fund	10/17/91	$ 168.8 million	Closed-ended fund
	Nuveen MI Quality Income Muni Fund	10/17/91	$ 150.0 million	Closed-ended fund
	Nuveen Ohio Quality Income Muni Fund	10/17/91	$ 60.0 million	Closed-ended fund
	Nuveen PA Quality Income Muni Fund	10/17/91	$ 93.8 million	Closed-ended fund
	Nuveen NJ Quality Income Muni Fund	10/17/91	$ 105.0 million	Closed-ended fund
	Nuveen TX Quality Income Muni Fund	10/17/91	$ 93.8 million	Closed-ended fund
	MicroProse, Inc.	10/03/91	$ 18.0 million	Computer games software
	The Bon-Ton Stores, Inc.	09/24/91	$ 45.5 million	Department stores
	Artisoft, Inc.	09/20/91	$ 80.0 million	Network software systems
	Nuveen Insured Muni Opportunity Fund	09/19/91	$ 1125.0 million	Closed-ended fund
	Mutual Assurance	09/04/91	$ 11.7 million	Property & casualty insurance
	Somatogen	08/02/91	$ 38.8 million	Human blood substitute
	Nuveen Quality Income Municipal Fund	06/19/91	$ 750.0 million	Closed-ended fund
	Outback Steakhouse, Inc.	06/18/91	$ 23.6 million	Restaurants
	Envoy Corp.	05/23/91	$ 20.0 million	Electronic processing service
	Nuveen Calif. Select Qual Municipal Fund	05/22/91	$ 300.0 million	Closed-ended fund
	Nuveen New York Select Qual Muni Fund	05/22/91	$ 300.0 million	Closed-ended fund
	Quantum Health Resources	04/30/91	$ 30.0 million	Therapy/support services
	Value Health, Inc.	04/04/91	$ 36.0 million	Health care benefits

LEAD UNDERWRITER & ADDRESS	ISSUER	PUBLIC OFFER DATE	OFFERING AMOUNT	BUSINESS
ALEX. BROWN & SONS INCORPORATED (continued)	Amsco Internantional, Inc.	03/26/91	$ 81.9 million	Sterilization / infection control
	Nuveen Select Quality Municipal Fund	03/21/91	$ 450.0 million	Closed-ended fund
	Atmel Corp.	03/19/91	$ 58.5 million	Integrated circuits
	Zilog, Inc.	02/27/91	$ 22.0 million	Standard integrated circuits
	Nuveen Florida Investment Qual Muni Fund	02/21/91	$ 210.0 million	Closed-ended fund
	Nuveen New Jersey Investment Qual Muni Fund	02/21/91	$ 153.8 million	Closed-ended fund
	Nuveen Penna. Investment Quality Muni Fund	02/21/91	$ 112.5 million	Closed-ended fund
	Alta Health Strategies, Inc.	01/22/91	$ 14.3 million	Health care management services
	Nuveen Insured Quality Muni. Fund	12/19/90	$ 495.0 million	Closed-ended fund
	Nuveen California Investment Quality Muni. Fund	11/20/90	$ 172.5 million	Closed-ended fund
	Nuveen New York Investment Quality Muni. Fund	11/20/90	$ 75.0 million	Closed-ended fund
	Gerrity Oil & Gas Corp.	08/15/90	$ 16.0 million	Oil drilling
	Allied Clinical Laboratories, Inc.	07/31/90	$ 22.1 million	Clinical testing laboratories
	IKOS Systems, Inc.	07/25/90	$ 20.3 million	Electronic computer systems
	O'Charley's, Inc.	07/19/90	$ 22.5 million	Franchised restaurants
	In-Store Advertising, Inc.	07/19/90	$ 38.0 million	Advertising promotion
	Swift Transportation Company	06/29/90	$ 20.6 million	Truckload carriers holding company
	Sundowner Offshore Services, Inc.	06/29/90	$ 11.7 million	Offshore well servicing
	Micrografx, Inc.	06/29/90	$ 21.3 million	Computer software
	AlCorp, Inc.	06/26/90	$ 21.4 million	Software engineering products
	Nuveen Investment Quality Muni. Fund	06/21/90	$ 450.0 million	Closed-ended fund
	Gensia Pharmaceuticals, Inc.	06/05/90	$ 30.8 million	Pharmaceuticals
	Mr. Coffee	05/31/90	$ 40.0 million	Coffee makers
	Mid-Amercian Waste Systems, Inc.	05/18/90	$ 72.0 million	Solid waste management
	Nuveen California Muni. Market Opp. Fund	05/18/90	$ 105.0 million	Closed-ended fund
	Nuveen New York Muni. Market Opp. Fund	05/18/90	$ 75.0 million	Closed-ended fund
	Orbital Sciences Corp.	04/24/90	$ 33.6 million	Space technology products
	Sanifill, Inc.	04/12/90	$ 19.0 million	Solid waste landfills
	Syntellect, Inc.	03/29/90	$ 28.0 million	Voice response systems
	Nuveen Municipal Market Opportunity Fund	03/22/90	$ 600.0 million	Closed-ended fund
	Integrated Systems, Inc.	03/06/90	$ 16.2 million	Software

LEAD UNDERWRITER & ADDRESS	ISSUER	PUBLIC OFFER DATE	OFFERING AMOUNT	BUSINESS
ALLEN & COMPANY INCORPORATED 711 Fifth Avenue New York, NY 10022	Savoy Pictures Entertainment, Inc. Syratech Corp. Envirogen, Inc. Right Start, Inc. Genelabs Technologies, Inc.	03/18/93 12/16/92 08/11/92 10/11/91 06/13/91	$ 52.9 million $ 37.4 million $ 8.6 million $ 11.5 million $ 25.6 million	Motion picture distribution Furniture and flatware Toxic waste biotechnology Mail order catalog service Biotechnology
ARTHUR W. WOOD COMPANY, INC. 185 Devonshire Street Suite 1100 Boston, MA 02110-1407	BKC Semiconductors, Inc.	08/20/92	$ 3.5 million	Semiconductor devices
BARINGTON CAPITAL GROUP, L.P. 730 Fifth Avenue - 12th Floor New York, NY 10019	Hypermedia Communications, Inc. Document Imaging Systems Corp.	03/09/93 12/08/92	$ 7.0 million $ 6.5 million	Communications & publishing Computer storage systems
BEAR, STEARNS & CO., INC. 245 Park Avenue New York, NY 10167	Consortium G Dina Group, Inc. Physician Corp. of America Wall Data, Inc. Watson Pharmaceuticals, Inc. Copley Pharmaceutical, Inc. Sportmart, Inc. Omega Healthcare Investors, Inc. Transportacion Maritima Mexicana Intermedia Communications of Florida, Inc. Men's Wearhouse, Inc. Diversicare, Inc. Jenny Craig, Inc. Stewart Enterprises, Inc. Osteotech, Inc. In Focus Systems, Inc. Chiles Offshore Corp.	03/31/93 03/29/93 03/15/93 02/17/93 10/14/92 10/05/92 08/07/92 06/10/92 04/30/92 04/14/92 11/08/91 10/29/91 10/09/91 07/17/91 12/20/90 05/24/90	$ 173.2 million $ 45.8 million $ 57.6 million $ 43.2 million $ 41.8 million $ 45.0 million $ 128.1 million $ 56.8 million $ 18.4 million $ 19.5 million $ 15.5 million $ 105.0 million $ 62.1 million $ 9.4 million $ 24.3 million $ 72.5 million	Trucks Health maintenance organization Connectivity software products Pharmaceutical products Over-the-counter drugs Sporting goods superstores Health care facilities Shipping & transportation Telephone services company Men's business attire Health services company Weight loss centers Death care industry services Bones & ligaments processor LCD color technology Oil & gas drilling
BERKELEY SECURITIES CORP. 11 Broadway New York, NY 10004	BitWise Designs, Inc.	05/13/92	$ 3.5 million	IBM compatible computers

LEAD UNDERWRITER & ADDRESS	ISSUER	PUBLIC OFFER DATE	OFFERING AMOUNT	BUSINESS
BLUNT ELLIS & LOEWI, INC. 111 East Kilbourn Avenue Milwaukee, WI 53202	Rocky Mountain Helicopters Templeton Global Utilities, Inc.	09/11/90 05/23/90	$ 7.0 million $ 36.0 million	Helicopter support services Closed-ended fund
CHATFIELD DEAN & CO., INC. 7935 East Prentice Avenue #200 Greenwood Village, CO 80111	Aspen Marine Group, Inc. Intervisual Books, Inc.	05/12/92 12/03/91	$ 5.1 million $ 5.1 million	Marine recreation services Childrens pop-up books
CHELSEA STREET SECURITIES, INC. 222 West Las Colinas Blvd. Suite 2000 Irving, TX 75039	LaTexResources, Inc.	11/09/92	$ 4.2 million	Oil & gas production
THE CHICAGO CORPORATION 208 South LaSalle Street Chicago, IL 60604	Exstar Financial Corp. DatEq Information Network, Inc.	12/18/92 11/06/91	$ 22.3 million $ 8.0 million	Insurance holding company Auto insurance support products
COHIG & ASSOCIATES, INC. 6300 South Syracuse Way Suite 430 Englewood, CO 80111	Soricon Corp. Marcum Natural Gas Services, Inc.	11/19/92 02/13/92	$ 4.0 million $ 3.9 million	Scanning technology Gas station fuel services
COMMONWEALTH ASSOCIATES One Exchange Plaza New York, NY 10006	Commonwealth Assoc. Growth Fund, Inc. Alamar Biosciences, Inc. Lukens Medical Corp. Providence Health Care, Inc. International Testing Services Mediware Information Systems, Inc. Star Multi Care Services, Inc. Express Cash International Corp. Gamma International, Ltd. Medical Nutrition	03/22/93 10/14/92 05/06/92 02/13/92 08/15/91 08/06/91 05/16/91 12/12/90 06/21/90 03/14/90	$ 21.0 million $ 4.3 million $ 8.3 million $ 13.1 million $ 5.2 million $ 4.6 million $ 4.7 million $ 3.6 million $ 6.3 million $ 2.6 million	Closed-ended fund Diagnostic equipment Disposable surgical products Nursing care Pipeline welding inspectors Computer-based information systems Temporary healthcare Pawn shops Bingo halls Weight control programs
CONTINENTAL BROKER-DEALER CORP. One Old Country Road Carle Place, NY 11514	MusicSource USA, Inc. Natural Child Care, Inc.	02/01/93 04/28/92	$ 5.7 million $ 4.9 million	Music data retrieval services Natural infant health care products

LEAD UNDERWRITER & ADDRESS	ISSUER	PUBLIC OFFER DATE	OFFERING AMOUNT	BUSINESS
CORPORATE SECURITIES GROUP, INC. 980 North Federal Highway - Suite 210 Boca Raton, FL 33432	Regenex, Inc.	08/16/90	$ 3.0 million	Chemicals
COVEY & CO., INC. 115 South Main Street Salt Lake City, UT 84111	Pinnacle Environmental, Inc.	05/17/90	$ 5.0 million	Industrial asbestos abatement
COWEN & CO. Financial Square New York, NY 10005	Applied Signal Technology, Inc. Metricom, Inc. Arch Communications Group, Inc. Telebit Corp.	03/26/93 05/01/92 01/17/92 04/27/90	$ 15.4 million $ 9.0 million $ 24.8 million $ 20.9 million	Telecommunications signal equipment Communications networking Telephone paging services Data transmission products
CRAIG-HALLUM, INC. 701 Fourth Avenue South 10th Floor Minneapolis, MN 55415	Odd's-N-End's, Inc. Universal International, Inc.	01/21/92 10/12/90	$ 5.3 million $ 4.9 million	Discount retail shops Wholesale merchandising
CROWELL, WEEDON & CO. 624 South Grand Avenue P.O. Box 54843 Terminal Annex Los Angeles, CA 90054	First Mortgage Corp.	04/16/92	$ 5.4 million	Mortgage banking
CRUTTENDEN & CO., INC. 18301 Von Karman - Suite 100 Irvine, CA 92715	Wilshire Technologies, Inc. Candy's Tortilla Factory, Inc.	11/24/92 08/09/91	$ 7.5 million $ 3.0 million	Disposable medical products Specialty foods

LEAD UNDERWRITER & ADDRESS	ISSUER	PUBLIC OFFER DATE	OFFERING AMOUNT	BUSINESS
D.H. BLAIR INVESTMENT BANKING CORP. 44 Wall Street New York, NY 10005	Magna-Lab, Inc.	03/30/93	$ 6.0 million	MRI devices
	Advanced Mammography Systems, Inc.	01/25/93	$ 7.7 million	Outpatient diagnostic services
	Health Image Media, Inc.	10/20/92	$ 6.6 million	Health magazines
	Life Medical Sciences	09/22/92	$ 6.0 million	Biomedical products
	Integrated Process Equipment Corp.	08/13/92	$ 5.3 million	Semiconductors
	Laser Video Network, Inc.	06/10/92	$ 6.3 million	Laser disc jukeboxes
	Applied Laser Systems	03/10/92	$ 7.2 million	Laser diode devices
	Las Vegas Entertainment Network, Inc.	02/20/92	$ 5.0 million	Television programming
	InfoNow Corp.	02/07/92	$ 6.9 million	Electronic distribution system
	SBS Engineering, Inc.	01/09/92	$ 4.0 million	Flight simulation systems
	Epigen, Inc.	12/10/91	$ 5.7 million	Pharmaceuticals
	Bradley Pharmaceuticals, Inc.	11/12/91	$ 4.5 million	Pharmaceuticals
	ENVIRx, Ltd.	11/12/91	$ 6.0 million	Environmental equipment
	Avitar, Inc.	07/22/91	$ 5.5 million	Pharmaceuticals
	Omega Environmental, Inc.	07/11/91	$ 6.0 million	Underground storage tanks
	Value Vision International, Inc.	06/28/91	$ 4.2 million	TV home shopping program
	Biomedical Waste Systems, Inc.	06/04/91	$ 6.0 million	Medical waste incineration
	Somanetics Corp.	03/20/91	$ 7.2 million	Medical diagnostic equipment
	Advanced Photonix, Inc.	02/11/91	$ 6.0 million	Photodetection devices
	Car Mart, Inc.	12/11/90	$ 4.2 million	Contract/automobile dealers
	Triple Threat Enterprises, Inc.	11/21/90	$ 3.2 million	Training/management for boxers
	Medenta Corp.	11/01/90	$ 4.0 million	Disposable testing products
	Prime Cellular, Inc.	08/02/90	$ 6.0 million	Construction consulting services
	CAP Rx, Ltd.	07/31/90	$ 4.0 million	Prescription drug insurance
	VIMRx Pharmaceuticals, Inc.	07/25/90	$ 5.0 million	Pharmaceuticals
	Builders Express, Inc.	06/07/90	$ 6.0 million	Home improvement stores
	Fountain Pharmaceuticals	05/15/90	$ 5.5 million	Encapsulation technology
	Lidak Pharmaceuticals	05/08/90	$ 5.0 million	Pharmaceuticals
	American Biogenetic Sciences, Inc.	05/01/90	$ 6.0 million	Genetic engineering
	Medicis Pharmaceutical	03/28/90	$ 8.9 million	Pharmaceutical products
	Interneuron Pharmaceuticals, Inc.	03/08/90	$ 8.5 million	Psychiatric pharmaceuticals
	Biomechanics Consulting	01/17/90	$ 4.4 million	Biomechanics consulting
DAKIN SECURITIES CORP. 505 Sansome Street - 8th Floor San Francisco, CA 94111	Sellectek, Inc.	12/10/92	$ 5.0 million	Computer information services

LEAD UNDERWRITER & ADDRESS	ISSUER	PUBLIC OFFER DATE	OFFERING AMOUNT	BUSINESS
DAIN BOSWORTH, INC. 60 South Sixth Street P.O. Box 1160 Minneapolis, MN 55440-1160	Union Bankshares, Ltd. Todhunter International, Inc. Bestop, Inc. Columbia Banking System, Inc. InterWest Savings Bank Fortis Corp. American Dental Laser, Inc. Sullivan Dental Products	03/09/93 10/13/92 08/13/92 06/16/92 07/12/91 06/28/91 06/18/91 04/18/90	$ 7.1 million $ 10.4 million $ 8.3 million $ 5.4 million $ 14.0 million $ 16.0 million $ 31.4 million $ 10.0 million	Bank holding company Citrus-based spirits Automobile soft tops Savings banks Savings bank Managed medical care services Dental lasers Dental supplies/products
DAIWA SECURITIES AMERICA, INC. One World Financial Center Tower A 200 Liberty Street New York, NY 10281-1003	Singapore Fund, Inc.	07/24/90	$ 36.0 million	Closed-ended fund

LEAD UNDERWRITER & ADDRESS	ISSUER	PUBLIC OFFER DATE	OFFERING AMOUNT	BUSINESS
DEAN WITTER REYNOLDS, INC. 2 World Trade Center New York, NY 10048	Dean Witter, Discover & Co.	02/22/93	$ 796.5 million	Securities brokerage services
	InterCapital CA Insured Municipal Income Trust	02/19/93	$ 195.0 million	Closed-ended fund
	InterCapital Insured Municipal Income Trust	02/19/93	$ 495.0 million	Closed-ended fund
	Developers Diversified Realty Corp.	02/02/93	$ 176.0 million	Real estate investment trust
	DF&R Restaurants, Inc.	01/27/93	$ 28.0 million	Restaurants
	ImageAmerica, Inc.	10/22/92	$ 16.1 million	Medical diagnostic services
	Equitrac Corp.	06/11/92	$ 16.5 million	Computer systems for law firms
	Krystal Co.	05/14/92	$ 25.2 million	Restaurants
	Lincare Holdings, Inc.	03/19/92	$ 46.9 million	Home oxygen therapy
	Toastmaster, Inc.	03/03/92	$ 43.1 million	Electric housewares
	SPS Transaction Services	02/25/92	$ 48.0 million	Point-of-sale transaction services
	Chem Trak, Inc.	02/19/92	$ 26.0 million	Testing equipment
	Intertape Polymer Group, Inc.	02/13/92	$ 17.0 million	Industrial plastic products
	Checkers Drive-In Restaurants, Inc.	11/15/91	$ 33.6 million	Fast food restaurant chain
	Supercuts, Inc.	10/30/91	$ 19.3 million	Haircutting salons
	Salton/Maxim Housewares Group, Inc.	10/09/91	$ 27.6 million	Home furnishings
	Government Technology Services, Inc.	09/20/91	$ 25.2 million	Computer hardware
	The Mediplex Group, Inc.	08/07/91	$ 41.8 million	Health care services
	American Biodyne, Inc.	07/12/91	$ 14.3 million	Mental health care services
	Software Spectrum, Inc.	07/11/91	$ 17.4 million	Computer software
	Coventry Corp.	04/16/91	$ 43.5 million	Managed helthcare & H.M.O.s
	Intercapital Insured Municipal Bond Trust	02/21/91	$ 69.0 million	Closed-ended fund
	The Blackstone Strategic Term Trust, Inc.	12/20/90	$ 500.0 million	Closed-ended fund
	Patriot Select Dividend Trust	07/24/90	$ 127.5 million	Closed-ended fund
	Allstate Municipal Income Opportunities Trust III	04/20/90	$ 100.0 million	Closed-ended fund
DICKINSON & CO. 405 6th Avenue - Suite 200 P.O. Box 9111 Des Moines, IA 50306-9111	New World Power Corp.	10/23/92	$ 7.0 million	Power generating systems

207

LEAD UNDERWRITER & ADDRESS	ISSUER	PUBLIC OFFER DATE	OFFERING AMOUNT	BUSINESS
DILLON, READ & CO., INC. 535 Madison Avenue New York, NY 10022	Physicians Health Services, Inc.	01/21/93	$ 52.5 million	Medical health plan services
	Summit Care Group	03/18/92	$ 22.1 million	Nursing care services
	Abbey Healthcare Group, Inc.	02/28/92	$ 41.3 million	Home healthcare services
	Intergroup Health Care Corp.	08/08/91	$ 47.1 million	Managed health care
	Hi-Lo Automotive, Inc.	05/09/91	$ 41.6 million	Auto parts & accessories
	CareNetwork, Inc.	03/26/91	$ 33.6 million	Health organization
	Vintage Petroleum, Inc.	08/03/90	$ 42.0 million	Crude oil & natural gas products
	Immune Response Corp.	05/02/90	$ 15.4 million	Pharmaceuticals
	Viking Office Products, Inc.	03/14/90	$ 24.2 million	Office supply sales
DONALD & CO. SECURITIES, INC. 136 East 57th Street New York, NY 10022	CM Communications, Inc.	01/11/90	$ 3.5 million	Cellular phones
DONALDSON & CO., INC. Eleven Piedmont Center Suite 200 Atlanta, GA 30305	Davidson & Associates, Inc.	03/31/93	$ 26.0 million	Educational software products
	Pillowtex Corp.	03/17/93	$ 54.6 million	Bedding products
	Argosy Gaming Co.	02/18/93	$ 114.0 million	Casinos
	Leviathan Gas Pipeline Partners, L.P.	02/11/93	$ 107.6 million	Natural gas
	Norand Corp.	02/01/93	$ 54.3 million	Electronic information systems
	MB Communications, Inc.	12/15/92	$ 33.8 million	Data communications products
	Kemet Corp.	10/21/92	$ 32.0 million	Capacitators for computers
	Tops Appliance City, Inc.	08/11/92	$ 26.3 million	Discount appliance retailer
	RHI Entertainment, Inc.	07/29/92	$ 25.7 million	Entertainment television business
	GTECH Holdings Corp.	07/22/92	$ 115.6 million	Lottery services
	Rexnord Corp.	07/01/92	$ 129.2 million	Ball & rolling bearings
	CrossComm Corp.	06/18/92	$ 29.3 million	Inter-networking products
	Basin Exploration, Inc.	05/13/92	$ 26.6 million	Oil & gas properties
	Syborn. Corp.	05/07/92	$ 90.4 million	Orthodontic & dental products
	Galey & Lord, Inc.	04/30/92	$ 29.0 million	Cotton apparel fabrics
	International Family Entertainment, Inc.	04/28/92	$ 120.0 million	Family programs for cable TV
	ERO, Inc.	04/07/92	$ 57.8 million	Children's products
	Chicago & North Western Holding Corp.	03/31/92	$ 143.5 million	Railroad holding company
	Musicland Stores Corp.	02/26/92	$ 188.9 million	Record & tape stores
	O W Office Warehouse, Inc.	05/14/91	$ 29.0 million	Retail office supply warehouse

208

LEAD UNDERWRITER & ADDRESS	ISSUER	PUBLIC OFFER DATE	OFFERING AMOUNT	BUSINESS
DONALDSON, LUFKIN & JENRETTE SECURITIES CORPORATION 140 Broadway New York, NY 10005	Viewlogic Systems, Inc. John B. Sanfilippo & Son, Inc. Alliance Imaging, Inc. The Latin American Equity Fund, Inc. Super Rite, Corp. Oxford Health Plans, Inc. Aes Corp. Ross Systems, Inc. Digital Systems International, Inc. Alliance Global Environment Fund, Inc.	12/17/91 12/03/91 11/08/91 10/22/91 09/23/91 08/08/91 06/25/91 04/25/91 06/08/90 05/23/90	$ 45.5 million $ 24.0 million $ 23.8 million $ 72.0 million $ 32.6 million $ 37.5 million $ 90.6 million $ 27.5 million $ 39.6 million $ 45.0 million	Software for electric products Nuts MRI services Closed-ended fund Groceries Health benefit plans Power plants Business software Telephone systems Closed-ended fund
DRAKE CAPITAL SECURITIES, INC. 1250 Fourth Street - 5th Floor P.O. Box 2146 Snata Monica, CA 90407	Voice Powered Technology International, Inc.	10/20/92	$ 5.5 million	Voice recognition products
DREXEL BURNHAM LAMBERT, INC. 60 Broad Street New York, NY 10004	Hadson Energy Resources Corp.	01/31/90	$ 26.0 million	Natural gas
ELLIOT, ALLEN & CO., INC. 461 Fifth Avenue New York, NY 10017	Hillside Bedding, Inc. Eco2, Inc.	02/11/93 10/22/92	$ 5.3 million $ 4.6 million	Discount bedding Solid waste & tire recycling
EMANUEL & COMPANY 110 Wall Street New York, NY 10005	Infu-Tech, Inc. Bio Time, Inc.	12/22/92 03/05/92	$ 8.0 million $ 5.0 million	Infusion therapy services Blood substitute solution
EQUITY SECURITIES TRADING CO., INC. 80 South Eighth Street - Suite 2820 Minneapolis, MN 55402	Gaming Corp. of North America Rimage Corp. Grand Casinos, Inc. Rochester Medical Corp.	02/22/93 11/04/92 10/09/91 11/05/90	$ 23.0 million $ 3.4 million $ 12.0 million $ 1.5 million	Gambling facilities & management Computer memory devices Gambling facilities & management Urinary catheters
EURO-ATLANTIC SECURITIES, INC. 777 Harbour Island Blvd. Suite 200 Tampa, FL 33602	Nova Technologies, Inc.	11/22/91	$ 2.6 million	Patient transfer system

LEAD UNDERWRITER & ADDRESS	ISSUER	PUBLIC OFFER DATE	OFFERING AMOUNT	BUSINESS
F.N. WOLF & CO., INC. 110 Wall Street New York, NY 10005	Noise Com, Inc. Implant Technology, Inc. Twin Star Productions, Inc.	10/21/91 12/17/90 01/24/90	$ 4.0 million $ 3.3 million $ 4.0 million	Noise source products Orthopedic products Consumer products via TV
FAHNESTOCK & CO., INC. 110 Wall Street New York, NY 10005	Premier Radio Networks, Inc. OTR Express, Inc.	04/28/92 01/22/92	$ 6.0 million $ 5.5 million	Radio programming Truckload motor carrier
FERRIS, BAKER WATTS, INC. 1720 Eye Street - N.W. Washington, DC 20006	Champion Industries, Inc.	01/21/93	$ 10.0 million	Optical goods stores
FIRST ALBANY CORP. 41 State Street P.O. Box 52 Albany, NY 12201	Medical Diagnostics, Corp. F.A. Tucker Group, Inc.	02/05/92 05/17/91	$ 11.5 million $ 7.7 million	Resonance imaging services Electric utility
FIRST BIRMINGHAM SECURITIES CORPORATION 1919 Morris Avenue - Suite 1200 Birmingham, AL 35203	LifeSouth, Inc.	01/29/90	$ 1.3 million	Health and life insurance

LEAD UNDERWRITER & ADDRESS	ISSUER	PUBLIC OFFER DATE	OFFERING AMOUNT	BUSINESS
FIRST BOSTON Park Avenue Plaza New York, NY 10055	Life Partners Group, Inc.	03/24/93	$ 258.4 million	Insurance holding company
	Saga Communications, Inc.	12/11/92	$ 23.0 million	Radio broadcasting company
	First Colony Holding Corp.	12/08/92	$ 212.8 million	Life insurance
	Monk-Austin, Inc.	11/20/92	$ 59.4 million	Leaf tabacco
	Acordia, Inc.	10/21/92	$ 37.7 million	Holding company
	Brilliance China Automotive Holdings Ltd.	10/09/92	$ 80.0 million	Minibuses
	Nu-kote Holding, Inc.	10/01/92	$ 44.4 million	Office printing devices
	John Alden Financial Corp.	09/25/92	$ 88.2 million	Insurance holding company
	Sports & Recreation, Inc.	09/16/92	$ 87.5 million	Sporting goods superstores
	Zoll Medical Corp.	07/16/92	$ 21.0 million	Cardiac devices
	CCP Insurance, Inc.	07/14/92	$ 84.0 million	Insurance holding company
	Salem Sportswear Corp.	06/03/92	$ 34.4 million	Sports apparel
	Arkansas Best Corp.	05/13/92	$ 175.8 million	Motor carrier holding company
	Dyersburg Corp.	05/12/92	$ 41.4 million	Fleece fabrics
	Morningstar Group, Inc.	04/24/92	$ 54.7 million	Frozen food products
	Stein Mart, Inc.	04/22/92	$ 42.3 million	Retail store chain
	AGCO Corp.	04/16/92	$ 63.0 million	Farm equipment & machinery
	Mohawk Industries, Inc.	04/01/92	$ 40.5 million	Woven & tufted carpets
	Protocol Systems, Inc.	03/24/92	$ 30.3 million	Patient monitor systems
	Health o Meter Products, Inc.	03/17/92	$ 35.0 million	Scales
	PolyMedica Industries, Inc.	03/05/92	$ 39.0 million	Polyurethane medical products
	Coleman Company, Inc.	02/26/92	$ 66.3 million	Heating, AC, and outdoor products
	Matrix Pharmaceuticals, Inc.	01/28/92	$ 52.5 million	Therapeutic implant devices

211

LEAD UNDERWRITER & ADDRESS	ISSUER	PUBLIC OFFER DATE	OFFERING AMOUNT	BUSINESS
FIRST BOSTON (continued)	Fischer Scientific International, Inc.	12/18/91	$ 98.6 million	Medical instruments & supplies
	Hamburger Hamlet Restaurant	11/21/91	$ 29.0 million	Full service restaurants
	Vitro, Sociedad Anonima	11/19/91	$ 111.7 million	Glass & household products
	Horace Mann Educators Corp.	11/15/91	$ 214.2 million	Multiline insurance
	NAMIC U.S.A. Corp.	11/07/91	$ 54.0 million	Medical products
	BET Holdings, Inc.	10/30/91	$ 72.3 million	Cable TV network
	Goody's Family Clothing, Inc.	10/25/91	$ 52.5 million	Family apparel store
	Gaylord Entertainment Co.	10/24/91	$ 156.8 million	Entertainment & communications
	The Argentina Fund, Inc.	10/11/91	$ 48.0 million	Closed-ended fund
	Genetic Therapy, Inc.	07/31/91	$ 14.0 million	Systems for gene therapy
	Interstate Bakeries Corp.	07/24/91	$ 200.0 million	Baker/bakery distributor
	Enquirer/Star Group, Inc.	07/19/91	$ 151.2 million	Periodicals
	Little Switzerland, Inc.	07/18/91	$ 54.7 million	Luxury items
	IHOP Corp.	07/12/91	$ 49.6 million	Family restaurants
	Tanknology Environmental	06/19/91	$ 14.9 million	Pollution control equipment & services
	Wheatley TXT Corp.	05/31/91	$ 36.0 million	Oil/gas pumps & valves
	Carlisle Plastics, Inc.	05/15/91	$ 74.3 million	Plastic products
	Haemonetics Corp.	05/09/91	$ 105.6 million	Biotech/process blood
	Take Care, Inc.	03/20/91	$ 47.5 million	Health services/HMO
	Sonic Corp.	02/28/91	$ 46.3 million	Drive-in chain
	BJ Services Co.	07/20/90	$ 135.0 million	Oilfield services
	Wet Seal, Inc.	07/03/90	$ 42.8 million	Women's clothing retailer
	RMI Titanium Co.	04/12/90	$ 75.0 million	Titanium sponge products
	DeVlieg-Bullard, Inc.	03/16/90	$ 30.0 million	Machine tools
	Scudder New Europe Fund, Inc.	02/09/90	$ 100.0 million	Closed-ended fund
FIRST EQUITY CORP. OF FLORIDA 1400 Miami Center 201 South Biscayne Blvd. Miami, FL 33131	Ezcony Interamerica, Inc.	08/06/92	$ 10.5 million	Electronics
FIRST HANOVER SECURITIES, INC. 71 Broadway - 15th Floor New York, NY 10006	Harmony Holdings, Inc.	11/13/91	$ 3.2 million	Motion picture/TV

LEAD UNDERWRITER & ADDRESS	ISSUER	PUBLIC OFFER DATE	OFFERING AMOUNT	BUSINESS
FIRST OF MICHIGAN CORP. 100 Renaissance Center 26th Floor Detroit, MI 48243	Pomeroy Computer Resources, Inc. Autocam, Corp. Spartan Motors, Inc.	04/03/92 10/29/91 07/02/91	$ 8.8 million $ 8.0 million $ 6.6 million	Computer hardware & software Special metal alloy components Custom heavy duty chassis
FURMAN SELZ, INC. 230 Park Avenue New York, NY 10169	LanOptics Ltd. Cellcor, Inc. Specialty Chemical Resources, Inc. Abaxis, Inc. Pacific Physician Services, Inc. GMIS	11/18/92 03/13/92 02/27/92 01/22/92 11/11/91 07/25/91	$ 18.9 million $ 22.0 million $ 24.0 million $ 23.9 million $ 18.7 million $ 16.3 million	Network management systems Chemical products Blood analyzer systems Cell therapy for AIDS treatment Managed health care services Database systems
GAINES, BERLAND, INC. 950 Third Avenue New York, NY 10022	Small's Oilfield Services Corp.	07/07/92	$ 4.9 million	Oilfield services
GILFORD SECURITIES, INC. 850 Third Avenue New York, NY 10022	International Canine Genetics, Inc. Sports/Leisure, Inc. Xenejenex, Inc.	03/24/93 10/28/91 02/09/90	$ 5.0 million $ 4.0 million $ 2.5 million	Canine reproduction services Unisex sports apparel Health care videos
G.K. SCOTT & CO., INC. One Fairchild Court Plainview, NY 11803	Electronic Technology Group, Inc.	03/12/90	$ 3.6 million	Electronic equipment
GKN SECURITIES CORP. 61 Broadway - 12th Floor New York, NY 10006	Information Systems Acquisition Corp. Complink, Ltd. Crocker Realty Investors, Inc. Neoprobe Corp. Bio Imaging Technologies, Inc. Trinity Capital Opportunity Corp. Financial Data Systems, Inc. Trinity Capital Enterprise, Corp. Restor Industries, Inc. Lancit Media Productions, Ltd. Robern Apparel, Inc.	03/26/93 03/10/93 01/21/93 11/10/92 06/18/92 05/14/92 12/04/91 09/12/91 08/12/91 06/19/91 04/03/91	$ 12.0 million $ 5.0 million $ 10.0 million $ 9.0 million $ 5.0 million $ 20.0 million $ 3.6 million $ 8.0 million $ 5.3 million $ 2.0 million $ 4.0 million	Acquisition company Computer networking products Real estate investment trust Cancer detection systems Biomedical computer imaging Financial publishing Investment company Blind pool company Pay telephones TV series and specials Skiwear and accessories

213

LEAD UNDERWRITER & ADDRESS	ISSUER	PUBLIC OFFER DATE	OFFERING AMOUNT	BUSINESS
GLOBAL AMERICA, INC. 110 Wall Street - 17th Floor New York, NY 10005	Auto Depot, Inc.	09/07/90	$ 9.0 million	Auto parts stores
	Mountaintop Corp.	06/29/90	$ 4.2 million	Liquor
	Cappucino's, Inc.	02/28/90	$ 5.0 million	Restaurants
GOLDMAN, SACHS & CO. 85 Broad Street New York, NY 10004	Gymboree Corp.	03/30/93	$ 43.3 million	Children's apparel
	Payless Cashways, Inc.	03/08/93	$ 357.0 million	Home improvement products
	Powersoft Corp.	02/03/93	$ 37.3 million	Software products
	Seacor Holdings, Inc.	12/17/92	$ 27.0 million	Oil & gas field services
	Haggar Corp.	12/10/92	$ 46.2 million	Men's apparel
	PeopleSoft, Inc.	11/18/92	$ 51.0 million	Resource management software
	Breed Technologies, Inc.	11/12/92	$ 105.4 million	Crash sensors
	Caraustar Industries, Inc.	10/01/92	$ 120.0 million	Management services
	Creative Technology Ltd.	08/03/92	$ 46.1 million	PC sound & video products
	Fleet Mortgage Group, Inc.	07/31/92	$ 161.0 million	Motgage banking
	Equitable Cos., Inc.	07/15/92	$ 315.0 million	Insurance holding company
	Ultramar Corp.	06/26/92	$ 392.3 million	Petroleum products & refining
	General Instrument Corp.	06/10/92	$ 264.0 million	Electronic systems & components
	Bed Bath & Beyond, Inc.	06/04/92	$ 85.0 million	Retail home furnishings
	Hook-SupeRx, Inc.	06/03/92	$ 77.0 million	Retail drugstores
	John Nuveen Co.	05/19/92	$ 144.0 million	Municipal securities company
	Boston Scientific Corp.	05/18/92	$ 319.6 million	Medical devices
	Reliance Electric Co.	05/05/92	$ 240.9 million	Transmission equipment
	Solo Serve	04/28/92	$ 31.2 million	Discount stores
	Younkers, Inc.	04/22/92	$ 77.1 million	Full line department stores
	Capital Re Corp.	04/08/92	$ 85.8 million	Insurance holding company
	Seragen, Inc.	04/01/92	$ 28.8 million	Therapeutic products
	United Retail Group, Inc.	03/10/92	$ 66.0 million	Women's apparel & accessories
	Cross Timbers Royalty Trust	02/27/92	$ 30.0 million	Oil & gas royalty trust
	Hospital Corp. of America	02/26/92	$ 584.8 million	Hospitals
	Scholastic, Inc.	02/24/92	$ 85.5 million	Educational books
	TNT Freightways Corp.	02/12/92	$ 195.0 million	Regional motor carrier
	Scotts Co.	01/31/92	$ 190.0 million	Do-it-yourself lawn care products

214

LEAD UNDERWRITER & ADDRESS	ISSUER	PUBLIC OFFER DATE	OFFERING AMOUNT	BUSINESS
GOLDMAN, SACHS & CO. (continued)	Attymax N.V.	12/17/91	$ 60.0 million	Pharmaceuticals
	Cytel, Corp.	11/22/91	$ 52.0 million	Immune system drugs
	Read-Rite Corp.	10/18/91	$ 40.6 million	Disk drive recording heads
	ShopKo Stores, Inc.	10/08/91	$ 198.0 million	Variety stores
	Tecnol Medical Products, Inc.	09/26/91	$ 41.3 million	Disposable medical products
	General Physics Corp.	09/25/91	$ 52.0 million	Management consulting & P.R.
	Technology Solution Co.	09/20/91	$ 45.0 million	Computer systems
	Sybase	08/13/91	$ 49.6 million	Software products
	Rogers Cantel Mobile Communications, Inc.	08/07/91	$ 127.5 million	Cellular telephone network
	MGIC Investment Corp.	08/06/91	$ 201.6 million	Mortgage insurance
	Royal Appliance Manufacturing	08/06/91	$ 70.1 million	Vacuum cleaners
	Wellfleet Communications, Inc.	07/30/91	$ 47.6 million	Internetworking products
	Exel Limited	07/18/91	$ 487.2 million	Excess liability insurance
	Societe Nationale Elf - Aquitaine	06/13/91	$ 182.7 million	Oil and gas
	BWIP Holding, Inc.	05/23/91	$ 92.8 million	Fluid tras/control equipment services
	Wisconsin Central Transporation Corp.	05/21/91	$ 34.7 million	Regional railroad
	Filene's Basement Corp.	04/30/91	$ 56.6 million	Discount department store
	AutoZone, Inc.	04/01/91	$ 59.8 million	Auto parts/accessories
	Destec Energy, Inc.	03/14/91	$ 240.0 million	Power producer
	Health Management Associates, Inc.	02/05/91	$ 40.8 million	Acute care hospitals
	MBNA Corp.	01/22/91	$ 689.3 million	Commercial bank
	American Waste Services, Inc.	10/04/90	$ 48.0 million	Waste disposal transportation
	Transatlantic Holdings, Inc.	06/15/90	$ 156.6 million	Property/casualty reinsurance
	K-Swiss, Inc.	06/04/90	$ 25.4 million	Athletic footwear
	Safeway, Inc.	04/25/90	$ 90.0 million	Food stores
	Santa Fe Energy Resources, Inc.	03/08/90	$ 169.7 million	Oil & gas production
	Teppco Partners, L.P.	02/28/90	$ 255.0 million	Oil & gas production
	Digital Sound Corp.	02/27/90	$ 40.0 million	Voice processing platform
	Reader's Digest Association, Inc.	02/14/90	$ 420.0 million	Periodicals
	Cabot Oil & Gas Corp.	02/07/90	$ 41.9 million	Natural gas
GRUNTAL & CO., INC. 14 Wall Street New York, NY 10005	Just Toys, Inc.	10/01/92	$ 11.6 million	Bendable plastic toys
	United States Paging Corp.	06/03/92	$ 6.0 million	Paging services
	Riddell Sports, Inc	06/27/91	$ 16.0 million	Football helmets
	R & B. Inc.	03/12/91	$ 11.4 million	Auto parts

215

LEAD UNDERWRITER & ADDRESS	ISSUER	PUBLIC OFFER DATE	OFFERING AMOUNT	BUSINESS
H.C. WAINWRIGHT & CO., INC. One Boston Place - 31st Floor Boston, MA 02108	DeWolfe Companies, Inc.	09/24/92	$ 5.4 million	Residential real estate
H.J. MEYERS & CO., INC. 356 N. Camden Drive Beverly Hills, CA 90210	Superconductor Technologies, Inc.	03/09/93	$ 15.0 million	Electronic products
	EduSoft Ltd.	07/14/92	$ 5.0 million	PC-based software products
	Intramed Labs, Inc.	06/09/92	$ 6.6 million	Miniature endoscopes
	Satellite Technology Management, Inc.	03/25/92	$ 16.3 million	Satellite communications network
	Anergen, Inc.	10/10/91	$ 14.0 million	Pharmaceuticals
	Magic Software Enterprises, Ltd.	08/28/91	$ 8.5 million	Software tools
	Laser Pacific Media Corp.	08/14/91	$ 6.6 million	Production services

216

LEAD UNDERWRITER & ADDRESS	ISSUER	PUBLIC OFFER DATE	OFFERING AMOUNT	BUSINESS
HAMBRECHT & QUIST, INC. One Bush Street San Francisco, CA 94104	Vical, Inc.	03/09/93	$ 10.0 million	Biological & biomolecular R&D
	Boca Research, Inc.	02/25/93	$ 30.0 million	Computer peripherals
	Molecular Dynamics, Inc.	02/05/93	$ 23.5 million	Medical & scientific equipment
	BioSurface Technology, Inc.	01/27/93	$ 30.0 million	Biological surfactants
	AutoImmune, Inc.	01/20/93	$ 39.0 million	Pharmaceutical products
	Microtest, Inc.	10/30/92	$ 33.4 million	Network diagnostic tools
	Platinum Software Corp.	10/22/92	$ 35.0 million	Management information software
	Universal Standard Medical Laboratories, Inc.	09/25/92	$ 20.0 million	Clinical lab services
	SOFTIMAGE	07/29/92	$ 16.2 million	Software products
	Kronos, Inc.	06/05/92	$ 18.0 million	Time allocation software
	Bio Circuits Corp.	05/14/92	$ 10.0 million	Biomaterials & related products
	VMARK Software, Inc.	05/14/92	$ 16.2 million	Computer software
	Chronimed, Inc.	03/20/92	$ 14.1 million	Drugs & medical products
	Premier Anesthesia, Inc.	03/04/92	$ 27.5 million	Anesthesiology services
	Heart Technology, Inc.	03/02/92	$ 68.4 million	Heart treatment devices
	American Business Information, Inc.	02/19/92	$ 34.5 million	Direct mail advertising
	Frame Technology Corp.	02/12/92	$ 28.0 million	Computer software
	DNX Corp.	12/11/91	$ 32.5 million	R & D therapeutic products
	Mitek Surgical Products, Inc.	10/25/91	$ 14.4 million	Surgical implants
	U.S. Robotics, Inc.	10/10/91	$ 46.8 million	Data communications products
	Barra, Inc.	10/01/91	$ 15.8 million	Financial software
	Dianon Systems, Inc.	07/31/91	$ 13.2 million	New technology tester
	Glycomed, Inc.	06/13/91	$ 16.1 million	Pharmaceuticals
	Immunologic Pharmaceutical Corp.	05/22/91	$ 20.0 million	Pharmaceuticals
	Cephalon, Inc.	04/25/91	$ 59.4 million	Pharmaceuticals
	Xyplex, Inc.	04/25/91	$ 28.0 million	Communication network systems
	Platinum Technology, Inc.	04/18/91	$ 37.5 million	System software/programs
	Vital Signs, Inc.	08/29/90	$ 12.8 million	Medical products
	Marcam Corp.	08/16/90	$ 17.6 million	Applications software & services
	Hologic, Inc.	03/01/90	$ 16.8 million	X-ray systems
HAMILTON INVESTMENTS, INC. 2 North LaSalle Street Chicago, IL 60602	HA-LO Industries, Inc.	10/28/92	$ 11.7 million	Advertising products

217

LEAD UNDERWRITER & ADDRESS	ISSUER	PUBLIC OFFER DATE	OFFERING AMOUNT	BUSINESS
HAMPSHIRE SECURITIES CORPORATION 919 Third Avenue New York, NY 10022	Paracelesian, Inc.	02/11/92	$ 5.5 million	Biotechnology company
HANIFEN, IMHOFF, INC. 1125 17th Street - Suite 1600 P.O. Box 5050 Denver, CO 80217-5050	OrthoLogic Corp. St. Mary Land & Exploration Co. Matritech, Inc.	01/28/93 12/16/92 07/09/92	$ 13.0 million $ 23.1 million $ 5.8 million	Medical equipment Crude petroleum & natural gas Cancer diagnostic products
HANOVER, STERLING & CO., LTD. 88 Pine Street Wall Street Plaza New York, NY 10005-1801	Mister Jay Fashions International, Inc. Blue Chip Computerware, Inc.	02/11/93 08/11/92	$ 2.0 million $ 2.0 million	Women's blouses Microcomputers
INTERSTATE/JOHNSON LANE CORPORATION 2700 NCNB Plaza 101 South Tyron Street Charlotte, NC 28280	Summit Financial Corp.	01/25/90	$ 5.5 million	Bank holding company
INVEMED ASSOCIATES, INC. 375 Park Avenue Suite 2205 New York, NY 10152	Cell Genesys, Inc. American Superconductor Corp.	01/26/93 12/11/91	$ 38.5 million $ 21.3 million	Biotechnology Superconducting wire products
INVESTORS ASSOCIATES, INC. 411 Hackensack Avenue Hackensack, NJ 07601	Chromatics International, Inc.	02/05/93	$ 5.8 million	General business services
J. EDMUND & CO. 1431 Brush Hill Road Milton, MA 02186	The Standish Care Company	02/06/92	$ 3.5 million	Senior housing & health services

LEAD UNDERWRITER & ADDRESS	ISSUER	PUBLIC OFFER DATE	OFFERING AMOUNT	BUSINESS
J.C. BRADFORD & CO. 330 Commerce Street Nashville, TM 37201	Rocky Shoes & Boots, Inc. Res-Care, Inc. Longhorn Steaks, Inc. Litchfield Financial, Inc. Meadowbrook Rehabilitation Group, Inc. Sholodge, Inc. Medaphis, Corp. American Healthcorp, Inc. ReLife, Inc. Community Health Systems, Inc.	02/03/93 12/15/92 03/31/92 02/25/92 02/13/92 02/12/92 10/09/91 08/13/91 07/23/91 03/07/91	$ 16.5 million $ 15.0 million $ 28.8 million $ 8.5 million $ 20.2 million $ 26.3 million $ 27.6 million $ 20.0 million $ 13.8 million $ 33.6 million	Men's footwear Support services for the disabled Steak restaurants Mortgage financing Rehabilitation services Inn franchisor Hospital & Physician management Diabetes treatment Rehab services for disabled Acute care hospitals
J.E. SHEEHAN & COMPANY, INC. 711 Fifth Avenue New York, NY 10022	Hoenig Group, Inc.	10/30/91	$ 15.0 million	Stock brokerage
J. GREGORY & COMPANY, INC. 833 Northern Boulevard Great Neck, NY 11021	New Day Beverage, Inc. ComCentral, Corp.	01/29/93 12/19/91	$ 5.0 million $ 3.0 million	Distilled liquors Telecommunications
J.P. MORGAN SECURITIES, INC. 60 Wall Street New York, NY 10260	Ace, Ltd. National Steel Corp. Riverwood International Corp.	03/24/93 03/23/93 06/17/92	$ 511.5 million $ 140.0 million $ 114.0 million	Liability insurance Flat-rolled steel products Paper & packaging products
J.W. GANT & ASSOCIATES, INC. 7600 East Orchard Road Suite 160 Englewood, CO 80111	Vital Living Products, Inc. Sheffield Industries, Inc. Beverly Hills Fan Co. Celebrity Resorts, Inc.	03/25/92 08/12/91 05/31/91 08/14/90	$ 4.3 million $ 4.0 million $ 3.0 million $ 3.5 million	Bottled drinking water Ladies hosiery Ceiling fans Sports resort
J.W. CHARLES SECURITIES, INC. 980 North Federal Highway Suite 210 Boca Raton, FL 33432	RailAmerica, Inc. Peachtree FiberOptics, Inc. All American Semiconductor, Inc. Suprema Specialties, Inc.	11/09/92 10/08/92 06/18/92 04/25/91	$ 3.9 million $ 3.5 million $ 3.5 million $ 3.5 million	Transportation holding company Plastic optical fiber Electronic components distributor Gourmet cheeses
JANNEY MONTGOMERY SCOTT, INC. 1601 Market Street Philadelphia, PA 19103	United American Healthcare Corp.	04/23/91	$ 11.9 million	Services to health plans

LEAD UNDERWRITER & ADDRESS	ISSUER	PUBLIC OFFER DATE	OFFERING AMOUNT	BUSINESS
JERSEY SECURITIES CORP. 28 West Grand Avenue Montvale, NJ 07645	Peerless Productions Ltd., Inc.	03/30/90	$ 2.1 million	Theatrical film producers
JOHN G. KINNARD & CO., INC. 1700 Northstar West Minneapolis, MN 55402	Title Wave Stores, Inc. Rottlund Co., Inc. Winthrop Resources Corp. AVECOR Cardiovascular, Inc. Serving Software, Inc. Olympic Financial Ltd. AudioScience, Inc. Computer Petroleum Corp. Education Alternatives, Inc. Ringer Corp.	03/17/93 10/29/92 06/24/92 03/26/92 03/18/92 01/30/92 06/11/91 05/21/91 04/25/91 09/19/90	$ 5.2 million $ 6.1 million $ 5.4 million $ 6.9 million $ 4.6 million $ 4.8 million $ 5.2 million $ 3.0 million $ 6.0 million $ 4.9 million	Home entertainment software Residential construction Computer leasing services Heart/lung devices Software for medical field Automobile installment loans High-tech hearing aids Information/customized news services Management/consulting service Environmental garden products
JOSEPHTHAL LYON & ROSS, INC. 6 East 43rd Street New York, NY 10017	SatCon Technology Corp. First Pacific Networks, Inc. Tapistron International, Inc. Sciclone Pharmaceuticals, Inc. MedSonic, Inc. Perfumania, Inc. Conceptronic, Inc. Embrex, Inc. AG Services of America, Inc.	11/12/92 07/22/92 06/24/92 03/17/92 01/23/92 12/19/91 12/04/91 11/07/91 08/01/91	$ 7.5 million $ 36.0 million $ 15.2 million $ 21.8 million $ 10.4 million $ 12.8 million $ 5.7 million $ 18.7 million $ 8.3 million	Machinery control systems Telecommunications technology Textile machinery Pharmaceuticals Scientific untrasonic products Perfume distributor Equipment to repair circuit boards Poultry bio-science/engineering products Crop inputs
KASHNER DAVIDSON SECURITIES CORP. 77 South Palm Avenue Sarasota, FL 34236	Lasersight, Inc. Omega Health Systems, Inc.	11/13/91 08/09/90	$ 4.5 million $ 2.3 million	Optical materials Eye care/surgery centers
KEEFE, BRUYETTE & WOODS, INC. Two World Trade Center - Suite 8566 New York, NY 10048	American Federal FSB Republic Bancorp Civic Bancorp	03/12/93 04/14/92 01/23/90	$ 54.3 million $ 10.0 million $ 7.0 million	Savings and loan association Commercial bank Commercial bank

LEAD UNDERWRITER & ADDRESS	ISSUER	PUBLIC OFFER DATE	OFFERING AMOUNT	BUSINESS
KEMPER SECURITIES, INC. 77 West Wacker Drive Chicago, IL 60601	Lifequest Medical, Inc. Cholestech Corp. M-Wave, Inc. Biosys RehabCare Corp.	08/20/92 06/26/92 03/31/92 03/09/92 06/26/91	$ 15.8 million $ 10.0 million $ 7.0 million $ 31.2 million $ 32.5 million	Vascular access devices Biomedical equipment Microwave components Natural bioinsecticides Outpatient care services
KENNEDY, MATHEWS, LANDIS, HEALY & PECORA, INC. 3636 IDS Center Minneapolis, MN 55402	Shuffle Master, Inc. Modami Services, Inc. MediVators, Inc. Ballistivet, Inc.	12/08/92 08/12/92 09/25/91 04/30/91	$ 6.4 million $ 5.0 million $ 5.3 million $ 6.2 million	Card shuffling systems Frozen yogurt products Disinfectors Ballistic implant system

LEAD UNDERWRITER & ADDRESS	ISSUER	PUBLIC OFFER DATE	OFFERING AMOUNT	BUSINESS
KIDDER PEABODY & CO., INC. 10 Hanover Square New York, NY 10005	Ethan Allen Interiors, Inc.	03/16/93	$ 132.4 million	Retail furniture stores
	Vision-Sciences, Inc.	12/15/92	$ 23.0 million	Endoscopic products
	Plaza Home Mortgage Corp.	10/02/92	$ 32.5 million	Mortgage financing
	Petroleum Heat and Power Co., Inc.	07/29/92	$ 44.0 million	Home heating oil
	Automotive Industries Holding, Inc.	05/01/92	$ 70.0 million	Automobile interior trim parts
	Kendall Square Research, Corp.	03/27/92	$ 44.0 million	Computer systems design
	Coastal Banc Savings Association	03/25/92	$ 28.1 million	Savings & loan association
	Dames & Moore, Inc.	03/05/92	$ 115.0 million	Environmental engineering consultant
	Opta Food Ingredients, Inc.	03/04/92	$ 20.4 million	Food ingredients
	Vitalink Pharmacy Services	03/03/92	$ 40.8 million	Pharmacy services
	Spectranetics Co.	01/21/92	$ 33.8 million	Laser/fiberoptic catheters
	CompUSA, Inc.	12/17/91	$ 72.7 million	Computer super-stores
	SLM International, Inc.	11/26/91	$ 36.8 million	Toys/sporting goods
	Atlantic Tele-Network, Inc.	11/14/91	$ 83.6 million	Telephone service
	National Rehabilitation Centers	11/06/91	$ 15.6 million	Musculoskeletal rehabs
	GranCare	10/31/91	$ 27.7 million	Long-term health care
	The Presley Companies	10/10/91	$ 56.0 million	Residential development
	Ezcorp, Inc.	08/27/91	$ 24.4 million	Pawn shops
	Vertex Pharmaceuticals, Inc.	07/24/91	$ 22.5 million	Pharmaceuticals
	Revell Monogram, Inc.	07/10/91	$ 17.1 million	Toy model kits
	OESI Power Corp.	05/10/91	$ 31.5 million	Geothermal power
	The Caldor Corp.	04/24/91	$ 86.5 million	Discount stores
	Citation Insurance Group	03/21/91	$ 16.6 million	Workers compensation insurance
	Environmental Elements Corp.	07/13/90	$ 40.8 million	Air pollution control systems
	Horsehead Resources Development Co.	06/29/90	$ 47.1 million	Inorganic waste recycling
	Delphi Financial Group, Inc.	03/13/90	$ 30.5 million	Insurance holding company
	Cii Financial, Inc.	03/07/90	$ 23.0 million	Workers compensation insurance
LADENBURG, THALMANN & CO., INC. 540 Madison Avenue New York, NY 10022	Nathan's Famous, Inc.	02/26/93	$ 13.5 million	Fast food restaurants
	American Insurance Group, Inc.	09/22/92	$ 16.0 million	Insurance holding company
	Value-Added Communications, Inc.	08/12/92	$ 14.6 million	Automated call processing services
	American Medical Response, Inc.	05/05/92	$ 25.5 million	Ambulance services
	All For A Dollar, Inc.	05/05/92	$ 18.0 million	Discount stores
	Jimbo's Jumbos, Inc.	12/06/91	$ 9.0 million	Peanuts
	Bally Gaming International, Inc.	11/11/91	$ 36.0 million	Game machines
	Rag Shops, Inc.	06/05/91	$ 9.4 million	Fabrics and crafts

LEAD UNDERWRITER & ADDRESS	ISSUER	PUBLIC OFFER DATE	OFFERING AMOUNT	BUSINESS
LAIDLAW EQUITIES, INC. 275 Madison Avenue - 12th Floor New York, NY 10016	Hi Tech Pharmacal Co., Inc. 3CI Complete Compliance Corp. Defense Software & Systems, Inc. Valley Systems, Inc.	08/03/92 04/14/92 02/11/92 06/11/91	$ 6.0 million $ 7.2 million $ 6.0 million $ 5.0 million	Pharmaceuticals Medical waste management Software services & products Industrial cleaning services
LAZARD FRERES & CO. One Rockefeller Plaza New York, NY 10020	Minerals Technologies, Inc. Smart & Final, Inc.	10/23/92 07/30/91	$ 166.4 million $ 95.0 million	Mineral based products Food services warehouse
LEGG MASON WOOD WALKER, INC. 111 South Calvert Street Baltimore, MD 21202	Sterling Bancshares, Inc. Hampshire Group Ltd.	10/22/92 06/17/92	$ 10.8 million $ 9.5 million	Bank holding company Clothing manufacturer

223

LEAD UNDERWRITER & ADDRESS	ISSUER	PUBLIC OFFER DATE	OFFERING AMOUNT	BUSINESS
LEHMAN BROS. PUERTO RICO, INC. Banco De Ponce Building Ground Level 268 Munoz Rivera Avenue Hato Rey, PR 00918	Orchard Supply Hardware Stores Corp.	03/30/93	$ 53.2 million	Hardware superstores
	Eastern American Natural Gas Trust	03/08/93	$ 110.7 million	Oil & gas company
	Tencor Instruments	03/08/93	$ 16.7 million	Inspection systems
	S3, Inc.	03/05/93	$ 30.0 million	Computer products
	Tecnomatix Technologies, Ltd.	02/25/93	$ 25.2 million	Computer software
	Preferred Income Management Fund	02/11/93	$ 120.0 million	Closed-ended fund
	Catalytica, Inc.	02/08/93	$ 16.8 million	Industrial process catalysts
	Proxima Corp.	02/03/93	$ 26.0 million	Liquid crystal displays for PCs
	Purolator Products Co.	12/14/92	$ 120.0 million	Filtration products
	HS Resources, Inc.	11/23/92	$ 39.9 million	Crude petroleum & natural gas
	Ligand Pharmaceuticals, Inc.	11/18/92	$ 41.3 million	Pharmaceuticals
	Santa Fe Energy Trust	11/12/92	$ 114.5 million	Special financing vehicle
	CMAC Investment Corp.	10/30/92	$ 139.5 million	Mortgage insurance
	Enterprise Oil plc	10/16/92	$ 135.0 million	Oil & gas exploration
	4th Dimension Software Ltd.	10/06/92	$ 24.6 million	Computer software
	USX-Delhi Group	09/25/92	$ 115.2 million	Natural gas producer
	Paco Pharmaceutical Services, Inc.	08/19/92	$ 35.0 million	Pharmaceutical packaging services
	Computervision Corp.	08/14/92	$ 240.0 million	CAD/CAM software
	Enron Liquids Pipeline L.P.	07/30/92	$ 130.0 million	Pipeline systems
	Ampex, Inc.	07/17/92	$ 14.4 million	Magnetic recording systems
	Allied Capital Commercial Corp.	06/30/92	$ 165.0 million	Real estate investment trust
	DR Horton, Inc.	06/05/92	$ 44.2 million	Single-family homes
	NetFRAME Systems, Inc.	06/04/92	$ 27.0 million	LAN equipment
	Quantum Restaurant Group, Inc.	06/03/92	$ 21.5 million	Restaurant chains
	Rival Co.	06/02/92	$ 23.1 million	Household appliances
	Hall-Mark Electronics Corp.	05/22/92	$ 35.2 million	Electronic components
	Holson Burnes Group, Inc.	05/20/92	$ 30.8 million	Photo albums
	Lida, Inc.	05/06/92	$ 23.0 million	Pile fabrics & knits
	Teledata Communication, Ltd.	04/16/92	$ 30.3 million	Telephone services
	First Data Corp.	04/09/92	$ 770.0 million	Information processing services
	BISYS Group, Inc.	03/19/92	$ 48.4 million	Data processing services
	Infinity Broadcasting Corp.	01/30/92	$ 107.2 million	Radio broadcasting
	Noel Group, Inc.	01/29/92	$ 88.0 million	Diverse holding company
	Sphinx Pharmaceuticals Corp.	01/23/92	$ 75.0 million	Cell membrane lipids

224

LEAD UNDERWRITER & ADDRESS	ISSUER	PUBLIC OFFER DATE	OFFERING AMOUNT	BUSINESS
LEHMAN BROS. PUERTO RICO, INC. (continued)	Pharmaceutical Marketing Services, Inc.	12/23/91	$ 52.5 million	Pharmaceutical distribution
	Lakehead Pipe Line Partners, LP	12/19/91	$ 373.9 million	Crude oil/natural gas
	Qualcomm, Inc.	12/13/91	$ 51.2 million	Space satellite communication equipment
	Century Cellular, Corp.	12/03/91	$ 40.8 million	Cellular phone system
	Agricultural Minerals, L.P.	11/26/91	$ 164.2 million	Fertilizers
	Seligman Quality Municipal Fund, Inc.	11/22/91	$ 60.0 million	Closed-ended fund
	Physician Computer Network, Inc.	11/21/91	$ 36.0 million	Medical programming for physicians
	Guaranty National Corp.	11/13/91	$ 72.5 million	Non-standard auto insurance
	Amphenol, Corp.	11/08/91	$ 127.7 million	Fiber optic connectors
	Total	10/24/91	$ 233.8 million	International oil and gas
	Lannet Data Communications, Ltd.	10/17/91	$ 36.4 million	Network hubs
	RP Scherer Corp.	10/11/91	$ 140.4 million	Drug delivery
	Sepracor, Inc.	09/20/91	$ 40.0 million	Pharmaceutical compounds
	Monro Muffler Brake, Inc.	07/29/91	$ 26.4 million	Undercar services
	Thermo Electron Technologies	07/24/91	$ 18.0 million	Optics and lasers R & D
	Idexx Corp.	06/21/91	$ 24.0 million	Biotech detection systems
	Preferred Income Fund	01/24/91	$ 100.5 million	Closed-ended fund
	Orthopedic Services, Inc.	07/10/90	$ 48.0 million	Artificial limbs
	Pool Energy Services Co.	04/17/90	$ 82.0 million	Oil & gas well maintenance
	Alliance New Europe Fund, Inc.	03/26/90	$ 189.0 million	Closed-ended fund
	Pride Companies, L.P.	03/23/90	$ 72.2 million	Petroleum refinery
A.M. LEVINE & CO., INC. 17 Battery Place New York, NY 10004	International Airline Support Group, Inc.	04/02/90	$ 2.4 million	Aircraft parts
LOVETT UNDERWOOD NEUHAUS & WEBB, INC. 909 Fannin Street Houston, TX 77010	Benchmark Electronics, Inc.	06/28/90	$ 9.6 million	Electronics
M.H. MEYERSON & CO., INC. 30 Montgomery Street Jersey City, NJ 07302	Globalink, Inc.	03/03/93	$ 5.0 million	Language translation through software
	Deprenyl USA, Inc.	01/17/92	$ 8.6 million	Photo-dynamic therapies
	Deprenyl Animal Health, Inc.	03/14/91	$ 3.6 million	Animal pharmaceuticals
	I-flow Corp.	02/01/90	$ 2.6 million	Drug infusion systems

225

LEAD UNDERWRITER & ADDRESS	ISSUER	PUBLIC OFFER DATE	OFFERING AMOUNT	BUSINESS
MALONE & ASSOCIATES, INC. 1401 17th Street - Suite 1550 Denver, CO 80202	Winners Circle, Inc. California Jamar, Inc.	07/10/90 04/26/90	$ 3.9 million $ 3.3 million	Clothing Laser systems
MANCHESTER RHONE SECURITIES CORP. 61 Broadway - Suite 2700 New York, NY 10006	First Cash, Inc.	04/25/91	$ 4.5 million	Pawn shops
MARCHE SECURITIES, INC. 512 Nicollet Mall - Suite 400 Minneapolis, MN 55402	Standard Platforms Holdings, plc.	09/28/90	$ 1.0 million	Data retrieval for processing
MATHEWS, HOLMQUIST & ASSOCIATES, INC. 100 N. 6th Street - Suite 306C Minneapolis, MN 55403	Celox Corp.	03/09/92	$ 4.6 million	Cell culture mediums
McDONALD & COMPANY SECURITIES, INC. 2100 Society Building Cleveland, OH 44114	Shoe Carnival, Inc.	03/16/93	$ 27.3 million	Specialty shoe stores

226

LEAD UNDERWRITER & ADDRESS	ISSUER	PUBLIC OFFER DATE	OFFERING AMOUNT	BUSINESS
MERRILL LYNCH, PIERCE, FENDER & SMITH, INC.	Bankers Life Holding Co.	03/25/93	$ 374.0 million	Health insurance
World Financial Center - Bldg. D	Citizens Corp.	03/19/93	$ 150.0 million	Property & casualty insurance
250 Vesey Street	Delaware Group, Inc.	03/18/93	$ 195.0 million	Investment trust
New York, NY 10281	Nuveen MA Premium Income Muni. Fund, Inc.	03/18/93	$ 62.3 million	Closed-ended fund
	Nuveen MD Premium Income Muni. Fund, Inc.	03/18/93	$ 78.8 million	Closed-ended fund
	Nuveen VA Premium Income Muni. Fund, Inc.	03/18/93	$ 78.0 million	Closed-ended fund
	Nuveen WA Premium Income Muni. Fund, Inc.	03/18/93	$ 31.5 million	Closed-ended fund
	Castle & Cooke Homes, Inc.	03/04/93	$ 81.0 million	Residential development
	Manufactured Home Communities, Inc.	02/24/93	$ 113.3 million	Real estate investment fund
	BlackRock Investment Qual. Muni. Trust, Inc.	02/19/93	$ 232.5 million	Closed-ended fund
	First USA, Inc.	02/17/93	$ 109.0 million	Credit cards
	Carr Realty Corp.	02/08/93	$ 149.6 million	Real estate investment trust
	Nine West Group, Inc.	02/02/93	$ 140.0 million	Women's shoes
	American Re Corp.	01/28/93	$ 287.7 million	Reinsurance services
	Wellpoint Health Networks, Inc.	01/27/93	$ 380.8 million	Health care plans
	Paragon Trade Brands, Inc.	01/26/93	$ 152.0 million	Paper diapers
	Duff & Phelps Utility & Corp. Bond Trust, Inc.	01/21/93	$ 360.0 million	Closed-ended fund
	Borg-Warner Securities Corp.	01/19/93	$ 61.1 million	Security services

227

LEAD UNDERWRITER & ADDRESS	ISSUER	PUBLIC OFFER DATE	OFFERING AMOUNT	BUSINESS
MERRILL LYNCH, PIERCE, FENDER & SMITH, INC. (continued)	Health Management Systems, Inc.	12/17/92	$ 30.0 million	Data processing services
	Snapple Beverage Corp.	12/14/92	$ 80.0 million	Iced teas & soft drinks
	Maybelline, Inc.	12/10/92	$ 87.4 million	Cosmetics company
	Hospitality Franchise Systems, Inc.	12/09/92	$ 76.8 million	Hotel franchisor
	Wellsford Residential Property Trust	11/19/92	$ 87.0 million	Real estate investment trust
	F&M Distributors, Inc.	09/24/92	$ 52.5 million	Discount drugstore chain
	Sunbeam-Oster Co., Inc.	08/18/92	$ 200.0 million	Household appliances
	Tadiran Ltd.	08/05/92	$ 81.2 million	Telecommunications equipment
	Pyxis Corp.	07/22/92	$ 56.0 million	Medical distribution systems
	North American Mortgage Co.	07/08/92	$ 63.3 million	Mortgage banking
	Bradlees, Inc.	07/01/92	$ 143.2 million	Discount department store chain
	Hafslund Nycomed A.S.	06/23/92	$ 74.7 million	Medical imaging products
	Banco Comercial Portugues S.A.	06/11/92	$ 80.3 million	Foreign commercial bank
	Franklin Quest Co.	06/02/92	$ 62.0 million	Productivity seminars
	First USA, Inc.	05/27/92	$ 38.0 million	Credit card holding company
	Waste Management International plc	04/06/92	$ 307.1 million	Waste management services
	Duff & Phelps Corp.	03/12/92	$ 54.0 million	Financial advisory services
	DSG International Limited	03/05/92	$ 48.5 million	Disposable diapers
	Callaway Golf Co.	02/27/92	$ 52.0 million	Golf clubs
	Living Centers of America, Inc.	02/13/92	$ 112.8 million	Health care centers
	CytoRad, Inc.	02/13/92	$ 35.0 million	Prostate cancer treatments
	ElectroCom Automation, Inc.	01/30/92	$ 147.2 million	Document processing systems
	National Re Holdings Corp.	01/29/92	$ 165.6 million	Insurance carrier
	Protein Design Labs, Inc.	01/28/92	$ 52.5 million	Antibody drugs
	Fleet Call, Inc.	01/27/92	$ 90.0 million	Specialized mobile radio systems

LEAD UNDERWRITER & ADDRESS	ISSUER	PUBLIC OFFER DATE	OFFERING AMOUNT	BUSINESS
MERRILL LYNCH, PIERCE, FENDER & SMITH, INC. (continued)	Healthtrust, Inc. - The Hospital Co.	12/12/91	$ 511.0 million	Hospitals
	Orbital Engine Corp., Ltd.	12/04/91	$ 105.1 million	Engineering technology
	Kimco Realty, Corp.	11/22/91	$ 128.0 million	REIT
	The Stop & Shop Companies, Inc.	11/22/91	$ 170.0 million	Retail stores
	MuniYield Fund, Inc.	11/21/91	$ 450.0 million	Closed-ended fund
	CENFED Financial Corp.	10/25/91	$ 8.8 million	Thrift holding company
	Health Care & Retirement, Corp.	10/17/91	$ 263.1 million	Long-term health care
	Maxum Health Corp.	09/19/91	$ 18.8 million	Medical diagnostic imaging services
	The Jundt Growth Fund, Inc.	08/23/91	$ 435.0 million	Closed-ended fund
	SyStemix, Inc.	08/06/91	$ 36.0 million	Cellular products
	The Singer Co. N.V.	08/01/91	$ 163.8 million	Consumer sewing machines
	Telecom Corp. of New Zealand	07/16/91	$ 237.1 million	Telecommunications services
	Marvel Entertainment Group, Inc.	07/15/91	$ 69.3 million	Comic books
	Kaiser Aluminum Corp.	07/11/91	$ 81.2 million	Aluminum products
	International Specialty Products, Inc.	06/24/91	$ 217.0 million	Chemical products
	Vigoro Group	05/20/91	$ 92.8 million	Nitrogen based fertilizer
	Ann Taylor Stores, Inc.	05/16/91	$ 127.4 million	Retail women's apparel stores
	Jones Apparel Group, Inc.	05/15/91	$ 63.0 million	Women's sportswear
	Duracell International, Inc.	05/01/91	$ 365.6 million	Alkaline batteries
	Regeneron Pharmaceuticals, Inc.	04/02/91	$ 99.0 million	Pharmaceuticals
	Medical Marketing Group, Inc.	03/26/91	$ 40.0 million	Marketing services
	Pamida Holdings, Inc.	09/18/90	$ 7.5 million	Retailer holding company
	Foundation Health Corp.	07/11/90	$ 41.3 million	Managed health care services
	The Thai Capital Fund, Inc.	05/22/90	$ 43.2 million	Closed-ended fund
	The Europe Fund, Inc.	04/26/90	$ 45.0 million	Closed-ended fund
	Geneva Steel	03/27/90	$ 62.0 million	Steel sheets
	G.T. Greater Europe Fund	03/22/90	$ 240.0 million	Closed-ended fund
	Sequola Systems	03/06/90	$ 18.1 million	Computer systems
	Intera Information Technologies Corp.	02/16/90	$ 16.6 million	Services to petroleum industry
	Taurus MuniCalifornia Holdings, Inc.	01/25/90	$ 51.0 million	Closed-ended fund
	Taurus MuniNew York Holdings, Inc.	01/25/90	$ 66.0 million	Closed-ended fund
	Luxottia Group, S.p.A.	01/23/90	$ 68.4 million	Eyeglass frames
	MAF Bancorp, Inc.	01/12/90	$ 7.6 million	Bank holding company

LEAD UNDERWRITER & ADDRESS	ISSUER	PUBLIC OFFER DATE	OFFERING AMOUNT	BUSINESS
MILLER, JOHNSON & KUEHN, INC. 1660 S. Highway 100 - Suite 228 Minneapolis, MN 55416	Recovery Engineering, Inc.	03/04/93	$ 4.0 million	Purification products
	Funco, Inc.	08/12/92	$ 5.0 million	Used Nintendo games
	Insignia System, Inc.	06/25/91	$ 5.1 million	Signs for retail merchants
	Selsmed Instruments, Inc.	03/20/91	$ 4.1 million	Cardiology instruments
	Everest Medical Corp.	12/06/90	$ 3.8 million	Electrosurgical devices
MONTGOMERY SECURITIES 600 Montgomery Street San Francisco, CA 94111	Inco Homes Corp.	03/31/93	$ 26.0 million	Residential construction
	Paralian Computer, Inc.	03/30/93	$ 27.0 million	Network servers & related software
	Southern Energy Homes, Inc.	03/12/93	$ 27.0 million	Manufactured homes
	Community Health Computing Corp.	03/09/93	$ 20.0 million	Info. systems for hospitals
	Resound Corp.	03/04/93	$ 21.3 million	Hearing devices
	Universal Electronics, Inc.	02/12/93	$ 31.2 million	Safety & security equipment
	CoCensys, Inc.	01/29/93	$ 22.6 million	Pharmaceuticals
	Creative Biomolecules, Inc.	12/17/92	$ 21.0 million	Pharmaceuticals
	President Riverboat Casinos, Inc.	12/11/92	$ 83.3 million	Riverboat casinos
	Micro Warehouse, Inc.	12/09/92	$ 51.3 million	Software direct marketer
	Miles Homes, Inc.	12/03/92	$ 22.5 million	Prefabricated buildings
	Cortech, Inc.	11/24/92	$ 32.0 million	Bio-pharmaceutical company
	Media Vision, Inc.	11/11/92	$ 45.0 million	Wholesale dental supplies
	Taco Cabana, Inc.	10/16/92	$ 36.5 million	Mexican patio cafes
	Cheesecake Factory, Inc.	09/17/92	$ 46.7 million	Casual restaurants
	StrataCom	07/21/92	$ 17.5 million	Telecommunication systems
	Eagle Hardware & Garden, Inc.	07/15/92	$ 42.0 million	Home improvement centers
	Micro Touch Systems, Inc.	06/30/92	$ 18.2 million	Touch screen computer systems
	Cardiovascular Imaging Systems, Inc.	05/18/92	$ 10.5 million	Imaging catheters
	Supermac Technology, Inc.	05/15/92	$ 18.0 million	Color graphic systems
	Valence Technology	05/07/92	$ 28.8 million	Rechargeable batteries
	Video Telecom Corp.	04/07/92	$ 27.6 million	Multimedia conference systems
	Damark International, Inc.	03/25/92	$ 33.9 million	Discounted merchandise
	Schuler Homes, Inc.	03/20/92	$ 69.8 million	Residential homes
	Lone Star Steakhouse & Saloon, Inc.	03/12/92	$ 18.9 million	Steak retaurants
	Day Runner, Inc.	03/11/92	$ 23.6 million	Diaries & organizers
	Univax Biologics, Inc.	02/04/92	$ 48.0 million	Biological products
	Allied Healthcare Products, Inc.	01/13/92	$ 16.0 million	Medical gases & respirator equipment

LEAD UNDERWRITER & ADDRESS	ISSUER	PUBLIC OFFER DATE	OFFERING AMOUNT	BUSINESS
MONTGOMERY SECURITIES (continued)	TRM Copy Centers	12/18/91	$ 18.3 million	Copy centers
	Genta, Inc.	12/17/91	$ 25.0 million	Pharmaceuticals
	Sam & Libby, Inc.	12/04/91	$ 39.9 million	Women's/children's footwear
	Centigram Communications Corp.	10/10/91	$ 19.4 million	Audio information systems
	Idec Pharmaceuticals Corp.	09/16/91	$ 45.0 million	Pharmaceuticals
	Vans, Inc.	08/22/91	$ 57.4 million	Casual shoes
	Video Lottery Technologies, Inc.	07/24/91	$ 39.9 million	Video lottery terminals
	Sun Television & Appliances, Inc.	07/17/91	$ 10.0 million	Retail appliance stores
	Bertucci's	06/28/91	$ 24.3 million	Restaurant chain
	Quarterdeck Office Systems	06/11/91	$ 34.0 million	Software products
	Cambridge Neuroscience Research, Inc.	06/06/91	$ 24.0 million	Pharmaceuticals
	Proteon, Inc.	06/04/91	$ 31.0 million	Computer network links
	Chipcom Corp.	05/03/91	$ 18.6 million	Computer network products
	Applied Immune Sciences, Inc.	05/02/91	$ 31.2 million	Pharmaceuticals
	Leslie's Poolmart	04/19/91	$ 27.8 million	Swimming pools/supplies
MORGAN, KEEGAN & CO., INC. Morgan Keegen Tower 50 Front Street Memphis, TN 38103	Varsity Spirit Corp.	01/28/92	$ 14.6 million	School apparel & accessories
	Ambar	12/12/91	$ 9.2 million	Environmental services
MORGAN STANLEY & CO., INC. 1251 Avenue of the Americas New York, NY 10020	Avid Technology, Inc.	03/11/93	$ 56.0 million	Video & audio editing systems
	Intuit, Inc.	03/11/93	$ 30.0 million	Software products
	Cyberonics, Inc.	02/10/93	$ 24.0 million	Medical equipment
	Gupta Corp.	02/04/93	$ 39.5 million	Computer software
	Dr. Pepper/Seven-Up Cos., Inc.	01/26/93	$ 247.8 million	Soft drink syrups
	Rhone-Poulenic, S.A.	01/26/93	$ 93.9 million	Chemicals & cosmetics
	General Nutrition Cos.	01/21/93	$ 56.8 million	Sports nutrition products

231

LEAD UNDERWRITER & ADDRESS	ISSUER	PUBLIC OFFER DATE	OFFERING AMOUNT	BUSINESS
MORGAN STANLEY & CO., INC. (continued)	Compuware Corp.	12/15/92	$ 153.3 million	Software products
	Taubman Centers, Inc.	11/20/92	$ 250.8 million	Real estate investment trust
	Corel Corp.	10/20/92	$ 29.5 million	Computer software
	Fritz Cos., Inc.	10/16/92	$ 38.3 million	Transportation logistics
	Tommy Hilfiger Corp.	09/22/92	$ 46.5 million	Men's sportswear
	American Residential Holding Corp.	08/14/92	$ 39.0 million	Mortgage holding company
	Wellcome plc	07/27/92	$ 1067.5 million	Pharmaceuticals
	British Bio-Technology Group plc	07/01/92	$ 15.2 million	Pharmaceuticals
	Authentic Fitness Corp.	06/25/92	$ 33.6 million	Swimwear & accessories
	Arrow International, Inc.	06/09/92	$ 36.0 million	Surgical supplies
	Network Computing Devices, Inc.	06/04/92	$ 24.0 million	Computer terminals
	Alcatel Alsthom	05/19/92	$ 236.3 million	Telecommunications equpiment
	Kohl's Corp.	05/18/92	$ 108.4 million	Department stores
	Natural Wonders	05/13/92	$ 18.8 million	Nature & science retailer
	Learning Co.	04/28/92	$ 22.0 million	Software for children
	Empresas ICA Sociedad Controlodora S.A. C.V.	04/08/92	$ 142.8 million	Home & industrial construction
	Sybron Chemical Industries, Inc.	03/31/92	$ 35.7 million	Orthodontic & dental products
	Xircom, Inc.	03/30/92	$ 40.6 million	Computer network products
	Cotec Industries, Inc.	03/25/92	$ 462.0 million	Auto & aerospace products
	Walker Interactive Systems, Inc.	03/25/92	$ 31.5 million	Computer software
	Burlington Industries Equity, Inc.	03/19/92	$ 469.4 million	Textile products
	Curaflex Health Services, Inc.	03/19/92	$ 39.0 million	Home infussion therapy
	Telios Pharmaceuticals, Inc.	03/19/92	$ 16.0 million	Pharmaceuticals
	El Paso Natural Gas Co.	03/12/92	$ 76.0 million	Natural gas company
	American Income Holding, Inc.	03/06/92	$ 69.2 million	Insurance holding company
	Foodmaker, Inc.	03/04/92	$ 180.0 million	Fast food restaurants
	Synopsys, Inc.	02/26/92	$ 28.8 million	Automation software
	Buttrey Food & Drug Stores Co.	02/13/92	$ 63.0 million	Food & drugs
	Amylin Pharmaceuticals, Inc.	01/17/92	$ 44.8 million	Hormonal drugs

LEAD UNDERWRITER & ADDRESS	ISSUER	PUBLIC OFFER DATE	OFFERING AMOUNT	BUSINESS
MORGAN STANLEY & CO., INC. (continued)	Perrigo, Inc.	12/16/91	$ 128.0 million	Pharmaceutical preparations
	Owens-Illinois, Inc.	12/11/91	$ 528.0 million	Packaging and glass products
	Retix	12/09/91	$ 25.2 million	Network software
	Bachman Information Systems, Inc.	11/26/91	$ 30.0 million	Software
	Joy Technologies, Inc.	11/15/91	$ 122.4 million	Mining equipment
	Morgan Stanley Emerging Markets Funds, Inc.	10/25/91	$ 60.0 million	Closed-ended fund
	The Warnaco Group, Inc.	10/11/91	$ 96.0 million	Men's & Women's apparel
	Treadco, Inc.	09/12/91	$ 40.0 million	Tires
	Mutual Risk Management Ltd.	06/25/91	$ 41.3 million	Risk management/insurance services
	Au Bon Pain, Inc.	06/06/91	$ 22.5 million	Retail bakeries
	Trans Canada Pipelines Ltd.	06/06/91	$ 86.5 million	Natural gas
	Isis Pharmaceuticals, Inc.	05/17/91	$ 25.0 million	Pharmaceuticals
	Medimmune, Inc.	05/08/91	$ 23.1 million	Pharmaceuticals
	Sierra Semiconductor Corp.	04/24/91	$ 32.0 million	Integrated circuits
	Radius, Inc.	08/21/90	$ 30.0 million	Graphics systems
	Xilinx, Inc.	06/12/90	$ 25.0 million	System software
	Curragh Resources, Inc.	05/24/90	$ 25.0 million	Lead & zinc mining/exploration
	Dynasty Classics Corp.	05/03/90	$ 28.5 million	Light fixtures
	Aspect Telecommunications Corp.	05/01/90	$ 29.0 million	Transaction processing systems
	VeriFone, Inc.	03/13/90	$ 52.8 million	Transaction automation systems
	Cisco Systems, Inc.	02/16/90	$ 50.4 million	Networking systems
NATWEST SECURITIES LIMITED 100 Wall Street New York, NY 10005	Chart Industries, Inc.	12/03/92	$ 42.2 million	Industrial equipment
	Regency Health Services, Inc.	06/26/92	$ 16.3 million	Healthcare facilities
NEEDHAM & COMPANY 400 Park Avenue New York, NY 10022	Leasing Solutions, Inc.	03/29/93	$ 5.0 million	Communications equipment
	IEC Electronics Corp.	02/12/93	$ 32.5 million	Customized electronics
	Rainbow Technologies, Inc.	09/12/91	$ 14.0 million	Software
	Meca Software, Inc.	07/19/90	$ 17.5 million	Software products
NEIDIGER, TUCKER, BRUNER, INC. 1675 Larimer #300 Denver, CO 80202	Internet Communications, Inc.	12/13/91	$ 2.6 million	Data communications equipment

233

LEAD UNDERWRITER & ADDRESS	ISSUER	PUBLIC OFFER DATE	OFFERING AMOUNT	BUSINESS
NOBLE INVESTMENT CO. OF PALM BEACH 1801 Clint Moore Rd. - Suite 110 Boca Raton, FL 33487	EV Environmental, Inc. Clucker's Wood Roasted Chicken, Inc. Heart Labs of America, Inc. Austin's International, Inc. Billy Blues Food Corp. Capitol Multimedia, Inc. Ocean Optique Distributors, Inc.	02/16/93 11/10/92 09/25/92 07/29/92 05/15/92 03/31/92 09/24/91	$ 3.5 million $ 3.9 million $ 5.1 million $ 4.9 million $ 5.0 million $ 4.6 million $ 5.125 million	Environmental testing services Restaurants Mobile cardiac services for hospitals Texas-style restaurants Texas-style restaurants Video & audio production Eyeglass frames
NOMURA SECURITIES INT'L., INC. 2 World Financial Center Building B New York, NY 10281-1198	Standard Management Corp. Compania Cervecerias Unidas S.A. Perceptron, Inc. Emerging Mexico Fund, Inc. Jakarta Fund Japan OTC Equity Fund, Inc.	02/02/93 09/23/92 08/20/92 10/02/90 04/10/90 03/14/90	$ 26.0 million $ 50.9 million $ 6.5 million $ 45.0 million $ 42.0 million $ 72.0 million	Insurance company Beverages Laser-based sensor systems Closed-ended fund Closed-ended fund Closed-ended fund
NORCROSS SECURITIES, INC. 645 E. Missouri Avenue - Suite 119 Phoenix, AZ 85012	Sheffield Medical Technologies, Inc. Reconditioned Systems, Inc.	02/11/93 12/18/92	$ 5.2 million $ 2.5 million	Biomedical products Modular workstation components
OAK RIDGE INVESTMENTS, INC. 233 N. Michigan Avenue Suite 1807 Chicago, IL 60601	Aerial Assault, Inc.	12/16/92	$ 4.0 million	Athletic shoes

LEAD UNDERWRITER & ADDRESS	ISSUER	PUBLIC OFFER DATE	OFFERING AMOUNT	BUSINESS
OPPENHEIMER & CO., INC. World Financial Center Oppenheimer Tower New York, NY 10281	Gilat Satelite Networks, Ltd.	03/26/93	$ 21.6 million	Satelite earth stations
	Gilat Satelite Networks, Ltd.	03/26/93	$ 6.0 million	Satelite earth stations
	Molten Metal Technology, Inc.	02/10/93	$ 42.0 million	Engineering services
	Municipal Partners Fund, Inc.	01/22/93	$ 75.0 million	Closed-ended fund
	Emerging Markets Income Fund	10/26/92	$ 46.5 million	Closed-ended fund
	Boomtown	10/23/93	$ 32.5 million	Gambling & betting services
	Banco Latinoamericano de Exportaciones, S.A.	09/24/92	$ 71.5 million	Specialized multinational bank
	Banco Latinoamericano de Exportaciones, S.A.	09/24/92	$ 16.5 million	Specialized multinational bank
	Arbor National Holdings, Inc.	08/07/92	$ 21.0 million	Mortgage holding company
	Kennedy-Wilson, Inc.	08/07/92	$ 26.3 million	Real estate auction company
	China Fund	07/10/92	$ 75.0 million	Closed-ended fund
	Finish Line, Inc.	06/09/92	$ 27.5 million	Athletic apparel retail chain
	Sapiens International Corp.	05/29/92	$ 33.4 million	Business software
	Sapiens International Corp.	05/29/92	$ 8.1 million	Business software
	BAESA	05/28/92	$ 52.8 million	Soft drinks
	Dura Pharmaceuticals, Inc.	02/06/92	$ 25.0 million	Prescription pharmaceuticals
	Ecoscience Corp.	02/05/92	$ 28.6 million	Natural pest control products
	Aames Financial Corp.	12/03/91	$ 13.5 million	Mortgage brokers
	The He-Ro Group, Ltd.	09/19/91	$ 29.9 million	Women's wear
	Lifetime Hoan Corp.	06/05/91	$ 18.6 million	Cutlery & kitchen tools
	Mexico Equity & Income Fund, Inc.	08/14/90	$ 64.8 million	Closed-ended fund
	Mexico Equity & Income Fund, Inc.	08/14/90	$ 7.2 million	Closed-ended fund
	European Warrent Fund, Inc.	07/17/90	$ 44.4 million	Closed-ended fund
	European Warrent Fund, Inc.	07/17/90	$ 27.6 million	Closed-ended fund
	NSC Corp.	06/12/90	$ 20.3 million	Asbestos abatement services
	IG Laboratories	05/02/90	$ 14.1 million	Genetic testing services
	Indonesia Fund, Inc.	03/01/90	$ 30.0 million	Closed-ended fund
	Indonesia Fund, Inc.	03/01/90	$ 30.0 million	Closed-ended fund
OSCAR GRUSS & SON, INCORPORATED 74 Broad Street New York, NY 10004	Magal Security Systems, Ltd.	03/23/93	$ 7.4 million	Computerized security systems

235

LEAD UNDERWRITER & ADDRESS	ISSUER	PUBLIC OFFER DATE	OFFERING AMOUNT	BUSINESS
PAINEWEBBER, INC. 1285 Avenue of the Americas New York, NY 10019	Nuveen FL Premium Income Muni. Fund 2, Inc.	03/18/93	$ 75.0 million	Closed-ended fund
	Nuveen Ins CA Premium Inc. Muni. Fund 2, Inc.	03/18/93	$ 171.0 million	Closed-ended fund
	Nuveen Ins NY Premium Inc. Muni. Fund 2, Inc.	03/18/93	$ 58.5 million	Closed-ended fund
	Nuveen MI Premium Income Muni. Fund 2, Inc.	03/18/93	$ 39.0 million	Closed-ended fund
	Nuveen NJ Premium Income Muni. Fund 2, Inc.	03/18/93	$ 66.0 million	Closed-ended fund
	Nuveen PA Premium Income Muni. Fund 2, Inc.	03/18/93	$ 94.5 million	Closed-ended fund
	Alamo Group, Inc.	03/18/93	$ 20.7 million	Grounds maintenance equipment
	Specialty Paperboard, Inc.	03/10/93	$ 36.7 million	Paper & paperboard products
	Washington Homes, Inc.	02/25/93	$ 27.0 million	Single family homes
	All-American Term Trust, Inc.	02/19/93	$ 180.0 million	Closed-ended fund
	Voyager AZ Muni. Income Fund, Inc.	02/19/93	$ 39.0 million	Closed-ended fund
	Voyager FL Muni. Income Fund, Inc.	02/19/93	$ 31.5 million	Closed-ended fund
	Voyager MN Muni. Income Fund II, Inc.	02/19/93	$ 94.5 million	Closed-ended fund
	Van Kempen Merritt Strategic Sector Muni. Trust	01/22/93	$ 142.5 million	Closed-ended fund

LEAD UNDERWRITER & ADDRESS	ISSUER	PUBLIC OFFER DATE	OFFERING AMOUNT	BUSINESS
PAINEWEBBER, INC. (continued)				
	United Waste Systems, Inc.	12/10/92	$ 16.8 million	Waste management services
	USA Classic, Inc.	11/20/92	$ 35.1 million	Outerwear
	Intelligent Surgical Lasers, Inc.	09/11/92	$ 6.4 million	Lasers for eye surgery
	Cantab Pharmaceuticals plc	06/30/92	$ 15.0 million	Biopharmaceutical R&D
	Financial Federal Corp.	05/28/92	$ 18.0 million	Equipment finance company
	Imperial Credit Industries, Inc.	05/18/92	$ 16.0 million	Mortgage banking
	Neozyme II/Genzyme Corp.	04/28/92	$ 63.0 million	Biotechnology company
	Catalina Marketing, Corp.	03/26/92	$ 36.0 million	Consumer marketing strategy
	Corvas International, Inc.	01/30/92	$ 30.0 million	Therapeutic agents
	Engle Homes, Inc.	01/21/92	$ 26.5 million	Single-family homes
	Tocor II/Centocor, Inc.	01/21/92	$ 70.0 million	Biomedical & genetic research
	Farrel Corp.	01/17/92	$ 14.3 million	Plastic processing equipment
	F & C International	12/13/91	$ 29.0 million	Fragrances
	World Acceptance Corp.	11/26/91	$ 21.0 million	Small loan consumer finance
	Athena Neurosciences, Inc.	11/07/91	$ 46.2 million	Pharmaceuticals
	CellPro, Inc.	09/24/91	$ 33.0 million	Pharmaceuticals
	The Blackstone Municipal Target...Trust	09/20/91	$ 400.0 million	Closed-ended fund
	Foxmeyer Corp.	08/29/91	$ 108.8 million	Drugs & drug proprietaries
	Capital Bancorporation, Inc.	08/08/91	$ 14.9 million	Bank holding company
	Special Devices, Inc.	08/07/91	$ 15.2 million	Aerospace devices
	R-Tek Corp.	07/26/91	$ 7.8 million	Recorded music
	Catherines Stores Corp.	07/24/91	$ 24.0 million	Women's apparel
	Teknekron Communications Systems, Inc.	07/18/91	$ 22.5 million	Software systems
	Micronics Computers, Inc.	07/17/91	$ 18.0 million	Systems circuit boards
	Freuhauf Trailer Corp.	06/28/91	$ 35.2 million	Truck trailers & parts
	Applied Extrusion Technologies, Inc.	06/06/91	$ 21.4 million	Thermoplastic nets
	Icos, Inc.	06/06/91	$ 31.2 million	Pharmaceuticals
	Cherokee, Inc.	06/05/91	$ 14.3 million	Clothing and apparel
	Moorco International, Inc.	06/04/91	$ 72.7 million	Fluid measurement control
	Sport Supply Group, Inc.	04/12/91	$ 23.8 million	Direct mail of sports equipment
	Maverick Tube Corp.	03/19/91	$ 21.6 million	Electric resistance pipe

237

LEAD UNDERWRITER & ADDRESS	ISSUER	PUBLIC OFFER DATE	OFFERING AMOUNT	BUSINESS
PAINEWEBBER, INC. (continued)	Neozyme Corp.	10/26/90	$ 46.0 million	Health care products
	Matrix Service Co.	09/26/90	$ 26.0 million	On-site refinery maintenance
	Arctco, Inc.	06/26/90	$ 35.2 million	Snowmobiles
	France Growth Fund, Inc.	05/10/90	$ 60.0 million	Closed-ended fund
	BE Avionics, Inc.	04/23/90	$ 15.4 million	Audio entertainment systems
	The Blackstone Advantage Term Trust, Inc.	04/20/90	$ 85.0 million	Closed-ended fund
	Advanced Logic Research	04/11/90	$ 39.0 million	Microcomputer systems
	Tetra Technologies	04/03/90	$ 23.5 million	Recycling/water treatment
	Bankers Corp.	03/16/90	$ 24.8 million	Bank holding company
	Tuboscope Corporation	03/13/90	$ 46.8 million	Oil pipeline services
	The Future Germany Fund, Inc.	02/27/90	$ 225.0 million	Closed-ended fund
	Growth Fund of Spain, Inc.	02/14/90	$ 129.6 million	Closed-ended fund
	The New Germany Fund, Inc.	01/24/90	$ 375.0 million	Closed-ended fund
PARADISE VALLEY SECURITIES, INC. 11811 N. Tatum - Suite 4040 Phoenix, AZ 85028	Reno Air, Inc.	05/28/92	$ 6.0 million	Regional airline
PARAGON CAPITAL CORP. 120 Wall Street - 28th Floor New York, NY 10005	Zams, Inc.	05/14/92	$ 3.8 million	Paper & party goods
	Natural Earth Technologies, Inc.	03/26/92	$ 5.0 million	Natural lawn & garden products
	Megacards, Inc.	10/10/91	$ 4.1 million	Sports cards
	Club-Theatre Network, Inc.	05/15/90	$ 6.5 million	Projection TV technology
PARKER/HUNTER, INC. 600 Grant Street - Suite 4000 Pittsburgh, PA 15219	Medrad Inc.	07/16/92	$ 12.0 million	Medical imaging products
PAULI & CO., INC. 232 S. Meramac Avenue St. Louis, MO 63105	Zoltek Cos., Inc.	11/06/92	$ 4.4 million	Carbon fibers
	D&K Wholesale Drug, Inc.	09/01/92	$ 4.6 million	Wholesale drug distributor
PAULSON INVESTMENT CO., INC. 811 S.W. Front Avenue Suite 200 Portland, OR 97204	Cree Research, Inc.	02/08/93	$ 11.6 million	Missile propulsion systems
	Farragut Mortgage Company, Inc.	02/25/92	$ 13.0 million	Mortgage banking
	Document Technologies, Inc.	02/14/92	$ 4.5 million	Document image processing systems
	With Design In Mind International, Inc.	05/10/91	$ 7.5 million	Gifts & novelties
	Pit Stop Auto Centers, Inc.	07/31/90	$ 4.0 million	Oil change service centers

LEAD UNDERWRITER & ADDRESS	ISSUER	PUBLIC OFFER DATE	OFFERING AMOUNT	BUSINESS
PENNSYLVANIA MERCHANT GROUP LTD. 259 Randor Chester Road - Suite 390 Randor, PA 19087	Ultralife Batteries, Inc.	12/23/92	$ 17.1 million	Lithium batteries
	ISG International Software Group Ltd.	12/17/92	$ 8.1 million	Computer productivity tools
	Air-Cure Environmental	12/16/92	$ 12.2 million	Environmental
	Affinity Biotech, Inc.	04/15/92	$ 12.0 million	Drug delivery systems
	Zynaxis, Inc.	01/30/92	$ 22.5 million	Biotechnology company
	Integrated Circuit Systems, Inc.	06/20/91	$ 10.7 million	Integrated circuits
PIPER JAFFRAY, INC. 222 South 9th Street Minneapolis, MN 55402	American Strategic Income Portfolio, III	03/18/93	$ 360.0 million	Closed-ended fund
	Kenfil, Inc.	01/28/93	$ 17.5 million	Wholesale computer hardware
	American Municipal Term Trust, Inc. III	11/19/92	$ 46.0 million	Closed-ended fund
	American Adjustable Rate Term Trust-1999	09/17/92	$ 165.0 million	Closed-ended fund
	Megafoods, Inc.	07/24/92	$ 14.0 million	Supermarket chain
	American Strategic Income Portfolio II	07/23/92	$ 270.0 million	Closed-ended fund
	Universal Hospital Services, Inc.	06/09/92	$ 13.6 million	Portable medical equipment
	Minnesota Municipal Term Trust II	04/16/92	$ 30.0 million	Closed-ended fund
	Braun's Fashions Corp.	03/31/92	$ 13.1 million	Women's apparel
	Endosonics Corp.	03/04/92	$ 41.3 million	Surgical instruments
	Agridyne Technologies, Inc.	02/14/92	$ 17.5 million	Biochemicals & insecticides
	American Adjustable Rate Term Trust-1998	01/23/92	$ 340.0 million	Closed-ended fund
	Cardiopulmonics, Inc.	01/17/92	$ 27.5 million	Cardiopulmonary products
	American Strategic Income Portfolio, Inc.	12/19/91	$ 67.5 million	Closed-ended fund
	American Municipal Term Trust, Inc. II	09/19/91	$ 70.0 million	Closed-ended fund
	Minnesota Municipal Term Trust, Inc.	09/19/91	$ 55.0 million	Closed-ended fund
	Fischer Imaging, Inc.	08/15/91	$ 21.7 million	X-ray apparatus
	Community First Bankshares	08/13/91	$ 18.3 million	Bank holding company
	American Adjustable Rate Term Trust-1997	07/17/91	$ 200.0 million	Closed-ended fund
	Regis Corp.	06/21/91	$ 44.4 million	Hair salons
	American Municipal Term Trust, Inc.	03/20/91	$ 75.0 million	Closed-ended fund
	American Adjustable Rate Term Trust, Inc.-1996	09/20/90	$ 55.0 million	Closed-ended fund
	The Pacific-European Growth Fund, Inc.	04/20/90	$ 36.0 million	Closed-ended fund
	American Adjustable Rate Term Trust, Inc.-1995	03/22/90	$ 100.0 million	Closed-ended fund

LEAD UNDERWRITER & ADDRESS	ISSUER	PUBLIC OFFER DATE	OFFERING AMOUNT	BUSINESS
THE PRINCIPAL/EPPLER, GUERIN & TURNER, INC. 1445 Ross Avenue - Suite 2300 P.O. Box 508 Dallas, TX 75221	Campo Electronics Appliances & Computers, Inc.	02/23/93	$ 19.6 million	Electronics stores
	ACE Cash Express, Inc.	12/02/92	$ 16.1 million	Check-cashing stores
	Amber's Stores	08/20/92	$ 8.4 million	Arts & crafts stores
	Encore Wire Corp.	07/16/92	$ 13.5 million	Copper electrical wire
	On The Border Cafes, Inc.	04/30/92	$ 11.5 million	Family restaurants
PRUDENTIAL-BACHE SECURITIES, INC. One Seaport Plaza 100 Gold Street New York, NY 10292	St. John Knits, Inc.	03/10/93	$ 147.2 million	Women's clothing
	Scandanavian Broadcasting System, S.A.	03/09/93	$ 54.0 million	Television broadcasting
	Equicredit Group	03/04/93	$ 49.0 million	Fixed rate consumer loans
	Nuveen Premium Muni. Income Fund 4, Inc.	02/19/93	$ 262.5 million	Closed-ended fund
	Chesapeake Energy Corp.	02/04/93	$ 27.6 million	Oil & gas
	Cone Mills Corp.	06/18/92	$ 48.0 million	Cotton & synthetic fabrics
	Optical Data Systems, Inc.	05/21/92	$ 17.1 million	Computer networking equipment
	Sports Town, Inc.	04/22/92	$ 22.8 million	Sporting good superstores
	First Western Corp.	03/17/92	$ 19.3 million	State commercial banks
	Enhanced Imaging Technologies, Inc.	03/03/92	$ 19.2 million	High quality visual image products
	Forstmann & Co., Inc.	02/26/92	$ 19.8 million	Wool fabrics
	Providential Corp.	02/10/92	$ 67.2 million	Sells reverse mortgage loans
	Blackstone North Am. Govt. Income Trust	12/20/91	$ 480.0 million	Closed-ended fund
	Duff & Phelps Util. Tax-Free Income Trust	11/21/91	$ 109.5 million	Closed-ended fund
	Custom Chrome, Inc.	11/05/91	$ 25.0 million	Parts for Harley Davidsons
	Body Drama, Inc.	10/10/91	$ 11.9 million	Women's lingerie
	Paging Network, Inc.	10/01/91	$ 100.8 million	Paging services
	York International Corp.	10/01/91	$ 184.0 million	Electric appliances
	The Money Store, Inc.	09/20/91	$ 35.2 million	Financial services
	Pharmohem Laboratories, Inc.	08/08/91	$ 17.0 million	Drug testing services
	Biomatrix, Inc.	08/06/91	$ 28.0 million	R & D therapeautic products
	Koll Management Services, Inc.	07/24/91	$ 11.0 million	Real estate management
	The Blackstone 1998 Term Trust, Inc.	04/23/91	$ 510.0 million	Closed-ended fund
	Failure Group. Inc.	08/17/90	$ 26.0 million	Consulting firm
	Offshore Pipelines, Inc.	07/25/90	$ 49.3 million	Marine construction
	Wahlco Environmental Systems, Inc.	04/25/90	$ 23.4 million	Gas conditioning systems
	Emerging Germany Fund, Inc.	03/29/90	$ 84.0 million	Closed-ended fund
	ACM Managed Multi-Market Trust, Inc.	01/19/90	$ 108.0 million	Closed-ended fund

LEAD UNDERWRITER & ADDRESS	ISSUER	PUBLIC OFFER DATE	OFFERING AMOUNT	BUSINESS
R.A.F. FINANCIAL CORP. One Norwest Center 1700 Lincoln Street - 32nd Floor Denver, CO 80203	Hibernia Foods plc H.D. Vest, Inc. Rentech, Inc.	10/22/92 11/21/91 04/18/91	$ 3.0 million $ 3.9 million $ 4.4 million	Beef for export Financial services Solids into fuels
R.G. DICKINSON & CO. 405 Sixth Avenue - Suite 200 P.O. Box 9111 Des Moines, IA 50306-9111	Trinity Biotechnology plc Interactive Network, Inc. TNC Media, Inc.	10/21/92 11/06/91 11/01/91	$ 5.4 million $ 18.0 million $ 4.8 million	Physical and biological research TV entertainment systems Pay-per-view TV production
R.J. STEICHEN & CO. 801 Nicollet Mall - Suite 1100 Minneapolis, MN 55402	Eltrax Systems, Inc. Digital Biometrics, Inc.	12/08/92 12/07/90	$ 4.1 million $ 2.1 million	Hospital information systems Fingerprint record products
R.F. LAFFERTY & CO., INC. 50 Broad Street New York, NY 10004	DiversiFax, Inc.	11/18/92	$ 5.0 million	Self-service fax machines
RAS SECURITIES CORP. 2 Broadway - 20th Floor New York, NY 10004	OCTuS, Inc. Transworld Home HealthCare, Inc. RCL Acquisition Corp. US Physical Therapy, Inc. CliniCorp. Inc.	01/15/93 12/07/92 07/29/92 05/28/92 01/13/92	$ 12.0 million $ 8.8 million $ 5.1 million $ 7.5 million $ 6.5 million	Computer systems design In-home health care M & A exchange of capital Physical therapy company Chiropractic offices & clinics
RAFFENSPERGER, HUGHES & CO., INC. 20 North Meridian Street Indianapolis, IN 46204	United Financial Bancorp, Inc. Shelby Couty Bancorp Wisconsin Pharmacal Company, Inc.	09/09/92 10/17/91 07/19/90	$ 4.6 million $ 1.7 million $ 6.6 million	Financial institution Financial institution Specialty chemicals
RAUSCHER PIERCE REFSENES, INC. 2500 RPR Tower - Lock Box 331 Plaza of the Americas Dallas, TX 75201	Celebrity, Inc. NCI Building Systems, Inc. Missimer & Associates, Inc.	12/16/92 04/03/92 12/20/91	$ 26.7 million $ 16.6 million $ 8.4 million	Artificial floral arrangements Metal building systems Environmental services

241

LEAD UNDERWRITER & ADDRESS	ISSUER	PUBLIC OFFER DATE	OFFERING AMOUNT	BUSINESS
RAYMOND JAMES & ASSOC., INC. 880 Carillon Parkway P.O. Box 12749 St. Petersburg, FL 33733-2749	GBC Technologies, Inc.	12/18/92	$ 12.1 million	Computer products
	Data Race, Inc.	10/07/92	$ 23.4 million	Data communications products
	Medical Resources, Inc.	09/03/92	$ 6.0 million	Diagnostic imaging services
	Amercian Funeral Servicies, Inc.	05/07/92	$ 18.0 million	Funeral homes & cemeteries
	Apple South, Inc.	11/21/91	$ 16.3 million	Dining restaurants
	Southwest Securities Group, Inc.	10/11/91	$ 12.5 million	Investment bank
	Crest Industries, Inc.	06/29/90	$ 8.1 million	Home improvement products
	Healthinfusion, Inc.	05/23/90	$ 6.4 million	Home infusion therapy
REICH & CO., INC. 500 Park Avenue New York, NY 10022	Zonagen, Inc.	03/25/93	$ 7.4 million	Female reproductive system products
	Hemagen Diagnostics, Inc.	02/04/93	$ 5.0 million	Diagnostic substances
	Computer Outsourcing Services, Inc.	01/19/93	$ 5.3 million	Data processing services
	Energy Research Corp.	06/25/92	$ 7.2 million	Energy generation & storage research
	Protein Polymer Technologies, Inc.	01/21/92	$ 9.4 million	Industrial organic chemicals
	Omni Films International, Inc.	08/01/91	$ 5.1 million	Wide-screen cinema systems
	National Medical Waste, Inc.	02/06/91	$ 6.0 million	Medical waste incineration
ROBERT TODD FINANCIAL CORP. 200 Garden City Plaza Garden City, NY 11530	IVF Amercia, Inc.	10/08/92	$ 5.4 million	In-vitro fertilization clinics
	Lifecell, Corp.	02/27/92	$ 6.2 million	Tissue transplant technology
	American Biomed, Inc.	10/22/91	$ 4.00 million	Medical research/cardiovascular devices
ROBERT W. BAIRD & CO., INC. 777 E. Wisconsin Avenue P.O. Box 672 Milwaukee, WI 53201	Chico's FAS, Inc.	03/24/93	$ 19.6 million	Casual clothing
	Marquette Electronics, Inc.	11/01/91	$ 32.9 million	Medical electronic equipment
	United Wisconsin Services, Inc.	10/24/91	$ 17.4 million	Group health care insurance
	Outlook Graphics Corp.	04/24/91	$ 20.1 million	Specialty printing

242

LEAD UNDERWRITER & ADDRESS	ISSUER	PUBLIC OFFER DATE	OFFERING AMOUNT	BUSINESS
ROBERTSON, STEPHENS & COMPANY 555 California Street Suite 2600 San Francisco, CA 94104	Liberty Technologies, Inc.	03/31/93	$ 16.2 million	Nuclear power diagnostic systems
	Brookstone, Inc.	03/25/93	$ 28.9 million	Specialty products
	Tricord Systems, Inc.	03/18/93	$ 33.0 million	Computer network servers
	Pacific Sunwear of California, Inc.	03/15/93	$ 23.4 million	Men's apparel
	NetWorth, Inc.	11/25/92	$ 17.6 million	LAN equipment
	McAfee Associates, Inc.	10/06/92	$ 41.6 million	Computer software
	Electronics for Imaging, Inc.	10/02/92	$ 38.3 million	Color imaging technology
	Banyan Systems, Inc.	08/06/92	$ 28.0 million	Computer network software
	Broadway & Seymour, Inc.	06/16/92	$ 10.4 million	Information technology
	RehabClinics, Inc.	06/05/92	$ 41.6 million	Physical therapy services
	Steris Corporation	06/01/92	$ 14.0 million	Infection prevention systems
	Software Etc. Stores, Inc.	04/22/92	$ 25.3 million	Computer software products
	Chipsoft, Inc.	04/03/92	$ 41.2 million	Business oriented software
	Cytotherapeutics, Inc.	03/25/92	$ 24.8 million	Medical research & development
	Advacare, Inc.	01/29/92	$ 63.8 million	Administrative management
	Whole Foods Market, Inc.	01/23/92	$ 23.4 million	Chain of supermarkets
	Gilead Sciences, Inc.	01/22/92	$ 75.0 million	Pharmaceutical company
	Ventritex, Inc.	01/22/92	$ 84.6 million	Medical products
	SyQuest Technology, Inc.	12/18/91	$ 24.2 million	Disk drive cartridges
	Tetra Tech Inc.	12/17/91	$ 14.7 million	Environmental engineering consultants
	Vitesse Semiconductor Corp.	12/11/91	$ 28.8 million	Digital circuits
	Advanced Interventional Systems, Inc.	11/06/91	$ 29.9 million	Laser systems-heart treatment
	Progress Software Corp.	07/30/91	$ 30.0 million	Computer programming language
	Meris Laboratories, Inc.	07/19/91	$ 19.7 million	Patient testing services
	Alkermes, Inc.	07/16/91	$ 17.5 million	Pharmaceuticals
	Cor Therapeutics, Inc.	06/27/91	$ 15.0 million	Biopharmaceuticals
	U.S. Homecare Corp.	06/05/91	$ 15.8 million	Home health care services
	Scigenics, Inc.	05/23/91	$ 40.0 million	Drugs for cancer treatment
	State of the Art, Inc.	05/23/91	$ 27.0 million	Microcomputer software
	Homedco Group, Inc.	05/02/91	$ 55.5 million	Home health care provider
	Cygnus Therapeutic Systems	01/31/91	$ 27.0 million	Transdermal drug transistors

LEAD UNDERWRITER & ADDRESS	ISSUER	PUBLIC OFFER DATE	OFFERING AMOUNT	BUSINESS
ROBERTSON, STEPHENS & COMPANY (continued)	Easel Corp.	08/09/90	$ 12.8 million	Computer graphics software
	Alias Research, Inc.	07/17/90	$ 28.6 million	Software products
	RasterOps	05/09/90	$ 22.4 million	Photo imaging products
	STOR Furnishings International, Inc.	04/27/90	$ 18.0 million	Furniture
	Pharmacy Management Services, Inc.	04/05/93	$ 30.0 million	Medical cost containment
	Tokos Medical Corporation	03/26/90	$ 24.0 million	Outpatient/home health care
THE ROBINSON-HUMPHREY CO., INC. 3333 Peachtree Road N.E. Atlanta, GA 30326	Brock Candy Co.	03/11/93	$ 28.0 million	Candies & fruit snacks
	Cryolife, Inc.	02/11/93	$ 15.0 million	Cryopreservation technology
	Midland Financial Group, Inc.	12/10/92	$ 29.4 million	Insurance holding company
	Books-A-Million, Inc.	11/02/92	$ 29.6 million	Book superstores
	American Studios, Inc.	09/17/92	$ 37.8 million	Portrait photography services
	National Vision Associates, Ltd.	05/19/92	$ 32.5 million	Retail vision centers
	Chromcraft Revington, Inc.	04/15/92	$ 27.5 million	Furniture
	Adesa Corp.	04/14/92	$ 32.0 million	Used car auctions
	Fred's, Inc.	03/18/92	$ 52.2 million	Discount general merchandise stores
	ARI Network Services, Inc.	11/15/91	$ 24.0 million	Computer network info. services
	LXE, Inc.	04/11/91	$ 10.5 million	Radio data communications
ROYCE INVESTMENT GROUP, INC. 113 Crossways Park Drive Woodbury, NY 117972	Ongard Systems, Inc.	08/11/92	$ 4.0 million	Infection control systems
	GraceCare Health Systems, Inc.	04/21/92	$ 5.4 million	Nursing care facilities
ROSENKRANTZ LYON & ROSS, INC. 6 East 43rd Street New York, NY 10017	Veterinary Centers of America, Inc.	10/10/91	$ 14.4 million	Veterinary clinics
	Medarex, Inc.	06/20/91	$ 13.8 million	Pharmaceuticals
	Credit Depot Corp.	04/19/91	$ 3.9 million	Mortgage broker
	Simitek Corp.	03/06/91	$ 11.7 million	Semiconductor memories
	Air-Cure Environmental	12/14/90	$ 4.0 million	Air pollution control systems
	Projectavision	07/24/90	$ 4.2 million	Solid state displays
	ACTV, Inc.	05/04/90	$ 4.7 million	Interactive TV & video technology
	Roberts Pharmaceuticals	01/23/90	$ 12.0 million	Pharmaceuticals
ROTAN MOSLE, INC. 700 Louisiana 3700 NCNB Bank Building Houston, TX 77002	First Seismic Corp.	09/18/90	$ 9.0 million	Seismic data
	Henley International, Inc.	02/02/90	$ 8.0 million	Physical therapy products

244

LEAD UNDERWRITER & ADDRESS	ISSUER	PUBLIC OFFER DATE	OFFERING AMOUNT	BUSINESS
S.D. COHN & CO., INC. 17 Battery Place - Suite 626 New York, NY 10004	Gotham Apparel Corp. Biospecifics Technologies Corp.	11/02/92 11/14/91	$ 3.6 million $ 3.6 million	Women's apparel Pharmaceuticals
S.G. WARBURG & CO., INC. 787 Seventh Avenue New York, NY 10019	Shaman Pharmaceuticals, Inc. Argus Pharmaceuticals, Inc.	01/27/93 07/10/92	$ 45.0 million $ 11.9 million	Pharmaceuticals Drugs for cancer treatment
SALOMON BROTHERS, INC. Seven World Trade Center New York, NY 10048	US Can Co. Global Industries, Ltd. Salomon Bros. High Income Fund, Inc. Life Reassurance Corp. of America Aracruz Celulose S.A. Valassis Communications, Inc. Enhance Financial Services Group, Inc. Margaretten Financial Corp. Citfed Bancorp BMC West, Inc. AMBAC, Inc. DeVry, Inc. Qual-Med, Inc. Value City Department Stores, Inc. Input/Output, Inc. Pac Rim Holding Corp. Grant-Norpac, Inc. Salomon Phibro Oil Trust Banner Aerospace, Inc. Coho Resources, Inc. Latin America Investment Fund, Inc. Compania de Telefonos de Chile, S.A. The Irish Investment Fund, Inc.	03/08/93 02/10/93 01/21/93 10/27/92 05/27/92 03/11/92 02/13/92 01/29/92 01/22/92 08/22/91 07/11/91 06/21/91 06/11/91 06/10/91 04/01/91 03/08/91 09/19/90 08/24/90 07/26/90 07/25/90 07/25/90 07/20/90 03/30/90	$ 66.6 million $ 36.3 million $ 60.0 million $ 186.7 million $ 92.8 million $ 319.3 million $ 77.6 million $ 255.0 million $ 19.6 million $ 12.8 million $ 292.0 million $ 21.2 million $ 59.1 million $ 73.1 million $ 39.2 million $ 19.9 million $ 41.0 million $ 74.4 million $ 105.0 million $ 45.5 million $ 45.0 million $ 66.7 million $ 30.0 million	Manufactures metal containers Water & sewage services Closed-ended fund Reinsurance Bleached wood pulp Print media products Financial guarantee insurance Holding company Mortgage banking Retail building materials Municipal bond insurance Technical institutes Health care services Department stores Seismic data acquisition system Workers compensation insurance Seismic data Oil investment vehicle Aviation products Oil & gas exploration Closed-ended fund Telecommunications Closed-ended fund
SANDS BROTHERS & CO., LTD. 101 Park Avenue New York, NY 10178	Semiconductor Packaging Materials Co., Inc.	12/20/91	$ 5.7 million	Stamps for electronics

245

LEAD UNDERWRITER & ADDRESS	ISSUER	PUBLIC OFFER DATE	OFFERING AMOUNT	BUSINESS
SCHNEIDER SECURITIES, INC. 104 Broadway Denver, CO 80203	Datawatch Corp. Aerodyne Products, Inc. Laser Vision Centers	05/28/92 07/18/91 04/03/91	$ 5.0 million $ 3.9 million $ 3.0 million	Computer workstations Automated systems Eye surgery center
SEIDLER AMDEC SECURITIES, INC. 515 South Figueroa Street Los Angeles, CA 90071-3396	Modtech, Inc.	07/19/90	$ 12.0 million	Modular classrooms
SHAMROCK PARTNERS, LTD. 111 Veterans Square Media, PA 19063	Nyer Medical Group, Inc.	06/09/92	$ 2.8 million	Medical products distributor
SHEARSON LEHMAN BROS., INC. American Express Tower World Financial Center New York, NY 10285-1900				
SMETEK, VAN HORN & CORMACK, INC. 1628 Marshall Houston, TX 77006-4122	Aphton Corp.	03/28/91	$ 7.0 million	Pharmaceuticals
SMITH BARNEY, HARRIS UPHAM & CO., INC. 1345 Avenue of the Americas New York, NY 10105	Amtrol, Inc. Hyperion 2005 Inv Grade Opp Term Trust Williams Coal Seam Gas Roalty Trust	03/18/93 02/19/93 01/13/93	$ 45.0 million $ 200.0 million $ 104.0 million	Plumbing & chemical containers Closed-ended fund Natural gas royalty trust

246

LEAD UNDERWRITER & ADDRESS	ISSUER	PUBLIC OFFER DATE	OFFERING AMOUNT	BUSINESS
SMITH BARNEY, HARRIS UPHAM & CO., INC. (continued)	Hayes Wheels International, Inc.	12/16/92	$ 125.4 million	Automobile wheels
	Student Loan Corp.	12/16/92	$ 48.6 million	Student loans
	Kranzco Realty Trust	11/12/92	$ 128.0 million	Real estate investment trust
	PennCorp Financial Group, Inc.	10/29/92	$ 83.1 million	Insurance underwriter
	Patterson Dental Co.	10/28/92	$ 48.0 million	Wholesale dental supplies
	Physicians Clinical Laboratory, Inc.	10/22/92	$ 12.0 million	Clinical laboratory services
	Discount Auto Parts, Inc.	08/18/92	$ 62.1 million	Autoparts superstores
	Triconex Corp.	03/19/92	$ 26.0 million	Computer software & hardware
	ISG Technologies, Inc.	03/06/92	$ 30.2 million	Computerized medical work stations
	I-Stat, Corp.	02/26/92	$ 55.5 million	Blood analysis equipment
	Roper Industries, Inc.	02/12/92	$ 37.5 million	Pumps & pumping equipment
	Integon Corp.	02/06/92	$ 99.1 million	Nonstandard auto insurance
	PCI Services, Inc.	01/28/92	$ 28.8 million	Pharmaceutical packaging
	Menley & James, Inc.	01/21/92	$ 26.0 million	Pharmaceutical products
	Magainin Pharmaceuticals, Inc.	12/11/91	$ 18.0 million	Pharmaceuticals
	Imclone Systems, Inc.	11/18/91	$ 35.0 million	Pharmaceuticals
	Sunbelt Nursery Group, Inc.	10/04/91	$ 27.2 million	Nurseries/lawn & garden supplies
	Mobley Environmental Services, Inc.	09/24/91	$ 27.2 million	Waste management services
	Curative Technologies, Inc.	06/28/91	$ 22.5 million	Biopharmaceutical products
	State Auto Financial Corp.	06/28/91	$ 22.7 million	Property & casualty insurance
	Coastal Healthcare Group, Inc.	06/20/91	$ 34.5 million	Contract management service
	Genesis Health Ventures, Inc.	06/19/91	$ 14.4 million	Health care services
	Pulse Engineering, Inc.	06/11/91	$ 26.8 million	Parts for LAN systems
	Danek Group, Inc.	05/16/91	$ 27.0 million	Spinal implants
	Integrated Health Services, Inc.	04/25/91	$ 52.5 million	Subacute medical care
	Brooktree Corp.	04/17/91	$ 42.0 million	Intergrated circuits
	Total Pharmaceutical Care	03/07/91	$ 19.6 million	Home infusion therapy
	Lunar Corp.	08/14/90	$ 15.0 million	Medical diagnostic equipment
	Bird Medical Technologies, Inc.	08/01/90	$ 16.0 million	Respiratory equipment
	Trimble Navigation, Ltd.	07/20/90	$ 30.0 million	Navigational instruments
	Fleer Corp.	06/05/90	$ 25.5 million	Baseball cards/candy
	Fingerhut Companies, Inc.	04/25/90	$ 82.5 million	Catalog & mail order houses
	Granite Construction, Inc.	04/20/90	$ 42.5 million	Heavy construction
	Pinkerton's	04/04/90	$ 28.0 million	Security service
	Seligman Select Municipal Fund, Inc.	02/15/90	$ 144.0 million	Closed-ended fund

LEAD UNDERWRITER & ADDRESS	ISSUER	PUBLIC OFFER DATE	OFFERING AMOUNT	BUSINESS
SOUTH RICHMOND SECURITIES, INC. 40 Rector Street - Suite 1810 New York, NY 10006	Telemed, Inc.	08/20/92	$ 5.0 million	Pregnancy home health care
STEPHENS, INC. 111 Center Street Little Rock, AR 72201	Danskin, Inc. USA Truck, Inc. Delta Queen Steamboat Co. Varsity Spirit Corp. Medicus Systems, Corp.	08/19/92 03/19/92 03/05/92 01/28/92 08/01/91	$ 39.0 million $ 13.1 million $ 48.6 million $ 14.6 million $ 7.2 million	Clothing manufacturer Irregular route carrier Steamboat river cruises School spirit products and services Healthcare facilities software
STIFEL, NICOLAUS, & CO., INC. 500 North Broadway St. Louis, MO 63102	Central Mortgage Bancshares, Inc.	10/22/92	$ 10.0 million	Bank holding company
STONEGATE SECURITIES, INC. 500 Crescent Court - Suite 270 Dallas, TX 75201	BioSafety Systems, Inc.	02/11/93	$ 3.6 million	Health care safety equipment
STRATTON OAKMONT, INC. 1979 Marcus Avenue - Suite 120 Lake Success, NY 11042	Out-Takes, Inc. Aquanatural Co. SMT Health Services, Inc. Nutrition Management Services Co. Healthcare Imaging Systems Lincon International, Inc. Ropak Laboratories IPS Health Care	03/10/93 12/02/92 03/04/92 01/29/92 11/12/91 08/13/91 05/16/91 01/16/91	$ 6.5 million $ 5.5 million $ 6.0 million $ 5.0 million $ 7.0 million $ 4.9 million $ 7.7 million $ 4.7 million	Portrait photography services Pollution control equipment Mobile X-ray facilities Health care facility food management MRI centers Industrial waste cleanup equipment Test kits for poison MRI servcies
STUART, COLEMAN & CO., INC. 11 West 42nd Street - 15th Floor New York, NY 10036	RT Industries, Inc.	06/17/92	$ 3.6 million	Brake friction products
THE STUART-JAMES CO., INC. 8055 E. Tufts Avenue Parkway #1200 Devnver, CO 80237	GB Foods Corp. Command Security Group Craftmade International Medgroup NDC Automation, Inc.	08/21/90 07/19/90 04/16/90 04/06/90 03/21/90	$ 4.3 million $ 3.8 million $ 3.5 million $ 3.4 million $ 2.4 million	Mexican restaurants Security guard services Ceiling fan & light kits Physical therapy Guided vehicle systems

248

LEAD UNDERWRITER & ADDRESS	ISSUER	PUBLIC OFFER DATE	OFFERING AMOUNT	BUSINESS
SUMMIT INVESTMENT CORPORATION International Centre - Suite 500 900 Second Avenue South Minneapolis, MN 55402	Casino Magic Corp. Sunrise Leasing Corp. Medamicus, Inc. Helix Biocore, Inc. (n/k/a ATS Medical, Inc.)	10/23/92 10/03/91 09/06/91 06/13/90	$ 18.5 million $ 5.0 million $ 3.6 million $ 5.6 million	Casinos Data processing equipment Medical devices Heart valves
SUTRO & CO., INC. 201 California Street San Francisco, CA 94104	Boomtown, Inc. ICU Medical, Inc. Glacier Water Services, Inc. Vidmark Corp.	10/23/92 03/31/92 03/13/92 06/29/90	$ 32.5 million $ 14.3 million $ 22.0 million $ 18.8 million	Casinos Disposable medical devices Coin-operated water dispensers Motion picture distributor
TEXAS CAPITAL SECURITIES, INC. 5085 Westheimer - Suite 4520 Houston, TX 77056	Hungarian Telephone and Cable Co. Universal Seismic Associates Mr. Bulb, Inc. Industrial Holdings, Inc.	12/24/92 05/11/92 04/14/92 01/15/92	$ 5.6 million $ 6.1 million $ 2.5 million $ 5.9 million	Local telephone & cable networks Scientific seismic data Efficient light bulbs Holding company
TEXAS SECURITIES 4200 South Hulen Street - Suite 536 Fort Worth, TX 76109	Spectral Diagnostics, Inc.	07/15/92	$ 3.9 million	In-vitro diagnostic antibodies
THOMAS JAMES ASSOC., INC. 1895 Mt. Hope Avenue P.O. Box 22719 Rochester, NY 14692	M-Systems Flash Disk Pioneers, Ltd. Xerographic Laser Images Corp. Palomar Medical Technologies, Inc. MRV Communications, Inc. XXsys Technologies, Inc. Network Imaging Corp. Sayett Group, Inc. Vision Ten, Inc. Bio-dyne Corp. Saratoga Brands, Inc. Sanborn, Inc. Excel Technology, Inc. Cybernetics Products, Inc. Acqua Group, Inc. DynaGen, Inc.	03/04/93 01/12/93 12/18/92 12/07/92 07/31/92 05/08/92 02/05/92 11/07/91 10/16/91 09/04/91 08/07/91 05/13/91 04/10/91 12/12/90 08/10/90	$ 4.6 million $ 5.0 million $ 6.6 million $ 5.1 million $ 6.0 million $ 6.0 million $ 8.0 million $ 4.7 million $ 3.3 million $ 4.4 million $ 3.8 million $ 4.1 million $ 4.5 million $ 3.0 million $ 4.0 million	Computer chips Laser imaging software Medical lasers Laser diodes Advanced material analysis devices TVs & refrigerators Hi-tech projection holding company Computerized work stations Exercise equipment Potato chips Industrial separation systems Laser systems Printed circuit boards Non-bottled water coolers Therapeutic products

LEAD UNDERWRITER & ADDRESS	ISSUER	PUBLIC OFFER DATE	OFFERING AMOUNT	BUSINESS
TUCKER ANTHONY, INC. One Beacon Street Boston, MA 02108	Chic by H.I.S., Inc. Brooktrout Technology, Inc. Kopin, Corp. Back Bay Restaurant Group, Inc. Peer Review Analysis, Inc.	02/18/93 10/20/92 04/15/92 03/13/92 12/05/91	$ 69.0 million $ 16.0 million $ 15.0 million $ 28.9 million $ 10.5 million	Denim apparel Fax machine software Digital imaging devices Family style restaurants Health care management programs
UNTERBERG HARRIS, L.P. 275 Battery Street - Suite 2980 San Francisco, CA 94111	On Assignment, Inc. Electronic Information Systems, Inc.	09/22/92 07/10/92	$ 11.9 million $ 8.6 million	Temporary laboratory help Telephone processing equipment
VAN KAMPEN MERRITT, INC. One Parkview Plaza Oakbrook Terrace, IL 60181				
VANTAGE SECURITIES, INC. 33 Wood Avenue South - 8th Floor Iselin, NJ 08830	Golden Eagle Group, Inc. R2 Medical Systems, Inc. CliniCom, Inc. Liuski International, Inc.	11/24/92 09/01/92 04/20/92 08/13/91	$ 4.0 million $ 4.8 million $ 6.5 million $ 7.7 million	Property & casualty insurance Cardiac electrodes Hospital on-line information systems Computers
VOLPE, WELTY & CO. One Maritime Plaza - 11th Floor San Francisco, CA 94111	Tro Learning, Inc. Walker Power, Inc. Acclaim Entertainment, Inc. Inforum, Inc. TriCare, Inc.	12/22/92 01/22/92 12/19/91 12/13/91 01/26/90	$ 20.0 million $ 9.4 million $ 17.0 million $ 22.0 million $ 10.4 million	Testing systems Electric power systems Video game cartridges Marketing information for hospitals Outpatient/home health care
W.B. MCKEE SECURITIES, INC. 3003 North Central Avenue Suite 100 Phoenix, AZ 85012	Care Concepts, Inc. Simula, Inc.	2/17/93 04/13/92	$ 4.2 million $ 5.0 million	Vehicles for the handicapped Air safety products
WEDBUSH MORGAN SECURITIES, INC. 1000 Wilshire Blvd. P.O. Box 30014 Los Angeles, CA 90030	Sport Chalet, Inc. Northrim Bank	11/19/92 11/06/90	$ 14.8 million $ 8.7 million	Sporting goods superstores Commercial bank

250

LEAD UNDERWRITER & ADDRESS	ISSUER	OFFERING AMOUNT	PUBLIC OFFER DATE	BUSINESS
WERBEL-ROTH SECURITIES, INC. 5560 W. Oakland Park Blvd. Fort Lauderdale, FL 33313	3Net Systems, Inc.	$ 5.0 million	08/10/92	Computer network systems
WERTHEIM SCHRODER & CO., INC. Equitable Center 787 Seventh Avenue New York, NY 10019-6016	Hahn Automotive Warehouse, Inc. Enzymatics, Inc. Holopak Technologies, Inc.	$ 17.5 million $ 11.9 million $ 16.0 million	01/20/93 05/14/92 09/20/91	Automotive parts Diagnostic devices Hot stamp foils (holograms)
WESSELS, ARNOLD & HENDERSON, L.P. 900 International Centre 920 Second Avenue South Minneapolis, MN 55402	Health Risk Management, Inc.	$ 15.4 million	12/19/90	Integrated health care services
WESTFIELD FINANCIAL CORP. 375 Park Avenue New York, NY 10152	Universal Self Care, Inc.	$ 4.7 million	12/11/92	Drugs for diabetes
WESTMINSTER SECURITIES, INC. 19 Rector Street New York, NY 10006	Bishop Equities South End Ventures Avalon Enterprises Carnegie Capital Corp., Inc. Elmwood Capital Corp. Harley Equities, Inc. Fulton Ventures, Inc. Sharon Capital Corp. West End Ventures, Inc.	$ 0.1 million $ 0.1 million $ 0.1 million $ 0.1 million $ 0.1 million $ 0.1 million $ 0.1 million $ 0.2 million $ 0.1 million	03/08/92 11/15/91 03/26/91 02/01/91 06/27/90 05/29/90 04/10/90 02/14/90 01/02/90	Blind pool Blind pool Blind pool Blind pool Blind pool Blind pool Blind pool Blind pool Blind pool
WESTONKA INVESTMENTS, INC. 12900 Whitewater Drive #180 Minnetonka, MN 55343	Environmental Technologies USA, Inc.	$ 4.0 million	10/23/92	Biodegradable products

LEAD UNDERWRITER & ADDRESS	ISSUER	PUBLIC OFFER DATE	OFFERING AMOUNT	BUSINESS
WHALE SECURITIES CO., L.P. 650 Fifth Avenue New York, NY 10019	Transcor Waste Services, Inc.	03/25/93	$ 5.0 million	Solid waste management services
	Saliva Diagnostic Systems, Inc.	03/04/93	$ 7.2 million	Saliva collection devices
	Consumer Portfolio Services, Inc.	10/22/92	$ 6.0 million	Auto contract broker
	CPI Aerostructures, Inc.	09/16/92	$ 5.0 million	Contract production of aircraft parts
	International Fast Food Corp.	05/21/92	$ 6.5 million	Burger Kings in Poland
	Ben Franklin Retail Stores, Inc.	04/28/92	$ 9.0 million	Variety and crafts stores
	Metrovision of North America, Inc.	12/17/91	$ 5.0 million	Videocable network
	Koo Koo Roo, Inc.	10/15/91	$ 6.3 million	Fast food restaurants
	Cellular Technical Services Co., Inc.	08/06/91	$ 5.0 million	Computer software
	Advanced Promotion Technologies, Inc.	06/26/91	$ 18.0 million	Point-of-sale marketing systems
	Integrated Waste Services, Inc.	05/14/90	$ 11.3 million	Non-hazardous waste services
	CMS-Data Corp.	05/08/90	$ 6.0 million	Software development
	Millfeld Trading Co., Inc.	01/19/90	$ 5.5 million	Footwear
WHEAT, FIRST SECURITIES, INC. 901 East Byrd Street P.O. Box 1357 Richmond, VA 23211	Mothers Work, Inc.	03/16/93	$ 16.3 million	Upscale maternity clothing
	Winston Furniture Company, Inc.	02/25/93	$ 31.2 million	Metal furniture
	Medquist, Inc.	05/04/92	$ 9.0 million	Home health care services
	Eskimo Pie Corp.	03/30/92	$ 49.7 million	Frozen pies

252

LEAD UNDERWRITER & ADDRESS	ISSUER	PUBLIC OFFER DATE	OFFERING AMOUNT	BUSINESS
WILLIAM BLAIR & CO. 135 South LaSalle Street Chicago, IL 60603	HCC Insurance Holdings, Inc.	10/28/92	$ 15.7 million	Property & casualty insurance
	Citation Computer Systems, Inc.	10/23/92	$ 6.3 million	Computer information systems
	IQ Software Corp.	10/15/92	$ 13.5 million	Analysis & report software
	Swing-N-Slide Corp.	08/28/92	$ 35.2 million	Playground equipment
	Alden Press Co.	08/18/92	$ 22.5 million	Catalogue printing
	Peak Technologies Group, Inc.	08/04/92	$ 18.7 million	Bar-code data collection systems
	Credit Acceptance Corp.	06/05/92	$ 26.0 million	Automobile finance company
	Theratech, Inc.	05/13/92	$ 9.4 million	Drug delivery products
	Buckle, Inc.	05/07/92	$ 23.0 million	Casual apparel
	Worthington Foods, Inc.	04/15/92	$ 21.0 million	Food specialties & substitutes
	Bell Sports Holding Corp.	04/09/92	$ 45.0 million	Bicycle accessories & helmets
	Gibralter Packaging Group, Inc.	03/05/92	$ 13.3 million	Paperboard packaging products
	International Jensen, Inc.	02/12/92	$ 19.0 million	Loudspeakers
	America Service Group, Inc.	11/21/91	$ 12.1 million	Correctional health care systems
	Insurance Auto Auctions, Inc.	11/20/91	$ 22.9 million	Recovered theft vehicles
	Barefoot Grass Lawn Service, Inc.	10/23/91	$ 34.4 million	Professional lawn care service
	Zebra Technologies Corp.	08/15/91	$ 44.0 million	Bar coding system equipment
	The Future Now	06/28/91	$ 17.5 million	Computer software and systems
	Symix Systems, Inc.	03/21/91	$ 15.0 million	Integrated management software
WILLIAM K. WOODRUFF & CO., INC. 7557 Rambler Road - Suite 112 Dallas, TX 75231	Calloway's Nursery, Inc.	06/26/91	$ 26.8 million	Retail garden centers

Firm Commitment IPO Underwritings involving from $5 million to under $10 million

filed with the SEC which were publicly offered between January 1, 1990 and March 31, 1993, listed by name of lead managing underwriter

FIRM COMMITMENT IPO'S JANUARY, 1990 THROUGH MARCH, 1993
FROM $ 5.0 MILLION TO $ 9.9 MILLION

LEAD UNDERWRITER & ADDRESS	ISSUER	PUBLIC OFFER DATE	OFFERING AMOUNT	BUSINESS
A.R. BARON & CO., INC. 1 Penn Plaza - Suite 4525 New York, NY 10119	Cypros Pharmaceutical Corp.	11/03/92	$ 6.3 million	Therapeutic drugs
A.S. GOLDMEN & CO., INC. 67 Wall Street New York, NY 10005-3192	Perma-Fix Environmental Services Managed-Health Benefits Corp.	12/08/92 08/11/92	$ 8.0 million $ 6.2 million	Pollution control services Health care cost services
ALLEN & COMPANY INCORPORATED 711 Fifth Avenue New York, NY 10022	Envirogen, Inc.	08/11/92	$ 8.6 million	Toxic waste biotechnology
BARINGTON CAPITAL GROUP, L.P. 730 Fifth Avenue - 12th Floor New York, NY 10019	Hypermedia Communications, Inc. Document Imaging Systems Corp.	03/09/93 12/08/92	$ 7.0 million $ 6.5 million	Communications & publishing Computer storage systems
BEAR, STEARNS & CO., INC. 245 Park Avenue New York, NY 10167	Osteotech, Inc.	07/17/91	$ 9.4 million	Bones & ligaments processor
BLUNT ELLIS & LOEWI, INC. 111 East Kilbourn Avenue Milwaukee, WI 53202	Rocky Mountain Helicopters	09/11/90	$ 7.0 million	Helicopter support services
CHATFIELD DEAN & CO., INC. 7935 East Prentice Avenue #200 Greenwood Village, CO 80111	Aspen Marine Group, Inc. Intervisual Books, Inc.	05/12/92 12/03/91	$ 5.1 million $ 5.1 million	Marine recreation services Childrens pop-up books
THE CHICAGO CORPORATION 208 South LaSalle Street Chicago, IL 60604	DatEq Information Network, Inc.	11/06/91	$ 8.0 million	Auto insurance support products
COMMONWEALTH ASSOCIATES One Exchange Plaza New York, NY 10006	Lukens Medical Corp. International Testing Services Gamma International, Ltd.	05/06/92 08/15/91 06/21/90	$ 8.3 million $ 5.2 million $ 6.3 million	Disposable surgical products Pipeline welding inspectors Bingo halls

256

LEAD UNDERWRITER & ADDRESS	ISSUER	PUBLIC OFFER DATE	OFFERING AMOUNT	BUSINESS
CONTINENTAL BROKER-DEALER CORP. One Old Country Road Carle Place, NY 11514	MusicSource USA, Inc.	02/01/93	$ 5.7 million	Music data retrieval services
COVEY & CO., INC. 115 South Main Street Salt Lake City, UT 84111	Pinnacle Environmental, Inc.	05/17/90	$ 5.0 million	Industrial asbestos abatement
COWEN & CO. Financial Square New York, NY 10005	Metricom, Inc.	05/01/92	$ 9.0 million	Communications networking
CRAIG-HALLUM, INC. 701 Fourth Avenue South 10th Floor Minneapolis, MN 55415	Odd's-N-End's, Inc.	01/21/92	$ 5.3 million	Discount retail shops
CROWELL, WEEDON & CO. 624 South Grand Avenue P.O. Box 54843 Terminal Annex Los Angeles, CA 90054	First Mortgage Corp.	04/16/92	$ 5.4 million	Mortgage banking
CRUTTENDEN & CO., INC. 18301 Von Karman - Suite 100 Irvine, CA 92715	Wilshire Technologies, Inc.	11/24/92	$ 7.5 million	Disposable medical products

257

LEAD UNDERWRITER & ADDRESS	ISSUER	PUBLIC OFFER DATE	OFFERING AMOUNT	BUSINESS
D.H. BLAIR INVESTMENT BANKING CORP. 44 Wall Street New York, NY 10005	Magna-Lab, Inc.	03/30/93	$ 6.0 million	MRI devices
	Advanced Mammography Systems, Inc.	01/25/93	$ 7.7 million	Outpatient diagnostic services
	Health Image Media, Inc.	10/20/92	$ 6.6 million	Health magazines
	Life Medical Sciences	09/22/92	$ 6.0 million	Biomedical products
	Integrated Process Equipment Corp.	08/13/92	$ 5.3 million	Semiconductors
	Laser Video Network, Inc.	06/10/92	$ 6.3 million	Laser disc jukeboxes
	Applied Laser Systems	03/16/92	$ 7.2 million	Laser diode devices
	Las Vegas Entertainment Network, Inc.	02/20/92	$ 5.0 million	Television programming
	InfoNow Corp.	02/07/92	$ 6.9 million	Electronic distribution system
	Epigen, Inc.	12/10/91	$ 5.7 million	Pharmaceuticals
	ENVIRx, Ltd.	11/12/91	$ 6.0 million	Environmental equipment
	Avitar, Inc.	07/22/91	$ 5.5 million	Pharmaceuticals
	Omega Environmental, Inc.	07/11/91	$ 6.0 million	Underground storage tanks
	Biomedical Waste Systems, Inc.	06/04/91	$ 6.0 million	Medical waste incineration-
	Somanetics Corp.	03/20/91	$ 7.2 million	Medical diagnostic equipment
	Advanced Photonix, Inc.	02/11/91	$ 6.0 million	Photodetection devices
	Prime Cellular, Inc.	08/02/90	$ 6.0 million	Construction consulting services
	VIMRx Pharmaceuticals, Inc.	07/25/90	$ 5.0 million	Pharmaceuticals
	Builders Express, Inc.	06/07/90	$ 6.0 million	Home improvement stores
	Fountain Pharmaceuticals	05/15/90	$ 5.5 million	Encapsulation technology
	Lidak Pharmaceuticals	05/08/90	$ 5.0 million	Pharmaceuticals
	American Biogenetic Sciences, Inc.	05/01/90	$ 6.0 million	Genetic engineering
	Medicis Pharmaceutical	03/28/90	$ 8.9 million	Pharmaceutical products
	Interneuron Pharmaceuticals, Inc.	03/08/90	$ 8.5 million	Psychiatric pharmaceuticals
DAKIN SECURITIES CORP. 505 Sansome Street - 8th Floor San Francisco, CA 94111	Sellectek, Inc.	12/10/92	$ 5.0 million	Computer information services
DAIN BOSWORTH, INC. 60 South Sixth Street P.O. Box 1160 Minneapolis, MN 55440-1160	Union Bankshares, Ltd.	03/09/93	$ 7.1 million	Bank holding company
	Bestop, Inc.	08/13/92	$ 8.3 million	Automobile soft tops
	Columbia Banking System, Inc.	06/16/92	$ 5.4 million	Savings banks

258

LEAD UNDERWRITER & ADDRESS	ISSUER	PUBLIC OFFER DATE	OFFERING AMOUNT	BUSINESS
DICKINSON & CO. 405 6th Avenue - Suite 200 P.O. Box 9111 Des Moines, IA 50306-9111	New World Power Corp.	10/23/92	$ 7.0 million	Power generating systems
DRAKE CAPITAL SECURITIES, INC. 1250 Fourth Street - 5th Floor P.O. Box 2146 Snata Monica, CA 90407	Voice Powered Technology International, Inc.	10/20/92	$ 5.5 million	Voice recognition products
ELLIOT, ALLEN & CO., INC. 461 Fifth Avenue New York, NY 10017	Hillside Bedding, Inc.	02/11/93	$ 5.3 million	Discount bedding
EMANUEL & COMPANY 110 Wall Street New York, NY 10005	Infu-Tech, Inc. Bio Time, Inc.	12/22/92 03/05/92	$ 8.0 million $ 5.0 million	Infusion therapy services Blood substitute solution
FAHNESTOCK & CO., INC. 110 Wall Street New york, NY 10005	Premier Radio Networks, Inc. OTR Express, Inc.	04/28/92 01/22/92	$ 6.0 million $ 5.5 million	Radio programming Truckload motor carrier
FIRST ALBANY CORP. 41 State Street P.O. Box 52 Albany, NY 12201	F.A. Tucker Group, Inc.	05/17/91	$ 7.7 million	Electric utility
FIRST OF MICHIGAN CORP. 100 Renaissance Center 26th Floor Detroit, MI 48243	Pomeroy Computer Resources, Inc. Autocam, Corp. Spartan Motors, Inc.	04/03/92 10/29/91 07/02/91	$ 8.8 million $ 8.0 million $ 6.6 million	Computer hardware & software Special metal alloy components Custom heavy duty chassis
GILFORD SECURITIES, INC. 850 Third Avenue New York, NY 10022	International Canine Genetics, Inc.	03/24/93	$ 5.0 million	Canine reproduction services

259

LEAD UNDERWRITER & ADDRESS	ISSUER	PUBLIC OFFER DATE	OFFERING AMOUNT	BUSINESS
GKN SECURITIES CORP. 61 Broadway - 12th Floor New York, NY 10006	Complink, Ltd. Neoprobe Corp. Bio Imaging Technologies, Inc. Trinity Capital Enterprise, Corp. Restor Industries, Inc.	03/10/93 11/10/92 06/18/92 09/12/91 08/12/91	$ 5.0 million $ 9.0 million $ 5.0 million $ 8.0 million $ 5.3 million	Computer networking products Cancer detection systems Biomedical computer imaging Investment company Pay telephones
GLOBAL AMERICA, INC. 110 Wall Street - 17th Floor New York, NY 10005	Auto Depot, Inc. Cappucino's, Inc.	09/07/90 02/28/90	$ 9.0 million $ 5.0 million	Auto parts stores Restaurants
GRUNTAL & CO., INC. 14 Wall Street New York, NY 10005	United States Paging Corp.	06/03/92	$ 6.0 million	Paging services
H.C. WAINWRIGHT & CO., INC. One Boston Place - 31st Floor Boston, MA 02108	DeWolfe Companies, Inc.	09/24/92	$ 5.4 million	Residential real estate
H.J. MEYERS & CO., INC. 356 N. Camden Drive Beverly Hills, CA 90210	EduSoft Ltd. Intramed Labs, Inc. Magic Software Enterprises, Ltd. Laser Pacific Media Corp.	07/14/92 06/09/92 08/28/91 08/14/91	$ 5.0 million $ 6.6 million $ 8.5 million $ 6.6 million	PC-based software products Miniature endoscopes Software tools Production services
HAMPSHIRE SECURITIES CORPORATION 919 Third Avenue New York, NY 10022	Paracelesian, Inc.	02/11/92	$ 5.5 million	Biotechnology company
HANIFEN, IMHOFF, INC. 1125 17th Street - Suite 1600 P.O. Box 5050 Denver, CO 80217-5050	Matritech, Inc.	07/09/92	$ 5.8 million	Cancer diagnostic products
INTERSTATE/JOHNSON LANE CORPORATION 2700 NCNB Plaza 101 South Tryon Street Charlotte, NC 28280	Summit Financial Corp.	01/25/90	$ 5.5 million	Bank holding company

LEAD UNDERWRITER & ADDRESS	ISSUER	PUBLIC OFFER DATE	OFFERING AMOUNT	BUSINESS
INVESTORS ASSOCIATES, INC. 411 Hackensack Avenue Hackensack, NJ 07601	Chromatics International, Inc.	02/05/93	$ 5.8 million	General business services
J.C. BRADFORD & CO. 330 Commerce Street Nashville, TM 37201	Litchfield Financial, Inc.	02/25/92	$ 8.5 million	Mortgage financing
J. GREGORY & COMPANY, INC. 833 Northern Boulevard Great Neck, NY 11021	New Day Beverage, Inc.	01/29/93	$ 5.0 million	Distilled liquors
JOHN G. KINNARD & CO., INC. 1700 Northstar West Minneapolis, MN 55402	Title Wave Stores, Inc. Rottlund Co., Inc. Winthrop Resources Corp. AVECOR Cardiovascular, Inc. AudioScience, Inc. Education Alternatives, Inc.	03/17/93 10/29/92 06/24/92 03/26/92 06/11/91 04/25/91	$ 5.2 million $ 6.1 million $ 5.4 million $ 6.9 million $ 5.2 million $ 6.0 million	Home entertainment software Residential construction Computer leasing services Heart/lung devices High-tech hearing aids Management/consulting service
JOSEPHTHAL LYON & ROSS, INC. 6 East 43rd Street New York, NY 10017	SatCon Technology Corp. Conceptronic, Inc. AG Services of America, Inc.	11/12/92 12/04/91 08/01/91	$ 7.5 million $ 5.7 million $ 8.3 million	Machinery control systems Equipment to repair circuit boards Crop inputs
KEEFE, BRUYETTE & WOODS, INC. Two World Trade Center - Suite 8566 New York, NY 10048	Civic Bancorp	01/23/90	$ 7.0 million	Commercial bank
KEMPER SECURITIES, INC. 77 West Wacker Drive Chicago, IL 60601	M-Wave, Inc.	03/31/92	$ 7.0 million	Microwave components
KENNEDY, MATHEWS, LANDIS, HEALY & PECORA, INC. 3636 IDS Center Minneapolis, MN 55402	Shuffle Master, Inc. Modami Services, Inc. MediVators, Inc. Ballistivet, Inc.	12/08/92 08/12/92 09/25/91 04/30/91	$ 6.4 million $ 5.0 million $ 5.3 million $ 6.2 milion	Card shuffling systems Frozen yogurt products Disinfectors Ballistic implant system

261

LEAD UNDERWRITER & ADDRESS	ISSUER	PUBLIC OFFER DATE	OFFERING AMOUNT	BUSINESS
LADENBURG, THALMANN & CO., INC. 540 Madison Avenue New York, NY 10022	Jimbo's Jumbos, Inc. Rag Shops, Inc.	12/06/91 06/05/91	$ 9.0 million $ 9.4 million	Peanuts Fabrics and crafts
LAIDLAW EQUITIES, INC. 275 Madison Avenue - 12th Floor New York, NY 10016	Hi Tech Pharmacal Co., Inc. 3CI Complete Compliance Corp. Defense Software & Systems, Inc. Valley Systems, Inc.	08/03/92 04/14/92 02/11/92 06/11/91	$ 6.0 million $ 7.2 million $ 6.0 million $ 5.0 million	Pharmaceuticals Medical waste management Software services & products Industrial cleaning services
LEGG MASON WOOD WALKER, INC. 111 South Calvert Street Baltimore, MD 21202	Hampshire Group Ltd.	06/17/92	$ 9.5 million	Clothing manufacturer
LOVETT UNDERWOOD NEUHAUS & WEBB, INC. 909 Fannin Street Houston, TX 77010	Benchmark Electronics, Inc.	06/28/90	$ 9.6 million	Electronics
M.H. MEYERSON & CO., INC. 30 Montgomery Street Jersey City, NJ 07302	Globalink, Inc. Deprenyl USA, Inc.	03/03/93 01/17/92	$ 5.0 million $ 8.6 million	Language translation through software Photo-dynamic therapies
MERRILL LYNCH, PIERCE, FENDER & SMITH, INC. World Financial Center - Bldg. D 250 Vesey Street New York, NY 10281	CENFED Financial Corp. Pamida Holdings, Inc. MAF Bancorp, Inc.	10/25/91 09/18/90 01/12/90	$ 8.8 million $ 7.5 million $ 7.6 million	Thrift holding company Retailer holding company Bank holding company
MILLER, JOHNSON & KUEHN, INC. 1660 S. Highway 100 - Suite 228 Minneapolis, MN 55416	Funco, Inc. Insignia System, Inc.	08/12/92 06/25/91	$ 5.0 million $ 5.1 million	Used Nintendo games Signs for retail merchants
MORGAN, KEEGAN & CO., INC. Morgan Keegan Tower 50 Front Street Memphis, TN 38103	Ambar	12/12/91	$ 9.2 million	Environmental services

LEAD UNDERWRITER & ADDRESS	ISSUER	PUBLIC OFFER DATE	OFFERING AMOUNT	BUSINESS
NEEDHAM & COMPANY 400 Park Avenue New York, NY 10022	Leasing Solutions, Inc.	03/29/93	$ 5.0 million	Communications equipment
NOBLE INVESTMENT CO. OF PALM BEACH 1801 Clint Moore Rd. - Suite 110 Boca Raton, FL 33487	Heart Labs of America, Inc. Billy Blues Food Corp. Ocean Optique Distributors, Inc.	09/25/92 05/15/92 09/24/91	$ 5.1 million $ 5.0 million $ 5.125 million	Mobile cardiac services for hospitals Texas-style restaurants Eyeglass frames
NOMURA SECURITIES INT'L., INC. 2 World Financial Center Building B New York, NY 10281-1198	Perceptron, Inc.	08/20/92	$ 6.5 million	Laser-based sensor systems
NORCROSS SECURITIES, INC. 645 E. Missouri Avenue - Suite 119 Phoenix, AZ 85012	Sheffield Medical Technologies, Inc.	02/11/93	$ 5.2 million	Biomedical products
OSCAR GRUSS & SON, INCORPORATED 74 Broad Street New York, NY 10004	Magal Security Systems, Ltd.	03/23/93	$ 7.4 million	Computerized security systems
PAINEWEBBER, INC. 1285 Avenue of the Americas New York, NY 10019	Intelligent Surgical Lasers, Inc. R-Tek Corp.	09/11/92 07/26/91	$ 6.4 million $ 7.8 million	Lasers for eye surgery Recorded music
PARADISE VALLEY SECURITIES, INC. 11811 N. Tatum - Suite 4040 Phoenix, AZ 85028	Reno Air, Inc.	05/28/92	$ 6.0 million	Regional airline
PARAGON CAPITAL CORP. 120 Wall Street - 28th Floor New York, NY 10005	Natural Earth Technologies, Inc. Club-Theatre Network, Inc.	03/26/92 05/15/90	$ 5.0 million $ 6.5 million	Natural lawn & garden products Projection TV technology
PAULSON INVESTMENT CO., INC. 811 S.W. Front Avenue Suite 200 Portland, OR 97204	With Design In Mind International, Inc.	05/10/91	$ 7.5 million	Gifts & novelties

263

LEAD UNDERWRITER & ADDRESS	ISSUER	PUBLIC OFFER DATE	OFFERING AMOUNT	BUSINESS
PENNSYLVANIA MERCHANT GROUP LTD. 259 Randor Chester Road - Suite 390 Randor, PA 19087	ISG International Software Group Ltd.	12/17/92	$ 8.1 million	Computer productivity tools
THE PRINCIPAL/EPPLER, GUERIN & TURNER, INC. 1445 Ross Avenue - Suite 2300 P.O. Box 508 Dallas, TX 75221	Amber's Stores	08/20/92	$ 8.4 million	Arts & crafts stores
R.G. DICKINSON & CO. 405 Sixth Avenue - Suite 200 P.O. Box 9111 Des Moines, IA 50306-9111	Trinity Biotechnology plc	10/21/92	$ 5.4 million	Physical and biological research
R.F. LAFFERTY & CO., INC. 50 Broad Street New York, NY 10004	DiversiFax, Inc.	11/18/92	$ 5.0 million	Self-service fax machines
RAS SECURITIES CORP. 2 Broadway - 20th Floor New York, NY 10004	Transworld Home HealthCare, Inc. RCL Acquisition Corp. US Physical Therapy, Inc. CliniCorp, Inc.	12/07/92 07/29/92 05/28/92 01/13/92	$ 8.8 million $ 5.1 million $ 7.5 million $ 6.5 million	In-home health care M & A exchange of capital Physical therapy company Chiropractic offices & clinics
RAFFENSPERGER, HUGHES & CO., INC. 20 North Meridian Street Indianapolis, IN 46204	Wisconsin Pharmacal Company, Inc.	07/19/90	$ 6.6 million	Specialty chemicals
RAUSCHER PIERCE REFSENES, INC. 2500 RPR Tower - Lock Box 331 Plaza of the Americas Dallas, TX 75201	Missimer & Associates, Inc.	12/20/91	$ 8.4 million	Environmental services
RAYMOND JAMES & ASSOC., INC. 880 Carillon Parkway P.O. Box 12749 St. Petersburg, FL 33733-2749	Medical Resources, Inc. Crest Industries, Inc. HealthInfusion, Inc.	09/03/92 06/29/90 05/23/90	$ 6.0 million $ 8.1 million $ 6.4 million	Diagnostic imaging services Home improvement products Home infusion therapy

LEAD UNDERWRITER & ADDRESS	ISSUER	PUBLIC OFFER DATE	OFFERING AMOUNT	BUSINESS
REICH & CO., INC. 500 Park Avenue New York, NY 10022	Zonagen, Inc. Hemagen Diagnostics, Inc. Computer Outsourcing Services, Inc. Energy Research Corp. Protein Polymer Technologies, Inc. Omni Films International, Inc. National Medical Waste, Inc.	03/25/93 02/04/93 01/19/93 06/25/92 01/21/92 08/01/91 02/06/91	$ 7.4 million $ 5.0 million $ 5.3 million $ 7.2 million $ 9.4 million $ 5.1 million $ 6.0 million	Female reproductive system products Diagnostic substances Data processing services Energy generation & storage research Industrial organic chemicals Wide-screen cinema systems Medical waste incineration
ROBERT TODD FINANCIAL CORP. 200 Garden City Plaza Garden City, NY 11530	IVF Amercia, Inc. Lifecell, Corp.	10/08/92 02/27/92	$ 5.4 million $ 6.2 million	In-vitro fertilization clinics Tissue transplant technology
ROYCE INVESTMENT GROUP, INC. 113 Crossways Park Drive Woodbury, NY 117972	GraceCare Health Systems, Inc.	04/21/92	$ 5.4 million	Nursing care facilities
ROTAN MOSLE, INC. 700 Louisiana 3700 NCNB Bank Building Houston, TX 77002	First Seismic Corp. Henley International, Inc.	09/18/90 02/02/90	$ 9.0 million $ 8.0 million	Seismic data Physical therapy products
SANDS BROTHERS & CO., LTD. 101 Park Avenue New York, NY 10178	Semiconductor Packaging Materials Co., Inc.	12/20/91	$ 5.7 million	Stamps for electronics
SCHNEIDER SECURITIES, INC. 104 Broadway Denver, CO 80203	Datawatch Corp.	05/28/92	$ 5.0 million	Computer workstations
SMETEK, VAN HORN & CORMACK, INC. 1628 Marshall Houston, TX 77006-4122	Aphton Corp.	03/28/91	$ 7.0 million	Pharmaceuticals
SOUTH RICHMOND SECURITIES, INC. 40 Rector Street · Suite 1810 New York, NY 10006	Telemed, Inc.	08/20/92	$ 5.0 million	Pregnancy home health care

LEAD UNDERWRITER & ADDRESS	ISSUER	PUBLIC OFFER DATE	OFFERING AMOUNT	BUSINESS
STEPHENS, INC. 111 Center Street Little Rock, AR 72201	Medicus Systems, Corp.	08/01/91	$ 7.2 million	Healthcare facilities software
STRATTON OAKMONT, INC. 1979 Marcus Avenue - Suite 120 Lake Success, NY 11042	Out-Takes, Inc. Aquanatural Co. SMT Health Services, Inc. Nutrition Management Services Co. Healthcare Imaging Systems Ropak Laboratories	03/10/93 12/02/92 03/04/92 01/29/92 11/12/91 05/16/91	$ 6.5 million $ 5.5 million $ 6.0 million $ 5.0 million $ 7.0 million $ 7.7 million	Portrait photography services Pollution control equipment Mobile X-ray facilities Health care facility food management MRI centers Test kits for poison
SUMMIT INVESTMENT CORPORATION International Centre - Suite 500 900 Second Avenue South Minneapolis, MN 55402	Sunrise Leasing Corp. Helix Biocore, Inc. (n/k/a ATS Medical, Inc.)	10/03/91 06/13/90	$ 5.0 million $ 5.6 million	Data processing equipment Heart valves
TEXAS CAPITAL SECURITIES, INC. 5085 Westheimer - Suite 4520 Houston, TX 77056	Hungarian Telephone and Cable Co. Universal Seismic Associates Industrial Holdings, Inc.	12/24/92 05/11/92 01/15/92	$ 5.6 million $ 6.1 million $ 5.9 million	Local telephone & cable networks Scientific seismic data Holding company
THOMAS JAMES ASSOC., INC. 1895 Mt. Hope Avenue P.O. Box 22719 Rochester, NY 14692	Xerographic Laser Images Corp. Palomar Medical Technologies, Inc. MRV Communications, Inc. XXsys Technologies, Inc. Network Imaging Corp. Sayett Group, Inc.	01/12/93 12/18/92 12/07/92 07/31/92 05/08/92 02/05/92	$ 5.0 million $ 6.6 million $ 5.1 million $ 6.0 million $ 6.0 million $ 8.0 million	Laser imaging software Medical lasers Laser diodes Advanced material analysis devices TVs & refrigerators Hi-tech projection holding company
UNTERBERG HARRIS, L.P. 275 Battery Street - Suite 2980 San Francisco, CA 94111	Electronic Information Systems, Inc.	07/10/92	$ 8.6 million	Telephone processing equipment
VANTAGE SECURITIES, INC. 33 Wood Avenue South - 8th Floor Iselin, NJ 08830	CliniCom, Inc. Liuski International, Inc.	04/20/92 08/13/91	$ 6.5 million $ 7.7 million	Hospital on-line information systems Computers

LEAD UNDERWRITER & ADDRESS	ISSUER	PUBLIC OFFER DATE	OFFERING AMOUNT	BUSINESS
VOLPE, WELTY & CO. One Maritime Plaza - 11th Floor San Francisco, CA 94111	Walker Power, Inc.	01/22/92	$ 9.4 million	Electric power systems
W.B. MCKEE SECURITIES, INC. 3003 North Central Avenue Suite 100 Phoenix, AZ 85012	Simula, Inc.	04/13/92	$ 5.0 million	Air safety products
WEDBUSH MORGAN SECURITIES, INC. 1000 Wilshire Blvd. P.O. Box 30014 Los Angeles, CA 90030	Northrim Bank	11/06/90	$ 8.7 million	Commercial bank
WERBEL-ROTH SECURITIES, INC. 5560 W. Oakland Park Blvd. Fort Lauderdale, FL 33313	3Net Systems, Inc.	08/10/92	$ 5.0 million	Computer network systems
WHALE SECURITIES CO., L.P. 650 Fifth Avenue New York, NY 10019	Transcor Waste Services, Inc. Saliva Diagnostic Systems, Inc. Consumer Portfolio Services, Inc. CPI Aerostructures, Inc. International Fast Food Corp. Ben Franklin Retail Stores, Inc. Metrovision of North America, Inc. Koo Koo Roo, Inc. Cellular Technical Services Co., Inc. CMS-Data Corp. Milfeld Trading Co., Inc.	03/25/93 03/04/93 10/22/92 09/16/92 05/21/92 04/28/92 12/17/91 10/15/91 08/06/91 05/08/90 01/19/90	$ 5.0 million $ 7.2 million $ 6.0 million $ 5.0 million $ 6.5 million $ 9.0 million $ 5.0 million $ 6.3 million $ 5.0 million $ 6.0 million $ 5.5 million	Solid waste management services Saliva collection devices Auto contract broker Contract production of aircraft parts Burger Kings in Poland Variety and crafts stores Videocable network Fast food restaurants Computer software Software development Footwear
WHEAT, FIRST SECURITIES, INC. 901 East Byrd Street P.O. Box 1357 Richmond, VA 23211	Medquist, Inc.	05/04/92	$ 9.0 million	Home health care services

267

LEAD UNDERWRITER & ADDRESS	ISSUER	PUBLIC OFFER DATE	OFFERING AMOUNT	BUSINESS
WILLIAM BLAIR & CO. 135 South LaSalle Street Chicago, IL 60603	Citation Computer Systems, Inc. Theratech, Inc.	10/23/92 05/13/92	$ 6.3 million $ 9.4 million	Computer information systems Drug delivery products

Firm Commitment IPO Underwritings below $5 million

filed with the SEC which were publicly offered between January 1, 1990 and March 31, 1993, listed by name of lead managing underwriter

FIRM COMMITMENT IPO'S JANUARY, 1990 THROUGH MARCH, 1993
UNDER $ 5.0 MILLION

LEAD UNDERWRITER & ADDRESS	ISSUER	PUBLIC OFFER DATE	OFFERING AMOUNT	BUSINESS
A.G. EDWARDS & SONS, INC. One North Jefferson St. Louis, MO 63103	Home Federal Savings Bank - MO	04/25/90	$ 2.1 million	Savings & loan
A.S. GOLDMEN & CO., INC. 67 Wall Street New York, NY 10005-3192	Princeton Dental Management Corp. Pet Products, Inc. Sports Heroes, Inc. Sports Media, Inc. Pamel Systems, Inc.	04/15/92 03/12/92 11/20/91 07/23/91 11/01/90	$ 4.2 million $ 4.3 million $ 4.5 million $ 3.8 million $ 4.0 million	Dental practices Beef dog treats Sports memorabilia Sports yearbooks Computer software
ARTHUR W. WOOD COMPANY, INC. 185 Devonshire Street Suite 1100 Boston, MA 02110-1407	BKC Semiconductors, Inc.	08/20/92	$ 3.5 million	Semiconductor devices
BERKELEY SECURITIES CORP. 11 Broadway New York, NY 10004	BitWise Designs, Inc.	05/13/92	$ 3.5 million	IBM compatible computers
CHELSEA STREET SECURITIES, INC. 222 West Las Colinas Blvd. Suite 2000 Irving, TX 75039	LaTexResources, Inc.	11/09/92	$ 4.2 million	Oil & gas production
COHIG & ASSOCIATES, INC. 6300 South Syracuse Way Suite 430 Englewood, CO 80111	Soricon Corp. Marcum Natural Gas Services, Inc.	11/19/92 02/13/92	$ 4.0 million $ 3.9 million	Scanning technology Gas station fuel services
COMMONWEALTH ASSOCIATES One Exchange Plaza New York, NY 10006	Alamar Biosciences, Inc. Mediware Information Systems, Inc. Star Multi Care Services, Inc. Express Cash International Corp. Medical Nutrition	10/14/92 08/06/91 05/16/91 12/12/90 03/14/90	$ 4.3 million $ 4.6 million $ 4.7 million $ 3.6 million $ 2.6 million	Diagnostic equipment Computer-based information systems Temporary healthcare Pawn shops Weight control programs

LEAD UNDERWRITER & ADDRESS	ISSUER	PUBLIC OFFER DATE	OFFERING AMOUNT	BUSINESS
CONTINENTAL BROKER-DEALER CORP. One Old Country Road Carle Place, NY 11514	Natural Child Care, Inc.	04/28/92	$ 4.9 million	Natural infant health care products
CORPORATE SECURITIES GROUP, INC. 980 North Federal Highway - Suite 210 Boca Raton, FL 33432	Regenex, Inc.	08/16/90	$ 3.0 million	Chemicals
CRAIG-HALLUM, INC. 701 Fourth Avenue South 10th Floor Minneapolis, MN 55415	Universal International, Inc.	10/12/90	$ 4.9 million	Wholesale merchandising
CRUTTENDEN & CO., INC. 18301 Von Karman - Suite 100 Irvine, CA 92715	Candy's Tortilla Factory, Inc.	08/09/91	$ 3.0 million	Specialty foods
D.H. BLAIR INVESTMENT BANKING CORP. 44 Wall Street New York, NY 10005	SBS Engineering, Inc. Bradley Pharmaceuticals, Inc. Value Vision International, Inc. Car Mart, Inc. Triple Threat Enterprises, Inc. Medenta Corp. CAP Rx, Ltd. Biomechanics Consulting	01/09/92 11/12/91 06/28/91 12/11/90 11/21/90 11/01/90 07/31/90 01/17/90	$ 4.0 million $ 4.5 million $ 4.2 million $ 4.2 million $ 3.2 million $ 4.0 million $ 4.0 million $ 4.4 million	Flight simulation systems Pharmaceuticals TV home shopping program Contract/automobile dealers Training/management for boxers Disposable testing products Prescription drug insurance Biomechanics consulting
DONALD & CO. SECURITIES, INC. 136 East 57th Street New York, NY 10022	CM Communications, Inc.	01/11/90	$ 3.5 million	Cellular phones
ELLIOT, ALLEN & CO., INC. 461 Fifth Avenue New York, NY 10017	Eco2, Inc.	10/22/92	$ 4.6 million	Solid waste & tire recycling
EQUITY SECURITIES TRADING CO., INC. 80 South Eighth Street - Suite 2820 Minneapolis, MN 55402	Rimage Corp. Rochester Medical Corp.	11/04/92 11/05/90	$ 3.4 million $ 1.5 million	Computer memory devices Urinary catheters

271

LEAD UNDERWRITER & ADDRESS	ISSUER	PUBLIC OFFER DATE	OFFERING AMOUNT	BUSINESS
EURO-ATLANTIC SECURITIES, INC. 777 Harbour Island Blvd. Suite 200 Tampa, FL 33602	Nova Technologies, Inc.	11/22/91	$ 2.6 million	Patient transfer system
F.N. WOLF & CO., INC. 110 Wall Street New York, NY 10005	Noise Com, Inc. Implant Technology, Inc. Twin Star Productions, Inc.	10/21/91 12/17/90 01/24/90	$ 4.0 million $ 3.3 million $ 4.0 million	Noise source products Orthopedic products Consumer products via TV
FIRST BIRMINGHAM SECURITIES CORPORATION 1919 Morris Avenue - Suite 1200 Birmingham, AL 35203	LifeSouth, Inc.	01/29/90	$ 1.3 million	Health and life insurance
FIRST HANOVER SECURITIES, INC. 71 Broadway - 15th Floor New York, NY 10006	Harmony Holdings, Inc.	11/13/91	$ 3.2 million	Motion picture/TV
GAINES, BERLAND, INC. 950 Third Avenue New York, NY 10022	Small's Oilfield Services Corp.	07/07/92	$ 4.9 million	Oilfield services
GILFORD SECURITIES, INC. 850 Third Avenue New York, NY 10022	Sports/Leisure, Inc. Xenejenex, Inc.	10/28/91 02/09/90	$ 4.0 million $ 2.5 million	Unisex sports apparel Health care videos
G.K. SCOTT & CO., INC. One Fairchild Court Plainview, NY 11803	Electronic Technology Group, Inc.	03/12/90	$ 3.6 million	Electronic equipment
GKN SECURITIES CORP. 61 Broadway - 12th Floor New York, NY 10006	Financial Data Systems, Inc. Lancit Media Productions, Ltd. Robern Apparel, Inc.	12/04/91 06/19/91 04/03/91	$ 3.6 million $ 2.0 million $ 4.0 million	Financial publishing TV series and specials Skiwear and accessories
GLOBAL AMERICA, INC. 110 Wall Street - 17th Floor New York, NY 10005	Mountaintop Corp.	06/29/90	$ 4.2 million	Liquor

LEAD UNDERWRITER & ADDRESS	ISSUER	PUBLIC OFFER DATE	OFFERING AMOUNT	BUSINESS
HANOVER, STERLING & CO., LTD. 88 Pine Street Wall Street Plaza New York, NY 10005-1801	Mister Jay Fashions International, Inc. Blue Chip Computerware, Inc.	02/11/93 08/11/92	$ 2.0 million $ 2.0 million	Women's blouses Microcomputers.
J. EDMUND & CO. 1431 Brush Hill Road Milton, MA 02186	The Standish Care Company	02/06/92	$ 3.5 million	Senior housing & health services
J. GREGORY & COMPANY, INC. 833 Northern Boulevard Great Neck, NY 11021	ComCentral, Corp.	12/19/91	$ 3.0 million	Telecommunications
J.W. GANT & ASSOCIATES, INC. 7600 East Orchard Road Suite 160 Englewood, CO 80111	Vital Living Products, Inc. Sheffield Industries, Inc. Beverly Hills Fan Co. Celebrity Resorts, Inc.	03/25/92 08/12/91 05/31/91 08/14/90	$ 4.3 million $ 4.0 million $ 3.0 million $ 3.5 million	Bottled drinking water Ladies hosiery Ceiling fans Sports resort
J.W. CHARLES SECURITIES, INC. 980 North Federal Highway Suite 210 Boca Raton, FL 33432	RailAmerica, Inc. Peachtree FiberOptics, Inc. All American Semiconductor, Inc. Suprema Specialties, Inc.	11/09/92 10/08/92 06/18/92 04/25/91	$ 3.9 million $ 3.5 million $ 3.5 million $ 3.5 million	Transportation holding company Plastic optical fiber Electronic components distributor Gourmet cheeses
JERSEY SECURITIES CORP. 28 West Grand Avenue Montvale, NJ 07645	Peerless Productions Ltd., Inc.	03/30/90	$ 2.1 million	Theatrical film producers
JOHN G. KINNARD & CO., INC. 1700 Northstar West Minneapolis, MN 55402	Serving Software, Inc. Olympic Financial Ltd. Computer Petroleum Corp. Ringer Corp.	03/18/92 01/30/92 05/21/91 09/19/90	$ 4.6 million $ 4.8 million $ 3.0 million $ 4.9 million	Software for medical field Automobile installment loans Information/customized news services Environmental garden products
KASHNER DAVIDSON SECURITIES CORP. 77 South Palm Avenue Sarasota, FL 34236	Lasersight, Inc. Omega Health Systems, Inc.	11/13/91 08/09/90	$ 4.5 million $ 2.3 million	Optical materials Eye care/surgery centers

273

LEAD UNDERWRITER & ADDRESS	ISSUER	PUBLIC OFFER DATE	OFFERING AMOUNT	BUSINESS
A.M. LEVINE & CO., INC. 17 Battery Place New York, NY 10004	International Airline Support Group, Inc.	04/02/90	$ 2.4 million	Aircraft parts
M.H. MEYERSON & CO., INC. 30 Montgomery Street Jersey City, NJ 07302	Deprenyl Animal Health, Inc. I-flow Corp.	03/14/91 02/01/90	$ 3.6 million $ 2.6 million	Animal pharmaceuticals Drug infusion systems
MALONE & ASSOCIATES, INC. 1401 17th Street - Suite 1550 Denver, CO 80202	Winners Circle, Inc. California Jamar, Inc.	07/10/90 04/26/90	$ 3.9 million $ 3.3 million	Clothing Laser systems
MANCHESTER RHONE SECURITIES CORP. 61 Broadway - Suite 2700 New York, NY 10006	First Cash, Inc.	04/25/91	$ 4.5 million	Pawn shops
MARCHE SECURITIES, INC. 512 Nicollet Mall - Suite 400 Minneapolis, MN 55402	Standard Platforms Holdings, plc.	09/28/90	$ 1.0 million	Data retrieval for processing
MATHEWS, HOLMQUIST & ASSOCIATES, INC. 100 N. 6th Street - Suite 306C Minneapolis, MN 55403	Celox Corp.	03/09/92	$ 4.6 million	Cell culture mediums
MILLER, JOHNSON & KUEHN, INC. 1660 S. Highway 100 - Suite 228 Minneapolis, MN 55416	Recovery Engineering, Inc. Selsmed Instruments, Inc. Everest Medical Corp.	03/04/93 03/20/91 12/06/90	$ 4.0 million $ 4.1 million $ 3.8 million	Purification products Cardiology instruments Electrosurgical devices
NEIDIGER, TUCKER, BRUNER, INC. 1675 Larimer #300 Denver, CO 80202	Internet Communications, Inc.	12/13/91	$ 2.6 million	Data communications equipment
NOBLE INVESTMENT CO. OF PALM BEACH 1801 Clint Moore Rd. - Suite 110 Boca Raton, FL 33487	EV Environmental, Inc. Clucker's Wood Roasted Chicken, Inc. Austin's International, Inc. Capitol Multimedia, Inc.	02/16/93 11/10/92 07/29/92 03/31/92	$ 3.5 million $ 3.9 million $ 4.9 million $ 4.6 million	Environmental testing services Restaurants Texas-style restaurants Video & audio production

274

LEAD UNDERWRITER & ADDRESS	ISSUER	PUBLIC OFFER DATE	OFFERING AMOUNT	BUSINESS
NORCROSS SECURITIES, INC. 645 E. Missouri Avenue - Suite 119 Phoenix, AZ 85012	Reconditioned Systems, Inc.	12/18/92	$ 2.5 million	Modular workstation components
OAK RIDGE INVESTMENTS, INC. 233 N. Michigan Avenue Suite 1807 Chicago, IL 60601	Aerial Assault, Inc.	12/16/92	$ 4.0 million	Athletic shoes
PARAGON CAPITAL CORP. 120 Wall Street - 28th Floor New York, NY 10005	Zams, Inc. Megacards, Inc.	05/14/92 10/10/91	$ 3.8 million $ 4.1 million	Paper & party goods Sports cards
PAULI & CO., INC. 232 S. Meramac Avenue St. Louis, MO 63105	Zoltek Cos., Inc. D&K Wholesale Drug, Inc.	11/06/92 09/01/92	$ 4.4 million $ 4.6 million	Carbon fibers Wholesale drug distributor
PAULSON INVESTMENT CO., INC. 811 S.W. Front Avenue Suite 200 Portland, OR 97204	Document Technologies, Inc. Pit Stop Auto Centers, Inc.	02/14/92 07/31/90	$ 4.5 million $ 4.0 million	Document image processing systems Oil change service centers
R.A.F. FINANCIAL CORP. One Norwest Center 1700 Lincoln Street - 32nd Floor Denver, CO 80203	Hibernia Foods plc H.D. Vest, Inc. Rentech, Inc.	10/22/92 11/21/91 04/18/91	$ 3.0 million $ 3.9 million $ 4.4 million	Beef for export Financial services Solids into fuels
R.G. DICKINSON & CO. 405 Sixth Avenue - Suite 200 P.O. Box 9111 Des Moines, IA 50306-9111	TNC Media, Inc.	11/01/91	$ 4.8 million	Pay-per-view TV production
R.J. STEICHEN & CO. 801 Nicollet Mall - Suite 1100 Minneapolis, MN 55402	Eltrax Systems, Inc. Digital Biometrics, Inc.	12/08/92 12/07/90	$ 4.1 million $ 2.1 million	Hospital information systems Fingerprint record products

275

LEAD UNDERWRITER & ADDRESS	ISSUER	PUBLIC OFFER DATE	OFFERING AMOUNT	BUSINESS
RAFFENSPERGER, HUGHES & CO., INC. 20 North Meridian Street Indianapolis, IN 46204	United Financial Bancorp, Inc. Shelby Couty Bancorp	09/09/92 10/17/91	$ 4.6 million $ 1.7 million	Financial institution Financial institution
ROBERT TODD FINANCIAL CORP. 200 Garden City Plaza Garden City, NY 11530	American Biomed, Inc.	10/22/91	$ 4.0 million	Medical research/cardiovascular devices
ROYCE INVESTMENT GROUP, INC. 113 Crossways Park Drive Woodbury, NY 117972	Ongard Systems, Inc.	08/11/92	$ 4.0 million	Infection control systems
ROSENKRANTZ LYON & ROSS, INC. 6 East 43rd Street New York, NY 10017	Credit Depot Corp. Air-Cure Environmental Projectavision ACTV, Inc.	04/19/91 12/14/90 07/24/90 05/04/90	$ 3.9 million $ 4.0 million $ 4.2 million $ 4.7 million	Mortgage broker Air pollution control systems Solid state displays Interactive TV & video technology
S.D. COHN & CO., INC. 17 Battery Place - Suite 626 New York, NY 10004	Gotham Apparel Corp. Biospecifics Technologies Corp.	11/02/92 11/14/91	$ 3.6 million $ 3.6 million	Women's apparel Pharmaceuticals
SCHNEIDER SECURITIES, INC. 104 Broadway Denver, CO 80203	Aerodyne Products, Inc. Laser Vision Centers	07/18/91 04/03/91	$ 3.9 million $ 3.0 million	Automated systems Eye surgery center
SHAMROCK PARTNERS, LTD. 111 Veterans Square Media, PA 19063	Nyer Medical Group, Inc.	06/09/92	$ 2.8 million	Medical products distributor
STONEGATE SECURITIES, INC. 500 Crescent Court - Suite 270 Dallas, TX 75201	BioSafety Systems, Inc.	02/11/93	$ 3.6 million	Health care safety equipment
STRATTON OAKMONT, INC. 1979 Marcus Avenue - Suite 120 Lake Success, NY 11042	Lincon International, Inc. IPS Health Care	08/13/91 01/16/91	$ 4.9 million $ 4.7 million	Industrial waste cleanup equipment MRI servcies

276

LEAD UNDERWRITER & ADDRESS	ISSUER	PUBLIC OFFER DATE	OFFERING AMOUNT	BUSINESS
STUART, COLEMAN & CO., INC. 11 West 42nd Street - 15th Floor New York, NY 10036	RT Industries, Inc.	06/17/92	$ 3.6 million	Brake friction products
THE STUART-JAMES CO., INC. 8055 E. Tufts Avenue Parkway #1200 Devnver, CO 80237	GB Foods Corp. Command Security Group Craftmade International Medgroup NDC Automation, Inc.	08/21/90 07/19/90 04/16/90 04/06/90 03/21/90	$ 4.3 million $ 3.8 million $ 3.5 million $ 3.4 million $ 2.4 million	Mexican restaurants Security guard services Ceiling fan & light kits Physical therapy Guided vehicle systems
SUMMIT INVESTMENT CORPORATION International Centre - Suite 500 900 Second Avenue South Minneapolis, MN 55402	Medamicus, Inc.	09/06/91	$ 3.6 million	Medical devices
TEXAS CAPITAL SECURITIES, INC. 5085 Westheimer - Suite 4520 Houston, TX 77056	Mr. Bulb, Inc.	04/14/92	$ 2.5 million	Efficient light bulbs
TEXAS SECURITIES 4200 South Hulen Street - Suite 536 Fort Worth, TX 76109	Spectral Diagnostics, Inc.	07/15/92	$ 3.9 million	In-vitro diagnostic antibodies
THOMAS JAMES ASSOC., INC. 1895 Mt. Hope Avenue P.O. Box 22719 Rochester, NY 14692	M-Systems Flash Disk Pioneers, Ltd. Vision Ten, Inc. Bio-dyne Corp. Saratoga Brands, Inc. Sanborn, Inc. Excel Technology, Inc. Cybernetics Products, Inc. Acqua Group, Inc. DynaGen, Inc.	03/04/93 11/07/91 10/16/91 09/04/91 08/07/91 05/13/91 04/10/91 12/12/90 08/10/90	$ 4.6 million $ 4.7 million $ 3.3 million $ 4.4 million $ 3.8 million $ 4.1 million $ 4.5 million $ 3.0 million $ 4.0 million	Computer chips Computerized work stations Exercise equipment Potato chips Industrial separation systems Laser systems Printed circuit boards Non-bottled water coolers Therapeutic products
VANTAGE SECURITIES, INC. 33 Wood Avenue South - 8th Floor Iselin, NJ 08830	Golden Eagle Group, Inc. R2 Medical Systems, Inc.	11/24/92 09/01/92	$ 4.0 million $ 4.8 million	Property & casualty insurance Cardiac electrodes

LEAD UNDERWRITER & ADDRESS	ISSUER	PUBLIC OFFER DATE	OFFERING AMOUNT	BUSINESS
W.B. MCKEE SECURITIES, INC. 3003 North Central Avenue Suite 100 Phoenix, AZ 85012	Care Concepts, Inc.	2/17/93	$ 4.2 million	Vehicles for the handicapped
WESTFIELD FINANCIAL CORP. 375 Park Avenue New York, NY 10152	Universal Self Care, Inc.	12/11/92	$ 4.7 million	Drugs for diabetes
WESTMINSTER SECURITIES, INC. 19 Rector Street New York, NY 10006	Bishop Equities South End Ventures Avalon Enterprises Carnegie Capital Corp., Inc. Elmwood Capital Corp. Harley Equities, Inc. Fulton Ventures, Inc. Sharon Capital Corp. West End Ventures, Inc.	03/08/92 11/15/91 03/26/91 02/01/91 06/27/90 05/29/90 04/10/90 02/14/90 01/02/90	$ 0.1 million $ 0.1 million $ 0.1 million $ 0.1 million $ 0.1 million $ 0.1 million $ 0.1 million $ 0.2 million $ 0.1 million	Blind pool Blind pool Blind pool Blind pool Blind pool Blind pool Blind pool Blind pool Blind pool
WESTONKA INVESTMENTS, INC. 12900 Whitewater Drive #180 Minnetonka, MN 55343	Environmental Technologies USA, Inc.	10/23/92	$ 4.0 million	Biodegradable products

278

Timetable for
Traditional IPO

TIMETABLE FOR AN INITIAL PUBLIC OFFERING

The following is a typical timetable for an IPO, which usually involves at least a four-month period:

PARTICIPANTS

Company:	CO
Underwriter:	U
Underwriters' Counsel:	UC
Company Counsel:	CC
Accountants:	A

SUMMARY OF KEY DATES

Organizational Meeting	January 7
Filing with SEC	Week of February 24
Receive SEC Comments	Week of March 23
Commence Marketing	Week of March 30
Offering	Week of April 13
Closing	Week of April 20

Date	Description of Action	Responsibility
January 7	Organizational Meeting	All Hands

1. Obtain name, address and phone number of all hands.
2. Discuss financial to be used in registration statement.
3. Assignment of responsibilities.
4. Selection of financial printer and bank note company.
5. Statements by officers and directors before, during and after registration period.
6. Discuss Board meetings, including dates, preparation of resolutions authority given to special or executive committees and power of attorney for interim amendment and price amendment.
7. Discuss Blue Sky considerations.
8. Discuss pre-filing press release.
9. Outline of prospectus.
10. Distribute underwriter's due diligence outline and document request.
11. Distribute internal Company projections.
12. Distribute last three years' financial statements.
13. Any other necessary action with respect to the offering:
    • Selection of directors
    • Status of audit

January 7–10	Company ceases further distribution of publicity relating to Company without prior clearance from CC and UC.	UC, CC
	Begin preparation of underwriting agreement and agreement among underwriters.	UC

Week of January 27	Begin review of corporate minute book and other relevant documents to be completed prior to filing.	UC, CC
	Prepare and distribute officer's and director's questionnaires to be returned prior to effective date.	CO, CC
	Contact printer, transfer agent and engraver.	CC
	Draft of Company financial distributed to working group.	CO, A
Week of February 3	Draft of S-1 and underwriting contracts distributed to working group.	CC, UC
	Drafting session/Site visits.	All Hands
	U receive draft of financial on acquisitions.	CO, A
	Due diligence with accountants on Company financial and acquisition financial.	U, UC
Week of February 10	Due diligence.	U, UC
	Next draft of registration statement, underwriting contracts distributed to working group.	CO, CC
	Drafting session with focus on acquisition disclosure.	All Hands
	Due diligence on Company.	U, UC
Week of February 17	Third draft of registration statement distributed to working group.	CO, CC
	Third drafting session.	All Hands
Week of February 24	Prepare and circulate draft news release relating to initial filing.	CO, CC
	Print registration statement and related documents in form ready for filing and arrange for signing where necessary.	CO
	Registration statement (together with exhibits, certified check for filing fee, powers of attorney, certified resolutions) filed with Securities and Exchange Commission ("SEC") in Washington, D.C.	CC
	Requisite copies of registration statement, preliminary prospectus and underwriting agreement, together with filing fee, to be mailed to National Association of Securities Dealers, Inc. ("NASD").	UC

	1934 Act Registration Statement on Form 8-A filed with SEC.	
	Acceleration requested to coincide with effectiveness of S-1.	
	Issue press release regarding filing.	CO, U
	Begin Blue Sky qualification.	UC
	Ascertain review status with SEC.	CC
	Begin preparation of road show presentation and schedule.	CO, U
Weeks of March 23 and March 30	Receive SEC comments (assume 30-day review at SEC).	All Hands
	File amendment #1 to S-1 and Acceleration Request. Prepare and clear press release relating to actual offering.	CO, U, CC
	Underwriters' questionnaires returned.	U
	Produce, execute and deliver letter to SEC notifying of clearance by NASD of underwriting arrangements.	UC
	SEC declares offering effective.	
	Underwriters commence distribution to prospective syndicate underwriters of an invitation accompanied by:	U
	1. Preliminary prospectus.	
	2. Proof of underwriting booklet.	
	3. Blue Sky memorandum.	
	4. Underwriters' questionnaire.	
	5. Underwriters' power of attorney.	
	Information meetings in various cities ("road show")	CO, U
Week of April 13	New Board of Special or Executive Committee designated by Board of Directors approves terms of offering, filing of price amendment and other necessary action.	CO
	Prepare prospectus.	All Hands
	CO and U agree on terms and other matters.	CO, U
	Sign up underwriters by power of attorney starting at 9:00 a.m. (EST).	U
	Issue press release with final terms of the offering.	CO, U
	Advise Blue Sky commissions where required.	UC

	File prospectus.	CC
	File final documents with NASD.	UC
	Tombstone advertisement is published.	U
Week of April 20	Closing	All Hands

<u>Preparation of Documents</u>   <u>Initial</u>
<u>Responsibility</u>

1.	Registration Statement	
	a. Cover page, stabilization language, underwriting section, back page	U
	b. Selected financial data	CO, A
	c. Capitalization	CO, A
	d. Remainder of prospectus, including summary page	CO, CC
	e. Part II of Registration Statement	
	• Item 14 Other expenses of Issuance and Distribution	CO, CC
	• Item 15 Indemnification of Directors and Officers	CO, CC
	• Item 16 Exhibits	CO, CC
	• Item 17 Undertakings	CO, CC
2.	Agreement among underwriters	U, UC
3.	Underwriting agreement	U, UC
4.	Underwriters' questionnaires	U, UC
5.	Powers of attorney (for underwriters)	U, UC
6.	Officers' and directors' questionnaires	CO, CC
7.	Opinion of counsel for the Company	CC
8.	Opinion of counsel for the Underwriters	UC
9.	Accountant's comfort letter	A
10.	Resolutions of Board of Directors, special or executive committees	CO, CC
11.	Press release—Initial filing	CC, U
	• Offering	CC, U
12.	Blue Sky memorandum	UC
13.	Tombstone advertisement	U
14.	Transmittal letters to SEC	CO, CC

Appendix 6

Excerpts from Regulation A Offering Circular of Real Goods Trading Corporation

dated June 21, 1993

OFFERING CIRCULAR
June 21, 1993
REAL GOODS TRADING CORPORATION
(Exact name of Company as set forth in Charter)

Type of securities offered: Common Stock
Maximum number of securities offered: 600,000
Minimum number of securities offered: Not applicable
Price per share: $6.00
Total proceeds: If maximum sold: $3,600,000
If minimum sold: Not applicable
(For use of proceeds and offering expenses, see Question Nos. 9 and 10)

Is a commissioned selling agent selling the securities in this offering? [x] Yes [ ] No. A portion of the offering may be sold by selling agents.

If yes, what percent is commission of price to public? 6% of selling price of shares sold by selling agent to selling agents' customers; 3% of selling price of shares sold by selling agents to the Company's customers. The Company believes that it will sell a significant portion of the shares without commission.

Is there other compensation to selling agent(s)? [x] Yes [ ] No
If one of the selling agents has sold at least $200,000 of securities, then that selling agent will be entitled to provide ongoing investor relations services for compensation related to the results of that agent's services and that selling agent will be reimbursed for certain due diligence costs.
(See questions No. 22.)

Is there a finder's fee or similar payment to any person? [ ] Yes [x] No (See Question No. 22)

Is there an escrow of proceeds until minimum is obtained? [x] Yes [ ] No (See Question No. 26). Escrow applies only to residents of Mississippi and Texas.

Is this offering limited to members of a special group, such as employees of the Company or individuals? [ ] Yes [x] No (See Question No. 25)

Is transfer of the securities restricted? [ ] Yes [x] No (See Question No. 25)
INVESTMENT IN SMALL BUSINESSES INVOLVES A HIGH DEGREE OF RISK, AND INVESTORS SHOULD NOT INVEST ANY FUNDS IN THIS OFFERING UNLESS THEY CAN AFFORD TO LOSE THEIR INVESTMENT IN ITS ENTIRETY. SEE QUESTION NO. 2 FOR THE RISK FACTORS THAT MANAGEMENT BELIEVES PRESENT THE MOST SUBSTANTIAL RISKS TO AN INVESTOR IN THIS OFFERING.

IN MAKING AN INVESTMENT DECISION INVESTORS MUST RELY ON THEIR OWN EXAMINATION OF THE PERSON OR ENTITY CREATING THE SECURITIES AND THE TERMS OF THE OFFERING, INCLUDING THE MERITS AND RISKS INVOLVED. THESE SECURITIES HAVE NOT BEEN RECOMMENDED BY ANY FEDERAL OR STATE SECURITIES COMMISSION OR REGULATORY AUTHORITY. FURTHERMORE, THE AUTHORITIES HAVE NOT PASSED UPON

286

2

THE ACCURACY OR THE ADEQUACY OF THIS DOCUMENT. ANY REPRESENTATION TO THE CONTRARY IS A CRIMINAL OFFENSE.

THE U.S. SECURITIES AND EXCHANGE COMMISSION DOES NOT PASS UPON THE MERITS OF ANY SECURITIES OFFERED OR THE TERMS OF THE OFFERING. NOR DOES IT PASS UPON THE ACCURACY OR COMPLETENESS OF ANY OFFERING CIRCULAR OR SELLING I 'TERATURE. THESE SECURITIES ARE OFFERED UNDER AN EXEMPTION FROM REGISTRA 1 1ON; HOWEVER, THE COMMISSION HAS NOT MADE AN INDEPENDENT DETERMINATION THAT THESE SECURITIES ARE EXEMPT FROM REGISTRATION.

This Company:
      [ ] Has never conducted operations.
      [ ] Is in the development stage.
      [x] Is currently conducting operations.
      [x] Has shown a profit in the last fiscal year.
      [ ] Other (Specify):
         (Check at least one, as appropriate)

SEE QUESTION NO. 2 FOR THE RISK FACTORS THAT MANAGEMENT BELIEVES PRESENT THE MOST SUBSTANTIAL RISKS TO AN INVESTOR IN THIS OFFERING.

This offering has been registered for offer and sale in the following states:

State	State file no.	Effective Date	State	State file no.	Effective Date
Alaska	93-01193	2/26/93	Montana	N.A.	4/8/93
Arizona	S-32568	6/14/93	Nebraska	246	2/24/93
California	5055173	2/25/93	Nevada	R93-29	*
Colorado	Exempt	2/26/93	New Hampshire	N.A.	4/1/93
Connecticut	SQ-22786	3/26/93	New Jersey	SR-7258	4/14/93
Delaware	N.A.	3/26/93	New Mexico	P930182	1/28/93
Dist. Columbia	Exempt	2/26/93	New York	S-25 81 45	2/26/93
Georgia	SEN930402128	2/5/93	North Carolina	799	*
Hawaii	N.A.	6/3/93	North Dakota	397	3/4/93
Idaho	43060	2/26/93	Ohio	81829	2/26/93
Illinois	9325199	3/19/93	Oklahoma	IA 354-93	*
Indiana	93004RQ	4/12/93	Oregon	93-00-11	3/1/93
Iowa	I-29155	3/29/93	Pennsylvania	92-12-14C	6/15/93
Kansas	93-S-1123	3/17/93	Rhode Island	N.A.	2/26/93
Kentucky	29062	5/24/93	South Carolina	RE6073	3/29/93
Louisiana	N.A.	3/26/93	South Dakota	N.A.	4/1/93
Maine	93-30-32	*	Texas	A 4179	4/13/93
Maryland	SR920675	3/18/93	Utah	2-6933/A17548-06	4/5/93
Massachusetts	930122-C	3/23/93	Vermont	1/22/93-01	*
Michigan	153236	*	Virginia	N.A.	*
Minnesota	R36415	*	Washington	C-35554	2/26/93
Mississippi	FI-93-02-002	4/30/93	West Virginia	N.A.	4/12/93
Missouri	N.A.	*			

N.A. Number not available
* State has not provided an effective date as of the date of this Offering Circular

3

TABLE OF CONTENTS

THIS OFFERING CIRCULAR CONTAINS ALL OF THE REPRESENTATIONS BY THE COMPANY
CONCERNING THIS OFFERING, AND NO PERSON SHALL MAKE DIFFERENT OR BROADER STATEMENTS
THAN THOSE CONTAINED HEREIN. INVESTORS ARE CAUTIONED NOT TO RELY UPON ANY
INFORMATION NOT EXPRESSLY SET FORTH IN THIS OFFERING CIRCULAR.

This Offering Circular, together with Financial Statements and other Attachments, consists of a total of 53
pages.

288

4

THE COMPANY

1. *Exact corporate name*: Real Goods Trading Corporation

   State and date of incorporation: California, 18 June 1990. Successor to proprietorship founded in 1986.

   Street address of principal office: 966 Mazzoni St., Ukiah, CA 95482

   Company Telephone Number: (707)468-9292   *Fiscal year*: 1 April - 31 March. Unless otherwise indicated, references to years are to the Company's fiscal year.

   Person(s) to contact at Company with respect to offering: John Schaeffer, President

RISK FACTORS

2. *List in the order of importance the factors which the Company considers to be the most substantial risks to   an investor in this offering in view of all facts and circumstances or which otherwise make the offering one   of high risk or speculative (i.e., those factors which constitute the greatest threat that the investment will be   lost in whole or in part, or not provide an adequate return).*

   (1) Dependence on Chief Executive Officer

   The Company's business is dependent, to a large extent, upon the services of John Schaeffer, founder, Chairman of the Board, President and Chief Executive Officer. The Company's operations could be adversely affected if, for any reason, Mr. Schaeffer ceases to be active in the Company's management. The Company has reduced this risk by retaining an experienced management team and insuring the life of Mr. Schaeffer for $1 Million. There can be no assurance, however, that the Company's efforts will be successful. John Schaeffer is 43 years old. For a description of the Company's management team, see questions 29-32.

   (2) Competition

   The mail order catalog business in the energy-efficiency and alternative energy fields is highly competitive. The Company competes primarily with other alternative energy mail order catalogs and secondarily with retail stores on the basis of price, breadth of product offerings, and information. Additionally, as alternative energy has become more accepted, some public utility companies are planning to enter the alternative energy production field. Wider public acceptance of alternative energy may draw additional competitors into the field. Several of the Company's competitors and potential competitors have financial resources superior to those of the Company. As these competitors enter the field, the Company's market share may fail to increase or may decrease despite the efforts of the Company to focus upon products unavailable elsewhere and to provide superior service. See 3(c) for further details on competition.

   (3) Recent Sales Results

   Catalog vendors such as the Company can control their growth to a greater extent than many other businesses by the rate at which they "prospect" - i.e. mail to rented lists. As the recent economic slowdown became clearer, the Company chose to reduce its prospecting, thus reducing its rate of sales growth from the substantial rate of prior years to a rate of 26% in fiscal 1992-93. While management believes that the Company can grow by prospecting, sales per catalog mailed to rented lists are generally materially lower than sales per catalog mailed to the Company's two-year buyer list. Thus, the cost of obtaining new customers may be greater than the cost of retaining current customers, and the productivity of new customers may be less than that of current customers.

5

(4) Weakening of Gasoline and Oil Prices

The Company believes that its sales are adversely affected by periods of decreased energy prices. The Company's products are less competitive in terms of price when energy prices are lower. Although the Company's sales have grown each year, during periods of high and low energy prices alike, any future declines in energy prices are likely to have an adverse effect upon sales.

(5) Reliance on Outside Suppliers

It has been the Company's policy not to manufacture or assemble any of the products it sells. Management believes this policy provides the most flexibility to meet customer needs, while reducing the Company's risk and its need for capital investments. However, because of this policy, the Company may experience delays in production and delivery which are beyond its control and which may result in canceled orders, reduced sales, and other events which may negatively affect income.

(6) Limit on Dividends

The Company currently has a line of credit for $400,000 with National Bank of The Redwoods. The business loan agreement pertaining to the line of credit prevents the Company from paying any dividends without the written consent of the bank. The Company has no present intention to pay dividends.

(7) Shareowners' Lack of Ability to Direct Corporate Actions

If all the shares being offered are sold, the Company's founders will still own 75.6% of the total shares outstanding. As a result, new shareowners will lack the ability to affect corporate actions.

(8) Increases in the Cost of Mailing and Paper

The Company spends significant amounts of money on paper for the production of catalogs and on mailing the catalogs and packages to its customers. Although the Company is satisfied with its current paper prices, there is no assurance that paper prices will not increase in the future. The United States Postal Service, which handles approximately 20% of the Company's orders, has increased rates in the past and the Company believes that similar increases are likely for shipments handled by United Parcel Service, Federal Express and the other carriers utilized by the Company. Higher costs of mailing, shipping and paper would increase the Company's cost of doing business and, to the extent such increases cannot be passed on to customers in the form of higher product or handling and shipping costs, could adversely affect its earnings.

(9) Potential State Sales Tax Liability

Various states have increasingly taken the position that mail order companies are responsible for collecting sales or use tax with respect to sales made to residents in their states even if the only contact with such states is the mailing of catalogs and products into such states. In 1992 the U.S. Supreme Court ruled that it is up to the U.S. Congress to decide whether sales tax may be charged to out of state customers by mail order companies. A subcommittee of the Ways and Means Committee of the House of Representatives is conducting hearings on legislation to require mail-order retailers to collect sales or use tax from out-of-state purchasers. Although the Company cannot predict the likelihood of passage of legislation or its final form, if such legislation is passed it could have an adverse effect upon the Company by increasing the Company's costs of doing business and by increasing the cost of its products to its customers.

(10) Reliance on Foreign Suppliers

6

In recent years, approximately 15% of the Company's inventory was manufactured by foreign sources. As a result, the Company is subject to the risks of doing business abroad, including adverse fluctuations in currency exchange rates (particularly those of the U.S. dollar against certain Asian currencies), changes in import duties or quotas and transportation, labor disputes and strikes. Although the Company has not experienced a material disruption of its operations to date, there is no assurance that this trend will continue. The occurrence of any one or more of the foregoing could adversely impact the Company's operations and earnings.

(11) Limited Trading Market

Since completion of its initial public offering in February 1992, a limited, order matching service has been provided in the Company's shares by Mutual Securities, Inc./Cowles, Sabol & Co., Inc., a broker-dealer registered with the SEC and under certain state securities laws ("the broker"). The broker uses its best efforts to execute orders to buy and sell the Company's shares upon request. This arrangement is, however, subject to the availability of persons known to the broker to be interested in selling or buying, and agreement upon a price for any transaction. During the year ended March 31, 1993, approximately 34,000 shares were traded in this manner through the broker. The broker does not maintain an inventory of the Company's stock or otherwise function as a "market maker" in the stock. California residents may not be solicited to buy or to sell the stock, which decreases the effectiveness of this order matching procedure. There is no contract or other agreement between the broker and the Company, and the broker may choose to cease this function at any time.

Upon completion of this offering, the Company believes that additional registered securities broker-dealers will execute orders to buy and sell the Company's shares and that they may function as "market makers," maintaining an inventory and soliciting orders to buy and sell the shares. If substantially all the shares being offered are sold, the Company believes it will meet the standards for having trading information about its shares quoted on the NASDAQ basic listing/"Small-Cap Issues" market, and it will apply for that status.

The Company's common stock has been accepted for trading on the Pacific Stock Exchange, through its proposed "SCOR" listing program pending approval of that program by the Securities and Exchange Commission. There can be no assurance of that approval. Upon approval from the Securities and Exchange Commission and upon the Company's registration under the Securities Exchange Act of 1934 and provided the Company continues to meet the applicable Pacific Stock Exchange requirements, the Company believes that its common stock will be listed on the Pacific Stock Exchange.

There is no assurance that any broker-dealers, including the broker, will maintain a market at any time or that the Company's trading information will be included in the NASDAQ system. There may be no organized trading market for the Company's common stock. Even if there is a trading market established, the ability of a shareowner to sell his or her shares will depend on the existence of persons interested in buying shares. There can be no assurance that people will be interested in buying the Company's stock.

(12) Dilution

Investors in the Company's shares being offered will pay a price per share considerably in excess of the cash originally invested by the founders, John and Nancy Schaeffer. In 1986, the Schaeffers began the business with $3,000 of capital. At March 31, 1993, the Company's "net tangible book value" (tangible assets of the Company, less its liabilities) was $1,154,600, equivalent to $0.41 per share outstanding at that date. After giving effect to the offering, assuming the sale of 600,000 shares at $6 per share, the net tangible book value will be $1.24 per share. This is a dilution in net tangible book value to investors who buy shares in this offering of $4.76 per share. (See Item 7 of this Offering Circular for a description of the offering price factors and the consideration for shares issued to the founders).

7

(13) Erosion of Revenues per Catalog over Time

While the Company is currently experiencing a rate 50% over the mail order industry average for revenues per catalog mailed, there can be no assurances that this high rate will continue. As the Company expands its mailing plan, it is likely that the revenues per catalog sent will decrease.

(14) Limited Retail Store Experience

The Company's marketing plan calls for the opening of three retail stores. The Company has limited experience with retail stores. There can be no assurance that the first store will be successful or, if it is successful, that other retail stores will be successful.

(15) New Construction

If a substantial number of the shares offered hereby are sold, the Company intends to use a substantial portion of the proceeds to construct a headquarters/warehouse/demonstration site. The Company does not have significant experience with projects of this magnitude and there can be no assurance that the Company will not experience material adverse effects such as cost overruns and delays.

Note: In addition to the above risks, businesses are often subject to risks not foreseen or fully appreciated by management. In reviewing this Offering Circular potential investors should keep in mind other possible risks that could be important.

BUSINESS AND PROPERTIES

3. *With respect to the business of the Company and its properties:*

   (a) Describe in detail what business the Company does and proposes to do, including what products or goods are or will be produced or services that are or will be rendered.

The Company's business is the sale of products and equipment that facilitate "independent living." This market consists of two primary segments - alternative energy and conservation. These products are principally marketed through the Company's catalogs and its Alternative Energy Sourcebook. Adjacent to its headquarters, the Company also has a showroom from which it makes retail sales.

Alternative Energy Market

Approximately 51% of the Company's business is generated from the alternative energy market. The Company believes it is the largest and oldest mail order supplier of alternative energy and energy-sensible products in the world. Through its catalogs (2,547,750 mailed in fiscal 1992-93) and its Alternative Energy Sourcebook™ (discussed later), it offers power systems for remote homes using alternative sources of energy including photovoltaic (solar-electric), hydro-electric, and wind-electric, as well as emerging alternative technologies like hydrogen fuel cells, and a new generation of photovoltaic cells. The Company endeavors to provide a full array of appliance systems components and technical service, for every aspect of living away from power lines. These products include battery storage systems, power conversion devices, charge controllers, meters, gasoline generators, low voltage water pumping systems, solar and propane gas water heaters, refrigerators, solar cooling devices, composting toilets, and a wide variety of low-voltage household appliances.

The traditional market for these power systems has been remote homes in excess of one quarter mile from the power companies' lines in the USA and, to a substantially lesser extent, in remote villages in third world countries. Foreign

8

sales account for approximately 2% of the Company's business. The Company has customers in over 100 countries. The Company also provides solar-electric systems for governmental agencies (approximately 2% of its business) including the United States Interior Department, the Bureau of Land Management, the U.S. Forest Service, and occasionally the military.

Conservation Market

In the past several years, the Company's mail order catalog has also been successful at marketing energy saving and conservation products to urban and suburban dwellers. This "conservation market" represents approximately 49% of the Company's business. These products include a full spectrum of energy-efficient lighting including outdoor and solar lighting; water saving devices including low flow showerheads, low-flush toilets, and faucet aerators; recycled paper products including toilet paper, paper towels, and facial tissue; and products used in recycling such as canvas and string bags, recycling bins, and paper recycling devices. To this same clientele, the Company markets non-toxic household products, water and air purification devices, magnetic radiation meters, and a large selection of solar toys, gifts, T-shirts and books.

The Company puts a great emphasis on education and produces and sells a wide variety of educational materials. Recognizing that the alternative energy field is relatively new and that misinformation is common, the Company publishes and periodically revises its Alternative Energy Sourcebook, a 500+ page textbook, that also includes nearly all of the products that the Company sells.

The AE Sourcebook is currently distributed by Ten Speed Press in Berkeley, California, which sells the book in 44 English speaking countries. The United States retail price is $16. The Company sells approximately 65,000 Sourcebooks annually. The Company also markets many books on specific aspects of alternative energy and conservation within its quarterly catalogs.

Retail Locations

The Company operates a showroom for its products at its headquarters in Ukiah. The showroom has become increasingly popular over the last year as, with little advertising, it has become known to mail order buyers and local shoppers alike. In-store customer traffic increased from an average of 10 sales per day in early 1990 to over 30 sales per day currently. In calendar 1990, showroom sales of $235,000 accounted for 5% of the Company's revenues. In fiscal 1993, showroom sales more than doubled to $608,448. Because of the showroom's success and many inquiries regarding retail representation, the Company is evaluating options for retail expansion. The company has tested consumer response to its merchandise premise with an educational kiosk located in two locations of a prominent "green" retailer, Terra Verde Trading Company of New York and Santa Monica. Considerable research will be devoted to this area as the Company seeks the best way to make its merchandise more available to consumers. The Company has entered into a letter of intent to acquire a retail location in Wisconsin.

The subject of retail expansion strategies has occupied significant management resources in the past year. In studying in great detail the geographic distribution of mail order sales, the San Francisco Bay Area has emerged as a prime market for opening a retail outlet. The Company will not open a store until other components of its strategy are in place and the results from retail tests, such as the one being conducted with Terra Verde, are fully understood. Background research is expected to be complete in mid calendar 1993. Additional expansion activities currently under consideration include:

- Establishing a destination retail location in conjunction with a new facility at a yet-to-be-determined site in Mendocino County, California, near the present company headquarters.

- Opening three prototype retail locations that can serve as models for either future expansion or franchising.

293

9

(b) *Describe how these products or services are to be produced or rendered and how and when the Company intends to carry out its activities. If the Company plans to offer a new product(s), state the present stage of development, including whether or not a working prototype(s) is in existence. Indicate if completion of development of the product would require a material amount of the resources of the Company, and the estimated amount. If the Company is or is expected to be dependent upon one or a limited number of suppliers for essential raw materials, energy or other items, describe. Describe any major existing supply contracts.*

The Company currently purchases from a vendor base of more than 200 suppliers. The Company's largest single product area is photovoltaic products. While there are many suppliers of photovoltaic modules, the Company has chosen to limit the majority of its purchases to the two with whom it has developed long term relationships. Because some of the products in the alternative energy field are new, the number of suppliers for these products is limited and the Company is dependent upon these manufacturers to perform according to their promises. The Company generally does not need to enter into long-term contracts with its suppliers as the merchandise is most often readily available. The Company currently has six-month non-binding open purchase orders with Carrizo Solar in Albuquerque, NM to purchase a large quantity of recycled photovoltaic modules and twelve-month non-binding open purchase orders with Solar Electric Specialties of Willits, California for purchase of Siemens photovoltaic modules. The Company has a 90 day return arrangement with its vendors for any of its products that are returned from customers in original condition. The Company has historically experienced product returns of 5-6% which management believes is not substantial in the industry.

The Company sources new products for its periodic catalogs through a variety of methods including attending specialized trade shows domestically and internationally, studying market trends, and evaluating the products of the many vendors that solicit the Company. The Company believes it is unique in gathering many new products and new product development ideas from its customers. It offers its customers a $25 reward for coming up with new products that it later includes in its catalogs and a $500 reward for product development ideas that the Company can have manufactured to later include in its product offerings on a proprietary basis.

The Company has pursued several co-development efforts with other companies. A product called the Solar SunShed has been offered for sale beginning in the fall of 1992. This effort took an existing garden shed engineered and marketed by the Gardeners' Supply Company of South Burlington, VT and solarized it with components sourced by Real Goods. The first units were shipped in September, 1992. The rationale of this project is to create an affordable (less than $2500) independently-powered structure that can be purchased by a person interested in energy independence, but who is not ready or willing to commit to living in a remote home location. It is expected that the market niche for this product will take several years to fully develop. The Company believes that the "Solar SunShed" will begin to bring the two markets of conservation and alternative energy together and enhance its overall product line to both markets. There can be no assurance that the "Solar SunShed" will be successful.

A second co-development project has taken place in the information field with Chelsea Green Publishing Company of Post Mills, VT. In this project a reference book on small wind systems has been customized to Real Goods specifications. Written by an acknowledged expert in the field (Paul Gipe), the book fills a conspicuous gap in the energy marketplace. The Company has sold more than a thousand copies of the best available wind generation reference, which contains information that is in some cases twenty years out of date. Not only will this Real Goods Guide to Small Wind Systems update the body of knowledge and give the Company a new product to sell, but it should also convince more people of the viability of small wind systems, thereby stimulating the need for equipment that the Company sells as well.

Both co-development projects have led to cross-marketing opportunities. In both instances the Company has been able to share consumerships with its co-venture partner, a technique that provides an extremely efficient and low-cost source of new inquiries and buyers.

(c) *Describe the industry in which the Company is selling or expects to sell its products or services and, where applicable, any recognized trends within that industry. Describe that part of the industry and the geographic*

294

10

area in which the business competes or will compete. Indicate whether competition is or is expected to be by price, service, or other basis. Indicate (by attached table if appropriate) the current or anticipated prices or price ranges for the Company's products or services, or the formula for determining prices, and how these prices compare with those of competitors' products or services, including a description of any variations in product or service features. Name the principal competitors that the Company has or expects to have in its area of competition. Indicate the relative size and financial and market strengths of the Company's competitors in the area of competition in which the Company is or will be operating. State why the Company believes that it can effectively compete with these and other companies in its area of competition.

The Company markets its products and services to two distinct, but closely related, markets. The first and traditional market consists of individuals who own or are purchasing a home away from utility company grid power and who want to produce their own electricity from alternative sources of energy. This market encompasses a wide range of humanity, ranging from people already living off the power grid, professionals who own second homes, suburban homeowners who are experimenting with independent energy, and even third world villages to whom independent power is a necessity. The largest geographic concentrations of this remote home market in the United States that the Company targets are in Northern California, Washington State, Colorado, Alaska, Hawaii, Oregon, upstate New York, and New England. There are also significant marketing opportunities in the South Pacific islands, East Africa, Indonesia, Central and South America, the Middle East, Mexico, and the Caribbean.

In this remote power market the Company competes primarily through its service capability and secondarily through competitive pricing. The Company writes and updates its Alternative Energy Sourcebook frequently. This 500+ page Sourcebook is the primary education and marketing vehicle that the Company uses to present its products. The Sourcebook is recognized as a comprehensive source of information on alternative energy systems and products. The Sourcebook is complemented by the Company's technical staff, who are fully trained in energy system sizing and who specialize in designing solar systems of all sizes. In order to stay price competitive, the Company maintains competitive research, and periodically offers sales or discounts on select merchandise. The Company generally sells its alternative energy products at a 30% profit margin in an effort to remain competitive.

The Company has several competitors in the alternative energy field. There are only two publicly traded alternative energy companies with which the Company competes. Photocomm, Inc. of Scottsdale, AZ, and Solar Electric Engineering of Santa Rosa, CA. Photocomm's revenues are approximately $10 million and Solar Electric's are approximately $1.7 million. Both are operating at a substantial loss. Other competitors include Alternative Energy Engineering of Redway, CA, with estimated retail sales of approximately $1 million, Backwoods Solar Electric, of Sandpoint, ID, with estimated retail sales of approximately $600,000 and Sunelco, of Hamilton, MT with estimated retail sales of approximately $1 million. The Company estimates the retail remote home market to be a $15-25 million per year business which is growing steadily at a rate of 10% per year. The Company now holds approximately an 18% market share. The Company believes that it enjoys a strong reputation within the industry.

The second market that the Company addresses is the energy conservation and ecological products market. These products include energy saving light bulbs, water conservation supplies, recycled and recycling products, water purification, toys, books, and gifts. This market is distinct from the previously discussed alternative energy market, in that its purchasers primarily live in urban and suburban areas. The "Green Market Alert," an environmental trade publication, estimates that this is currently a $34 billion per year market, only a small portion of which ($45 million) is sold via mail order. The leading competitor, with catalog sales of approximately $7 million, is Seventh Generation of Colchester, VT. After several years of dramatic increases, their sales growth has slowed in the past two years. Other competitors include Save Energy Co., of San Francisco, CA with annual sales of approximately $1 million, and several other very small catalogers. Industry observers, as reported in the Green Market Alert, project that sales of conservation products via catalog channels will triple by 1996. The environmental segment is the more volatile of the two markets. A recent Roper Organization study on environmentalism commissioned by S.C. Johnson and Son pointed out that 78% of adults say that our nation must "make a major effort to improve the quality of our environment." At the moment, recycling appears to be the most rapidly growing pro-environmental behavior. Between March 1989 and February 1990, the share of Americans who say they regularly recycle bottles and cans

11

rose from 41% to 46%, and the share who regularly recycle newspapers rose from 20% to 26%.

The Roper study broke down the American population into five basic segments: True-Blue Greens, Greenback Greens, Sprouts, Grousers, and Basic Browns. The first three market segments comprise the primary target for the environmental and energy conservation segment of the Company's market.

True-Blue Greens (11% of the adult population) have strong environmental concerns and are leaders in the environmental movement. 59% regularly recycle newspapers. *Greenback Greens* (11% of the adult population) are most willing to pay more money for environmentally safe products. They will pay 20% more for environmentally safe products, compared with 7% for the general public. *Sprouts* (26% of the adult population) are the all important "swing" group that represent a future environmental target market. The Company competes in this market by using consumer education and quality service, as the market is not as yet overly price sensitive. The Company is widely considered one of the originators in what is known as the "socially responsible marketplace" and has the reputation of being thoughtful and environmentally responsible.

A number of new small competitors have emerged in the market place, as well as established companies newly selling into this market, such as the Sharper Image. Over 250 "green" stores, selling earth-friendly merchandise, have opened in the past two years. The Company believes that its strength lies in its complete array of alternative energy products, backed by full technical service and its full roster of communications vehicles, such as the Alternative Energy Sourcebook. As mentioned before, the Company sells alternative energy hardware products at a lower margin (approximately 30%) and sells its gift, educational, and energy conservation items at a higher margin (approximately 50%) as these items are typically sold at higher margins by the competition. The Company believes that most of its products are priced at or below the competition's price. The Company's average margin for the period of 1 April 1992 through 31 March 1993 was 45.3%, which is on the upper end of the mail order industry average, which (according to Robert Morris Associates' 1992 report on Retailers - Catalog & Mail-Order Houses) ranges from 38.5% to 43.0%. The Company has been averaging 39.74% gross profit margin (60.26% cost of goods sold), 18% for publicity expense, 23% for operating expense, and 1-5% pre-tax profit over the last several years. The range on the margin percentage varies between 38-43.6%, and the margin has improved in each of the past three years.

Note: Because this Offering Circular focuses primarily on details concerning the Company rather than the industry in which the Company operates or will operate, potential investors may wish to conduct their own separate investigation of the Company's industry to obtain broader insight in assessing the Company's prospects.

(d) *Describe specifically the marketing strategies the Company is employing or will employ in penetrating its market or in developing a new market. Set forth in response to Question No. 4 below the timing and size of the results of this effort which will be necessary in order for the Company to be profitable. Indicate how and by whom its products or services are or will be marketed (such as by advertising, personal contact by sales representatives, etc.), how its marketing structure operates or will operate and the basis of its marketing approach, including any market studies. Name any customers that account for, or based upon existing orders will account for, a major portion (20% or more) of the Company's sales. Describe any major existing sales contracts.*

As one of the original "green" marketers, the Company believes it has an advantage in the market, but one that will become more fragile as the market becomes more saturated. The Company believes its position can be maintained and strengthened by enhancing its credibility and positive image in the alternative energy field by several marketing strategies.

The goals of these marketing strategies are to enhance the Company's position as an industry leader, to actively communicate this position to the consumer, and to convince the consumer that the Company can satisfy all of his/her energy saving equipment needs, thereby committing the customer to Real Goods by isolating him/her from other competitors.

12

The tactics that the Company will use to achieve its marketing goals are as follows:

1. Create educational vehicles that expose the consumer to the critical issues of energy and environment. These efforts have included:

    - The Declaration of Energy Independence, a document that the Company authored, that more than 20,000 consumers signed in conjunction with the first declared "Off the Grid Day," a national holiday when people were asked to disconnect from the power grid. This year for Off the Grid Day, the Company is planning a National Home Tour of alternatively-powered dwellings. This is scheduled for October 1993 and will give local media a convenient way of reporting on the application of energy independence in their particular region.

    - Establishment of the "Institute For Independent Living." The Institute provides interactive seminars in energy independence. Begun in 1992, each available session of the Institute sold out, encouraging the company to expand its schedule for 1993, appoint a full-time "Dean," establish a more permanent campus, and to begin the creation of specifically designed educational materials. Institute students convene at the Company from all around the country to learn about all aspects of independent living. Students receive intensive hands-on training on the sizing and installation of photovoltaic systems. The Company has offered six weekend and one week-long seminars in 1993 to accommodate 140 students. As of the date of this Offering Circular, all workshops are nearly sold out. Since this is a new program for the Company, there can be no assurance that it will be successful.

    - Creation of a "Real Goods For Real Kids on Real Planets™" program to promote energy awareness among young people. This program enables local non-profit, environmentally oriented organizations to raise funds by selling planet-friendly products and letting Real Goods handle the messy mechanics of order fulfillment. Four prototype organizations have signed on to date, and based on their experience the program will be fine-tuned and expanded in 1993. Preliminary discussions have already begun with several large children's organizations. Since this is a new program for the Company, there can be no assurance that it will be successful.

    - Co-publication (with Chelsea Green Publishing) of the *Real Goods Guide to Small Wind Systems (described previously)*. Chelsea Green has published some of the nation's most-respected environmental books, including BEYOND THE LIMITS and THE MAN WHO PLANTED TREES. A roster of educational titles related to independent living is planned for joint publication by the two companies, giving Real Goods new products to sell, exposure of its name in book stores, and educational properties that facilitate the cause of independent living.

    - In addition to these activities Real Goods is an active participant in energy-related fairs, forums, and exhibitions. The Company sponsored the Tour de Sol (a race from Albany to Boston of solar-electric vehicles), displayed at Eco-Expos in Los Angeles, Denver, New York, and San Francisco, co-sponsored the Solar Energy Expo and Rally, and attended numerous conferences related to socially active businesses.

    - Real Goods acquired the direct marketing assets of a competitor, Rising Sun Enterprises of Boulder, CO. Among these was an informative booklet that the Company has renamed "The Book of Light" and re-issued under its own name. It is hoped that this piece can be further refined and used as the basis for a co-publishing project with the Chelsea Green Publishing Company.

2. Communicate directly to the consumer via:

    - **The Real Goods Color Catalog**. This piece continued to improve in 1993, with new product, new photography and a design "face-lift" to help clarify merchandise categories.

    - **The Real Goods News**. This three-times-a-year publication is the Company's journal of independent living.

13

In addition to products for sale, the News contains editorial features, columns, staff and customer profiles, and the popular Reader's Forum, where Real Goods customers are given their turn on the soap box to express their views about the Company, the government, or the environment.

- **The Real Stuff Newsletter.** This simple newsletter is for subscribers and shareowners only and offers a behind-the-scenes look at what's going on at the Company. It also offers special buying opportunities on close-outs and overstocks and has proved to be extremely profitable and helpful to consumers.

- **The Alternative Energy Sourcebook.** This 500+ page book represents the core of the Company's offering. The Company believes that it is very well regarded in the industry as the definitive text on alternative energy systems. It offers guidance to the novice on conception, feasibility, and design of alternative power systems as well as a full compendium of accessories and products for every aspect of independent living. The Company prints up to 75,000 Sourcebooks annually, and distributes the book in over 100 countries. The book is updated more or less annually.

- **Media Advertising.** The Company offers its goods and services as well as its Alternative Energy Sourcebook to the general public via small space advertising in relevant periodical publications such as Garbage Magazine, Harrowsmith Magazine, the Utne Reader, E Magazine, the Mother Earth News, Home Power Magazine and other avenues that reach prospective customers.

- **Public Relations Programs.** The company sends regular press releases to its file of environmentally-oriented media. Two recent programs that have been successful have been the "Real Relief" program offering special discounts and priority shipment to victims of natural disasters like Hurricanes Andrew and Iniki (in Florida and Hawaii). For Christmas a "Solar Sultan's" package, offering a complete package for independent living anywhere in the world, attracted great media interest.

- An experimental mailing, in the Fall of 1992, focusing on an expanded roster of educational materials related to environmental fields, is being tested to see if more targeted merchandising efforts hold promise for further segmentation of the customer population. More sophisticated segmentation of the market will be key to the Company's abilities to meet its growth objectives. It will allow the Company to mail more efficiently and environmentally responsibly and benefit its relationships with its customers.

3. Establish Owners' Programs that promote customer loyalty.

The Company's primary marketing vehicle for penetrating its market is its catalogs. The Company mails its main color catalog six times per year: January, April, June, August, September, and October. Typically, the October mailing is the largest and encompasses the holiday season, with this one catalog accounting for as much as 35% of annual revenues. The Company mails its "Real Goods News" three times each year to its two-year buyer file and to its recent inquiries. The Company mails its "Real Stuff" newsletter four times each year to its shareowners and subscribers. In fiscal 1992-93 the Company mailed 2,547,750 catalogs, an average of 280,000 catalogs in each mailing, compared to 1.6 million in the previous fiscal year. Of these, approximately 1,588,000 went to the Company's own mailing list and the balance went to highly targeted prospective customers. The Company's mailing list consists of a 100,000 customer two-year buyer file (customers who have ordered within 24 months), 10,000 subscribers (explained later), and approximately 150,000 inquirers in the last 24 months. The Company mails to each subscriber a minimum of thirteen times per year, and to each buyer and inquirer a minimum of nine times per year. Prospective customers come from mailing lists rented from competitors and market segments that have been shown to be highly profitable in the past. The rate of return for the catalogs the Company has sent out far exceeds the average for direct mail companies. All Company marketing vehicles are used to aggressively promote sales of the Alternative Energy Sourcebook, which portrays the full range of the Company's products. The Sourcebook generally produces an average order over ten times that of the catalogs.

14

The Company also rents its mailing list to other non-competitive, responsible, and environmentally-conscious companies for mailings.

All shareowners on the Company's records receive 5% discounts on all purchases from the Company. The Company reserves the right to change or discontinue the program in the future.

The **Alternative Energy Sourcebook** is unique to the Company and is not easily duplicated by competitors. It enhances the overall credibility of the Company and is featured prominently in all catalogs and media ads. The Company distributes the Sourcebook through Ten Speed Press, of Berkeley, CA and will continue to aggressively promote the book through energy writers, environmental columnists, and other mail order catalogs that feature energy and environmental goods.

The Company is continuing its innovative Subscriber Program that it began in 1989 in response to the many very committed customers that it found in its customer base. These subscribers tend to take their energy independence more seriously. They're committed to the Company as their energy saving resource and the Company returns that commitment. The Company solicits a one-time fee from Subscribers, who receive the Company's Subscriber Newsletter, **The Real Stuff**, four times every year which contains special pricing, close out bargains, customer profiles, and lots of news. Subscribers get a free copy of the **Alternative Energy Sourcebook** and other benefits that return the initial investment in future savings. Subscribers have an average order 60% higher than the average customer and order at a frequency rate up to 50% greater. Subscribers tend to be loyal to the Company and their support will be strongly targeted in the future. Expanding the Subscriber base and finding new ways to reward these customers for their loyalty will continue to be high priorities for the Company.

The Company conducted a customer survey of 2,000 of its customers (350 subscribers and 1650 general) in March of 1991 that confirmed its beliefs about the uniqueness of the subscriber customer base, as well as solidified its understanding of its general customer base. Some of the analyses from that survey are described in the charts on the next page. The average customer (non-subscriber and subscriber) purchased $169 worth of merchandise from the Company and placed an average of two orders. This average order is about three times higher than comparable direct mail companies which typically have an average order of $40 to $60. However the subscribers purchased an average of $469 with three orders and non-subscribers purchased an average of $121 with two orders. Further, subscribers showed the strongest interest and purchase intent for practical equipment-oriented product categories. The Company's customer survey revealed that the typical customer is 40.8 years old, has a median annual household income of $38,450, (both fairly typical), but the Company's average customer has a far higher level of education than the US average, with nearly 95% having attended college and a full 44% having attended graduate school.

The Company has collected its information on customer profile, customer demographics, past sales results, and industry trends into an in-house database. The information contained in this database guides the Company in its decisions regarding retail expansion, mail order strategies, and even creative design. The purpose of this intelligence-gathering effort is to lay the foundation for future growth.

Because the Company sells in the environmental marketplace, many of its customers are by nature counter-cultural in habits. They resist the proliferation of mail order materials and eschew traditional means of shopping (such as shopping malls). This both creates opportunity for the Company, but also creates some unique marketing challenges as well. The Company hopes that from the creation of its database, the capabilities of its new computer system, and an intelligent strategic overview it will be able to reduce waste circulation by targeting its communications vehicles more precisely to the preferences of the specific audience.

Nine separate consumer profiles, each with corresponding strategy, have been created. In the coming year

15

the communications vehicles will be altered so that content and style are suitable for a specific purpose, and will be phased into operation. Through the use of such database marketing, the Company hopes to be able to identify consumer segments that can then be grown through more traditional means of rental lists and media advertising.

16

Demographic Analysis From the Company's
March 1991 Customer Survey

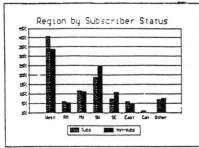

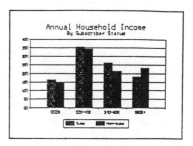

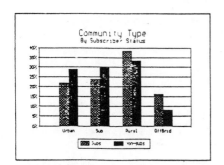

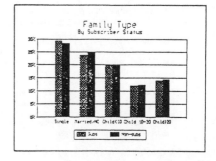

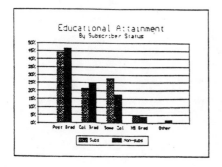

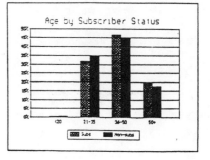

17

The Company's public relations efforts have been intensified in recent years, and will continue to be an important part of the overall marketing mix. The number of inquiries increased from 2,000 per month to over 10,000 per month from 1990 to 1993. This has been accomplished largely on the development of innovative programs that have been aggressively communicated to the environmental press.

The following programs are typical of the Company activities that have drawn attention from the media to the Company's overall mission of promoting independent living:

- "Real Relief"- was spawned in the wake of natural disasters Hurricanes Andrew and Iniki, to provide alternative energy equipment to people living in federal disaster areas. In addition to promoting customer loyalty, the Company is experiencing positive feedback from the general public for its efforts during a time of need.

- The Billion Pound Goal describes the effort of the Company to reduce the production of greenhouse gases through the actions of its staff and customers. As of May 1, 1993, the Company believes that its customers have prevented the production of over 500 million pounds of carbon dioxide from being spewed into the atmosphere, putting it more than 50% ahead of schedule toward its billion pound goal.

- The National Independent Home Tour (planned for October 16, 1993) will give local journalists a chance to observe, personally, the way alternative energy lifestyles are being lived in their locale. Because this is a new program, there can be no assurance that it will be successful.

- The Declaration of Energy Independence, authored by the Company, was delivered to White House Officials by Presidential candidate, Jerry Brown.

These and many other efforts have kept Real Goods prominently in the public eye. Press coverage has included a segment on CBS's "This Morning", several mentions in INC. Magazine, The New York Times and The Wall Street Journal. Numerous radio interviews, including several on National Public Radio, and articles in smaller media have produced a continual flow of new inquirers interested in Real Goods. Most recently the Company was cited by a prominent consumer magazine as one of the best places to buy energy-efficient lighting. The Company believes it uses its small media budget efficiently. Magazines have been targeted by subject and circulation efficiency, with different creative aspects targeted for specific interest groups including alternative energy, counterculture, environment, and economic (energy savers). The Company is continually in the process of refining its marketing effort from both a strategic and tactical standpoint in order to better target its message to specific groups of consumers.

(e) *State the backlog of written firm orders for products and/or services as of a recent date (within the last 90 days) and compare it with the backlog of a year ago from that date.*

As of: 3/31/93 $66,710
As of: 3/31/92 $41,882

Explain the reason for significant variations between the two figures, if any. Indicate what types and amounts of orders are included in the backlog figures. State the size of typical orders. If the Company's sales are seasonal or cyclical, explain.

Although backlogs are considered healthy in the manufacturing industry, in the mail order industry, backorders are generally a symptom of inefficiency and create additional costs and risks of lost sales. Backlogged orders in the mail order business are "backorders." The Company has over 200 vendors for the products that it carries in its catalogs. When a vendor fails to deliver as promised and the customer has paid for an order, a backorder is created. The Company attempts to keep its backorders at any given time to less

18

than 10% of its total orders which is considered the industry standard. The Company is able to achieve this goal the vast majority of the time. The backorder figures above are within normal tolerance for the mail order industry.

(f) *State the number of the Company's present employees and the number of employees it anticipates it will have within the next 12 months. Also, indicate the number by type of employee (i.e., clerical, operations, administrative, etc.) the Company will use, whether or not any of them are subject to collective bargaining agreements, and the expiration date(s) of any collective bargaining agreement(s). If the Company's employees are on strike, or have been in the past three years, or are threatening to strike, describe the dispute. Indicate any supplemental benefits or incentive arrangements the Company has or will have with its employees.*

The Company currently employs 59 employees, of which 11 are general and administrative, 43 are in operations and 5 are in clerical or data processing. Of the 43 operations employees, 31 are full time staff and 12 are part time or temporary. In peak periods of order activity such as the fall/Christmas season, the Company typically employs up to 25 additional temporary employees. The Company presently intends to increase its staff in the next twelve months, as necessary. At the end of that period, the Company has budgeted to have 69 employees; 16 in general and administrative positions, 47 in operations (of which 35 will be full time and 12 temporary or part time) and 6 in clerical or data processing. The Company's projections for increased staffing needs are somewhat dependent upon the success of this public offering, and if less than the maximum amount is raised, the Company would limit its staff increases accordingly. There can be no assurances that the Company's business will grow to require such a staffing increase. At present, the Company's benefit package consists of a medical plan, vacation, sick leave, 401-K retirement plan, a 125-S child care and medical flex plan, and employee discounts on merchandise for all full time employees. The Company has adopted a stock option plan which it intends to implement in the next 12 months for some of its key employees. The Company is not subject to any collective bargaining agreements at present, and no employees have been on strike, or threatened to strike since the Company's inception.

(g) *Describe generally the principal properties (such as real estate, plant and equipment, patents, etc.) that the Company owns, indicating also what properties it leases and a summary of the terms under those leases, including the amount of payments, expiration dates and the terms of any renewal options. Indicate what properties the Company intends to acquire in the immediate future, the cost of such acquisitions and the sources of financing it expects to use in obtaining these properties, whether by purchase, lease or otherwise.*

The Company currently leases both its operations facilities in Ukiah, an 8,000 square foot office / customer service / showroom / administration complex under a lease that expires at the end of March 1994, and a 7,500 square foot warehouse/distribution center facility, under a lease that expires at the end of September 1993. While the Company could continue renting the existing warehouse/distribution space, it has negotiated a lease of a 14,000 square foot warehouse/distribution space in Ukiah for one year beginning July 1, 1993, with options to renew. The Company is leasing its $25,000 Mitel telephone system and its $10,000 warehouse racking and shelving system. The lease on the Mitel telephone system runs until October, 1993, at which time the Company may elect to purchase it for fair market value or 15% of the original purchase price, which ever is lower. The lease on the warehouse racking and shelving system runs until October, 1994 at which time the Company may elect to purchase the system for $1. The Company owns part of its current computer system, an IBM-compatible Novell network with 25 work stations and a 750 mB fixed disk, which runs the Company's communication, administrative, marketing and accounting functions. The Company leases the balance of its computer hardware and software system that is used for order entry, inventory control, and back end catalog circulation analysis for $3,700 per month. The lease runs until October 1, 1997 at which time the Company may elect to purchase the system for fair market value.

Although there is no assurance thereof, the Company believes that it will begin to strain its current facilities by the end of 1993 and will outgrow its facilities by the Spring of 1994. The Company's long term strategic planning calls for a consolidation of its current facilities (the warehouse is currently two blocks away from the main operation) into one large location. It has been determined that the Company requires 5-10 acres of land upon which it can build a 15,000 square foot warehouse with expansion capabilities to 75,000 square feet, a 10,000 square foot administrative/operations/training headquarters, and a 3,000 square foot showroom facility. The Company believes that this proposed Company Headquarters facility will be adequate for expansion of all the Company's plans for at least 10 years. The Company has determined that a good location for such a facility is adjacent to the U.S. Highway 101 corridor between Hopland and Willits, where maximum visibility is afforded to the 50,000+ vehicles that pass by daily. There can be no assurance that it can procure suitable land for an agreeable price or that it can obtain all necessary approvals and other resources to proceed with the plan described below.

The Company believes that it is in its best interests to build this "destination facility" as a showpiece of alternative energy and sustainable, non-toxic building practices so that it can be a living monument to sustainability. The Company has begun its search for a suitable property site and has initiated discussions with several world-class environmentally oriented architects.

In choosing a building system, the Company believes it is important to consider the embodied energy of the materials. For instance, timber buildings require significantly less energy to produce than concrete and steel buildings. The Company would endeavor to design a project that could repay its embodied energy mortgage over time by generating more energy than it took to build it, providing a model for others to follow. Local materials as well as recycled materials would be utilized wherever feasible.

The current plan is to have the entire complex off-the-grid and powered by a photovoltaic array along with whichever other suitable renewable energy sources are available at the sight including wind and hydro power systems. Passive solar and subterranean cooling strategies would be employed to cool interior thermal mass at night and evaporative cooling in the day would be designed into the buildings to minimize or totally eliminate energy-hogging air conditioning loads. The contents of the warehouse could be used to help mitigate thermal loads and in-the-slab radiant heating could be further utilized for increased efficiency. Planting the roof to insulate against thermal loads and merging the building with the landscape would be considered and daylighting would be utilized for the entire warehouse. Appropriate eye-level views to the exterior to increase the sense of the outdoors in the warehouse interior would further be employed.

The Company is considering a plan to treat all site-generated wastewater and perhaps other waste water (RVs, local housing) on the site. This type of treatment system would provide for an onsite aquaculture system allowing the Company to grow heavy metal absorbing vegetation and shrimp for food. A well would be considered with a PV powered pump to maintain self-sufficiency and avoid city water hookup costs.

The Company's buildings at the new location will embody all the concepts espoused by its philosophy of sustainability, and safe and sane non-toxic building materials. The showroom will showcase all of the items within the Company's product line in actual use wherever possible. The Company will endeavor to make the entire site of its headquarters remarkable, unique, and slightly outrageous so as to develop the site as a demonstration farm. The development might well include an exterior "commons" or "oasis" area with lush vegetation, sustainable agriculture, a possible aviary, and a solar greenhouse to accommodate agriculture in the winter months.

Outbuildings, currently sold by the Company such as geodesic domes, yurts, and earth-sheltered housing could be placed on the property for the dual function of showing the structures for sale as well as housing a segment of the "Institute for Independent Living." The Institute, which was highly successful in its debut sessions of 1992, endeavors to teach all aspects of independent living to interested students. The possibility of including a building as an alternative energy "bed and breakfast" is being discussed where interested customers could come to spend a night experiencing living off-the-grid. The Company believes that this project is so unique and

20

educational and has the potential to be such a futuristic model of building and conducting business that it could very well become a tourist attraction and environmental center for Northern California.

By purchasing 5-10 acres, the Company would allow enough room for any expansion it foresees in the near future. The Company would target moving into the new warehouse, offices and retail space by the spring of 1994. The Company estimates that a project of this scope would take nine months to plan and nine months to build. The following are estimates of costs for this project:

5-10 Acres of Land	$300,000
Warehouse Construction (15,000 sf @ $20/sf)	$300,000
Warehouse Equipment	$ 20,000
Office Construction (10,000 sf @ $65/sf)	$650,000
Office Furniture (50 people @ $300/person)	$ 15,000
Showroom Construction (3,000 sf @ $35/sf)	$105,000
Showroom Fixturing (3,000 sf @ $120/sf)	$360,000
Architect (@ 15% of Construction Costs)	$155,000
Energy System	$ 75,000
Parking & Paving	$ 20,000
Landscaping	$ 25,000
Relocation Expenses	$ 15,000

Total Expenses for Construction, etc.   **$2,040,000**

The Company has been in contact with the Small Business Administration (SBA) about its construction packages for small businesses. The Company has received encouragement that it will qualify for a $1 million construction loan at the current rate of 8% amortized over 20 years. The Company would capitalize the building project with $1 million from the proceeds from this stock offering and would seek to borrow $1 million from SBA for the construction loan, although there can be no assurances that at the time of application the loan will be approved or that interest rates will remain at their current levels. See "Use of Proceeds."

(h) *Indicate the extent to which the Company's operations depend or are expected to depend upon patents, copyrights, trade secrets, know-how or other proprietary information and the steps undertaken to secure and protect this intellectual property, including any use of confidentiality agreements, covenants-not-to-compete and the like. Summarize the principal terms and expiration dates of any significant license agreements. Indicate the amounts expended by the Company for research and development during the last fiscal year, the amount expected to be spent this year and what percentage of revenues research and development expenditures were for the last fiscal year.*

The Company's **Alternative Energy Sourcebook** and its name are copyrighted and trademarked. The Company protects its customer list through limiting access to its computer system, proprietary information agreements with its employees, and appropriate list rental agreements. The Company keeps its vendor files under internal control. The Company is spending approximately $30,000 in the current fiscal year for research and development of new products. It intends to increase this amount to $75,000 in the next year and expend more energy and staff time into new product research. The Company sent its President, John Schaeffer, and its new product development manager, Jeff Oldham to the Guangzhou Trade Fair in China last year and has attended trade fairs in Europe this year. It plans to greatly expand its new product searches to keep its product offerings fresh and on the cutting edge.

(i) *If the Company's business, products, or properties are subject to material regulation (including environmental regulation) by federal, state, or local governmental agencies, indicate the nature and extent of regulation and its effects or potential effects upon the Company.*

305

21

The Company is not subject to any material regulation beyond that generally required for a retail catalog sales business.

(j) *State the names of any subsidiaries of the Company, their business purposes and ownership, and indicate which are included in the Financial Statements attached hereto.*

The Company has no subsidiaries.

(k) *Summarize the development of the Company (including any material mergers or acquisitions) during the past five years, or for whatever lesser period the Company has been in existence. Discuss any pending or anticipated mergers, acquisitions, spin-offs or recapitalization. If the Company has recently undergone a stock split, stock dividend or recapitalization in anticipation of this offering, describe (and adjust historical per share figures elsewhere in this Disclosure Document accordingly).*

The Company began operations in October, 1986 as a sole proprietorship owned by John Schaeffer. The first mail order catalog was sent to 3,000 people at that time and sales for the first three months ended 31 December 1986 were $29,831. Three catalog mailings went out in calendar 1987 to approximately 30,000 people with total sales of $250,397. Besides Mr. Schaeffer, one employee was hired in 1987. In 1988, the catalog expanded to 64 pages and the Company began renting mailing lists from like minded companies. It sent out a total of 100,000 catalogs and sales in 1988 were $726,407. By the end of 1988 there were three employees. In 1989, mailing list rentals continued and three catalogs were sent to a total of approximately 350,000 people. By the end of 1989 there were a total of 14 employees and sales were $1,933,008. In 1990, the Company continued to expand and incorporated on 18 June 1990. Upon incorporation the Company employed 32 people and mailed 213,000 catalogs; sales prior to incorporation were $1,994,522. Audited sales for fiscal 1991 (the period beginning June 18, 1990 and ending March 31, 1991) were $3,993,451, 512,500 catalogs were mailed, and the Company had 45 employees at year end. In fiscal 1992 April 1, 1991 through March 31, 1992) sales expanded to $6,178,476 and there were 46 employees. Fiscal 1993 sales were $7,778,282, catalogs mailed totaled 2,547,750, and there were 56 employees at year end.

Growth in the key elements of the business since its inception was as follows:

(Calendar years 1986 through 1990 are unaudited - Fiscal years 1991 through 1993 are audited)

Year	Revenues	Catalogs Mailed	Employees
1986*	$ 29,381	3,000	1
1987	$ 250,397	30,000	2
1988	$ 726,407	100,000	3
1989	$1,933,008	350,000	14
1990**	$1,994,522	213,000	32
1991***	$3,993,451	512,500	45
1992	$6,178,476	1,588,000	46
1993	$7,778,282	2,547,750	56

 * 1986 figures include operations for 3 months only.
 ** The Company incorporated June 18, 1990. Figures shown represent the period January 1, 1990 through June 17, 1990.
 *** Revenues shown represent audited results of the period from June 18, 1990 through the fiscal year ended March 31, 1991.

4. (a) *If the Company was not profitable during its last fiscal year, list below in chronological order the events which in management's opinion must or should occur or the milestones which in management's opinion the*

22

Company must or should achieve in order for the Company to become profitable, and indicate the expected manner of occurrence or the expected method by which the Company will achieve the milestones.

Not applicable.

(b) *State the probable consequences to the Company of delays in achieving each of the events or milestones within the above time schedule, and particularly the effect of any delays upon the Company's liquidity in view of the Company's then anticipated level of operating costs. (See Question Nos. 11 and 12.)*

Not applicable.

Note: After reviewing the nature and timing of each event or milestone, potential investors should reflect upon whether achievement of each within the estimated time frame is realistic and should assess the consequences of delays or failure of achievement in making an investment decision.

OFFERING PRICE FACTORS

If the securities offered are common stock, or are exercisable for or convertible into common stock, the following factors may be relevant to the price at which the securities are being offered.

5. *What were net, after-tax earnings for the last fiscal year?*

Per share based upon average number of shares outstanding:
In fiscal 1993 the company earned $43,470 in the aggregate or $.016 per share.

6. *If the Company had profits, show offering price as a multiple of earnings. Adjust to reflect for any stock splits or recapitalization, and use conversion or exercise price in lieu of offering price, if applicable.*

Offering Price Per Share

Net After-Tax Earnings   (price/earnings multiple) = 386
Last Year Per Share

7. (a) *What is the net tangible book value of the Company? (If deficit, show in parenthesis.) For this purpose, net tangible book value means total assets (exclusive of copyrights, patents, goodwill, research and development costs and similar intangible items) minus total liabilities.*

$1,154,660 as of March 31, 1993.
Per share based upon number of shares outstanding as of March 31, 1993: $.406.

If the net tangible book value per share is substantially less than this offering (or exercise or conversion) price per share, explain the reasons for the variation.

In February 1992 the Company closed an offering of 200,000 shares of its common stock at $5.00 per share. Subsequently, in the very limited trading market, the Company's common stock was bought and sold at $5.50 per share. Nevertheless, since there has been only a limited trading market in the Company's shares, the offering price is inherently arbitrary and is not necessarily related to any future value. Management believes that, since the Company is an ongoing retail business, tangible assets such as land, buildings and machinery are not as important in determining value as intangible assets such as customer relationships, employee team, reputation and product knowledge.

307

23

(b) *State the dates on which the Company sold or otherwise issued securities during the last 12 months, the amount of such securities sold, the number of persons to whom they were sold, any relationship of such persons to the Company at the time of sale, the price at which they were sold and, if not sold for cash, a concise description of the consideration. (Exclude bank debt.)*

From the commencement of this offering through the date of this Offering Circular, the Company has sold 245,606 shares to 1,617 members of the public.

8. (a) *What percentage of the outstanding shares of the Company will the investors in this offering have?* (Assume exercise of options, warrants or rights and conversion of convertible securities.)

If the maximum is sold: 17.7%
If the minimum is sold: Not applicable[1]

(b) *What post-offering value is management attributing to the entire Company by establishing the price per security set forth on the cover page (or exercise or conversion price if common stock is not offered)? (Total outstanding shares after offering times offering price, or exercise or conversion price if common stock is not offered.)*

If maximum is sold: Approximately $20,382,960
If minimum is sold: Not applicable[1]

(For above purposes, assume convertible securities are converted and outstanding options exercised in determining "shares".)

Note: After reviewing the above, potential investors should consider whether or not the offering price (or exercise or conversion price, if applicable) for the securities is appropriate at the present stage of the Company's development.

---

[1]Note - The Company has established no minimum for this offering, however securities regulators in Mississippi and Texas have required the Company to establish an escrow account with respect to residents of their states until the proceeds exceed $1,800,000. Without an escrow requirement, securities regulators in Iowa and Massachusetts have established a minimum of $1,800,000 for residents of their states and the Nebraska securities regulator has established a minimum of $2,160,000 for Nebraska residents.

24

USE OF PROCEEDS

9. The following table sets forth the use of the proceeds from this offering assuming $1,800,000 sold and if $3,600,000 is sold.

	If $1,800,000 Sold		If $3,600,000 Sold	
	Amount	%	Amount	%
Total Proceeds:	$1,800,000	100%	$3,600,000	100%
Less Offering Expenses:				
Commissions & Finder's Fees*	$15,000	.8%	$115,000	3.2%
Legal & Accounting:	$90,000	5.0%	$90,000	2.5%
Printing & Advertising:	$50,000	2.8%	$50,000	1.4%
Other (specify) Consulting:	$39,000	2.2%	$66,000	1.8%
Postage:	$50,000	2.8%	$50,000	1.4%
Filing Fees:	$15,000	.8%	$15,000	0.4%
Net Proceeds from Offering:	$1,541,000	85.6%	$3,214,000	89.3%

* If only the minimum is sold, a $15,000 commission is estimated assuming the Company will be able to raise $1,500,000 from its customers and will pay a 5% commission on the additional $300,000 to an outside broker/dealer. It is further assumed that if the Company succeeds in selling the entire $3.6 million worth of shares, a $115,000 commission will need to be paid to an outside broker dealer. There can be no assurance that the assumptions will prove to be true.

As of June 21, 1993, the Company has raised $1,473,636 and has set no minimum necessary to close this offering. However the securities regulators from Mississippi and Texas have required the Company to establish an escrow account with respect to residents of their states until the proceeds exceed $1,800,000. Without an escrow requirement, securities regulators in Iowa and Massachusetts have established a minimum of $1,800,000 for residents of their states and the Nebraska securities regulator has established a minimum of $2,160,000 for Nebraska residents. If less than $1,800,000 is received, the "Office/Warehouse/Showroom" complex will be scaled back to acquiring the land, but just building a destination retail/demonstration store and Real Goods will continue to lease office and warehouse space until such time as it can afford to build them.

"The payment for consulting is for services provided by Drew Field and Lorne Groe, including planning, scheduling and budgeting; drafting and reviewing materials; training staff; managing several parts of the process; preparing filings with the SEC and state securities administrators and responding to comments; coordinating with auditors and other service providers. The amount was negotiated by the Company to depend partially upon the amount of proceeds from this offering."

25

Use of Net Proceeds:

The Company presently intends to open a retail store in the San Francisco Bay Area (approximately 2,000 square feet), a second retail store in a smaller urban area (approximately 1,600 square feet), and a third store in a more rural area (approximately 1,200 square feet). The Company may alter its plans as necessary or appropriate. The Company's goal is to develop profitable retail models in three demographic locations that it can later evaluate and consider the possibility of further company stores or possible franchising.

The Company estimates that the Bay Area store would cost approximately $160,000 for renovation and displays ($80/square foot) and $200,000 for inventory. The Company estimates the second store (1,600 square feet) would cost $120,000 for renovation and $150,000 for inventory and that the third, more rural store (1,200 square feet) would cost $80,000 for renovation and $100,000 for inventory. The Company currently is a party to a letter of intent to purchase the more rural store in Wisconsin. There can be no assurance that such stores will be opened or that they will be successful.

If $1,800,000 Sold		If $3,600,000 Sold	
Amount	%	Amount	%
$360,000	20.0%	$690,000	19.2%

The Company presently intends to take steps to significantly increase its universe of mail order buyers. There can be no assurance that the Company will be successful. The Company currently has approximately 100,000 two-year buyers (customers who have purchased in the last two years). Each mail order buyer purchases on average $4 per catalog mailed for each of the 9 catalogs mailed per year, accounting for approximately $3,600,000 in annual revenues. The Company, through its test mailings to prospects, has determined that many more potential customers exist that would likely be receptive to its product offerings and philosophy. Through the rental of mailing lists, the Company is able to deliver a catalog to these new potential customers for approximately $0.36 each, including printing, mailing, and list rental. By mailing its catalog to 2,500,000 potential customers, the Company believes it can acquire 50,000 new buyers at a conservative 2% pull rate. The cost of such a mailing over the next year would be $900,000. At current buyer levels of purchases, these additional new 50,000 buyers would bring in an additional $1,800,000 in annual revenues at an average of $4 per catalog for 9 catalogs per year. Because it believes that these new customers would not perform as well as its long established "core" customers, the Company believes that new customers would experience an approximate 20% "fall-off" from its already established customers. This would amount to $3.20 per new customer per catalog for each of its 9 catalogs per year or a total increase in annual revenues of $1,440,000. The Company believes that expanding its universe of buyers would strengthen its position as the leading environmental cataloger and have the effect of significantly increasing revenues.

If $1,800,000 Sold		If $3,600,000 Sold	
Amount	%	Amount	%
$200,000	11.1%	$900,000	25%

The Company intends to purchase 5-10 acres of land and relocate its headquarters to this property. The Company plans to build a 15,000 square foot warehouse, a 10,000 square foot office complex, and a 3,000 square foot showroom facility to showcase its merchandise and provide a kinetic example of its products and philosophies in action (see section 3-G under Business and Properties). The Company intends to finance this proposed $2 million project with $1 million in capital from this offering and $1 million in debt from an SBA loan. There can be no assurance that the Company will locate appropriate land at an appropriate cost or that it will obtain the referenced debt financing.

26

If $1,800,000 Sold		If $3,600,000 Sold	
Amount	%	Amount	%
$700,000	38.9%	$1,000,000	27.8%

The Company sees great potential with its Institute for Independent Living following its successful debut season of 1992. If the offering is more than modestly successful, the Company intends to allocate $75,000 for the Institute's expansion, which would go for facilities improvements, educational materials, production of instructional videos and the possible purchase of a school bus that would take the Institute on the road around the country. The funds would be used further to publish several books that would serve as textbooks for the Institute.

If $1,800,000 Sold		If $3,600,000 Sold	
Amount	%	Amount	%
$0	0%	$75,000	2.1%

The balance of funds will be used for additions to working capital that may be made (although actual allocations will depend upon management's judgment at the time cash becomes available): [1]

	If $1,800,000 Sold		If $3,600,000 Sold	
	Amount	%	Amount	%
Increase in average inventory	$100,000		$200,000	
Increase in annual payroll	$100,000		$150,000	
Other	$ 81,000		$199,000	
	$281,00	15.6%	$549,000	15.2%
Total Use of Net Proceeds:	$1,541,000	100%	$3,214,000	100%

[1] The amounts disclosed in this table are management's best estimate of the use of working capital. Actual allocations may vary depending on the circumstances present at the time of expenditure. The increase in average inventory assumes a decrease in the number of turns per year from 8 down to 6.4, still more than double the industry standard (according to Robert Morris Associates). The Company intends to increase its average inventory from a current level of $700,000 to $900,000. The Company intends to hire within the next year a merchandising director, a buyer, retail store manager and several clerical employees.

Note: After reviewing the portion of the offering allocated to the payment of offering expenses, and to the immediate payment to management and promoters of any fees, reimbursements, past salaries or similar payments, a potential investor should consider whether the remaining portion of his investment, which would be that part available for future development of the Company's business and operations, would be adequate.

10. (a) *If material amounts of funds from sources other than this offering are to be used in conjunction with the proceeds from this offering, state the amounts and sources of such other funds, and whether funds*

311

27

are firm or contingent. If contingent, explain.

If the Company is able to locate suitable land for its new headquarters, it plans to seek debt financing to improve the land as planned. While the company believes that an SBA loan would be the most suitable debt source, there can be no assurance that it will be forthcoming. In its absence, the Company would seek other funding sources and, if none is available, it might terminate the project.

(b) *If any material part of the proceeds is to be used to discharge indebtedness, describe the terms of such indebtedness, including interest rates. If the indebtedness to be discharged was incurred within the current or previous fiscal year, describe the use of the proceeds of such indebtedness.*

Not applicable

(c) *If any material amount of the proceeds is to be used to acquire assets, other than in the ordinary course of business, briefly describe and state the cost of the assets and other material terms of the acquisitions. If the assets are to be acquired from officers, directors, employees or principal shareowners of the Company or their associates, give the names of the persons from whom the assets are to be acquired and set forth the cost to the Company, the method followed in determining the cost, and any profit to such persons.*

See "Use of Proceeds".

(d) *If any amount of the proceeds is to be used to reimburse any officer, director, employee or shareowner for services already rendered, assets previously transferred, monies loaned or advanced, or otherwise, explain:*

Not applicable

11. *Indicate whether the Company is having or anticipates having within the next 12 months any cash flow or liquidity problems.*

No.

Whether or not it is in default or in breach of any note, loan, lease or other indebtedness or financing arrangement requiring the Company to make payments.

No.

Indicate if a significant amount of the Company's trade payables have not been paid within the stated trade term.

No.

State whether the Company is subject to any unsatisfied judgments, liens or settlement obligations and the amounts thereof.

No.

Indicate the Company's plans to resolve any such problems.

Not Applicable.

28

12. *Indicate whether proceeds from this offering should satisfy the Company's cash requirements for the next 12 months, and whether it will be necessary to raise additional funds. State the source of additional funds, if known.*

Proceeds from the current offering will satisfy the Company's cash requirements for the next 12 months. A line of credit from the bank will facilitate response to seasonal inventory demands and is required to be completely repaid for thirty days every year. However, if the company proceeds with the headquarters consideration described above, debt financing will be necessary to fund construction.

29

CAPITALIZATION

13. *Indicate the capitalization of the Company as of the most recent practicable date and as adjusted to reflect the sale of the minimum and maximum amount of securities in this offering and the use of the net proceeds here from:*

	Amount Outstanding As of: March 31, 1993:	As Adjusted If $1,800,000 sold	If $3,600,000 sold
Debt:			
Short-term debt	$0	$0	$0
Long-term debt	$0	$0	$0
Total Debt	$0	$0	$0
Shareowners' equity:			
Preferred stock (without par value)	$0	$0	$0
Common stock (without par value) (number of shares)	$921,602 (2,797,160)	$2,462,602 (3,097,160)	$4,135,602 (3,397,160)
Additional paid in capital	$0	$0	$0
Retained earnings	$76,758	$76,758	$76,758
Total shareowners' equity	$1,154,660	$2,539,360	$4,212,360
Total Capitalization	**$1,154,660**	**$2,539,360**	**$4,212,360**

Number of Shares Authorized:	10,000,000 Common 1,000,000 Preferred

Number of preferred shares authorized: 1,000,000 shares without par value; none issued.

Number of common shares authorized: 10,000,000 shares, without par value.

Number of common shares reserved to meet conversion requirements or for the issuance upon exercise of options, warrants or rights: 600,000 are reserved for issuance under existing stock option plan. There are no options, warrants or rights outstanding.

30

DESCRIPTION OF SECURITIES

14. *The securities being offered hereby are*:

    [x] Common Stock
    [ ] Preferred or Preference Stock
    [ ] Notes or Debentures
    [ ] Units of two or more type of securities composed of:
    [ ] Other:

15. *These securities have*:

    Yes No
    [x] [ ] Cumulative voting rights
    [ ] [x] Other special voting rights
    [ ] [x] Preemptive rights to purchase in new issues of shares
    [ ] [x] Preference as to dividends or interest
    [ ] [x] Preference upon liquidation
    [ ] [x] Other special rights or preferences (specify):

    Explain:

16. *Are the securities convertible?* [ ] Yes [x] No

17. (a) *If securities are notes or other types of debt securities*: Not Applicable.

    (b) *If notes or other types of debt securities are being offered and the Company had earnings during its last fiscal year, show the ratio of earnings to fixed charges on an actual and pro forma basis for that fiscal year. "Earnings" means pre-tax income from continuing operations plus fixed charges and capitalized interest. "Fixed charges" means interest (including capitalized interest), amortization of debt discount, premium and expense, preferred stock dividend requirements of majority owned subsidiary, and such portion of rental expense as can be demonstrated to be representative of the interest factor in the particular case. The pro forma ratio of earnings to fixed charges should include incremental interest expense as a result of the offering of the notes or other debt securities.*

    Not applicable.

    Note: Care should be exercised in interpreting the significance of the ratio of earnings to fixed charges as a measure of the "coverage" of debt service, as the existence of earnings does not necessarily mean that the Company's liquidity at any given time will permit payment of debt service requirements to be timely made. See Question Nos. 11 and 12. See also the Financial Statements and especially the statement of Cash Flows.

18. *If securities are Preference or Preferred stock*:
    Are unpaid dividends cumulative? [ ] Yes [ ] No
    Are securities callable? [ ] Yes [ ] No Explain:

    Not applicable

315

31

19. *If securities are capital stock of any type, indicate restrictions on dividends under loan or other financing arrangements or otherwise*:

The Company currently may not pay dividends on stock without the consent of the bank holding its $400,000 line of credit. The Company's Business Loan Agreement with its regular bank, National Bank of the Redwoods, requires the bank's written consent before any dividends may be paid (other than dividends payable in stock).

20. *Current amount of assets available for payment of dividends (if deficit must be first made up, show deficit in parenthesis)*: $76,758 as of March 31, 1993, subject to approval of the bank.

PLAN OF DISTRIBUTION

21. *The selling agents (that is, the persons selling the securities as agent for the Company for a commission or other compensation) in this offering are*:

American National Securities, Inc., Beverly Hills, CA, Walnut Street Securities, Inc., St. Louis, MO, and Progressive Asset Management, Inc., Oakland, CA.

22. *Describe any compensation to selling agents or finders, including cash, securities, contracts or other consideration, in addition to the cash commission set forth as a percent of the offering price on the cover page of this Offering Circular. Also indicate whether the Company will indemnify the selling agents or finders against liabilities under the securities laws. ("Finders" are persons who for compensation act as intermediaries in obtaining selling agents or otherwise making introductions in furtherance of this offering.)*

Compensation will be paid only to any registered securities broker-dealer selected by the Company, and then only as a percent of the offering price. (The Company will pay 6% for shares sold by them to their customers and 3% for shares sold by them to the Company's customers). An additional 1% will be paid on shares sold by Progressive Asset Management to the Company's customers for ongoing investor relations services if those sales exceed $200,000, and Progressive Asset Management will, at that time, be entitled to reimbursement of up to $5,000 in due diligence expenses. No compensation related to sales of shares will be paid to any employees of the Company. The Company will indemnify the selling agents against liabilities for claimed misstatements or omissions in this Offering Circular.

23. *Describe any material relationships between any of the selling agents or finders and the Company or its management.*

Not applicable
Note: After reviewing the amount of compensation to the selling agents or finders for selling the securities, and the nature of any relationship between the selling agents or finders and the Company, a potential investor should assess the extent to which it may be inappropriate to rely upon any recommendation by the selling agents or finders to buy the securities.

24. *If this offering is not being made through selling agents, the names of persons at the Company through which this offering is being made:*

This offering is being made through selling agents (see question 21 above). In addition, this offering is being made directly by the Company through written announcements, under the direction of John Schaeffer, the Company's president and CEO. The Company will publish announcements of the offering in its catalogs and newsletters, and will mail copies of the announcement to its shareowners and customers. The announcements will provide the very limited information permitted under applicable securities laws and will give the Company's telephone number for requesting this Offering Circular. Similar announcements will be published in other selected media and mailed to

316

32

other selected individuals.

Offering Circular will be accompanied by a Share Purchase Agreement and a return envelope. Assistance in connection with the offering will be available from the selling agents and from John Schaeffer, President of the company, and Anne Mayea, its shareowner relations coordinator.

25. *If this offering is limited to a special group, such as employees of the Company, or is limited to a certain number of individuals (as required to qualify under Subchapter S of the Internal Revenue Code) or is subject to any other limitations, describe the limitations and any restrictions on resale that apply*:

The offering is being made only to persons for whom the amount invested does not exceed ten percent of the net worth of such persons (excluding principal residence and its furnishings and automobiles) including the net worth of spouse, if applicable.

Will the certificates bear a legend notifying holders of such restrictions? [ ] Yes [x] No

26. (a) *Name, address and telephone number of independent bank or savings and loan association or other similar depository institution acting as escrow agent if the proceeds are escrowed until minimum proceeds are raised*: National Bank of the Redwoods (707)573-4800, 111 Santa Rosa Avenue, Santa Rosa, CA 95402. The states of Texas and Mississippi have requested that funds received from investors residing in these states be held in an Escrow Account until such time as $1,800,000 has been raised. Through June 21, 1993, the Company has received subscriptions for 245,606 shares and $1,473,636 in aggregate.

    (b) *Date at which funds will be returned by escrow agent if minimum proceeds are not raised*: November 30, 1993.

    Will interest on proceeds during escrow period be paid to investors? [ ] Yes [x] No

27. *Explain the nature of any resale restrictions on presently outstanding shares, and when those restrictions will terminate, if this can be determined:*

As a condition of registering shares in the initial public offering with state securities administrators, the Company's founders, John and Nancy Schaeffer, agreed to place 900,512 of their shares into an escrow. Those shares may only be released from escrow upon the occurrence of certain events such as the Company's earning at least $0.25 per share in each of two consecutive years, or earning an average of $0.25 per share for five consecutive years, or after the Company's shares have traded in certain stock markets at a price of at least $8.75 for at least 90 consecutive trading days. This requirement has been imposed by the Securities Division of the Department of Licensing of the State of Washington.

Sales by the Schaeffers of any non-escrowed shares are restricted by Rule 144 under the federal Securities Act of 1933, as amended. Generally, they may not sell more than 1% of the total shares of the Company outstanding within any three-month period, but if the number of shares being traded increases substantially, an alternative limit could apply, that is, the average weekly trading volume of the shares during the four calendar weeks preceding the date on which notice of the sale is filed. Rule 144 has additional requirements as to the manner of sale, notice and availability of current public information about the Company.

DIVIDENDS, DISTRIBUTION AND REDEMPTIONS

28. *If the Company has within the last five years paid dividends, made distributions upon its stock or redeemed any securities, explain how much and when:*
Not Applicable.

33

OFFICERS AND KEY PERSONNEL OF THE COMPANY

29. *Chief Executive Officer*:   *Title*:   President

   Name: **John Schaeffer** *Age*:   43

   Office Street Address: 966 Mazzoni St., Ukiah, CA 95482

   Telephone No.:   (707)468-9292

   Names of employers, titles and dates of positions held during past five years with an indication of job responsibilities.

   Founded the Company in 1986. Ran all aspects of organization for three years; after increasing management depth, has focused on Marketing and Merchandising departments.

   Education (degrees, schools, and dates): B.A., Anthropology, University of California at Berkeley, 1971

   Also a Director of the Company? [x] Yes [ ] No

   Indicate amount of time to be spent on Company matters if less than full time: Full Time.

30. *Chief Operating Officer*:

   Title: Executive Vice President and Chief Operating Officer

   Name: **David C. Smith**   *Age*:   50

   Office Street Address: 966 Mazzoni St., Ukiah, CA 95482

   Telephone No.:   (707)468-9292

   Names of employers, titles and dates of positions held during past five years with an indication of job responsibilities.

   Real Goods Trading Corporation; Ukiah, CA
   Executive Vice President and Chief Operating Officer
   1993 - Present
   Responsible for all operational divisions of the company, including warehouse, distribution, phone agents, customer service, technical support, data processing, and retail store.

   Self employed writing, researching, and establishing a publishing company.
   1991 - 1993

   Medical Self Care, Inc.
   President, Chief Executive Officer
   1988 - 1991

   Smith & Hawken, Ltd.
   Co-Founder, President, Chief Operations Officer

34

1979 - 1988

Education (degrees, schools, and dates):

No formal degrees.

Also a Director of the Company? [x] Yes [ ] No

Indicate amount of time to be spent on Company matters if less than full time: Full Time.

31. *Chief Financial Officer*:

    Title: Controller and Chief Financial Officer

    Name: **James T. Robello**   *Age*:   47

    Office Street Address: 966 Mazzoni St. Ukiah, CA 95482

    Telephone No.:   (707)468-9292

    Names of employers, titles and dates of positions held during past five years with an indication of job responsibilities.

Real Goods Trading Corporation; Ukiah, CA
Controller and Chief Financial Officer
1991 - Present
Responsible for all financial and administrative functions including financial forecasting and planning, expense control, accounting, purchasing, human resources, banking relations, insurance, strategic planning, and facilities.

Cray Research, Inc.; San Ramon, CA
Business Manager II, Western/Asia Pacific Region
1989-1991
Responsible for all financial and administrative functions for 15 western states, Australia, and the Far East for this $250 + million division. Responsibilities included financial forecasting and planning, expense control, accounting, human resources, contract administration, strategic planning, and facilities.

Cray Research, Inc.; San Ramon, CA
Business Manager I
1985-1989
Responsible for all financial and administrative functions for 13 western states. Responsibilities included financial forecasting and planning, expense control, accounting, human resources, contract administration, strategic planning, and facilities.

Cray Research, Inc.; San Ramon, CA
Business Controls Manager, Western Region
1983-1985

Responsible for all financial functions for 9 western states. Responsibilities included financial forecasting and planning, expense control, accounting, strategic planning, and facilities.

Education (degrees, schools, and dates): B.B.A., Finance & Business Environment; University of Oregon; 1967

35

Also a Director of the Company? [ ] Yes [x] No

Indicate amount of time to be spent on Company matters if less than full time:

Full Time

32. *Other Key Personnel*:

    Title: Marketing Director

    Name: **Stephen Morris**   *Age*:   45

    Office Street Address: 41 South Main Street, Randolph, VT 05060

    Telephone No.:   (802) 728-3180

    Names of employers, titles and dates of positions held during past five years with an indication of job responsibilities.

    Sole Proprietor of Stephen Morris Associates, providing sales and marketing consulting service. 1990-Present

    Prior: 1978-1990, Sales Manager; Director of Sales and Distribution; Vice President, Sales and marketing for Vermont Castings, Inc. of Randolph, Vermont.

    Indicate amount of time to be spent on Company matters if less than full time:

    Minimum of 40 hours per month

    The Company has a well-educated technical staff of six with over 100 years of combined experience with off-the-grid living products. These technicians are trained to do the sizing of alternative energy systems all over the world and produce competitive price quotations with solar sizing computer software.

DIRECTORS OF THE COMPANY

33. *Number of Directors*: 3

    If Directors are not elected annually, or are elected under a voting trust or other arrangement, explain:

    Not applicable

34. *Information concerning outside or other Directors (i.e., those not described above)*:

    Name: **Michael Potts** *Age*:   48

    Office Street Address: 966 Mazzoni Street, Ukiah, CA 95482

    Telephone No.:   (707) 468-9292

    Names of employers, titles and dates of positions held during past five years with an indication of job responsibilities.

36

Self employed consultant specializing in adapting computer technology and office automation to the needs of growing enterprises without losing sight of the human values involved; his special interest is in small, self-generated businesses working in socially responsible ways. Michael is a member of several mail order catalog networks.

1987 - 1992

Real Goods Trading Company
Manager of Information Services
1989 - 1991 (Less than full time)

Education (degrees, schools, and dates): BA degree in Irish Literature; Harvard College; 1967.

35. (a) *Have any of the Officers or Directors ever worked for or managed a company (including a separate subsidiary or division of a larger enterprise) in the same business as the Company?* [x] Yes] No

David C. Smith was formerly a director and President of Smith & Hawken, Ltd., a catalog retailer of garden products. In addition, he was formerly President and Chief Executive Officer of Medical Self Care, Incorporated, a catalog retailer of health products.

(b) *If any of the Officers, Directors or other key personnel have ever worked for or managed a company in the same business or industry as the Company or in a related business or industry, describe what precautions, if any, (including the obtaining of releases or consents from prior employers) have been taken to preclude claims by prior employer for conversion or theft of trade secrets, know-how or other proprietary information.*

David C. Smith has no non-compete agreements or other legal restraints regarding proprietary business information from previous employers.

No proprietary information from former employers is applicable to the Company's business.

(c) *If the Company has never conducted operations or is otherwise in the development stage, indicate whether any of the Officers or Directors has ever managed any other company in the start-up or development stage and describe the circumstances, including relevant dates.*

Not applicable

(d) *If any of the Company's key personnel are not employees but are consultants or other independent contractors, state the details of their engagement by the Company.*

Stephen Morris, of Stephen Morris Associates, serves as Marketing Manager for the Company on an hourly basis with a $1,500 monthly guarantee.

(e) *If the Company has key man life insurance policies on any of its Officers, Directors or key personnel, explain, including the names of the persons insured, the amount of insurance, whether the insurance proceeds are payable to the Company and whether there are arrangements that require the proceeds to be used to redeem securities or pay benefits to the estate of the insured person or to a surviving spouse.*

The Company has a life insurance policy for John Schaeffer in the amount of $1,000,000.

36. *If a petition under the Bankruptcy Act or any State insolvency law was filed by or against the Company or its Officers, Directors or other key personnel, or a receiver, fiscal agent or similar officer was appointed by a court for the business or property of any such persons, or any partnership in which any of such persons was*

321

37

general partner at or within the past five years, or any corporation or business association of which any such person was an executive officer at or within the past five years, set forth below the name of such persons, and the nature and date of such actions.

Not applicable

Note: After reviewing the information concerning the background of the Company's Officers, Directors and other key personnel, potential investors should consider whether or not these persons have adequate background and experience to develop and operate this Company and to make it successful. In this regard, the experience and ability of management are often considered the most significant factors in the success of a business.

PRINCIPAL SHAREOWNERS

37. *Principal owners of the Company (those who beneficially own directly or indirectly 10% or more of the common and preferred stock presently outstanding) starting with the largest common shareowner. Include separately all common stock issuable upon conversion of convertible securities (identifying them by asterisk) and show average price per share as if conversion has occurred. Indicate by footnote if the price paid was for a consideration other than cash and the nature of any such consideration.*

Name: John & Nancy Schaeffer

Office Street Address: 966 Mazzoni Street, Ukiah, CA

Telephone No.: (707)468-9292

Principal occupation: President of the Company

Class of Shares: Common

Average Price Per Share: $.03. The consideration was the transfer of the assets of a going business.

No. of Shares Now Held: 2,569,109 including 900,512 shares held in escrow

% of Total: 91.8%

No. of Shares Held After Offering, if All Securities Sold: 2,569,109

% of Total: 75.6%

38. *Number of shares beneficially owned by Officers and Directors as a group*:

Before offering: 2,571,909 shares 91.9% of total outstanding) including 900,512 shares held in escrow

After offering: Assuming $3,600,000 sold: 2,571,909 shares 75.6% of total outstanding)
Assuming $1,800,000 sold: 2,571,909 shares 83.0% of total outstanding)

(Assume all options exercised and all convertible securities converted.)

38

MANAGEMENT RELATIONSHIPS, TRANSACTIONS AND REMUNERATION

39. (a) *If any of the Officers, Directors, key personnel or principal shareowners are related by blood or marriage, please describe.*

   John & Nancy Schaeffer are married.

   (b) *If the Company has made loans to or is doing business with any of its Officers, Directors, key personnel or 10% shareowners, or any of their relatives (or any entity controlled directly or indirectly by any of such persons) within the last two years, or proposes to do so within the future,explain. (This includes sales or lease of goods, property or services to or from the Company, employment or stock purchase contracts, etc.) State the principal terms of any significant loans, agreements, leases, financing or other arrangements.*

   The Company lent $47,609 to John Schaeffer on a demand basis. This promissory note which had a principal amount of up to $72,000, was executed on 1 July 1990 and bore an interest rate of 9% annually. The note was paid off in full on 25 August, 1992 including $6,740 in accumulated interest. Any future loans to officers, directors, 5% shareowners, or affiliates will be for a bona fide business purpose and approved by a majority of the disinterested members of the Board of Directors. Any future transactions with such persons will be on terms no less favorable to the company than could be obtained from unaffiliated third parties.

   (c) *If any of the Company's Officers, Directors, key personnel or 10% shareowners has guaranteed or co-signed any of the Company's bank debt or other obligations, including any indebtedness to be retired from the proceeds of this offering, explain and state the amounts involved.*

   John Schaeffer has signed personal guarantees to National Bank of the Redwoods in Santa Rosa for the Company's $400,000 line of credit.

40. (a) *List all remuneration by the Company to Officers, Directors and key personnel for the last fiscal year*:

Chief Executive Officer:	$70,061
Chief Operating Officer:	$58,963
Chief Accounting Officer:	$56,355
Directors as a group:	$0
(Three persons)	

   (b) *If remuneration is expected to change or has been unpaid in prior years, explain*:

   Remuneration is expected to be paid in Fiscal Year ending 31 March 1994.

Chief Executive Officer:	$72,000
Chief Operating Officer:	$83,000
Chief Accounting Officer:	$60,000

   Not applicable.

   (c) *If any employment agreements exist or are contemplated, describe*:

   John Schaeffer has an employment agreement with the Company providing a salary of $72,000 annually to be CEO and President of the Company. The contract is automatically renewed for an additional year.

323

39

41. (a) *Number of shares subject to issuance under presently outstanding stock purchase agreements, stock options, warrants or rights*: None. The Company will not grant options in excess of 10% of the outstanding shares for a one year period following the qualification date of this offering.

    Indicate which have been approved by shareowners. State the expiration dates, exercise prices and other basic terms for these securities: None. The exercise prices for any option must be at least 85% of the fair market value of the shares on the date the option was granted.

    (b) *Number of common shares subject to issuance under existing stock purchase or option plans but not yet covered by outstanding purchase agreements, options or warrants*: 600,000

    (c) *Describe the extent to which future stock purchase agreements, stock options, warrants or rights must   be approved by shareowners.*

    Shareowner approval would be necessary only to increase the authorized number of shares, not for any specific stock purchase agreements, stock options, warrants or rights.

42. *If the business is highly dependent on the services of certain key personnel, describe any arrangements to assure that these persons will remain with the Company and not compete upon any termination:*

    The business currently is highly dependent on the services of John Schaeffer, who will continue to be the majority shareowner of the Company. There is an employment contract with Mr. Schaeffer in effect. No other arrangements for retaining his services are considered necessary.

    Note: After reviewing the above, potential investors should consider whether or not the compensation to management and other key personnel directly or indirectly, is reasonable in view of the present stage of the Company's development.

LITIGATION

43. *Describe any past, pending or threatened litigation or administrative action which has had or may have a material effect upon the Company's business, financial condition, or operations, including any litigation or action involving the Company's Officers, Directors or other key personnel. State the names of the principal parties, the nature and current status of the matters, and amounts involved. Give an evaluation by management or counsel, to the extent feasible, of the merits of the proceedings or litigation and the potential impact on the Company's business, financial condition, or operations.*

    Not Applicable.

FEDERAL TAX ASPECTS

44. *If the Company is an S corporation under the Internal Revenue Code of 1986, and it is anticipated that any significant tax benefits will be available to investors in this offering, indicate the nature and amount of such anticipated tax benefits and the material risks of their disallowance. Also, state the name, address and telephone number of any tax advisor that has passed upon these tax benefits. Attach any opinion or any description of the tax consequences of an investment in the securities by the tax advisor.*

    The Company is not an S corporation.

    Name of Tax Advisor: Deloitte & Touche

40

Address: 50 Fremont Street
                    San Francisco, CA 94105

Telephone No.: (415) 247-4000

Note: Potential investors are encouraged to have their own personal tax consultant contact the tax advisor to review details of the tax benefits and the extent that the benefits would be available and advantageous to the particular investor.

MISCELLANEOUS FACTORS

45. *Describe any other material factors, either adverse or favorable, that will or could affect the Company or its business (for example, discuss any defaults under major contracts, any breach of bylaw provisions, etc.) or which are necessary to make any other information in this Disclosure Document not misleading or incomplete.*

With rapidly increasing power company utility rates, which have been increasing at close to 10% every year, the market is expanding to the suburban sphere as the costs of solar-electric power approach the costs of power company rates on a 30-year amortized basis. If existing trends continue, electric rate analysts predict that in five to fifteen years solar-electric power will be cost competitive with electric grid power. Pacific Gas and Electric Company (P.G.&E), a Northern California utility company, has increased its rates at approximately 10% per year each of the last three years and has estimated that 10% of its power will be generated by photovoltaic modules in the next ten years.

52

MANAGEMENT'S DISCUSSION AND ANALYSIS OF CERTAIN RELEVANT FACTORS

47. *If the Company's financial statements show losses from operations, explain the causes underlying these losses and what steps the Company has taken or is taking to address these causes.*

Not Applicable

48. *Describe any trends in the Company's historical operating results. Indicate any changes now occurring in the underlying economics of the industry or the Company's business which, in the opinion of Management, will have a significant impact (either favorable or adverse) upon the Company's results of operations within the next 12 months, and give a rough estimate of the probable extent of the impact, if possible.*

Real Goods has been profitable since its inception. The Company's rapid growth has been a result of investments in developing and growing its customer mailing list. Additionally, substantial investments have been made developing the Company's infrastructure to support a rapidly growing business. For the fiscal year ended March 31, 1992, the Company's Earnings From Operations were $22,078. The Company had Net Other Expenses of $12,075 which were primarily due to interest paid during the year. The Company's fiscal 1992 Earnings Before Income Taxes were $10,003, and Net Earnings were $5,603.

Net sales for the fiscal year ended March 31, 1993 increased 25.9% to $7,778,282 due to the increased circulation of catalogs. Cost of Goods Sold increased 22.2%, which represented a decrease as a percentage of sales from 56.4% to 54.7% because the Company was able to achieve certain purchasing economies and because of the continuing shift in the product mix toward higher margin merchandise.

Selling, general and administrative expenses increased 29.4% to $3,459,927 due to the increased circulation of catalogs, accelerating the expense write-off period of catalogs from six months to four months, more accurately reflecting the catalog life, increased levels of sales activity, participation in trade shows, and establishment of the Institute for Independent Living.

The increase in sales and gross margin offset higher operating expenses and the Company's earnings from operations increased 173.9% to $60,469. The Company's interest expense decreased 86.4% to $3,463 due to the retirement of long and short term debt with the proceeds of the Company's first stock offering. Other income increased 29.5% to $2,242, while interest income decreased 13.7% to $10,024 due to lower interest rates and the retirement of the note receivable from stockholder. Income taxes of $25,802 were accrued in fiscal 1993, while just $4,400 was accrued the previous year.

As a result of the foregoing, the Company's net earnings for the fiscal 1993 increased 675.8% to a profit of $43,470.

Note: At the end of fiscal 1993 the Company reclassified mail list rental income as an offset to mail list rental expense in accordance with generally accepted accounting principles. At that time, prior years statements were restated for reporting consistency.

Management believes that the Company's current infrastructure will support planned levels of growth. The Company plans to make selective additional investments in the future which may have short term negative effects.

In the longer term, the Company's plan is to increase its gross margin on sales as well as the dollar amount of sales. If achieved, this combination of better margin and higher sales volume would result in increased profits. There can be no assurance that the Company will increase either its gross margins or total sales.

See responses to Questions 3(a), 3(c), and 3(d), above that discuss in detail the current market for the Company's products and industry trends. The Company's sales increased at a rate of 150-200% in the start up phase during our first three years of operations. The Company had sales growth of 33% in its fourth year of operations and growth of 25.9% in its fifth year. The Company is planning a sales increase of about 24.9% for the current fiscal year. There can be no assurance that sales will increase at all. Electric company rates are expected to continue to increase at the current rate of approximately 10% per year, with the result that the demand for the Company's alternative energy products should significantly increase. The Company has put significant attention toward increasing its gross profit margin which it expects will have a positive effect toward overall profitability in the next 12 months.

53

49. *If the Company sells a product or products and has had significant sales during its last fiscal year, state the existing gross margin (net sales less cost of such sales as presented in accordance with generally accepted accounting principles) as a percentage of sales for the last fiscal year:*

45.26%

What is the anticipated gross margin for next year of operations?

Approximately 46.5%, although there can be no assurance thereof.

If this is expected to change, explain. Also, if reasonably current gross margin figures are available for the industry, indicate these figures and the source or sources from which they are obtained.

The Company's gross profit margin for the fiscal year ending 31 March 1993 was 45.26%. The Company has budgeted its gross profit margin for the next fiscal year of operations to be 46.5%, although no assurances can be given that it will achieve this. According to Robert Morris Associates' 1992 report on Retailers - Catalog & Mail-Order Houses, the gross profit margin for the industry ranges from 38.5% to 43.0%. The Company expects gross profit margin to improve by 1.26% due to a change in mix of products sold favoring high margin products. This change in mix is expected as a result of the company increasing its mailings of color catalogs (with generally higher margin products), more than it is increasing the mailings of the Real Goods News catalogs and Real Stuff mailers (generally lower margin products). The fiscal 1994 mailing plan calls for mailing 3,347,000 color catalogs, 485,000 Real Goods News catalogs, and 46,000 Real Stuff mailers.

50. *Foreign sales as a percent of total sales for last fiscal year:*

2%

Domestic government sales as a percent of total domestic sales for last fiscal year: 2%. Explain the nature of these sales, including any anticipated changes:

Approximately 2% of the Company's sales for the last fiscal year were to foreign customers and approximately 2% of sales were to U.S. government agencies. These sales mostly involved photovoltaic modules and alternative energy systems. The Company expects these percentages to increase slightly, but not significantly, in the next fiscal year.

Form U-7
(contains the SCOR form)

SMALL CORPORATE OFFERING
REGISTRATION FORM (Form U-7)
as adopted by NASAA on April 29, 1989

Instructions For Use of Form U-7
(Not Part of Disclosure Document)

I.   **Introduction**

Form U-7 has been developed pursuant to the Small Business Investment Incentive Act of 1980 (now contained in Section 19 of the Securities Act of 1933) which prescribes State and Federal cooperation in furtherance of the policies expressed in that Act of a substantial reduction in costs and paperwork to diminish the burden of raising investment capital, particularly by small business, and a minimum interference with the business of capital formation.

Form U-7 is the general registration form for corporations registering under state securities laws securities that are exempt from registration with the Securities and Exchange Commission (the "SEC") under Rule 504 of Regulation D. It is designed to be used by Companies, the attorneys and accountants for which are not necessarily specialists in securities regulation.

Historically, state legislatures have generally followed two approaches to the regulation of public offerings of securities such as those made under Form U-7. Some states deal solely with the disclosure made to investors. In addition to disclosure, other states also apply substantive fairness standards to public offerings in order to assure that the terms and structure of the offering are fair to investors. In particular, those standards are designed to require the promoters of the enterprise to share its potential risks and rewards fairly with the public investors. Those standards vary from state to state and as a general rule must be complied with by a Company in order to register its securities in those states.

You may anticipate receiving comments from examiners in many of the states in which Form U-7 registration is sought. Depending upon the regulatory approach taken by the state, those comments may be limited to requests for disclosure of additional information or may also require that certain terms of the offering be modified to comply with the state's substantive fairness criteria. Failure to resolve outstanding comments can lead to denial of an application for registration.

A Company, prior to using Form U-7, may wish to contact the staff of the securities administrator of each state in which the offering is to be filed to review applicable substantive fairness standards. It may be possible to arrange a prefiling conference with the administrator's staff. The states that apply such standards may identify those standards in an appendix to these instructions or may use other means to make them available.

II.   **Qualification for Use of Form**

To be eligible to use Form U-7, a Company must comply with each of the following requirements.

A.   The Company must be a corporation organized under the laws of one of the states or possessions of the United States which engages in or proposes to engage in a business other than petroleum exploration or production or mining or other extractive industries. "Blind pool" offerings and other offerings for which the specific business or properties cannot now be described are ineligible to use Form U-7.

B.   The securities may be offered and sold only on behalf of the Company, and Form U-7 may not be used by any selling security-holder (including purchasing underwriters in a firm commitment underwriting) to register his securities for resale.

C.   The offering price for common stock (and the exercise price, if the securities are options, warrants or rights for, and the conversion price if the securities are convertible into, common stock) must be equal to or

330

greater than $5.00 per share. By execution of the application and filing of the U-7 in any state, the Company thereby agrees with the Administrator that the Company will not split its common stock, or declare a stock dividend, for two years after effectiveness of the registration; provided, however, that in connection with a subsequent registered public offering, the Company may upon application and consent of the administrator take such action.

D.   The Company may engage selling agents to sell the securities. Commissions, fees, or other remuneration for soliciting any prospective purchaser in this state in connection with this offering may only be paid to persons who, if required to be registered, the Company believes, and has reason to believe, are appropriately registered in this state.

E.   This form shall not be available for the securities of any Company if the Company or any of its Officers, Directors, 10% stockholders, promoters or any selling agents of the securities to be offered, or any officer, director or partner of such selling agent: (i) has filed a registration statement which is the subject of a currently effective registration stop order entered pursuant to any state's securities law within five years prior to the filing of the application for registration hereunder; (ii) has been convicted within five years prior to the filing of the application for registration hereunder of any felony or misdemeanor in connection with the offer, purchase or sale of any security or any felony involving fraud or deceit, including, but not limited to, forgery, embezzlement, obtaining money under false pretenses, larceny, or conspiracy to defraud; (iii) is currently subject to any state administrative enforcement order or judgment entered by that state's securities administrator within five years prior to the filing of the application for registration hereunder or is subject to any state's administrative enforcement order or judgment in which fraud or deceit, including but not limited to making untrue statements of material facts and omitting to state material facts, was found and the order or judgment was entered within five years prior to the filing of the application for registration hereunder; (iv) is subject to any state's administrative enforcement order or judgment which prohibits, denies, or revokes the use of any exemption from registration in connection with this offer, purchase, or sale of securities; (v) is currently subject to any order, judgment, or decree of any court of competent jurisdiction temporarily or preliminarily restricting or enjoining, or is subject to any order, judgment or decree of any court of competent jurisdiction, permanently restraining or enjoining, such party from engaging in or continuing any conduct of practice in connection with the purchase or sale of any security or involving the making of any false filing with the state entered within five years prior to the filing of the application for registration hereunder; (vi) the prohibitions of paragraphs (i) - (iii) and (v) above shall not apply if the person subject to the disqualification is duly licensed or registered to conduct securities related business in the state in which the administrative order or judgment was entered against such person or if the broker-dealer employing such party is licensed or registered in this state and the Form B-D filed with this state discloses the order, conviction, judgment, or decree relating to such person. No person disqualified under this subsection may act in a capacity other than that for which the person is licensed or registered; and (vii) any disqualification caused by this section is automatically waived if the state securities administrator or agency of the state which created the basis for disqualification determines upon a showing of good cause that it is not necessary under the circumstances that registration be denied.

If any of the circumstances in clauses (ii), (iii) or (v) of the preceding paragraph has occurred more than five years from the date of the application for registration hereunder, these circumstances should be described in response to Question 45 as a Miscellaneous Factor.

F.   Use of the Form is available to any offering of securities by a Company, the aggregate offering price of which within or outside this state shall not exceed $1,000,000, less the aggregate offering price for all securities sold within the twelve months before the start of, and during the offering of, the securities under SEC Rule 504 in reliance on any exemption under section 3(b) of the Securities Act of 1933 or in violation of section 5(a) of that act. The Form is not available to a Company that is an investment company (including mutual funds) or is subject to the reporting requirements of § 13 or §15(d) of the Securities Exchange Act of 1934.

ii

331

G. The Company shall file with the SEC a Form D of Regulation D under the Securities Act of 1933 claiming exemption of the offering from registration under such act pursuant to Rule 504. A copy of the Form D with appropriate state signature pages shall be filed with the administrator at the same time as filed with the SEC.

III. General Requirements For Use of Form

A. The Form U-7 when properly filled in, signed and submitted, together with the exhibits scheduled below and a Form U-1 Uniform Application to Register Securities, constitutes an application for registration for the states listed at the bottom of the cover page of the Form. There should be filed with each state there listed a signed original of the Form, together with an executed Form U-1 and a signed original of the consent to service of process constituting Exhibit 7. Any references in the Form U-1 to SEC registration and effectiveness should be disregarded and Questions 6 and 8(a) of the Form U-1 are inapplicable. The Form U-1 should set forth the amount of securities being registered in that state and the method of calculating the filing fee, and there should be enclosed a check for the amount of the filing fee. Each state must separately declare the registration effective by an order to that effect unless that state has some other procedure applicable to registration on Form U-7. Once registration is effective as to a given state, the effective date should be noted at the bottom of the cover page of the Form. Any changed or revised Disclosure Document must also be signed.

B. Each question in each paragraph of the Form should be responded to. If the question or series of questions is inapplicable, so indicate. Each answer should be clearly and concisely stated and in the space provided; however, notwithstanding the specificity of the questions, responses should not involve nominal, immaterial or insignificant information.

C. If the provided space is insufficient, additional space should be created by cutting and pasting the Form to add more lines or by putting the Form on a word processor and adding more lines in this or a similar manner. Irrespective of which method is used, care should be taken to assure that the Form is accurately and completely reproduced. Smaller type size should not be used, and script or italic type styles should be avoided.

D. There must be submitted to the administrator an opinion of an attorney licensed to practice in a state or territory of the United States that the securities to be sold in the offering have been duly authorized and when issued upon payment of the offering price will be legally and validly issued, fully paid and nonassessable and binding on the Company in accordance with their terms.

E. The Disclosure Document on Form U-7 constitutes the offering circular or prospectus and the Form once filled out, filed and declared effective may be reproduced by the Company by copy machine or otherwise for dissemination to potential investors. (The Company is cautioned to control the copying and distribution to preclude inaccurate or unreadable copies from being used and to prevent other unauthorized uses for which the Company may nevertheless be deemed responsible.) These Instructions are not part of the Disclosure Document and should not be included. Reproduced copies should be on white paper and should be stapled or secured in the left margin without a cover of any type.

F. The Company should expect that the office of the administrator may have comments and questions concerning the answers set forth on the Form and that changes may be required to be made to the answers before the registration is declared effective. Comments and questions may either be included in a letter or made by telephone communication initiated by the office of the administrator in response to the filing.

G.   No offers or sales may be made in this state until the registration has been declared effective by the administrator. To make offers or sales before the registration is effective could lead to a stop order or other proceeding which would preclude use of the Form in this or any other state and could give rise to a right of rescission by investors enforceable against management, principal stockholders and the selling agents as well as the Company. When the registration has been declared effective in this state, offers and sales may be made in this state even though registration in other states has not been declared effective. This Disclosure Document must be delivered to each investor before the sale is made, e.g. (a) before any order is entered; (b) any subscription agreement is signed; or (c) any part of the purchase price is received. The registration statement will be effective only for the same time period specified in the order of the administrator, which may be different for different states; however, no registration statement shall remain effective in a particular state for a period greater than one year.

H.   After the registration has been declared effective, and while the offering is still in progress, if any portion of the Form should need to be changed or revised because of a material event concerning the Company or the offering to make it accurate and complete, it shall be so changed, revised, or supplemented. If changed, revised or supplemented, (including an addition on the cover page of another state in which the offering has been registered) the Form as so changed, revised or supplemented, clearly marked to show changes from the previously filed version, should be filed and cleared with the administrator of this state before use. If any of the changes or revisions are of such significance that they are material to the making of an investment decision by an investor, and if the minimum proceeds have not been raised, after filing with and clearance by the administrator, the Disclosure Document on this Form as so changed, revised or supplemented should be recirculated to persons in this state that have previously subscribed, and they should be given the opportunity to rescind or reconfirm their investment.

I.   Options, warrants and similar rights to purchase securities constitute a continuous offering of the underlying securities during the exercise period and require the securities to be registered and the Disclosure Document to be kept continuously current throughout the exercise period through the use of the above amendment procedure or by means of a supplement, as appropriate. Upon any change, revision or supplement to the Disclosure Document, a copy must be promptly furnished to the holders of options, warrants and similar rights.

J.   Any and all supplemental selling literature or advertisements announcing the offering should be filed by the Company and cleared with the securities administrator of each state prior to publication or circulation within that state. An announcement should not be a sales motivation device and should normally contain no more than the following: (1) the name of the Company, (2) characterization of the Company as indicated on the Cover Page of the Disclosure Document, (3) address and telephone number of the Company, (4) a brief indication in ten words or less of the Company's business or proposed business, (5) the number and type of securities offered and the offering price per security, (6) the name, address and telephone number of any selling agent authorized to sell the securities, (7) a statement that the announcement does not constitute an offer to sell or solicitation of an offer to purchase and that any such offer must be made by official Disclosure Document, (8) how a copy of the Disclosure Document may be obtained, and (9) the Company's corporate logo. Clip and return coupons requesting a copy of the Disclosure Document are permitted in printed announcements. (For example, an announcement in "tombstone" format with a black-lined border and using the following language would ordinarily be acceptable: "50,000 shares, common stock; $5 per share; (Logo) XYZ Corporation, a development stage database computer software company now conducting operations, Midtown, Ohio; Selling agent: ABC Securities, 1234 Main Street, Midtown, Ohio, (321) 123-4567; This announcement does not constitute an offer to sell or the solicitation of an offer to buy the securities, which offer may be made only by means of an official Disclosure Document; A copy of the Disclosure Document may be obtained by contacting the selling agent at the above address and telephone number." Similarly, a classified advertisement using the following language would ordinarily be acceptable: "Common stock of XYZ Corporation, a development stage database computer software company now conducting operations, Midtown, Ohio. Price $5 per share. Total offering 50,000 shares. This announcement does not constitute an offer to sell or the solicitation of an offer to buy the securities, which offer may be made only by means of an official Disclosure Document. A copy of the Disclosure Document may be obtained by contacting the Company, Industrial Park, Suite 12B, 456 Mill Road, Midtown, Ohio, (321) 321-4321.")

The issuance of any but routine press releases or the granting of interviews to news media during, or at about the same time of, an offering could constitute indirect advertising, which if not precleared with the securities administrator would be prohibited. Any unusual news article or news program featuring the Company during this period, particularly if present or future earnings, or the pending offering, are mentioned, could delay or cause suspension of the effectiveness of the registration and disrupt the offering. Consequently any such news article or news program, no matter by whom it may be initiated, should generally be discouraged during this period.

IV.   **Instructions as to Specific Captions and Questions**

BE VERY CAREFUL AND PRECISE IN ANSWERING ALL QUESTIONS. GIVE FULL AND COMPLETE ANSWERS SO THAT THEY ARE NOT MISLEADING UNDER THE CIRCUMSTANCES INVOLVED. DO NOT DISCUSS ANY FUTURE PERFORMANCE OR OTHER ANTICIPATED EVENT UNLESS YOU HAVE A REASONABLE BASIS TO BELIEVE THAT IT WILL ACTUALLY OCCUR WITHIN THE FORSEEABLE FUTURE.   IF ANY ANSWER REQUIRING SIGNIFICANT INFORMATION IS MATERIALLY INACCURATE, INCOMPLETE OR MISLEADING, THE COMPANY, ITS MANAGEMENT AND PRINCIPAL STOCKHOLDERS MAY HAVE LIABILITY TO INVESTORS. THE SELLING AGENTS SHOULD EXERCISE APPROPRIATE DILIGENCE TO DETERMINE THAT NO SUCH INACCURACY OR INCOMPLETENESS HAS OCCURRED, OR THEY ALSO MAY BE LIABLE.

A.   Cover Page. The Cover Page of the Disclosure Document is a summary of certain essential information and should be kept on one page if at all possible. For purposes of characterizing the Company on the cover page, the term "development stage" has the same meaning as that set forth in Statement of Financial Accounting Standards No. 7 (June 1, 1975).

B.   Risk Factors. The Company should avoid generalized statements and include only those factors which are unique to the Company. No specific number of risk factors is required to be identified. If more than 16 significant risk factors exist, add additional lines and number as appropriate. Risk factors may be due to such matters as cash flow and liquidity problems, inexperience of management in managing a business in the particular industry, dependence of the Company on an unproven product, absence of an existing market for the product (even though management may believe a need exists), absence of an operating history of the Company, absence of profitable operations in recent periods, an erratic financial history, the financial position of the Company, the nature of the business in which the Company is engaged or proposes to engage, conflicts of interest with management, arbitrary establishment of offering price, reliance on the efforts of a single individual, or absence of a trading market if a trading market is not expected to develop. Cross references should be made to the Questions where details of the risks are described.

C.   Business and Properties. The inquiries under Business and Properties elicit information concerning the nature of the business of the Company and its properties. Make clear what aspects of the business are presently in operation and what aspects are planned to be in operation in the future. The description of principal properties should provide information which will reasonably inform investors as to the suitability, adequacy, productive capacity and extent of utilization of the facilities used in the enterprise. Detailed descriptions of the physical characteristics of the individual properties or legal descriptions by metes and bounds are not required and should not be given.

As to Question 4, if more than five events or milestones exist, add additional lines as necessary. A "milestone" is a significant point in the Company's development or an obstacle which the company must overcome in order to become profitable.

D.   Offering Price Factors. Financial information in response to Questions 5, 6 and 7 should be consistent with the Financial Statements. Earnings per share for purposes of Question 5 should be calculated by dividing earnings for the last fiscal year by the weighted average of outstanding shares during that year. No calculations should be shown for periods of less than one year or if earnings are negative or nominal. For purposes of Question 8, the "offering price" of any options, warrants or rights or convertible securities in the offering is the respective exercise or conversion price.

E.   Use of Proceeds. Use of net proceeds should be stated with a high degree of specificity. Suggested (but not mandatory) categories are: leases, rent, utilities, payroll (by position or type), purchase or lease of specific items of equipment or inventory, payment of notes, accounts payable, etc., marketing or advertising costs, taxes, consulting fees, permits, professional fees, insurance and supplies. Categories will vary depending on the Company's

v

334

plans. Use of footnotes or other explanation is recommended where appropriate. Footnotes should be used to indicate those items of offering expenses that are estimates. Set forth in separate categories all payments which will be made immediately to the Company's executive officers, directors and promoters, indicating by footnote that these payments will be so made to such persons. If a substantial amount is allocated to working capital, set forth separate sub-categories for use of the funds in the Company's business.

If any substantial portion of the proceeds has not been allocated for particular purposes, a statement to that effect as one of the Use of Net Proceeds categories should be included together with a statement of the amount of proceeds not so allocated and a footnote explaining how the Company expects to employ such funds not so allocated.

F.   Plan of Distribution. In Question 26 if the proposed business of the Company requires a minimum amount of proceeds to commence, or to proceed with, the business in the manner proposed, there shall be established an escrow with a bank or savings and loan association or other similar depository institution acting as independent escrow agent with which shall be immediately deposited all proceeds received from investors until the minimum amount of proceeds has been raised. Any failure to deposit funds promptly into the escrow shall be grounds for enforcement proceedings against the persons involved. The date at which the funds will be returned by the escrow agent if the minimum proceeds are not raised shall not be later than one year from the date of effectiveness of the registration in this state.

G.   Capitalization. Capitalization should be shown as of a date no earlier than that of the most recent Financial Statements provided pursuant to Question 46. If the Company has mandatory redeemable preferred stock, include the amount thereof in "long term debt" and so indicate by footnote to that category in the capitalization table.

H.   Officers and Key Personnel of the Company. The term "Chief Executive Officer" means the officer of the Company who has been delegated final authority by the board of directors to direct all aspects of the Company's affairs. The term "Chief Operating Officer" means the officer in charge of the actual day-to-day operations of the Company's business. The term "Chief Financial Officer" means the officer having accounting skills who is primarily in charge of assuring that the Company's financial books and records are properly kept and maintained and financial statements prepared.

The term "key personnel" means persons such as vice presidents, production managers, sales managers, or research scientists and similar persons, who are not included above, but who make or are expected to make significant contributions to the business of the Company, whether as employees, independent contractors, consultants or otherwise.

I.   Principal Stockholders. If shares are held by family members, through corporations or partnerships, or otherwise in a manner that would allow a person to direct or control the voting of the shares (or share in such direction or control - as, for example, a co-trustee) they should be included as being "beneficially owned." An explanation of these circumstances should be set forth in a footnote to the "Number of Shares Now Held."

J.   Management Relationships, Transactions and Remuneration. For purposes of Question 39(b), a person directly or indirectly controls an entity if he is part of the group that directs or is able to direct the entity's activities or affairs. A person is presumptively a member of a control group if he is an officer, director, general partner, trustee or beneficial owner of a 10% or greater interest in the entity. In Question 40, the term "Cash" should indicate salary, bonus, consulting fees, non-accountable expense accounts and the like. The column captioned "Other" should include the value of any options or securities given, any annuity, pension or retirement benefits, bonus or profit-sharing plans, and personal benefits (club memberships, company cars, insurance benefits not generally available to employees, etc.). The nature of these benefits should be explained in a footnote to this column.

K.   Financial Statements. Attach to the Disclosure Document for the Company and its consolidated subsidiaries, a balance sheet as of the end of the most recent fiscal year. If the Company has been in existence for less than one fiscal year, attach a balance sheet as of the date within 135 days of the date of filing the registration statement. If the first effective date of state registration, as set forth on the Cover Page of this Disclosure Document, is within 45 days after the end of the Company's fiscal year and financial statements for the most recent fiscal year are not available, the balance sheet may be as of the end of the preceding fiscal year and there shall be included an

vi

335

additional balance sheet as of an interim date at least as current as the end of the Company's third fiscal quarter of the most recently completed fiscal year. Also attach, for the Company and its consolidated subsidiaries and for its predecessors, statements of income and cash flows and statements of changes in stockholders' equity for the last fiscal year preceding the date of the most recent balance sheet being attached, or such shorter period as the Company (including predecessors) has been in existence. In addition, for any interim period between the latest reviewed or audited balance sheet and the date of the most recent interim balance sheet being attached, provide statements of income and cash flows. Financial statements shall be prepared in accordance with generally accepted accounting principles. If the Company has not conducted significant operations, statements of receipts and disbursements shall be included in lieu of statements of income. Interim financial statements may be unaudited. All other financial statements shall be audited by independent certified public accountants; provided, however, that if each of the following four conditions are met, such financial statements in lieu of being audited may be reviewed by independent certified public accountants in accordance with the Accounting and Review Service Standards promulgated by the American Institute of Certified Public Accountants: (a) the Company shall not have previously sold securities by means of an offering involving the general solicitation of prospective investors by means of advertising, mass mailings, public meetings, "cold call" telephone solicitation or any other method directed toward the public, (b) the Company has not been previously required under federal or state securities laws to provide audited financial statements in connection with any sale of its securities, (c) the aggregate amount of all previous sales of securities by the Company (exclusive of debt financings with banks and similar commercial lenders) shall not exceed $1,000,000, and (d) the amount of the present offering does not exceed $500,000.

If since the beginning of its last fiscal year the Company has acquired another business, provide a pro forma combined balance sheet as of the end of the fiscal year, and a pro forma combined statement of income as if the acquisition had occurred at the beginning of the Company's last fiscal year, if any of the following exists: (a) the investments in and advances to the acquired business by the Company and its subsidiaries' (other than the acquired business) exceeds 20% of the Company's assets on its consolidated balance sheet at the end of the Company's last fiscal year, (b) the Company's and its subsidiaries (other than the acquired business') proportionate share of the total assets (after intercompany eliminations) of the acquired business exceeds 20% of the assets on the consolidated balance sheet, or (c) the Company's and its subsidiaries' (other than the acquired business') equity in income from continuing operations before income taxes, extraordinary items and cumulative effect of a change in accounting principle, of the acquired business exceeds 20% of such income of the Company and its consolidated subsidiaries for the Company's last fiscal year.

The financial statements should reflect all stock splits (including reverse stock splits), stock dividends and recapitalizations even if they have occurred since the date of the financial statements.

V.   **Exhibits**

There shall be filed with the Administrator at the same time as the filing of the Form U-7 copies of each of the following documents to the extent applicable as exhibits to which the Administrator may refer in reviewing the Form U-7 and which will be available for public inspection by any person upon request.

1.   Form of Selling Agency Agreement.

2.   Company's Articles of Incorporation or other Charter documents and all amendments thereto.

3.   Company's By-Laws, as amended to date.

4.   Copy of any resolutions by directors setting forth terms and provisions of capital stock to be issued.

5.   Any indenture, form of note or other contractual provision containing terms of notes or other debt, or of options, warrants or rights to be offered.

6.   Specimen of security to be offered (including any legend restricting resale).

vii

7.   Consent to service of process (Form U-2) accompanied by appropriate corporate resolution (Form U-2A).

8.   Copy of all advertising or other materials directed to or to be furnished investors in the offering.

9.   Form of escrow agreement for escrow of proceeds.

10.   Consent to inclusion in Disclosure Document of Accountant's report.

11.   Consent to inclusion in Disclosure Document of Tax Advisor's opinion or description of tax consequences.

12.   Consent to inclusion in Disclosure Document of any evaluation of litigation or administrative action by counsel.

13.   Form of any Subscription Agreement for the purchase of securities in this offering.

14.   Opinion of Counsel required in paragraph III. D. of these Instructions.

15.   Schedule of residence street addresses of Officers, Directors and principal stockholders.

16.   Work Sheets showing computations of responses to Questions 6, 7(a), 8(a), 8(b) and 17(b), using forms attached to these Instructions.

15000267.MIS

FORM U-7
DISCLOSURE DOCUMENT

_____
(Exact name of Company as set forth in Articles of Incorporation or Charter)

Type of securities offered: _____

Maximum number of securities offered: _____

Minimum number of securities offered: _____

Price per security: $_____

Total proceeds: If maximum sold: $_____

  If minimum sold: $_____

       (For use of proceeds and offering expenses, see Question Nos. 9 and 10)

Is a commissioned selling agent selling the securities in this offering? [ ] Yes [ ] No

If yes, what percent is commission of price to public? _____%.

Is there other compensation to selling agent(s)? [ ] Yes [ ] No

Is there a finder's fee or similar payment to any person? [ ] Yes [ ] No (See Question No. 22)

Is there an escrow of proceeds until minimum is obtained? [ ] Yes [ ] No (See Question No. 26)

Is this offering limited to members of a special group, such as employees of the Company or individuals?
[ ] Yes [ ] No (See Question No. 25)

Is transfer of the securities restricted? [ ] Yes [ ] No (See Question No. 25)

INVESTMENT IN SMALL BUSINESSES INVOLVES A HIGH DEGREE OF RISK, AND INVESTORS SHOULD NOT INVEST ANY FUNDS IN THIS OFFERING UNLESS THEY CAN AFFORD TO LOSE THEIR INVESTMENT IN ITS ENTIRETY. SEE QUESTION NO. 2 FOR THE RISK FACTORS THAT MANAGEMENT BELIEVES PRESENT THE MOST SUBSTANTIAL RISKS TO AN INVESTOR IN THIS OFFERING.

IN MAKING AN INVESTMENT DECISION INVESTORS MUST RELY ON THEIR OWN EXAMINATION OF THE ISSUER AND THE TERMS OF THE OFFERING, INCLUDING THE MERITS AND RISKS INVOLVED. THESE SECURITIES HAVE NOT BEEN RECOMMENDED BY ANY FEDERAL OR STATE SECURITIES COMMISSION OR REGULATORY AUTHORITY. FURTHERMORE, THE FOREGOING AUTHORITIES HAVE NOT CONFIRMED THE ACCURACY OR DETERMINED THE ADEQUACY OF THIS DOCUMENT. ANY REPRESENTATION TO THE CONTRARY IS A CRIMINAL OFFENSE.

This Company:

      [ ]   Has never conducted operations.

      [ ]   Is in the development stage.

      [ ]   Is currently conducting operations.

      [ ]   Has shown a profit in the last fiscal year.

      [ ]   Other (Specify):_____

          (Check at least one, as appropriate)

This offering has been registered for offer and sale in the following states:

State	State File No.	Effective Date
_____	_____	_____
_____	_____	_____
_____	_____	_____
_____	_____	_____

U-7:4/29/89

1

TABLE OF CONTENTS

THIS DISCLOSURE DOCUMENT CONTAINS ALL OF THE REPRESENTATIONS BY THE COMPANY CONCERNING THIS OFFERING, AND NO PERSON SHALL MAKE DIFFERENT OR BROADER STATEMENTS THAN THOSE CONTAINED HEREIN. INVESTORS ARE CAUTIONED NOT TO RELY UPON ANY INFORMATION NOT EXPRESSLY SET FORTH IN THIS DISCLOSURE DOCUMENT.

This Disclosure Document, together with Financial Statements and other Attachments, consists of a total of _____ pages.

3

339

THE COMPANY

1.   Exact corporate name: _____

_____

State and date of incorporation: _____

_____

Street address of principal office: _____

_____

Company Telephone Number: (___) _____

Fiscal year: _____   _____
              (month)   (day)

Person(s) to contact at Company with respect to offering: _____

Telephone Number (if different from above): (___) _____

RISK FACTORS

2.   List in the order of importance the factors which the Company considers to be the most substantial risks to an investor in this offering in view of all facts and circumstances or which otherwise make the offering one of high risk or speculative (i.e., those factors which constitute the greatest threat that the investment will be lost in whole or in part, or not provide an adequate return).

    (1) _____

    (2) _____

    (3) _____

    (4) _____

    (5) _____

    (6) _____

4

(7) _____
   _____
   _____
(8) _____
   _____
   _____
   _____
(9) _____
   _____
   _____
   _____
(10) _____
   _____
   _____
   _____
(11) _____
   _____
   _____
   _____
(12) _____
   _____
   _____
   _____
(13) _____
   _____
   _____
   _____
(14) _____
   _____
   _____
   _____
(15) _____
   _____
   _____
   _____
(16) _____
   _____
   _____
   _____

Note: In addition to the above risks, businesses are often subject to risks not foreseen or fully appreciated by management. In reviewing this Disclosure Document potential investors should keep in mind other possible risks that could be important.

5

BUSINESS AND PROPERTIES

3.   With respect to the business of the Company and its properties:

(a)   Describe in detail <u>what</u> business the Company does and proposes to do, including what products or goods are or will be produced or services that are or will be rendered.

_____
_____
_____
_____
_____
_____
_____
_____
_____
_____
_____
_____
_____

(b)   Describe <u>how</u> these products or services are to be produced or rendered and how and when the Company intends to carry out its activities. If the Company plans to offer a new product(s), state the present stage of development, including whether or not a working prototype(s) is in existence. Indicate if completion of development of the product would require a material amount of the resources of the Company, and the estimated amount. If the Company is or is expected to be dependent upon one or a limited number of suppliers for essential raw materials, energy or other items, describe. Describe any major existing supply contracts.

_____
_____
_____
_____
_____
_____
_____
_____

(c)   Describe the industry in which the Company is selling or expects to sell its products or services and, where applicable, any recognized trends within that industry. Describe that part of the industry and the geographic area in which the business competes or will compete.

Indicate whether competition is or is expected to be by price, service, or other basis. Indicate (by attached table if appropriate) the current or anticipated prices or price ranges for the Company's products or services, or the formula for determining prices, and how these prices compare with those of competitors' products or services, including a description of any variations in product or service features. Name the principal competitors that the Company has or expects to have in its area of competition. Indicate the relative size and financial and market strengths of the Company's competitors in the area of competition in which the Company is or will be operating. State why

6

342

the Company believes that it can effectively compete with these and other companies in its area of competition.

_____
_____
_____
_____
_____
_____
_____
_____

Note: Because this Disclosure Document focuses primarily on details concerning the Company rather than the industry in which the Company operates or will operate, potential investors may wish to conduct their own separate investigation of the Company's industry to obtain broader insight in assessing the Company's prospects.

(d)   Describe specifically the marketing strategies the Company is employing or will employ in penetrating its market or in developing a new market. Set forth in response to Question 4 below the timing and size of the results of this effort which will be necessary in order for the Company to be profitable. Indicate how and by whom its products or services are or will be marketed (such as by advertising, personal contact by sales representatives, etc.), how its marketing structure operates or will operate and the basis of its marketing approach, including any market studies. Name any customers that account for, or based upon existing orders will account for, a major portion (20% or more) of the Company's sales. Describe any major existing sales contracts.

_____
_____
_____
_____
_____
_____
_____
_____

(e)   State the backlog of written firm orders for products and/or services as of a recent date (within the last 90 days) and compare it with the backlog of a year ago from that date.

As of: _____/_____/_____ $_____
       (a recent date)

As of: _____/_____/_____ $_____
       (one year earlier)

Explain the reason for significant variations between the two figures, if any. Indicate what types and amounts of orders are included in the backlog figures. State the size of typical orders. If the Company's sales are seasonal or cyclical, explain.

_____
_____
_____
_____
_____

7

343

(f) State the number of the Company's present employees and the number of employees it anticipates it will have within the next 12 months. Also, indicate the number by type of employee (i.e., clerical, operations, administrative, etc.) the Company will use, whether or not any of them are subject to collective bargaining agreements, and the expiration date(s) of any collective bargaining agreement(s). If the Company's employees are on strike, or have been in the past three years, or are threatening to strike, describe the dispute. Indicate any supplemental benefits or incentive arrangements the Company has or will have with its employees.

_____
_____
_____
_____
_____
_____
_____
_____

(g) Describe generally the principal properties (such as real estate, plant and equipment, patents, etc.) that the Company owns, indicating also what properties it leases and a summary of the terms under those leases, including the amount of payments, expiration dates and the terms of any renewal options. Indicate what properties the Company intends to acquire in the immediate future, the cost of such acquisitions and the sources of financing it expects to use in obtaining these properties, whether by purchase, lease or otherwise.

_____
_____
_____
_____
_____
_____
_____
_____

(h) Indicate the extent to which the Company's operations depend or are expected to depend upon patents, copyrights, trade secrets, know-how or other proprietary information and the steps undertaken to secure and protect this intellectual property, including any use of confidentiality agreements, covenants-not-to-compete and the like. Summarize the principal terms and expiration dates of any significant license agreements. Indicate the amounts expended by the Company for research and development during the last fiscal year, the amount expected to be spent this year and what percentage of revenues research and development expenditures were for the last fiscal year.

_____
_____
_____
_____
_____
_____
_____

8

344

(i)   If the Company's business, products, or properties are subject to material regulation (including environmental regulation) by federal, state, or local governmental agencies, indicate the nature and extent of regulation and its effects or potential effects upon the Company.

_____
_____
_____
_____
_____
_____
_____
_____
_____

(j)   State the names of any subsidiaries of the Company, their business purposes and ownership, and indicate which are included in the Financial Statements attached hereto. If not included, or if included but not consolidated, please explain.

_____
_____
_____
_____
_____
_____
_____
_____
_____

(k)   Summarize the material events in the development of the Company (including any material mergers or acquisitions) during the past five years, or for whatever lesser period the Company has been in existence. Discuss any pending or anticipated mergers, acquisitions, spin-offs or recapitalizations. If the Company has recently undergone a stock split, stock dividend or recapitalization in anticipation of this offering, describe (and adjust historical per share figures elsewhere in this Disclosure Document accordingly).

_____
_____
_____
_____
_____
_____
_____
_____
_____

4.   (a)   If the Company was not profitable during its last fiscal year, list below in chronological order the events which in management's opinion must or should occur or the milestones which in

9

management's opinion the Company must or should reach in order for the Company to become profitable, and indicate the expected manner of occurrence or the expected method by which the Company will achieve the milestones.

Event or Milestone	Expected manner of occurrence or method of achievement	Date, or number of months after receipt of proceeds, when should be accomplished
(1)		
(2)		
(3)		
(4)		
(5)		

(b)   State the probable consequences to the Company of delays in achieving each of the events or milestones within the above time schedule, and particularly the effect of any delays upon the Company's liquidity in view of the Company's then anticipated level of operating costs. (See Question Nos. 11 and 12) _____

Note: After reviewing the nature and timing of each event or milestone, potential investors should reflect upon whether achievement of each within the estimated time frame is realistic and should assess the consequences of delays or failure of achievement in making an investment decision.

10

OFFERING PRICE FACTORS

If the securities offered are common stock, or are exercisable for or convertible into common stock, the following factors may be relevant to the price at which the securities are being offered.

5. What were net, after-tax earnings for the last fiscal year? (If losses, show in parenthesis.)

    Total $_____   ($_____ per share)

6. If the Company had profits, show offering price as a multiple of earnings. Adjust to reflect for any stock splits or recapitalizations, and use conversion or exercise price in lieu of offering price, if applicable.

    $$\frac{\text{Offering Price Per Share}}{\text{Net After-Tax Earnings Last Year Per Share}} = \text{_____ (price/earnings multiple)}$$

7. (a) What is the net tangible book value of the Company? (If deficit, show in parenthesis.) For this purpose, net tangible book value means total assets (exclusive of copyrights, patents, goodwill, research and development costs and similar intangible items) minus total liabilities.

        $_____   ($_____ per share)

    If the net tangible book value per share is substantially less than this offering (or exercise or conversion) price per share, explain the reasons for the variation.

    _____
    _____
    _____
    _____

    (b) State the dates on which the Company sold or otherwise issued securities during the last 12 months, the amount of such securities sold, the number of persons to whom they were sold, any relationship of such persons to the Company at the time of sale, the price at which they were sold and, if not sold for cash, a concise description of the consideration. (Exclude bank debt.)

    _____
    _____
    _____
    _____
    _____
    _____
    _____
    _____
    _____

11

347

8.　(a)　What percentage of the outstanding shares of the Company will the investors in this offering have? (Assume exercise of outstanding options, warrants or rights and conversion of convertible securities, if the respective exercise or conversion prices are at or less than the offering price. Also assume exercise of any options, warrants or rights and conversions of any convertible securities offered in this offering.)

If the maximum is sold: _____%

If the minimum is sold: _____%

(b)　What post-offering value is management implicitly attributing to the entire Company by establishing the price per security set forth on the cover page (or exercise or conversion price if common stock is not offered)? (Total outstanding shares after offering times offering price, or exercise or conversion price if common stock is not offered.)

If maximum is sold:　$_____ *

If minimum is sold:　$_____ *

(For above purposes, assume outstanding options are exercised in determining "shares" if the exercise prices are at or less than the offering price. All convertible securities, including outstanding convertible securities, shall be assumed converted and any options, warrants or rights in this offering shall be assumed exercised.)

* These values assume that the Company's capital structure would be changed to reflect any conversions of outstanding convertible securities and any use of outstanding securities as payment in the exercise of outstanding options, warrants or rights included in the calculation. The type and amount of convertible or other securities thus eliminated would be: _____. These values also assume an increase in cash in the Company by the amount of any cash payments that would be made upon cash exercise of options, warrants or rights included in the calculations. The amount of such cash would be: $_____.

Note: After reviewing the above, potential investors should consider whether or not the offering price (or exercise or conversion price, if applicable) for the securities is appropriate at the present stage of the Company's development.

12

348

USE OF PROCEEDS

9.   (a)   The following table sets forth the use of the proceeds from this offering:

	If Minimum Sold		If Maximum	
	Amount	%	Amount	%
Total Proceeds	$_____	100%	$_____	100%
Less: Offering Expenses				
Commissions and Finders Fees	_____	___	_____	___
Legal & Accounting	_____	___	_____	___
Copying & Advertising	_____	___	_____	___
Other (Specify): _____	_____	___	_____	___
Net Proceeds from Offering	$_____	___	$_____	___
Use of Net Proceeds				
_____	$_____	___%	$_____	___%
_____	_____	___	_____	___
_____	_____	___	_____	___
_____	_____	___	_____	___
_____	_____	___	_____	___
_____	_____	___	_____	___
Total Use of Net Proceeds	$_____	100%	$_____	100%

(b)   If there is no minimum amount of proceeds that must be raised before the Company may use the proceeds of the offering, describe the order of priority in which the proceeds set forth above in the column "If Maximum Sold" will be used.

_____

_____

_____

Note: After reviewing the portion of the offering allocated to the payment of offering expenses, and to the immediate payment to management and promoters of any fees, reimbursements, past salaries or similar payments, a potential investor should consider whether the remaining portion of his investment, which would be that part available for future development of the Company's business and operations, would be adequate.

10.   (a)   If material amounts of funds from sources other than this offering are to be used in conjunction with the proceeds from this offering, state the amounts and sources of such other funds, and whether funds are firm or contingent. If contingent, explain.

_____

_____

13

(b)   If any material part of the proceeds is to be used to discharge indebtedness, describe the terms of such indebtedness, including interest rates. If the indebtedness to be discharged was incurred within the current or previous fiscal year, describe the use of the proceeds of such indebtedness.

_____

_____

_____

(c)   If any material amount of the proceeds is to be used to acquire assets, other than in the ordinary course of business, briefly describe and state the cost of the assets and other material terms of the acquisitions. If the assets are to be acquired from officers, directors, employees or principal stockholders of the Company or their associates, give the names of the persons from whom the assets are to be acquired and set forth the cost to the Company, the method followed in determining the cost, and any profit to such persons.

_____

_____

_____

_____

(d)   If any amount of the proceeds is to be used to reimburse any officer, director, employee or stockholder for services already rendered, assets previously transferred, or monies loaned or advanced, or otherwise, explain:

_____

_____

_____

11.   Indicate whether the Company is having or anticipates having within the next 12 months any cash flow or liquidity problems and whether or not it is in default or in breach of any note, loan, lease or other indebtedness or financing arrangement requiring the Company to make payments. Indicate if a significant amount of the Company's trade payables have not been paid within the stated tradeterm. State whether the Company is subject to any unsatisfied judgments, liens or settlement obligations and the amounts thereof. Indicate the Company's plans to resolve any such problems.

_____

_____

_____

_____

12.   Indicate whether proceeds from this offering will satisfy the Company's cash requirements for the next 12 months, and whether it will be necessary to raise additional funds. State the source of additional funds, if known.

_____

_____

_____

_____

14

350

CAPITALIZATION

13. Indicate the capitalization of the Company as of the most recent balance sheet date (adjusted to reflect any subsequent stock splits, stock dividends, recapitalizations or refinancings) and as adjusted to reflect the sale of the minimum and maximum amount of securities in this offering and the use of the net proceeds therefrom:

	Amount Outstanding		
	As of:	As Adjusted	
	/ / (date)	Minimum	Maximum
Debt:			
Short-term debt (average interest rate _____%)	$_____	$_____	$_____
Long-term debt (average interest rate _____%)	$_____	$_____	$_____
Total debt	$_____	$_____	$_____
Stockholders equity (deficit):			
Preferred stock - par or stated value (by class of preferred in order of preferences)			
_____	$_____	$_____	$_____
_____	$_____	$_____	$_____
_____	$_____	$_____	$_____
Common stock--par or stated value	$_____	$_____	$_____
Additional paid in capital	$_____	$_____	$_____
Retained earnings (deficit)	$_____	$_____	$_____
Total stockholders equity (deficit)	$_____	$_____	$_____
Total Capitalization	$_____	$_____	$_____

_____

Number of preferred shares authorized to be outstanding:

Class of Preferred	Number of Shares Authorized	Par Value Per Share
_____	_____	$_____
_____	_____	$_____
_____	_____	$_____

Number of common shares authorized: _____ shares. Par or stated value per share, if any: $_____

Number of common shares reserved to meet conversion requirements or for the issuance upon exercise of options, warrants or rights: _____ shares.

15

351

DESCRIPTION OF SECURITIES

14. The securities being offered hereby are:

      [ ]   Common Stock
      [ ]   Preferred or Preference Stock
      [ ]   Notes or Debentures
      [ ]   Units of two or more types of securities, composed of:

      [ ]   Other: _____

15. These securities have:

Yes	No	
[ ]	[ ]	Cumulative voting rights
[ ]	[ ]	Other special voting rights
[ ]	[ ]	Preemptive rights to purchase in new issues of shares
[ ]	[ ]	Preference as to dividends or interest
[ ]	[ ]	Preference upon liquidation
[ ]	[ ]	Other special rights or preferences (specify): _____

Explain: _____

16. Are the securities convertible? [ ] Yes [ ] No
    If so, state conversion price or formula. _____
        Date when conversion becomes effective: __/__/__
        Date when conversion expires: __/__/__

17. (a) If securities are notes or other types of debt securities:
      (1) What is the interest rate? _____%
          If interest rate is variable or multiple rates, describe: _____

      (2) What is the maturity date? __/__/__
          If serial maturity dates, describe: _____

      (3) Is there a mandatory sinking fund? [ ] Yes [ ] No Describe: _____

      (4) Is there a trust indenture? [ ] Yes [ ] No
          Name, address and telephone number of Trustee _____

      (5) Are the securities callable or subject to redemption?
          [ ] Yes [ ] No Describe, including redemption prices: _____

      (6) Are the securities collateralized by real or personal property?
          [ ] Yes [ ] No Describe: _____

16

(7) If these securities are subordinated in right of payment of interest or principal, explain the terms of such subordination. _____

_____

How much currently outstanding indebtedness of the Company is senior to the securities in right of payment of interest or principal? $_____.
How much indebtedness shares in right of payment on an equivalent (pari passu) basis? $_____.
How much indebtedness is junior (subordinated) to the securities? $_____.

(b) If notes or other types of debt securities are being offered and the Company had earnings during its last fiscal year, show the ratio of earnings to fixed charges on an actual and pro forma basis for that fiscal year. "Earnings" means pretax income from continuing operations plus fixed charges and capitalized interest. "Fixed charges" means interest (including capitalized interest), amortization of debt discount, premium and expense, preferred stock dividend requirements of majority owned subsidiary, and such portion of rental expense as can be demonstrated to be representative of the interest factor in the particular case. The pro forma ratio of earnings to fixed charges should include incremental interest expense as a result of the offering of the notes or other debt securities.

	Last Fiscal Year		
	Actual	Pro Forma	
		Minimum	Maximum
"Earnings" = "Fixed Charges"	_____	_____	_____
If no earnings, show "Fixed Charges" only	_____	_____	_____

Note: Care should be exercised in interpreting the significance of the ratio of earnings to fixed charges as a measure of the "coverage" of debt service, as the existence of earnings does not necessarily mean that the Company's liquidity at any given time will permit payment of debt service requirements to be timely made. See Question Nos. 11 and 12. See also the Financial Statements and especially the Statement of Cash Flows.

18. If securities are Preference or Preferred stock:
Are unpaid dividends cumulative? [ ] Yes [ ] No
Are securities callable? [ ] Yes [ ] No Explain: _____

_____
_____

Note: Attach to this Disclosure Document copies or a summary of the charter, bylaw or contractual provision or document that gives rise to the rights of holders of Preferred or Preference Stock, notes or other securities being offered.

19. If securities are capital stock of any type, indicate restrictions on dividends under loan or other financing arrangements or otherwise:

_____
_____
_____

20. Current amount of assets available for payment of dividends (if deficit must be first made up, show deficit in parenthesis): $_____.

17

353

PLAN OF DISTRIBUTION

21. The selling agents (that is, the persons selling the securities as agent for the Company for a commission or other compensation) in this offering are:

Name: _____   Name: _____

Address: _____   Address:_____

_____   _____

Telephone No. ( )   Telephone No. ( )

22. Describe any compensation to selling agents or finders, including cash, securities, contracts or other consideration, in addition to the cash commission set forth as a percent of the offering price on the cover page of this Disclosure Document. Also indicate whether the Company will indemnify the selling agents or finders against liabilities under the securities laws. ("Finders" are persons who for compensation act as intermediaries in obtaining selling agents or otherwise making introductions in furtherance of this offering.)

_____
_____
_____
_____

23. Describe any material relationships between any of the selling agents or finders and the Company or its management.

_____
_____
_____
_____

Note: After reviewing the amount of compensation to the selling agents or finders for selling the securities, and the nature of any relationship between the selling agents or finders and the Company, a potential investor should assess the extent to which it may be inappropriate to rely upon any recommendation by the selling agents or finders to buy the securities.

24. If this offering is not being made through selling agents, the names of persons at the Company through which this offering is being made:

Name: _____   Name: _____

Address: _____   Address:_____

_____   _____

Telephone No. ( )   Telephone No. ( )

25. If this offering is limited to a special group, such as employees of the Company, or is limited to a certain number of individuals (as required to qualify under Subchapter S of the Internal Revenue Code) or is subject to any other limitations, describe the limitations and any restrictions on resale that apply:

_____
_____
_____
_____

Will the certificates bear a legend notifying holders of such restrictions?
[ ] Yes [ ] No

18

26. (a) Name, address and telephone number of independent bank or savings and loan association or other similar depository institution acting as escrow agent if proceeds are escrowed until minimum proceeds are raised:

_____

_____

_____

_____

(b) Date at which funds will be returned by escrow agent if minimum proceeds are not raised: ___

_____

Will interest on proceeds during escrow period be paid to investors?
[ ] Yes   [ ] No

27. Explain the nature of any resale restrictions on presently outstanding shares, and when those restrictions will terminate, if this can be determined:

_____

_____

_____

_____

Note: Equity investors should be aware that unless the Company is able to complete a further public offering or the Company is able to be sold for cash or merged with a public company that their investment in the Company may be illiquid indefinitely.

DIVIDENDS, DISTRIBUTIONS AND REDEMPTIONS

28. If the Company has within the last five years paid dividends, made distributions upon its stock or redeemed any securities, explain how much and when:

_____

_____

_____

_____

_____

_____

_____

_____

_____

19

355

OFFICERS AND KEY PERSONNEL OF THE COMPANY

29.   Chief Executive Officer: Title:_____

Name: _____   Age: _____

Office Street Address: _____
_____
_____

Telephone No.: (   ) _____

Name of employers, titles and dates of positions held during past five years with an indication of job responsibilities.

_____
_____
_____

Education (degrees, schools, and dates): _____
_____

Also a Director of the Company [   ] Yes   [   ] No

Indicate amount of time to be spent on Company matters if less than full time:

_____
_____
_____

30.   Chief Operating Officer: Title: _____

Name: _____   Age: _____

Office Street Address: _____
_____
_____

Telephone No.: (   ) _____

Names of employers, titles and dates of positions held during past five years with an indication of job responsibilities.

_____
_____
_____

Education (degrees, schools, and dates): _____

Also a Director of the Company? [   ] Yes   [   ] No

Indicate amount of time to be spent on Company matters if less than full time:

_____
_____
_____

20

356

31.   Chief Financial Officer: Title: _____

        Name: _____   Age: _____

        Office Street Address: _____

                                              _____

                                              _____

        Telephone No.: (_____) _____

        Names of employers, titles and dates of positions held during past five years with an indication of job responsibilities.

        _____

        _____

        _____

        Education (degrees, schools, and dates): _____

        Also a Director of the Company? [ ] Yes [ ] No

        Indicate amount of time to be spent on Company matters if less than full time:

        _____

        _____

        _____

32.   Other Key Personnel:

        (A)   Name: _____   Age: _____

                Title: _____

                Office Street Address: _____

                                      _____

                                      _____

                Telephone No.: (_____) _____

                Names of employers, titles and dates of positions held during past five years with an indication of job responsibilities.

                _____

                _____

                _____

                Education (degrees, schools, and dates): _____

                Also a Director of the Company? [ ] Yes [ ] No

        Indicate amount of time to be spent on Company matters if less than full time:

        _____

        _____

        _____

21

(B) Name: _____   Age: _____

Title: _____

Office Street Address: _____
_____
_____

Telephone No.: (_____) _____

Names of employers, titles and dates of positions held during past five years with an indication of job responsibilities.

_____
_____
_____

Education (degrees, schools, and dates): _____
_____

Also a Director of the Company? [ ] Yes [ ] No

Indicate amount of time to be spent on Company matters if less than full time:

_____
_____
_____

DIRECTORS OF THE COMPANY

33. Number of Directors: _____ If Directors are not elected annually, or are elected under a voting trust or other arrangement, explain:

_____
_____
_____

34. Information concerning outside or other Directors (i.e. those not described above):

(A) Name: _____   Age: _____

Office Street Address: _____
_____
_____

Telephone No.: (_____) _____

Names of employers, titles and dates of positions held during past five years with an indication of job responsibilities.

_____
_____
_____

Education (degrees, schools, and dates): _____
_____

22

(B)   Name: _____   Age: _____

Office Street Address: _____

_____

_____

Telephone No.: (_____) _____

Names of employers, titles and dates of positions held during past five years with an indication of job responsibilities.

_____

_____

_____

Education (degrees, schools, and dates):   _____

_____

(C)   Name: _____   Age: _____

Office Street Address: _____

_____

_____

Telephone No.: (_____) _____

Names of employers, titles and dates of positions held during past five years with an indication of job responsibilities.

_____

_____

_____

Education (degrees, schools, and dates): _____

_____

35.   (a)   Have any of the Officers or Directors ever worked for or managed a company (including a separate subsidiary or division of a larger enterprise) in the same business as the Company? [ ] Yes [ ] No

Explain: _____

_____

_____

(b)   If any of the Officers, Directors or other key personnel have ever worked for or managed a company in the same business or industry as the Company or in a related business or industry, describe what precautions, if any, (including the obtaining of releases or consents from prior employers) have been taken to preclude claims by prior employers for conversion or theft of trade secrets, know-how or other proprietary information.

_____

_____

_____

_____

23

359

(c)   If the Company has never conducted operations or is otherwise in the development stage, indicate whether any of the Officers or Directors has ever managed any other company in the start-up or development stage and describe the circumstances, including relevant dates.

_____
_____
_____
_____

(d)   If any of the Company's key personnel are not employees but are consultants or other independent contractors, state the details of their engagement by the Company.

_____
_____
_____

(e)   If the Company has key man life insurance policies on any of its Officers, Directors or key personnel, explain, including the names of the persons insured, the amount of insurance, whether the insurance proceeds are payable to the Company and whether there are arrangements that require the proceeds to be used to redeem securities or pay benefits to the estate of the insured person or to a surviving spouse.

_____
_____
_____

36.   If a petition under the Bankruptcy Act or any State insolvency law was filed by or against the Company or its Officers, Directors or other key personnel, or a receiver, fiscal agent or similar officer was appointed by a court for the business or property of any such persons, or any partnership in which any of such persons was general partner at or within the past five years, or any corporation or business association of which any such person was an executive officer at or within the past five years, set forth below the name of such persons, and the nature and date of such actions.

_____
_____
_____

Note: After reviewing the information concerning the background of the Company's Officers, Directors and other key personnel, potential investors should consider whether or not these persons have adequate background and experience to develop and operate this Company and to make it successful. In this regard, the experience and ability of management are often considered the most significant factors in the success of a business.

24

360

PRINCIPAL STOCKHOLDERS

37. Principal owners of the Company (those who beneficially own directly or indirectly 10% or more of the common and preferred stock presently outstanding) starting with the largest common stockholder. Include separately all common stock issuable upon conversion of convertible securities (identifying them by asterisk) and show average price per share as if conversion has occurred. Indicate by footnote if the price paid was for a consideration other than cash and the nature of any such consideration.

	Class of Shares	Average Price Per Share	No. of Shares Now Held	% of Total	No. of Shares Held After Offering if All Securities Sold	% of Total
Name:						
	____	____	____	___	____	__
	____	____	____	___	____	__
Office Street Address:						
Telephone No.						
(___) _____						
Principal occupation:						
Name:						
	____	____	____	___	____	__
	____	____	____	___	____	__
Office Street Address:						
Telephone No.						
(___) _____						
Principal occupation:						

25

361

	Class of Shares	Average Price Per Share	No. of Shares Now Held	% of Total	No. of Shares Held After Offering if All Securities Sold	% of Total
Name:						
	_____	____	____	__	_____	__
	_____	____	____	__	_____	__

Office Street Address:
_____
_____
_____

Telephone No.
(___) _____

Principal occupation:
_____

Name:
_____ _____ ____ ____ __ _____ __
_____ ____ ____ __ _____ __

Office Street Address:
_____
_____
_____

Telephone No.
(___) _____

Principal occupation:
_____

38.   Number of shares beneficially owned by Officers and Directors as a group:

Before offering: _____ shares   (_____% of total outstanding)

After offering: a) Assuming minimum securities sold:_____ shares
                                                   (_____% of total outstanding)

                    b) Assuming maximum securities sold: _____ shares
                                                   (_____% of total outstanding)
(Assume all options exercised and all convertible securities converted.)

MANAGEMENT RELATIONSHIPS, TRANSACTIONS AND REMUNERATION

39.   (a)   If any of the Officers, Directors, key personnel or principal stockholders are related by blood or marriage, please describe.

_____
_____
_____
_____
_____

26

362

(b)   If the Company has made loans to or is doing business with any of its Officers, Directors, key personnel or 10% stockholders, or any of their relatives (or any entity controlled directly or indirectly by any of such persons) within the last two years, or proposes to do so within the future, explain. (This includes sales or lease of goods, property or services to or from the Company, employment or stock purchase contracts, etc.) State the principal terms of any significant loans, agreements, leases, financing or other arrangements.

_____
_____
_____
_____
_____
_____
_____
_____

(c)   If any of the Company's Officers, Directors, key personnel or 10% stockholders has guaranteed or co-signed any of the Company's bank debt or other obligations, including any indebtedness to be retired from the proceeds of this offering, explain and state the amounts involved.

_____
_____
_____

40.   (a)   List all remuneration by the Company to Officers, Directors and key personnel for the last fiscal year:

	Cash	Other
Chief Executive Officer	$_____	$_____
Chief Operating Officer	_____	_____
Chief Accounting Officer	_____	_____
Key Personnel: _____	_____	_____
_____	_____	_____
Others: _____	_____	_____
_____	_____	_____
_____	_____	_____
Total:	$_____	$_____

Directors as a group
(number of persons ___) $_____ $_____

(b)   If remuneration is expected to change or has been unpaid in prior years, explain:

_____
_____
_____
_____

27

(c)   If any employment agreements exist or are contemplated, describe:

_____
_____
_____
_____
_____

41.   (a)   Number of shares subject to issuance under presently outstanding stock purchase agreements, stock options, warrants or rights: _____ shares (____% of total shares to be outstanding after the completion of the offering if all securities sold, assuming exercise of options and conversion of convertible securities). Indicate which have been approved by shareholders. State the expiration dates, exercise prices and other basic terms for these securities:

_____
_____
_____
_____
_____

(b)   Number of common shares subject to issuance under existing stock purchase or option plans but not yet covered by outstanding purchase agreements, options or warrants: _____ shares.

(c)   Describe the extent to which future stock purchase agreements, stock options, warrants or rights must be approved by shareholders.

_____
_____
_____
_____

42.   If the business is highly dependent on the services of certain key personnel, describe any arrangements to assure that these persons will remain with the Company and not compete upon any termination:

Note: After reviewing the above, potential investors should consider whether or not the compensation to management and other key personnel directly or indirectly, is reasonable in view of the present stage of the Company's development.

LITIGATION

43.   Describe any past, pending or threatened litigation or administrative action which has had or may have a material effect upon the Company's business, financial condition, or operations, including any litigation or action involving the Company's Officers, Directors or other key personnel. State the names of the principal parties, the nature and current status of the matters, and amounts involved. Give an evaluation by management or counsel, to the extent feasible, of the merits of the proceedings or litigation and the potential impact on the Company's business, financial condition, or operations.

_____
_____
_____
_____
_____

28

FEDERAL TAX ASPECTS

44.   If the Company is an S corporation under the Internal Revenue Code of 1986, and it is anticipated that any significant tax benefits will be available to investors in this offering, indicate the nature and amount of such anticipated tax benefits and the material risks of their disallowance. Also, state the name, address and telephone number of any tax advisor that has passed upon these tax benefits. Attach any opinion or any description of the tax consequences of an investment in the securities by the tax advisor.

_____
_____
_____
_____
_____
_____

Name of Tax Advisor: _____
Address: _____
_____
Telephone No. (_____) _____

Note: Potential investors are encouraged to have their own personal tax consultant contact the tax advisor to review details of the tax benefits and the extent that the benefits would be available and advantageous to the particular investor.

MISCELLANEOUS FACTORS

45.   Describe any other material factors, either adverse or favorable, that will or could affect the Company or its business (for example, discuss any defaults under major contracts, any breach of bylaw provisions, etc.) or which are necessary to make any other information in this Disclosure Document not misleading or incomplete.

_____
_____
_____
_____
_____
_____

FINANCIAL STATEMENTS

46.   Attach reviewed or audited financial statements for the last fiscal year and unaudited financial statements for any interim periods thereafter. If since the beginning of the last fiscal year the Company has acquired another business the assets or net income of which were in excess of 20% of those for the Company, show pro forma combined financial statements as if the acquisition had occurred at the beginning of the Company's last fiscal year.

The Company does hereby agree to provide to investors in this offering for five years (or such longer period as required by law) hereafter annual financial reports containing a balance sheet as of the end of the Company's fiscal year and a statement of income for said fiscal year, all prepared in accordance with generally accepted accounting principles and accompanied by an independent accountant's report. If the Company has more than 100 security holders at the end of the fiscal year, the financial statements shall be audited.

29

365

MANAGEMENT'S DISCUSSION AND ANALYSIS OF CERTAIN RELEVANT FACTORS

47.   If the Company's financial statements show losses from operations, explain the causes underlying these losses and what steps the Company has taken or is taking to address these causes.

_____
_____
_____

_____

48.   Describe any trends in the Company's historical operating results. Indicate any changes now occurring in the underlying economics of the industry or the Company's business which, in the opinion of Management, will have a significant impact (either favorable or adverse) upon the Company's results of operations within the next 12 months, and give a rough estimate of the probable extent of the impact, if possible.

_____
_____
_____

_____

49.   If the Company sells a product or products and has had significant sales during its last fiscal year, state the existing gross margin (net sales less cost of such sales as presented in accordance with generally accepted accounting principles) as a percentage of sales for the last fiscal year: _____%.
What is the anticipated gross margin for next year of operations? Approximately _____%.
If this is expected to change, explain. Also, if reasonably current gross margin figures are available for the industry, indicate these figures and the source or sources from which they are obtained.

_____
_____
_____

_____

50.   Foreign sales as a percent of total sales for last fiscal year: _____%. Domestic government sales as a percent of total domestic sales for last fiscal year: _____%.
Explain the nature of these sales, including any anticipated changes:

_____
_____
_____

30

SIGNATURES:

A majority of the Directors and the Chief Executive and Financial Officers of the Company shall sign this Disclosure Document on behalf of the Company and by so doing thereby certify that each has made diligent efforts to verify the material accuracy and completeness of the information herein contained. By signing this Disclosure Document, the Chief Executive and Chief Financial Officers agree to make themselves, the Company's books and records, copies of any contract, lease or other document referred to in the Disclosure Document, or any other material contract or lease (including stock options and employee benefit plans), except any proprietary or confidential portions thereof, and a set of the exhibits to this Disclosure Document, available to each investor prior to the time of investment, and to respond to questions and otherwise confirm the information contained herein prior to the making of any investment by such investor.

The Chief Financial Officer signing this form is hereby certifying that the financial statements submitted fairly state the Company's financial position and results of operations, or receipts and disbursements, as of the dates and period(s) indicated, all in accordance with generally accepted accounting principles consistently applied (except as stated in the notes thereto) and (with respect to year-end figures) including all adjustments necessary for fair presentation under the circumstances.

Chief Executive Officer: Directors:

_____   _____

Title: _____   _____

                                 _____

Chief Financial Officer: _____

_____   _____

Title: _____   _____

31

Notes

1. October 19, 1992, p. 92.
2. According to Financial Accounting Standards Bulletin No. 14, the following factors should consider (among others) in determining whether products and services are related (and, therefore, be grouped into a single industry segment) or unrelated (and, therefore, should be separated into two or more industry segments):

    a. The nature of the product. Related products or services have similar purposes or end uses. Thus, they may be expected to have similar rates of profitability, similar degrees of risk, and similar opportunities for growth.

    b. The nature of the production process. Sharing of common or interchangeable production or sales facilities, equipment, labor force, or service group or use of the same or similar basic raw materials may suggest that products or services are related. Likewise, similar degrees of labor intensiveness or similar degrees of capital intensiveness may indicate a relationship among products or services.

    c. Markets and marketing methods. Similarity of geographic marketing areas, types of customers, or marketing methods may indicate a relationship among products or services. For instance, the use of a common or interchangeable sales force may suggest a relationship among products or services. The sensitivity of the market to price changes and to change in general economic conditions may also indicate whether products or services are related or unrelated.

3. See Appendices 3 and 4 of this book.
4. Only two years are required in Forms SB-1 and SB-2 Registration Statements that can be used by a "small business issuer".
5. It may be necessary to give Class A stock a dividend and liquidation preference to permit registration of the Class A stock under certain state securities laws. The extent of the preferences are subject to negotiation with state securities law administrators. California normally prohibits two classes of common stock with unequal voting rights.
6. Richard Carter and Steven Manaster, "Initial Public Offerings and Underwriter Reputation," *The Journal of Finance* Vol. XLV, No. 4 (September 1990), 1045–1067; James M. Johnson and Robert E. Miller, "Investment Banker Prestige and the Underpricing of Initial Public Offerings," *Financial Management* 17 (Summer 1988), 19–29; Robert Perez, *Inside Investment Banking*: New York (Praeger Publishers, 1984);

S. L. Hayes, "Investment Banking: Power Structure in Flux," *Harvard Business Review* (March/April 1971), 136–152.

7. *The Wall Street Journal,* January 15, 1986, p. 1.

8. See Ronald J. Gilson & Reiner H. Kraakman, "The Mechanisms of Market Efficiency", 70 VA. L. Rev. 549, 618–621 (1984).

9. Stephen P. Ferris, Janine S. Hiller, Glenn A. Wolfe and Elizabeth S. Cooperman, "An Analysis and Recommendation for Prestigious Underwriter Participation in IPOs," *The Journal of Corporation Law,* (Spring 1992), 581–603.

10. 283 F.Supp. 643 (1968).

11. The prospectus is part I of the Form S-1 registration statement. Part II of the Form S-1 registration statement contains a breakdown of the expenses of the offering, information about the indemnification of directors and officers, information about recent sales of unregistered securities, and exhibits, financial statement schedules and undertakings. The Form S-1 also includes a cover page and a cross-reference sheet, which are not part of the prospectus. The cover page contains information about the number of shares being registered, the registration fee, the agent for service of process, and similar information.

12. In describing developments, information must be given as to matters such as the following: the year in which the registrant was organized and its form of organization; the nature and results of any bankruptcy, receivership, or similar proceedings with respect to the registrant or any of its significant subsidiaries; the nature and results of any other material reclassification, merger, or consolidation of the registrant or any of its significant subsidiaries; the acquisition or disposition of any material amount of assets other than the ordinary course of business; and any material changes in the mode of conducting the business.

13. The term "liquidity" refers to the ability of an enterprise to generate adequate amounts of cash to meet the enterprise's needs for cash. Except where it is otherwise clear from the discussion, the registrant must indicate those balance sheet conditions or income or cash flow items that the registrant believes may be indicators of its liquidity condition. Liquidity generally must be discussed on both a long-term and short-term basis. The issue of liquidity must be discussed in the context of the registrant's own business or businesses. For example, a discussion of working capital may be appropriate for certain manufacturing, industrial or related operations but might be inappropriate for a bank or public utility.

14. An accredited investor includes certain institutional investors and (among others): (a) any natural person whose individual net worth, or joint net worth with that person's spouse, exceeds $1 million at the time of purchase; and (b) any natural person who had an individual income in excess of $200,000 in each of the two most recent years or joint income with that person's spouse in excess of $300,000 in each of those years and has a reasonable expectation of reaching the same income level in the current year.

15. Id.

16. The company must agree to not split its common stock, or declare a stock dividend, for two years after the effective date of the registration.

17. This risk can be hedged by obtaining written warranties and representations from the shell's promoters and escrowing their stock or other compensation received in connection with the merger.

18. Approximately 4,000 of the over 13,000 stocks listed in the Pink Sheets are traded in the "OTS Bulletin Board," which is a computerized trading system.

19. CUSIP is the trademark for a system that identifies specific security issuers—and their issues—stocks, bonds, notes, etc., of corporate, municipal, state and federal issues, and selected foreign issues. Under the CUSIP plan, a CUSIP number is permanently assigned to each issue and will identify that single issue and no other. It provides brokers, banks, exchanges and institutions with a uniform number that is used in all phases of their security dealings—comparisons, wire communications, transaction reports, delivery

tickets, transfer, proxy and price services, dividend claims and bookkeeping—and eliminates the confusion and delays that arise from a multitude of numbering systems. CUSIP is the acronym for the Committee on Uniform Security Identification Procedures of the American Bankers Association.

20. Once the company has less than 300 securityholders, the company can deregister the class of securities and cease being subject to the reporting provisions of the 1934 Act.

21. 15 U.S.C. 78p (1981).

22. Rules 16a-2 and 16a-3 under the 1934 Act.

23. Section 3(a)(11) of 1934 Act and Rule 16a-1(d) under the 1934 Act.

24. Instruction 4(a)(i) to Form 4.

25. Id.

26. Rule 16a-3(f)(1) under the 1934 Act.

27. Rule 16a-3(f)(2) under the 1934 Act.

28. Section 16(a) of the 1934 Act.

29. Rule 16a-3(h) under the 1934 Act.

30. Rule 16a-3(e) under the 1934 Act.

31. Rule 405 of Items S-K.

32. 15 U.S.C. § 78u(d)(3) (West Supp. 1991).

33. 15 U.S.C. § 78p (1981).

34. *Perfect Photo, Inc. v. Grabb,* 205 F. Supp. 569 (E.D. Pa. 1962). *See also* 5 Louis Loss & Joel Seligman, Securities Regulation 2383 (3d ed. 1989).

35. *Adler v. Klawans,* 267 F.2d 840 (2d Cir. 1959). But see *Foremost-McKesson, Inc. v. Provident Securities Co.,* 423 U.S. 232 (1976), holding that a 10 percent beneficial owner was not covered by Section 16(b) where he was not such an owner before the initial purchase. See also Rule 16a-2(c) under the 1934 Act. Rule 16a-2(a) under the 1934 Act provides that Section 16 does not apply to transactions by directors and officers occurring within 6 months before they become an officer or director.

36. *Blau v. Mission Corp.,* 212 F.2d 77 (2d Cir. 1954); *Blau v. Albert,* 157 F.Supp. 816 (S.D.N.Y. 1957); *Benisch v. Cameron,* 81 F.Supp. 882 (S.D.N.Y. 1948). *See generally* 5 Loss & Seligman, *supra* note 34, at 2330–31.

37. The motivation of the shareholder in bringing the suit is legally irrelevant. *Magida v. Continental Can Co.,* 12 F.R.D. 74 (S.D.N.Y. 1951). *See also Magida v. Continental Can Co.,* 231 F.2d 843 (2d Cir. 1956); 5 Loss & Seligman, *supra* note 34, at 2333.

38. Rule 16b-6(a) under the 1934 Act.

39. *Newmark v. RKO General, Inc.,* 425 F.2d 348 (2d Cir. 1970), *cert denied* 400 U.S. 854 (1970); cf. Rule 16b-7 under 1934 Act.

40. *Trancale v. Blumberg,* 80 F.Supp. 387 (S.D.N.Y. 1948); 5 Loss & Seligman, *supra* note 31, at 2353–64; Rule 16b-6(a) under the 1934 Act.

41. *Matas v. Siess,* 467 F.Supp. 217 (S.D.N.Y. 1979). *Cf. Rosen v. Drisler,* 421 F.Supp. 1282 (S.D.N.Y. 1976); *Freedman v. Barrow,* 427 F.Supp. 1129 (S.D.N.Y. 1976). But see Rule 16a-1(c)(3), which provides an exclusion for stock appreciation rights exercisable only for cash provided that certain other conditions are met.

42. Rule 16a-1(a)(2) under the 1934 Act.

43. Rule 16a-1(a)(2)(ii)(A) and (e) under the 1934 Act.

44. *Smolowe v. Delendo Corp.,* 136 F.2d 231 (2d Cir. 1943), *cert. denied,* 320 U.S. 751 (1943).

45. Op. Gen. Counsel, Release No. 34–116 (1935); *Prager v. Sylvestri,* 449 F.Supp. 425, (S.D.N.Y. 1978).

46. *Smolowe v. Delendo Corp., supra note* 44. *But cf. Morales v. Lukens, Inc.* CCH Fed. Sec. L.Rep. ¶ 91,676 (S.D.N.Y. 1984) holding that profit on two simultaneous but separate sales made at different prices should be calculated on the basis of the average price for all of the stock, based on testimony that the two sales were part of a single plan of disposition negotiated at a single price for the entire block. See Rule 16b-6(c) under the

1934 Act, which provides certain rules for determining the recoverable profits in transactions involving so-called "derivative securities" (e.g., stock options, warrants and convertible stock).

47. *Gratz v. Claughthon*, 187 F.2d 46 (2d Cir. 1951), *cert. denied*, 341 U.S. 920 (1951).
48. *Smolowe v. Delendo Corp., supra* note 44.
49. *Kern County Land Co. v. Occidental Petroleum*, 411 U.S. 582 (1973).
50. 15 U.S.C. § 78p (1971).
51. 15 U.S.C. § 78ff (1981).
52. *SEC v. Texas Gulf Sulphur Co.*, 401 F.2d 833 (2d Cir. 1968), *cert. denied sub. nom. Coates v. SEC.*, 394 U.S. 976 (1969); 312 F.Supp. 77 (S.D.N.Y. 1970), *aff'd in relevant part*, 446 F.2d 1301 (2d Cir. 1971), *cert. denied* 404 U.S. 1005 (1971).
53. Id.
54. 8 Loss & Seligman, *supra* note 31, at 3740–58.
55. 8 Loss & Seligman, *supra* note 34, at 3680–3729.
56. 8 Loss & Seligman, *supra* note 34, at 3584–98. *Cf. Chiarella v. U.S.*, 445 U.S. 222 (1980); *Dirks v. SEC*, 463 U.S. 646 (1983). *But see SEC v. Materia*, 745 F.2d 197 (2d Cir. 1984), *cert denied*, 471 U.S. 1053 (1985); *U.S. v. Newman*, 664 F.2d 12 (2d Cir. 1981); *SEC v. Lund*, 570 F.Supp. 1397 (C.D.Cal. 1983).
57. *Ernst & Ernst v. Hochfelder*, 425 U.S. 185 (1976); A. Bromberg and L. Lowenfels, Securities Fraud and Commodities Fraud, § 8.4, p. 204.131 et seq. (1992).
58. A. Bromberg, supra note 57.
59. *TSC Industries, Inc. v. Northway, Inc.*, 426 U.S. 438 (1976). A Bromberg, *supra* note 54, at § 8.3, p.199.
60. *See Chiarella v. U.S.*, 445 U.S. 222 (1980); *SEC v. Materia*, 745 F.2d 197 (2d Cir. 1984), *cert denied*, 471 U.S. 1053 (1985); *U.S. v. Newman*, 664 F.2d 12 (2d Cir. 1981).
61. 15 U.S.C. § 78 c,o,t,u and ff (1981).
62. *SEC v. Shattuck Denn Mining Corp.*, 297 F.Supp. 470 (S.D.N.Y. 1968).
63. *SEC v. Texas Gulf Sulphur Co., supra* note 52.
64. *Elkind v. Liggett & Myers, Inc.*, 472 F.Supp. 123 (S.D.N.Y. 1978), *aff'd in part and rev'd in part*, 635 F.2d 156 (2d Cir. 1980).
65. *See SEC v. Bausch & Lomb Incorporated*, 565 F.2d 8 (2d Cir. 1977); *Faberge, Inc.*, 188 SEC News Digest LR–5548 (October 2, 1972).
66. 15 U.S.C. § 78m(d) and (g) (1981).
67. Sec. 13(d)(6)(B).
68. *GAF Corporation v. Milstein*, 453 F.2d 709 (2d Cir. 1971), *cert. denied*, 406 U.S. 910 (1972).
69. Rule 13d-5(b)(1) under the 1934 Act.
70. Sec. 13(d)(2). *See Cooper Laboratories, Inc.*, Release No. 34-22171 (June 26, 1985) (amendment filed five business days after obligation to amend was not prompt).
71. Rule 13d-3 under the 1934 Act.
72. Rule 13d-1(c) under the 1934 Act.
73. *See* Release No. 33–6456 (March 4, 1983); *In the matter of Bruns, Nordeman & Co.*, 40 SEC 653 (1961).
74. *See* Release No. 34–23611 (September 11, 1986); Release No. 33–6456 (March 4, 1983); *American Electronic Laboratories, Inc.*, 1971–1972 CCH ¶ 78,783.
75. 15 U.S.C. § 78 m(b)(2)(1981); 15 U.S.C. § 78 dd-1(1981).
76. *See* generally, D. Ruder, *Multiple Defendants in Securities Law Fraud Cases: Aiding and Abetting, Conspiracy, in Pari Delicto, Indemnification and Contribution*, 120 U.Pa. L. Rev. 597 (1972).
77. *Gould v. American Hawaiian Steamship Company*, 535 F.2d 761 (3d Cir. 1976).
78. *Brennan v. Midwestern United Life Insurance Co.*, 259 F.Supp. 673 (N.D. Ind. 1966), 286 F.Supp. 702 (N.D. Ind. 1968), *aff'd*, 417 F.2d 147 (7th Cir. 1969), cert denied, 397 U.S. 989 (1970).

79. *See, Report of Investigation in the matter of National Telephone Co., Inc.,* relating to activities of the outside directors of National Telephone Co., Inc., Release No. 34-14380 (January 16, 1978).
80. Securities Act Release No. 5223 (January 11, 1972).
81. Rule 144(d)(2)(ii) under the 1933 Act.
82. If Form 144 is not required to be filed because of an exemption, the four weeks is measured from the date of receipt of the order to execute the transaction by the broker or the date of execution of the transaction directly with a market maker.
83. No filing is required if the amount of securities to be sold during any period of three months does not exceed 500 shares or other units and the aggregate sale price does not exceed $10,000. Likewise, sales made pursuant to Rule 145(d) (in general applicable to sales by control persons of acquired companies) do not require the filing of Form 144.
84. Rule 144(k) under the 1933 Act.
85. *See, e.g. David D. Wexler* (available August 19, 1981); *Hellman, Ferri Investment Associates* (available November 16, 1981).

Index